THE MAN BETWEEN

THE MAN BETWEEN

A Biography of Carol Reed

Nicholas Wapshott

Chatto & Windus
LONDON

Published in 1990 by
Chatto & Windus Ltd
20 Vauxhall Bridge Road
London SW1V 2SA

A CIP catalogue record for this book is available
from the British Library

ISBN 0 7011 3353 8

Typeset at The Spartan Press Ltd,
Lymington, Hants
Printed in Great Britain by
Mackays of Chatham plc,
Chatham, Kent

Contents

List of Illustrations

For Louise

Acknowledgements

This life of Sir Carol Reed could not have made much progress without the consent and co-operation of his son Max, to whom I am most grateful. Few biographers have enjoyed such freedom from interference from the key member of a subject's family.

Others, too, have ensured that the more intimate aspects of Carol Reed's life have not gone unrecorded. Those who helped me piece together what Reed was like as a father and husband include Max Reed, Reed's stepdaughter Tracy Reed, his secretary Dorli Percival, Judy Campbell Birkin, her son Andrew and Sir John Birkin. For information about Reed's schooldays I must thank P. Pollak and R. B. Mallion of the King's School, Canterbury. What Reed was like as a young man was discovered with the help of Edgar Wallace's daughters Pat and Penelope, Lyn M. Hoser and Daphne du Maurier's son, Kits Browning.

To bring together the details of Reed's working life, none have been more helpful and encouraging than Graham Greene, whose fondness for Reed led him to answer repeated enquiries with generosity and politeness. Others who helped reveal important insights into Reed's life and career include Michael Powell, Alec Guinness, Rex Harrison, Eric Ambler, Garson Kanin, Helen Cherry, Rachel Kempson, Mrs James Mason, Auberon Waugh, Jeremy Saunders, Gordon Richards, Peggy Ashcroft and Colin Sorensen.

I am also indebted to Donat Gallagher, Martin Scorsese, Jay Cocks, Hugo Vickers, Penelope Gilliat, Aidan Crawley, Elizabeth Longford, Michael Hordern, John Mills, Bryan Forbes, Anthony Marreco, Peter Ustinov, Anna Kythreotis, Corin Redgrave and Phyllis Calvert. There are numerous other friends and associates of Reed who have helped me enormously but do not wish to be named.

The staff of the British Film Institute have been continually helpful, among them Elaine Burrows, John Gillett, Sheila Whitaker and Wilf Stevenson.

It would have been impossible to have discovered so much about Carol Reed were it not for the patient and diligent research of Amy Nicolson, who warrants special thanks. Her work was ably supplemented by Amelia Hill.

And I have received useful and friendly advice from Carmen Callil, my publisher, Jonathan Burnham and Robert Lacey.

For permission to reproduce excerpts from copyright material I am grateful to the following: W. H. Allen & Co. plc for *Over My Shoulder* by Jessie Matthews; The Bodley Head Ltd for *Emlyn* by Emlyn Williams; Campbell Thomson & McLaughlin Ltd for *Here Lies* by Eric Ambler, © 1985 by Eric Ambler, published by Weidenfeld & Nicolson Ltd/Fontana; Curtis Brown on behalf of the Estate of Daphne du Maurier for *I'll Never Be Young Again* © Daphne du Maurier 1932; Hamish Hamilton Ltd for *Anything for a Quiet Life* by Jack Hawkins, © Jack Hawkins 1973, *Edgar Wallace* by Margaret Lane, © Margaret Lane 1964, *Before I Forget* by James Mason, © James Mason 1981, and *Blessings in Disguise* by Alec Guinness, © Alec Guinness 1985; William Heinemann Ltd for *Dear Me* by Peter Ustinov; Macmillan Publishers Ltd for *Rex: An Autobiography* by Rex Harrison; Penguin Books Ltd for *The Actor's Life: Journals 1956–1976* by Charlton Heston (Allen Lane, 1979), © Charlton Heston, 1976, 1978; Laurence Pollinger Ltd, William Heinemann Ltd and The Bodley Head Ltd for *The Fallen Idol* by Graham Greene; Laurence Pollinger Ltd and The Bodley Head Ltd for *Ways of Escape* by Graham Greene; George Weidenfeld & Nicolson Ltd for *In My Mind's Eye* by Michael Redgrave and *The Letters of Evelyn Waugh*, edited by Mark Amory.

I would like to thank the British Film Institute – their Stills Library and Reference Library in particular – for help in researching and providing photographs. I also wish to thank the following for permission to reproduce photographs: Hamish Hamilton Ltd, from *The Great Lover* by Madeleine Bingham (2); Victor Gollancz Ltd (6); The Rank Organisation plc (8, 11); The Beaton Archive and Sotheby's, London (10); Weintraub Entertainment (Administration) Ltd (13, 14, 15 and 16); Columbia Pictures Industries Inc. (17, 18 and 20).

Nicholas Wapshott
London, March 1990

Introduction

Towards the end of his life, Carol Reed was contemplating the script of a film about the life of J. M. Barrie, written by Andrew Birkin, the son of Reed's friend Judy Campbell Birkin. He turned to his wife, Penelope Dudley Ward, and said: 'But Pemp, I love children, but no one wants to make a film about me . . .' It was a remark which revealed a great deal about Reed. He never expected anyone to be interested enough in his life to attempt to record it, nor would he have invited such a venture.

Despite an extraordinary career, first acting, then directing for the stage and ultimately making films, he had a low opinion of his achievements. For Reed, film-making was more a craft than an act of creativity. His approach was one of technical perfection and he attempted to conceal the personal elements which none the less coloured his work. He had little regard for those directors who made films smothered with autobiographical traces. He found the French 'Nouvelle Vague', which had made a virtue of the notion of a film's authorship, self-indulgent, and he was contemptuous of those who loaded their films with political or social messages. His own pictures were never evangelical and even those, like *The Stars Look Down*, with an undeniable moral, he insisted could as easily have been made to reflect the opposite point of view.

This reluctance to acknowledge his own personality stemmed directly, as did so much else, from having grown up the illegitimate child of an ostentatious public figure, his father the great Victorian-Edwardian actor-manager, Sir Herbert Beerbohm Tree. Tree was the head of two families, one with his wife Maud, the other with his mistress May Reed, Carol's mother. As a result, all Herbert and May's children maintained a lifelong reticence about their parents and childhood.

As a schoolboy, Carol found he could not resist telling friends how great a man his father was, but his boasting caused

3

embarrassment to his headmaster who sent for his mother to forbid Carol to mention Tree again. This reprimand proved traumatic for Reed, who submerged the memory of his roots for the rest of his life, talking about his early life only to his brothers and sister and to his second wife, Pempie. As his career blossomed and his fame attracted the press, he refused to be drawn on his early years, always disguising the truth to protect his parents. He extended this self-denial to his own private life, which soon became almost as complicated as that of his father.

However, Reed's films do include hints of his personality. During school holidays he would wander backstage in his father's theatre and the actors all made him welcome, so he persistently used in his films actors from the Victorian and Edwardian stage. A child participating in, but perhaps not understanding, the world of adults also provides a recurring theme in his pictures. Yet few Reed films reveal his eccentric character or his extraordinary network of personal friends. Reed's reticence, which Andrew Birkin has described as 'cultivated naivety', has left him with a reputation for diffidence, which is far from the case, and his meticulously planned working method has alienated those who prefer their directors to display the extravagance of their characters on the screen.

Reed's compulsive secrecy about himself and his family have not made it easy to trace his life. He was not a great letter-writer, nor did he keep a diary. Although successful for most of his life, he kept well away from the limelight, sheltering behind a genuine shyness. He did little to disabuse those who wrote that he was really a bland technician whose personal affairs were not worth exploring. It was a deceit which he was able to maintain as long as he was alive. Researching the life of Carol Reed, therefore, I have occasionally felt like a picture restorer removing the years of grime and varnish applied by others to reveal a lost masterpiece. Here is a life so rich and colourful that it is hard to credit that it has taken so many years for it to be written.

It is, of course, very British to deride success and ignore home-grown genius, and there is little doubt that Reed enjoyed the privacy which such grudging attitudes allowed. But it is unforgivable that one of the most important British film-makers should have been misunderstood and ignored for so long. When he died in 1976, the obituary in the *Washington Post* gave a clear verdict of his place in history. It said: 'Sir Carol and Alfred Hitchcock have been the most famous and respected film-makers to emerge from the British motion picture industry', which, assuming that the writer had ignored the fact that Charles Chaplin was British, gives an indication of how quickly we forget our great men.

His three films made immediately after the Second World War, *Odd Man Out*, *The Fallen Idol* and *The Third Man*, can hardly be matched for quality of direction, photography and performances. His failure to sustain the power and energy of this high period of creativity had more to do with the collapse of the British film industry than with a decline in his creative powers. Reed spent the last twenty-five years of his life patching together deals with American companies, which both sapped his energy and ensured that his talent would be compromised. Ironically, if, like Michael Powell and Emeric Pressburger, he had virtually stopped making films when British money dried up, his reputation would not have been diminished by the memory of his flawed final pictures.

1

The Family Tree

Hanging in the opulent gloom of the Garrick Club in London is a portrait of Sir Herbert Beerbohm Tree in the role of Falstaff. Sir Herbert as Sir John appears in romping mood, with a woman on each arm. While he holds the actress Ellen Terry firmly in one embrace, he is amorously gripping Madge Kendal in another.

This picture of Tree, trapped between two competing women, looking over his shoulder to flirt with one while he hugs the second, must have caused some titters among the members of the Garrick, for the pose accurately reflected the complication of Tree's own private life.

Tree adored women and, as a true late-Victorian, he saw nothing of virtue in respectable monogamy nor anything wrong with taking advantage of the extraordinary attraction to women of all ages which his powerful good looks and his fame granted him. But, as in the portrait of Falstaff, there were, among all the women that he encouraged to love him and to whom he in turn swore his love, two women above the others in his genuine affections.

The first was his wife Maud, the mother of his three Tree daughters and an actress of considerable fame. There is little doubt that the most important woman in his life was Maud Holt, later to become Lady Tree, for there was in her independent frame of mind a perfect match and partner for Tree's wayward character. She was an anchor for him, a standard by which to judge all other women and a sounding board for his wildest ideas. Most important to him, and the reason that, despite everything, there was no prospect of divorce, Maud Tree was as bloody-minded and as maverick a character as Tree himself. She appeared on stage with him and understood his trade like few others. She was also a rival to him, challenging his decision not to continue casting her opposite him by hiring another theatre and mounting a competing production to deflect attention from his efforts. Maud was his public partner and she revelled in his fame, throwing parties and playing the grand hostess.

Tree respected Maud like no other woman, except one. That woman was Beatrice May Pinney, a young woman whom he took as his mistress, set up in a large house on Putney Hill and with whom he made the conventional home and married life he was never to achieve with Maud. She was the antithesis of Maud and was happy to remain in the background, satisfied to be Tree's true love and the woman to whom he went home to live a regular domestic life. She happily forwent the glamour and the attention which Maud craved. While Maud took the title Lady Tree and became a close friend of the leading lights of society, May Pinney quietly kept house.

Herbert and May had five sons and a daughter, one of whom was Carol Reed (May Pinney had renamed herself May Reed). To a great extent, May was Tree's true wife, while Maud became his mistress. The one was reliable and homely; the other a Shavian 'new woman' who enjoyed a career and a life independent of her husband.

The eulogy written by Maud little more than two months after Tree's death in 1917, in a compilation of similar testaments assembled by Tree's half-brother Max Beerbohm, hints at this eccentric and inverted life which Tree had engineered for himself. It is a more honest and unsentimental account of their time together than might be expected from a grieving Edwardian widow, not least considering the time of its publication, so soon after the great man's demise and so early in the Great War when the cult of heroic death had reached a pitch of self-immolating indulgence.

Maud did, indeed, love her husband. She loved him despite everything and she pays tribute to his fine qualities as a husband and father and as a creative actor and entertaining character. But still she does not shrink from making plain the true nature of their life together. Perhaps she found that even the hypocrisy of the Edwardian age could not extend to hiding the mixed pleasures of life with Tree from the large number of friends and acquaintances who knew already about the tribulations of being the wife of such a monstrous egotist.

The book of memories by those who had worked with or were related to Tree was intended primarily for those who knew him.

That the Trees' marriage was difficult and unconventional was well known not only by theatrical people but also by the gossip-consuming public. Tree was such a celebrated personality in such a public trade that his deeds were the talk of the bars and parlours of London.

It was well known that Herbert Tree had caused his wife distress by casting women other than her in his plays, to her loud and jealous complaints, and that he was perhaps the most accomplished womaniser in the whole of London, making little attempt to keep his affairs secret. The dome room at the top of Tree's theatre, His Majesty's in the Haymarket, which he had built for himself in 1897, was a legendary temple to the seduction of young women.

In such circumstances it was generally assumed that Tree's wife was not so much to be pitied as admired for brazening out her husband's infidelities and forging a successful acting career of her own. Indeed, Maud was so forceful a character that it was unclear to many who collected tittle-tattle about the Tree marriage whether Herbert's indiscretions were the cause or the result of his fiery wife's behaviour.

Maud's extensive account of their life together, entitled 'Herbert and I', still contained the traditional humbug which would normally be associated with such a venture. It paid sincere tribute in the most glowing terms to Tree as a person, as a husband and as an inspiration to Maud and her daughters. As a tribute from an actress and sentimentalist to her dead actor husband, it indulges in the hyperbole of theatrical celebrations to ensure that Herbert's extravagant and ostentatious life was not underplayed. And there is also the ethos of the age which dictated that all great men were to be described in triumphal terms which might have fitted a Roman emperor. Such was the example set by the old Queen, Victoria, at the death of her own dear Albert.

But beneath the veneer of convention, Maud made clear that life with Tree, although fascinating, thrilling and, for her, the most wonderful experience, was by no means always a pleasure.

Their life together had begun happily enough. When Maud Holt first encountered Tree, at a fancy dress ball in 1881, she was eighteen and a student of Greek, Latin and mathematics at

Queen's College, Harley Street, with the ambition of winning a place at Girton College, Cambridge. Tree was tall, slim, with bright red hair and pale turquoise eyes turning to green. Aged twenty-nine, he had a confident bearing and a slightly exotic air which often caused him to be cast as a foreigner.

Whether through laziness or because his actor's life caused him to spend so much time in disguise while going about his business, he did not arrive at the party in fancy dress and appeared, in Maud's words, a 'tall, pale, youthful creature' with 'a voice whose wistful cadence haunted the hearer'.

She already knew of him as an actor and challenged him at this first meeting with the words: 'But you cannot possibly be the old man who acts in *Forget-Me-Not*?' He said that he was, and although they spoke for some time, the only thing Maud remembered was that she hoped to meet him again to resubmit herself to his 'haunting personality'.

It was perhaps, in the light of subsequent events, a portent that it was not Herbert but Maud who took the romantic initiative by writing to Tree in May 1881 and asking him, in a roundabout way, whether he would come and see her acting in an amateur production so that he might advise her whether she had any future on the stage. Maud, who lived away from her parents in rooms monitored by an aged matron, must have been a modern, forward woman to make such an ambiguous proposal.

It was equally a portent that Tree, having established a means of attracting young women to him, discovered that there was no easier way of finding lovers than to respond to such inviting overtures. Maud's letter was similar to many others from unknown women which were to continue to arrive despite his marriage.

Tree waited some months before responding to Maud's advances. At first he declined an invitation to see her act, as he was in Birmingham, performing at the Prince of Wales's Theatre. Maud had rather given up hope of ever receiving a more encouraging reply when, towards the end of summer, he wrote again. It was a short letter containing a terse piece of advice and a tantalising but irritatingly unspecific promise of a future meeting. 'My Dear Miss Holt,' he wrote. 'Don't go on the stage unless you feel you must. How are you? We shall meet in the autumn. Yours sincerely, H.B.T.'

By the winter, without warning or invitation, Tree had visited Miss Holt at her rooms above a shop at 10 Orchard Street, near Marble Arch.

Tree was an actor and a romantic, but particularly useful when wooing young women was his professional speciality, romantic acting. His wooing technique was to bombard his chosen victim with love letters and with readings of Victorian romantic verse, delivered in a dreamy murmur. The poems, with titles such as 'In the Mission Garden' and 'Aux Italiens', were often heavily imbued with quasi-religious sentiment.

His performance certainly touched the impressionable Maud Holt, who fell in love with Tree over a prolonged succession of visits which came at increasingly short intervals until they were taking tea at least once a week. Mrs Newman, Maud's self-appointed chaperone, with whom she shared her lodgings, was rarely far away and often insisted on sitting in on these tea-time meetings. Maud was distracted from her Greek studies while Tree explained to her his theatrical ambitions, which amounted at the time to little more than the hope of staging a modest one-act tragedy called *Merely Players*, with a plot similar to *I Pagliacci*, in which, he flatteringly suggested, Maud should play the female lead.

At the beginning of February 1882, the relationship encountered a hiccup as Tree attempted a sexual advance which the proper, or perhaps wily, Maud repelled. By the 7th he was asking forgiveness for his forwardness and asking whether he might call her by her Christian name. By the 12th, leaning on the mantelpiece upstairs in Orchard Street, Tree took Maud's hand in his and proposed marriage. She hesitated before accepting, coolly considering what it would mean for her university course, what her close sister Emma would think of the arrangement and, the most important issue, what it would be like to be married to an actor, and in particular an actor like Tree.

Two days later, as romance would have it on St Valentine's day, the couple walked together from the home of Maud's parents in Richmond to Herbert Tree's family at Clanricarde Gardens, a cul-de-sac off the Bayswater Road, and declared that they had become engaged. Tree slipped onto Maud's finger a diamond ring which he had found in Kensington Gardens as a child. He had first given it to his mother who, on her deathbed, had returned it to him, saying he was to give it to his future wife. Maud was greeted wholeheartedly into the bosom of the Beerbohm family home, where she and Herbert would spend each Sunday.

The family that Maud was to marry into was first recorded through the paternal line at the beginning of the eighteenth century. Frederick Beerbohm was a merchant in Pomerania. His son, Ernest Joachim Beerbohm, moved to Memel on the Baltic before marrying his wife Roerdanz, the daughter of a family in the timber business. For backing Frederick the Great of Prussia against Russia, the Kaiser awarded Edward a property called Bernsteinbruch in Brandenburg. It is now called Pelcczye and, since 1945, has been part of west Poland. In 1763 Roerdanz gave birth to Ernest Henry Beerbohm, who twenty-two years later married Henriette Amalie Radke, a German of Slav origins. Henriette gave birth to eleven children, the last of which, born in 1810, was Julius Ewald Beerbohm, Tree's father. He was educated at Schnepfeuthal in Thuringia, at the age of eighteen travelled to France to take up the study of commerce and two years later emigrated to Britain and began trading in corn in the City of London, eventually becoming a member of the Baltic Exchange.

After many years living as a bachelor in St James's Square, at the age of thirty-nine he married Constantia Draper, the daughter of a clerk at Lloyd's. Constantia gave birth to three sons and a daughter and died before she reached thirty. The first son was Ernest, who took off for the Cape Colony, where he became a sheep farmer and married a local woman, a black whom the Beerbohm family referred to, without irony, as a 'brunette'. The third son was Julius, who travelled to Patagonia, wrote an account of his journey and also poetry, none of it published.

The middle son was born on 17 December 1852 at 2 Pembridge Villas, Kensington, and was named by his parents Herbert Draper Beerbohm. At the start of his acting career, Herbert renamed himself Herbert Beerbohm Tree, explaining to his father, who thought little of the stage, that he intended to climb to the very top of his chosen trade.

Tree's father subsequently married his dead wife's sister in Switzerland, and they had four daughters and then one son,

Max Beerbohm, the novelist, critic and wit, who was thus both Herbert Beerbohm Tree's brother and his cousin.

Herbert Beerbohm and his two brothers were all educated first at Mrs Adams's dame-school at Frant, near Tunbridge Wells in Kent, then at Dr Stone's school, King's Square, Bristol. Their father, however, decided that a good German education was needed and the trio were sent to the grim regime of his old school at Schnepfeuthal. The experience left a lasting impression on Herbert, who reacted against all unnecessary spartanism for the rest of his life.

On his return to Britain, Herbert was expected by his father to become a clerk in the family business, by now a thriving concern. He was to work as a corn merchant for eight years. His ambition from the age of seventeen, however, was to become an actor, and he hurled himself into amateur dramatics. Performing with groups calling themselves the Erratics, the Irrationals, the Bettertons and the Philothespians, he soon became notorious for his accurate and humorous impressions of the leading actors of the day, including Henry Irving. His diary records his theatre-going experiences, among them his first sight of Ellen Terry, as Portia in the Bancroft management's production of *The Merchant of Venice* at the Prince of Wales theatre.

He was compiling a cuttings book of notices of his own stage appearances to tout around to professional managements, but for the most part his amateur work in theatres on the fringe of London was a dispiriting affair. A friend, T. Murray Ford, described the young Tree as 'a lanky youth acting with amateurs at Dalston and Haggerston. He was reserved, almost sullen, but keen and deep in love with his art . . . His father had told young Beerbohm that he must stick to business and leave acting alone, and the lad was on his beam-ends at times, and not too proud to borrow an occasional half-crown from the waitresses of Crosby Hall [a restaurant in Bishopsgate].'

When, after appearing as Grimaldi in a charity show at the Globe Theatre in 1878, Herbert was offered a place in the touring Bijou Comedy Company, he abandoned his father's work in favour of an actor's life. This short tour led to the offer by Henry Neville of a London job and from then on 'Mr H. B. Tree' was a permanent presence on the London stage, only leaving the capital on tours with established professional companies.

In 1880, the year before he met Maud, Tree returned to London to take the part by which Maud was to recognise him at the fancy dress party, that of Prince Maleotti in a revival of Genevieve Ward's *Forget-Me-Not*. Tree was heavily made-up to look older and was generally praised for his performance. He was next to play before the Prince of Wales in *L'Aventurier*, dining with the prince and his mistress Lily Langtry after the show, and he was a great popular success in *Where's the Cat?* and *The Colonel*, in both of which he shamelessly imitated Oscar Wilde. He was appearing in *The Colonel* in Birmingham when he wrote to Maud that he was unable to come to see her perform.

By 1882 he was confident that he could earn his living as an actor and could support a wife. Some of Maud's friends, including her influential sister Emmie and her eldest brother Willie, thought differently. Although an increasing number of young gentlemen had taken to the stage, it was by no means a respectable trade. Willie Holt, on lunching with Tree, considered that his frayed cuffs were indication enough that he was not a suitable husband for his sister, and told Maud so on his return. She took no notice. However, Herbert's enemies kept Maud fully informed of any gossip or rumour they could find to try to alter her determination to marry him.

The tensions of the engagement are evident in the almost daily correspondence between them. Maud soon discovered that an actor's temperament was not always easy to endure. She appeared with Herbert in a one-act play at the Trees' home and learned for the first time that sharing a stage with him was awkward for anyone, and would prove doubly difficult for an actress who was also Tree's wife. He became angry with her, criticised her and made her very upset.

His letter of apology gives a flavour of the first of what was to be a lifetime's vicious arguments. 'I should not like you to know me as I was tonight,' he wrote. 'You see the excitement and whirl of acting makes one break through one's own ideas of what is correct . . . I am so sorry you should have witnessed that exhibition of brutal temper.' But in another letter he showed that in one thing at least he was to be generous and sensitive to her wishes, by allowing her her own acting career. 'In regard to your going on stage,' he wrote, 'my mind is filled with doubts.' However, he considered it likely that he would never be able to provide her with true happiness and 'so you shall do as you please'.

Soon those of Maud's friends who opposed the marriage began souring the engagement by telling her of rumours of Tree's previous relationships. There had certainly been women in his life. In his twenty-nine years he had come across many amorous opportunities and taken full advantage of them. One of the earliest recorded conquests was Cornelie d'Anka, an actress who had taken the lead role in *Madame Favart* in which Tree was playing Count Pontsable. Tree thought little of her as an actress, complaining that she hadn't learnt her lines and that he had to keep prompting her. Within a week, however, he was recording in his diary that there was 'a great deal of good' in her, a euphemism for the fact that she was game for sexual exploits.

Another name to appear in his diary, at a place where two pages were later torn out, was 'Rose', though who she was remains a mystery. And there were other lovers who did not feature in the pages of Tree's diary. However, while wooing Maud it appears that Tree promised his wayward days were over.

Then came the incident of the Liberty's silk scarf which Herbert gave as a birthday present to Myra Home, the lover and later the wife of the dramatist Arthur Wing Pinero. The scarf was, apparently, an innocent gift, but Tree went out of his way to imply that it was nothing of the sort. His efforts at invoking jealousy, however, went badly awry. First, before sending the scarf he asked Maud her opinion of it and she replied that it was too good for Myra Home. Ignoring this hint, Tree took a page of Maud's notepaper, headed with a large 'M' monogram, and, in front of Maud, proceeded to decorate the capital letter with flowers and expand it into the name Myra.

A storm broke. Salvos passed between them in the form of dramatic letters. Tree's grovelling apology for the misunderstood scarf revealed that his personal morality was going to prove hard for Maud to live with. 'It is so difficult,' he wrote, 'to act strictly according to the cruel letter of what is considered the right thing to do. I assure you most solemnly that I have not broken through the spirit of what is right in doing what I have done.'

In June 1882 he was again defending his behaviour from gossip linking him with other women. This time Maud was so hurt that she sent back his engagement ring. Tree bombarded her with letters begging forgiveness. 'If any lies have been told about me, I hope you won't believe them. Tell me what you have heard – I have no fear,' he wrote.

The matter plainly had some substance, for Tree eventually apologised to Maud, this time to her face, although he backed up the apology with a letter in which he described his ambiguous position. 'You shall not regret your forgiveness – the forgivers are more blessed than the deceivers – although I can hardly be said to have deceived. I do think you were carried away by those feelings for which I love you the more – but which perhaps spring from your inexperience of the world. I have done nothing since our engagement for which you could really blame me.'

Maud was eager to overcome the breach between them, and when the apology came by hansom cab she smartly got into it and asked the driver to take her to Tree's lodgings on Hampstead Heath. It was a passionate and tearful reunion.

The next month Maud agreed to accompany her ailing sister to the spa of Aix-les-Bains, which did not please Herbert. What is worse, Maud's doubts about her fiancé's infidelity reasserted themselves. Again Tree had to write an unapologetic apology for something in his past.

His impatience with the virginal Maud was beginning to show. 'I was foolish – perhaps weak – but not vicious or dishonourable. I gave you to understand, when I first asked you to care for me, that my past life had not been entirely unworldly. I repented what I had done, and you forgave me. I have endeavoured to make every reparation for the error committed before I knew you, and I have been true and loyal to you.' He told her that she must choose between him and her family and friends. It was unfair to continue to taunt him with old rumours about old flames.

Before he had time to send the letter, a telegram arrived from Aix, demanding that he come at once to see her. He set off by train, boat and train and took a suite in the Grand Hotel at Aix. He appeared to be in no hurry to assure Maud that all was well. After taking a leisurely sulphur bath, he announced himself by letter.

She decided to punish him for his lack of urgency. To his distress, she did not reply. Having just crossed Europe to see Maud at her insistence, Tree became angry and wrote her an ultimatum. He would do exactly as she demanded, even if she wished to break off their engagement. He would return to London and they would never see each other again. All he wanted was her decision one way or the other. Maud eventually relented and they spent the next two weeks together.

Their love affair was plainly something of a daring and dangerous game, with manufactured dramas and melodramatic situations which suited the age and particularly fitted the romantic prelude to a marriage between two Victorian actors. However, it took place at the cost of an honest appraisal of what such a marriage would entail. Whether they fooled themselves and each other into thinking that their marriage would be tranquil and ordered after such a tempestuous engagement is impossible to know.

The next point of difference between them was over the company Tree liked to keep. In Maud's absence abroad, Tree had joined a theatrical troupe known as the Costume Society, with the hope of making money. The leading light of the Society was E. W. Godwin, the fashionable architect, who was better known in London for being the father of Ellen Terry's two children, although she remained married to the artist George Frederick Watts. Godwin, who designed houses in Chelsea for James McNeill Whistler and Oscar Wilde and who first laid out the arts and crafts colony of Bedford Park in Chiswick, was already an acquaintance of Tree before his engagement, but Maud had forbidden the friendship to continue. She was hostile to the licentiousness enjoyed by Tree's bohemian friends. Her Richmond respectability was showing through.

Maud's response to Tree joining the Costume Society was indicative of the atmosphere that was to pervade their marriage. She attacked him over his association with Godwin, but used it as a bargaining counter in establishing her own freedom. (Later she revealed that 'I had a stupid, narrow-minded kind of jealousy about (Godwin). I wanted Herbert in a glass case, and I used to think that Mr Godwin tried to get him out.')

Maud wrote that she had an 'intense objection' to Tree mixing with Godwin on a day-to-day basis and invoked the impeccable sensibilities of her ailing sister as evidence of the unsuitability of the liaison. 'Today for the first time Emmie asked me who this Mr Godwin was – and when I told her "the architect" she was quite horrified – utterly disgusted at the idea of my ever having known such a man.' She went on: 'He is such a man as she would no more shake hands with than with a snake, and is as sorry as you know I am for you, whom she so likes, to know such a man.'

Maud gave Tree an ultimatum. 'I warn you, you will have to choose between him and me.' If he were to persist, which she could not prevent 'any more than I can forbid you London which holds Mr Godwin', she would return to her studies – which Tree had told her he wished her to abandon. They would take up just four afternoons and one morning a week. 'So, after my little outburst, dear, I come round to your way of thinking.'

Tree was taken aback by such a skilful counter and wrote from the Criterion Theatre: 'I absolutely forbid you to take up your college work.' He demanded to know what Emmie Holt had heard about Godwin. And he did not like the way his fiancée was directing her remarks at him: 'It is not right, or becoming.' After all, she would be his wife before long.

The following morning he added a second letter to the envelope. 'I am going to telegraph you this morning that the College scheme is out of the question . . . It is for me to use my judgment in regard to my own business affairs.' The Costume Society could make him several hundred pounds a year, and that was the main reason for him joining it. Godwin had been a good friend to him in the past. Tree then made what was to be the first of many vain attempts to curtail Maud's activities and have her behave like a conventional Victorian wife. 'Maud, I expect you to allow me to have a certain authority over your actions – or endless misunderstandings may arise. I am to be the breadwinner, not you. I should not like you to further worry yourself with my work – and if you once set this precedent, there is no knowing what your whims may lead you to!'

During August 1882 Tree took rooms suitable for a first married home on the first floor of No. 2 Old Burlington Street, Mayfair, for three guineas a week. The preparations for the imminent marriage were well on the way.

Four days before the wedding, 'only 4 more days before you will be my own entirely – when no chaperone can say "Nay"' – he wrote her a loving, joshing note, but one which contained an unintentional irony. He had taken to calling her 'Dear Child', or in this case 'Dear Childie, I am writing you a few lines after the theatre to beg you to take great, great care of yourself for the next few days – be very careful at crossings, so as not to be run over – for you know what expenses I have incurred in the way of procuring a licence, which is not transferable, by the way.'

The marriage ceremony was extraordinary, not least because the best man, in the absence of Tree's brother Julius who was in Spain, was the ten-year-old Max Beerbohm, who has left a touching record of it. He had always regarded two of his stepbrothers, being so much older than him, as exceptional characters. Julius he considered a god; Herbert merely a hero. Then 'in some early month of '84,' according to Beerbohm's account, 'my classification of the two brothers underwent a sudden change.' Herbert became a god; Julius a mere hero.

The reason for this transformation was that Herbert was engaged to be married, and for the young Beerbohm 'being married had always seemed to me an even finer thing, a thing even more essential to the full glory of the adult state, than having a moustache.'

Maud had chosen for the date of the marriage her favourite sister Emmie's birthday, 16 September 1882, and it was to take place from the Trees' country home of Thurnham Court in Kent, where she was to spend the night before the wedding.

Beerbohm remembered 'the two triumphal arches of flowers and branches, one at the gate of the garden, the other at the gate of the little church hard by'. Young Max posted himself outside the church an hour before the service, waiting for the groom to arrive from London, where he had been performing the night before. When Herbert appeared, top-hatted, his skin appeared so pale that Max asked: 'Have you lost the ring?' He had not, but plainly the ordeal of a wedding ceremony was more arduous to Tree than a theatrical opening.

Maud covered her agitation by busying herself about the house. When Herbert asked to have a few words with his wife-to-be she proved to be too busy decorating the house with flowers to take him very seriously. For Herbert, however, her inability to break off what she was doing to have a few serious words about the importance of what they were committing themselves to was an omen. Looking back on that day after his death, Maud thought 'the contrasts of our moods that marriage morning has often recurred to me as laying bare the lightness of my temperament and the unguessed, ungauged depths of his.' It was a simple service, and at the moment when Herbert whispered the marriage vows, Maud felt 'there crept into my heart a new kind of love – a protecting love – the passionate longing to guard from harm that one feels towards a little child.'

The celebrations over, the couple embarked upon a marriage which was to be quite different from that promised on the wedding day. It was, first and foremost, as with so many acting partnerships, continually and unavoidably peripatetic, which led to an extraordinary confusion and disorientation in their affairs.

Soon the couple had left Old Burlington Street for a series of hotels, ending up in a house at 4 Wilton Street in Belgravia. Then, finding at the end of a theatrical run that they had no income, the house was let while they moved first into Maud's sister Emmie's rooms, then to lodgings on Haverstock Hill. The couple fell deep into debt. Before long Tree was employed again and he returned to Wilton Street while Maud, persistently unwell, went to live in the country. It was the first of many separations.

Although Herbert and Maud appeared together in amateur theatricals during the early years of their marriage, Maud quickly struck out on her own, in defiance of her husband's wishes. After the first night of *The Millionaire*, in which Maud appeared in a red wig, Herbert stalked through their home with his face fully lathered, cut-throat razor in hand, exclaiming: 'I hope it doesn't mean that you will be more famous than I. I couldn't have that.'

Before long the Trees joined the Chelsea artistic community, moving to a house in Cheyne Walk. Herbert found success in *The Private Secretary* at the Globe, mainly through brilliant and ingenious ad-libbing, and then as Macari in Hugh Conway's *Called Back*, the first of the great roles which established his reputation and for which theatrical historians still remember him. The early years of marriage were a time of happiness for the couple as they gained a circle of increasingly famous friends: W. S. Gilbert, Oscar Wilde, Hamilton Synge, J. Comyns Carr, Edward Bell, A. K. Moore, even the once-reviled E. W. Godwin.

In July 1884 their first child, Viola, was born. Tree was very fond of Viola and his two subsequent legitimate children. He personally taught Viola to ride a horse and to swim and told her the stories of the German myths, passed down to him by his father. He holidayed with Maud and Viola and would take Viola to spend a week or so in the country when Maud was committed to a part on the London stage.

For Tree, *Called Back* was followed by *The School for Scandal*, in which he played Joseph Surface in a cast which included Lily Langtry, with whom he was also to play the character part of an old Anglo-Indian in *Peril*. The Tree family kept on the move, leaving Chelsea for North Audley Street in Mayfair, then a flat above the Prince of Wales Theatre, then Tree took lodgings back in Wilton Street while Maud took Viola on a trip to Egypt with the W. S. Gilberts. They then rented a house at Ascot in the Berkshire countryside, followed by one in Rosary Gardens, Chelsea, moving next to Bournemouth, where they acted together in *Othello*, *The Merchant of Venice* and *The School for Scandal*.

Shortly afterwards, on their return to Rosary Gardens, Tree took the lease on the Comedy Theatre in Panton Street, transforming himself from a mere character actor to an actor-manager with a theatre and work entirely of his own choosing.

The Trees became celebrities in their own right, throwing and attending parties with the most fashionable names of the day, and becoming part of the scene recorded by George du Maurier in *Punch*. Maud relaxed into her new position as the independent actress wife of Henry Irving's principal rival, and was happy to boast of the company she kept: 'Our life brimmed with laughter, for we were constantly in the company of that King of Mirth, Comyns Carr, of W. S. Gilbert (who could not speak without uttering a witticism), F. C. Burnand, George Grossmith, Oscar Wilde, John Toole, the Hares, the Kendals, the Bancrofts, the Peruginis – all the joy of the London world.' And 'then there were the Pineros, the Jeunes, the Charles Lawrences, the Manners, the d'Oyly Cartes, Arthur Sullivan, the Boughtons, the [Hamilton] Tennants, the Lionel Tennysons, Frederick Locker, Whistler. If it was a coterie, what a coterie!'

It was a full and confusing time for the Trees. There were weddings, where Gladstone could be seen, New Year parties, with 'Sargent, Tadema, Galsworthy, Pinero, Ellen Terry, Barrie, Ray Lankester, Mason, Anthony Hope, Benson, Burne-Jones, Sylvia du Maurier . . . Henry James and Harry and Laurence Irving', the dinner parties thrown by 'the Seymour Trowers, the George Broughtons, the Carl Meyers, the Morel Mackenzies, the de la Rues and the Heilbuts' and parties in the studios of 'Tadema, Leighton, Millais, Watts, Poynter, Burne-Jones and Alfred Gilbert'.

Living first at New Cavendish Street, Mayfair, then at The Grange on Hampstead Heath, Maud was too busy name-dropping, partying and acting, often in a different theatre from Tree, to notice that her husband was not always coming straight home at nights. Yet she hinted after his death that she was aware of what was going on, or at least that others kept her informed, when she wrote: 'All Herbert's friends were my friends; the theatre, whether or no I acted, seemed mine as much as his. I sang my existence away; sang, house-hunted, devised clothes, collected furniture, read a little, laughed incessantly – had a silly habit of pirouetting through life . . . "You take things so lightly," was [Herbert's] gentle comment, his severest reproof. But he marvelled at the unconquerable rebound of what I called my india-rubber ball of a heart.'

First at the Comedy and then the Haymarket, the career of Herbert Tree became a catalogue of highly lucrative successes interspersed with the odd notorious failure. He was best known and loved by a large, clamorous public for his character parts, particularly those in which ingenious make-up trans-formed his instantly recognisable features into those of a stranger. A mark of his fame and popularity can be gleaned from this notice of his appearance in his first production at the Comedy, *The Red Lamp*:

With loose-lipped, fleshy face, the white eyelids, low, over expressionless pale eyes, cat-footed, though rather pon-derous in build he walked on to the stage, stick in hand. For just one moment the eyes flashed, he thrust the stick viciously beneath the sofa – an action incredibly swift, and he was again immobile, enigmatic and unrecognised in his own theatre, until an individuality of enunciation revealed the amazing disguise, and cheers rang out.

In the autumn of 1887 Tree took a lease on the Haymarket Theatre and transferred *The Red Lamp* to it. There he produced a string of popular successes in which he cast himself, and sometimes Maud, in prominent roles. The range of plays at the Haymarket in which Tree chose to project himself was intended by him to challenge the position of Henry Irving as Britain's most versatile and brilliant actor. It was an audacious assault upon the great man's standing and Tree did not find it easy to convert critics to his cause, not least because Irving had silenced many of them by taking out expensive options on their translations of foreign plays.

Irving's regime at the Lyceum was well established and serious in intent. He was openly dismissive of Tree's talents. Tree's choice of plays was alternately classical, challenging Irving on his home ground of Shakespearean heroics, deliberately modern and, in the case of Ibsen, difficult for a popular audience. Tree retained his sense of excitement about the theatre, even when it became his trade, and he was an evangelist, hoping to share his own enthusiasm for plays with his public. He was also relentlessly, unashamedly, commercial.

His attitude was revealed in his remark: 'It's no good giving the public what they want. Give them what you want them to want, and in time they'll want it.' His procession of unlikely plays at the Haymarket included: *The Merry Wives of Windsor*, with himself as Falstaff, commemorated in the Garrick Club portrait; W. S. Gilbert's *Comedy and Tragedy*; W. E. Henley and Robert Louis Stevenson's *Beau Austin*; Henry Arthur Jones's *The Dancing Girl*; *Hamlet*, with himself as the Prince of Denmark and Maud as Ophelia; Oscar Wilde's *A Woman of No Importance*; Ibsen's *An Enemy of the People*; a dramatisation of George du Maurier's novel *Trilby*; and *Henry IV, Part I*, Tree again playing Falstaff.

Bernard Shaw was ultimately convinced by Tree's attempt at educating the public through entertaining renditions of unlikely plays, even if as a drama critic he was often highly critical of Tree's interpretation of parts. He wrote that his 'notion of feeding the popular drama with ideas, and gradually educating the public by classical matinees, financed by the spoils of the popular plays in the evening bill, seems to have been the right one.'

Merry Wives was Tree's first attempt at Shakespeare. He kept more closely to the original text than Irving, but succeeded in winning an unlikely audience to Shakespeare by the power of his own interpretation of a part and the spectacular nature of the music and stage effects. His Falstaff was portrayed in a playful, nimble manner, with a pneumatic paunch which, to his consternation, deflated during previews at Crystal Palace.

Tree's friends had warned him against Shakespeare, arguing the contemporary theatrical wisdom that 'Shakespeare spells ruin', so Tree introduced the play slowly to his theatre, at first only at quiet periods of the week, Monday evenings and Wednesday afternoon matinees. As the production and his performance began to gather a good reputation, so Tree increased its frequency and introduced it into the mainstream of his repertory.

Tree's next attempt at Shakespeare, *Hamlet*, was a more obvious pitch at Irving's crown, for Irving's rendition had become a legendary exercise in the mass hypnotism of an audience by an actor at the top of his powers. Tree's attempt to follow was considerably less successful. Not that the public thought it so, for they came to see Tree in whatever guise he wished to adopt. The critics, however, could barely find a good word to say. Shaw gave Tree a great deal of advice, but the remark which became the talk of London was that of W. S. Gilbert, to Tree himself: 'My dear fellow, I never saw anything so funny in my life, and yet it was not in the least vulgar.' Tree filled the stage with children, whose purpose eluded even Maud, who wandered the stage as the mad Ophelia, extravagantly strewing real flowers about her.

When the success of Oscar Wilde's *Lady Windermere's Fan* became evident, Tree wrote to ask Wilde whether he would write a play for the Haymarket company. The assumption that there would be a leading part in the new play for Tree himself was implicit in the invitation, which led Wilde to remark to Tree: 'As Herod in my *Salome* you would be admirable. As a peer of the realm in my latest dramatic device, pray forgive me if I do not see you.'

Wilde hesitated because the character of Lord Brancaster (later changed to Lord Illingworth) which Tree would undoubtedly have played was based upon himself. Tree recorded this conversation:

Wilde: This witty aristocrat whom you wish to assume in my play is quite unlike anyone who has been on the stage before. He is like no one who has existed before.
Tree: My God! He must be supernatural.
Wilde: He is certainly not natural. He is a figure of art. Indeed, if you can bear the truth, he is myself.

Tree persisted in his demand that Wilde's next comedy should be produced at his theatre and Wilde, who knew the Trees well and had dined with them at the Haymarket, relented, although he was nervous about Tree's reputation as a free adapter of other people's works. In a letter of condolence to Tree about the death of his father, who had died in the summer of 1892, Wilde announced that, although the American rights of his new play had been sold, the English rights were free. 'If you will send me your dates I would read it to you somewhere about the end of this month.'

The Trees were at the Central Station Hotel in Glasgow, on tour with *Hamlet*, when Wilde arrived with the completed manuscript of the play he was calling at the time 'Mrs Arbuthnot'. He stayed, Maud remembered, for three days of 'delighted listening, planning, and – inevitable in his society – laughter, badinage, partridges, oysters, champagne'. But for Maud, a little of Wilde went a long way. 'I remember how glad we were, Herbert and I, when some smart invitation recalled him.'

Tree's attitude to Wilde was more generous than that of his wife. He admired Wilde's wit and, when starting out on his acting career, had flattered Wilde by lampooning him in the pages of *Punch*. Tree also considered himself a wit, with some justification, though he was no match for Wilde, with whom he did not attempt to compete.

As a mark of his admiration, he recorded some of the witticisms which Wilde had made to him:

'Wonderful man, Columbus,' said a New Yorker.
'Why?' asked Wilde.

'He discovered America.'
'Oh no! It had been discovered before, but it was always
hushed up.'

And:

Wilde: I shall always regard you as the best critic of my plays.
Tree: But I have never criticised your plays.
Wilde: That's why.

Tree welcomed Wilde to sit in the auditorium while rehearsals for *A Woman of No Importance* took place at the
Haymarket at the end of March 1893. When Tree's biographer
Hesketh Pearson asked him whether the production had been
with the assistance of Wilde, Tree joked: 'No, with the interference of Wilde.'

The partnership worked well, even if Wilde had some doubts
about Tree's extravagant acting style, but he was confident
enough of Tree's judgement to strike out a long diatribe against
puritanism which was to have been delivered by Lord Illingworth at the beginning of the third act. The lines, omitted from
the production and the published text, might have been written
by Tree himself.

My dear boy, the real enemy of modern life, of everything that
makes life lovely and joyous and coloured for us, is Puritanism, and the Puritan spirit. There is the danger that lies
ahead of the age, and most of all in England. Every now and
then this England of ours finds that one of its sores shows
through its rags and shrieks for the nonconformists. Caliban
for nine months of the year, it is Tartuffe for the other three.
Do you despise a creed that starves the body, and does not
feed the soul? Why, I tell you, Gerald, that the profligate, the
wildest profligate who spills his life in folly, has a better,
saner, finer philosophy of life than the Puritan has. He, at any
rate, knows that the aim of life is the pleasure of living, and
does in some way realise himself, be himself. Puritanism is the
hideous survival of the self-mutilation of the savage, man in
his madness making himself the victim of his monstrous
sacrifice. Profligate, Gerald, you will never be; you will choose
your pleasures too carefully, too exquisitely for that. But
Puritanism you will always reject. It is not a creed for a

gentleman. And, as a beginning, you will make it your ideal
to be a dandy always.

A Woman of No Importance was followed by a production of
Ibsen's *An Enemy of the People*, in which Tree played Dr Stock-
man. It was by no means a conventional rendition of Ibsen, but
then Tree had few examples to imitate, as this was one of the first
Ibsen productions on the English stage. Again the play was
introduced at a matinee, and Tree attempted to make it as
palatable to the public as possible. It became one of his favourite
productions and was regularly revived in his repertory. His
admiration for Ibsen was almost unique, for there was a great
deal of hostility to the message of the plays. Tree, however,
found something in Ibsen which others didn't, and he was alone
in Britain in his contribution of three guineas towards a
seventieth-birthday gift of a drinking-cup for Ibsen. Shaw's
comment was that Tree 'must feel rather like a man in morning
dress at a smart dinner-party, for no other manager compromised himself by meddling in the business'.

On their annual tour of provincial theatres in 1894, the Trees
went to Edinburgh, where they were summoned to perform
before Queen Victoria at Balmoral. For Tree this was an
extraordinary honour, and after the performance he was presented to the queen; for Maud it was much more. Whatever the
tribulations of living with Tree, this was her reward as she came
before what she described as 'her gentle touch, her sweet voice,
her simple personality, the power, wisdom and might of
England'.

Maud and Herbert had been married scarcely three years
when, unknown to Maud, he began his long affair with May
Pinney, setting up a parallel household in Putney. The stormy
Tree marriage, however, persisted through the nineties and in
December 1894, ten years after the birth of Viola, they had their
second child, named apparently without irony Felicity.

After Tree's death, Bernard Shaw wrote to Maud and described to her the predicament in which she had found herself:

Nobody. . . can form the faintest notion of how awful a thing
it is to be married to a man of genius, especially when you

have twice his brains. You have to keep yourself sane, like
Robinson Crusoe, by continually striking a balance between the good and evil in your lot, like this:

Good: I am in the thick of everything. I know all sorts of
interesting people, and am courted by them. I have the
continually renewed excitement of great events like
splendid productions, as if I were a queen with a
coronation every three months. I am the happiest of
women.

Evil: But I am married to Herbert; and Herbert is married to
his theatre, to his destiny, to his work, and to everyone
who plays on his feelings or his vanity. Married to a
Monster and can't even have the Monster all to myself! I
am the wretchedest of women.

In January 1895 Herbert and Maud embarked upon what
appeared to both of them to be the final episode of their
marriage: their first tour of the United States. Most of Tree's
company had gone on ahead and the couple were only
accompanied by Max Beerbohm and a theatre colleague, both
of whom kept themselves entirely to themselves until they
reached the quay in New York.

Maud wrote, sadly, of that significant Atlantic crossing: 'For
the first time for many years, I had Herbert completely to
myself. To me this was a return of the golden age, and I
appreciated and loved every hour of that eight days' journey.'
Tree was subdued and 'wistfully inclined to be waited upon
and looked after, so that it made Heaven for her who had
fretted under his more mercurial and elusive moods. How I
adored and looked back upon the long-drawn days of that
week! Days that never came again, though something very
near them was the last fortnight of his life.' She reminded him,
in the Greek of her early studies, of the expression 'Call no wife
happy until she has her husband safe under a linseed poultice',
for only in that way can she be sure to have a monopoly of his
attentions.

When the ship tied up in Manhattan, the press embarked in
droves to interview the arriving celebrity. According to Maud,
they 'elbowed me out of existence and blotted out my pageant. I
was discovered in our state-room weeping among our boxes,

because my happy, cherished hours were over. Herbert dried my tears and promised me that everything should come again: but it never did.'

2

I am But a Broken Reed

The love affair between Herbert Tree and May Pinney was a romantic tragedy which might never have come about but for a strange accident. Fate plays a part in the creation of each life, but in this instance the life of Carol Reed can be traced to a solitary piece of chance. Had Herbert Tree been more efficient at tidying up a day's work with his papers, his life-long affair with May Pinney would never have taken place and neither Carol nor his brothers and sister would have been born.

In 1892, ten years after Tree had married Maud, Beatrice May Pinney, aged just seventeen, went to the Haymarket Theatre to see Tree in *The Dancing Girl*, a serious modern drama by Henry Arthur Jones who, with Arthur Wing Pinero and Oscar Wilde, was one of the London stage's three most successful dramatists during the 1890s. Tree had hoped to benefit from an association with Jones and had staged his play *Wealth* in 1889, but the production made a loss. He resumed the association with *The Dancing Girl*, which was to run for three hundred performances – a record for such a serious piece of work.

It was during a rehearsal for the play that one of the many amusing incidents concerning Tree took place. Jones, in desperation at Tree's interpretation of a line, had cried: 'No, no, no,' to which Tree had said: 'Don't repeat yourself.' 'I must if you won't listen,' said Jones. Tree replied: 'Repetition breeds listlessness. By the time you said your last "no" I had forgotten what the first was about.' Jones, barely containing his anger, went along with his tormentor: 'Very well. I'll be content with one. No!' 'No what?'

Having seen Tree in *The Dancing Girl*, May Pinney wrote to him confessing that she had fallen in love with him and asking whether they might meet. He replied to her, as he replied to many other young women in a similar plight, that a meeting was out of the question, but thanking her all the same. Although

Tree was married, with a wife who prominently shared his limelight, this did not prevent a shoal of young female admirers from falling in love with him from the stalls of the Haymarket.

What differentiated May Pinney from the rest was the determination with which she persisted in her romantic sexual fantasy. She was adamant that only a meeting would satisfy her ardour, and she wrote again to Tree, who was shortly to leave with Maud, Viola and her nurse on their annual holiday to Marienbad, his favourite spa resort. He enjoyed every aspect of the place, was first at the Pump Room in the early morning, then, according to Maud, 'took baths, drank waters, drove, walked, dreamed in the pine-forest, wrote, studied, made friends, lived and laughed and sang away industriously idle days' before going out each evening to the theatre or the opera.

Always a man with too much work to do, yet always as polite as possible with his loyal followers, he swept all of his unresolved paperwork into a suitcase and took it to Austria with him. There, in a hotel room, he trudged through his unfinished business. He came across the young Miss Pinney's second letter, read it and was touched by it, but considered that there was no future in any relationship she might suggest. He therefore decided not to reply, and threw her letter in the hearth, along with the other waste paper of his day's work. Before leaving for a walk he set a match to the pile and all trace of the girl's proposal went up in flames. Or so he imagined.

Whether it was by pure chance or because he gave more thought to the young woman as he took his walk around the spa, he returned to his hotel room to discover that a corner of one of the letters had not been burnt with the rest. It contained the address of May Pinney, to whom, he decided, he would write. Fate had spared her message to him, so Fate must be obeyed.

Tree wrote to May Pinney from his Marienbad hotel room and agreed to meet her. The implication to both of them was quite plain. Thus, he and May became lovers, and soon she became pregnant and gave birth to their son Claude, who took his father's true surname, Beerbohm. May became Tree's permanent mistress and was maintained by him in a house on Putney Hill.

It is a touching and deeply romantic story. How true it is is difficult to know, for the teller of this implausible tale was Tree himself, via the memory of another young woman with whom he was to have a long affair, Olivia Truman. We can assume, in the circumstances, that Tree embroidered the truth about May's approach to him. Olivia knew of the existence of Lady Tree, but he was telling his newest lover how he also came to have a well-established mistress. Tree's charm was able to ward off the threat of embarrassment in such a situation, and he did this by telling with an equal mixture of candour, pathos and romance the story of the formation of his second family.

The three most important women in Tree's life delivered themselves to him in the same way, first falling in love with him on the stage, then writing to him, then meeting him briefly. The pattern was so familiar that Maud, revealing a sense of humour much to her credit, used to say: 'Herbert's affairs start with a compliment and end with a confinement.'

In the early 1890s, May Pinney changed her name to Reed, as she explained many years later, 'Because I was but a broken Reed at the foot of the mighty Tree.' Her second son, Robin, and her third, Vivian Guy, born in March 1904, and all the subsequent children were named Reed.

The home in which Tree established his second family on Putney Hill was a strange, single-storeyed house called Daisyfield. He bought it from the painter John Brett after 1895, by which time May had two children by Tree. Brett had designed the house to his own, rather eccentric, specifications. Beatrix Potter once visited Brett there: 'His house is a curiosity, planned by himself, all on one floor, in the ecclesiastical cruciform, without fireplaces – or originally doors, but it was so uncomfortable that they added some.' Olivia Truman, who, although a rival, became friendly with May, thought it 'a curious house all on one floor with very large, rather mysterious rooms opening out of each other divided by curtains – and intensely quiet – except for the children's voices.'

Tree's marriage to Maud had lost most of its meaning by 1896 when he set out alone on his second American tour. Herbert found it difficult to avoid sexual liaisons with women who thrust themselves at him, while Maud demanded inappropriate roles in his plays. To retaliate she set up her own productions in direct opposition, forcing him to take notice. As they both grew older, Herbert would hire theatres for Maud to act in, simply in order to keep her away from His Majesty's. There were stormy scenes both at home and in the theatre, yet still Tree maintained an affectionate loyalty to her. He appeared to prefer bigamy to complete separation and, although he explored divorce a number of times, he never found the right moment to abandon Maud. He was also very fond of his Tree daughters and, in an attempt to have a legitimate son, tried for a third child with Maud during 1896. She was pregnant when he crossed the Atlantic.

During this rare period of reconciliation, Herbert rewarded his wife by appointing her to the committee administering the construction of his new theatre, Her Majesty's, which was being built across the road from the Haymarket. Viola Tree vividly remembered the early days of Her Majesty's. 'He was justly proud of it,' she wrote, 'as it gradually dropped its scaffolding and emerged, a tall, cream-coloured building, with a bronze dome, which we hoped would turn green with time. He and I used to look up at it, and then walk to the top of the Haymarket and look down at it, and one of us would say: "I think it's a little greener today, don't you?"'

While Tree was in America, Maud received an anonymous letter informing her about her husband's other family. Whether this was the first time that she discovered about May it is hard to tell, but it is perhaps significant that Maud always referred to May's children as Herbert's 'American sons'.

Tree was at the Lafayette Square Opera House in Washington D.C., preparing Gilbert Parker's dramatisation of his own novel *The Seat of the Mighty*, when Maud's angry letters caught up with him. He adopted his usual defence of assaulting the source of the gossip to avoid addressing the substance of the allegations. 'Don't worry, sweet one, about that horrid letter,' he wrote. 'It was evidently written by some enemy of yours – for who but a cruel and depraved wretch could send such a letter knowing your condition. Please don't give it another thought.'

Within a week he had written a second letter, again reassuring his wife that all was well. 'I am not flirting with anyone and you may rely on my being good. I have been worrying myself about that horrible letter – if you get any more, do not worry yourself by reading them, promise me, but send them to Webb [his business solicitor] or to George Lewis [his personal lawyer].' He wrote that he had no idea who had been sending the letters and he concluded, 'If I had known, I would have made you come with me.'

In a subsequent letter, Tree wrote extravagantly of his love for his wife and his daughters. 'I took your picture to bed last night and Viola's and Felicity's and prayed for my darlings.' By January he was in Philadelphia and was still apologising. 'It was madness to let you stay behind . . . Oh, my dear sweet Maud, by the time you get this letter all will probably be over – I hope you will not suffer – you know that I shall always be thinking of you and wishing that I could be by to hold your dear hand. Sometimes I think I cannot stay – but that I must take the first steamer to London, regardless of everything. Maud darling, I hope you have not been making yourself unhappy about me – you must know that you are sure of my love.'

Later that month Iris Tree was born. The fact that she was not a boy appears to have been significant in ensuring that the Tree marriage would never revive. Herbert and Maud had both hoped for a son as both were conscious that there was no male heir. According to Maud, 'It had been quite settled and determined beforehand that the new baby should be the boy of the family, for both Herbert and I longed for a son; but the frost of our disappointment was soon melted away by the calm and inextinguishable sunshine of the newcomer.' To give Tree credit, he was devoted to all his children equally, whichever their sex, and was particularly encouraging to the girls, urging them to work if they wished.

Maud could not be blamed for not producing a boy, but her personal behaviour was far from blameless. While displaying indignation at the prospect of Herbert's adultery, she had been making love to the actor Lewis Waller, himself a married man. Herbert had heard the rumours about Maud's love affair and had tackled her on the subject. It was an awkward and somewhat unconvincing performance on Tree's behalf to complain of his wife's infidelities when he was enjoying so many himself. Perhaps it was a question of the degree of indiscretion which Tree considered appropriate in such a public marriage, perhaps simply the double standard of a man who cannot bear to see his wife follow his own example. Whatever the reason, Tree confronted Maud with the fact and drew out of her an explanation and an assurance that nothing had gone on.

Tree took off to Marienbad for his annual indulgence, leaving Maud behind. He wrote to her from Austria that her affectionate words had made him both happy and sad, and confessed that he had not fully understood her for a long time and that this might be his fault. This was the moment when both concluded that a bargain must be struck. Maud would continue directing his social arrangements, would administer his principal residence and would be intimately involved in his theatre work, particularly the running of his new theatre. He, however, was to be allowed his own private life.

He spent the rest of his life bobbing between Maud's house, the fixed domestic circumstances of Daisyfield and his private rooms at the top of his new theatre. Maud laid the foundation stone of Her Majesty's Theatre in 1895 and it slowly rose up opposite the Haymarket Theatre. It was designed in the French style by the architect C. J. Phipps. On the top floor was a sumptuous suite of rooms in which Tree would live and in which he could entertain his lovers. He moved into it in 1900.

The interior of the dome was split into two rooms: one a banqueting suite, the scene of all Tree's first-night parties, with food delivered from the Carlton restaurant next to the theatre; the other was a sitting room, with his bed concealed in the wall. Viola remembered that the dome 'consisted of a high banqueting-hall, ending in rafters and what might have been a belfry, and a small inner room, which he always said was very characteristic of himself. This, however, was his own modest estimate, for it really was nothing more than an ordinary comfortable room, distinguished only by a frieze running round it, painted with scenes from *Twelfth Night*, *The Tempest* and *The Taming of the Shrew*. Underneath the frieze were bookshelves containing large illustrated books.'

Tree was not tidy. 'The interesting books and papers were piled up with his methodical untidiness on chair, sofas and desks: the room had a nice glow of hard work; there was nothing stale or burnt out about it.' Tree had built a central London palace for himself, with the dome room his private domain.

Maud's affair with Lewis Waller continued, and was even encouraged by Tree in 1898 when he awarded the actor a three-year contract. Life at Her Majesty's must have been very complicated, with Waller abandoning a successful version of *The*

Three Musketeers, in which his wife was playing the lead female part, in order to be bought out for a huge sum by Tree, his rival as an actor-manager and Maud's cuckolded husband.

Maud was unhappy with the small role in *The Three Mus-keteers* which Herbert had found for her and wished instead to play the part taken by Mrs Waller in the original production. Even when it fell vacant, Tree declined Maud's offer to take it up, adding to a state of affairs, entirely engineered by Tree, which was already brimming over with latent hysteria. Maud made her displeasure felt by sitting in the wings and bawling. It is little wonder that Tree enjoyed retreating to the tranquillity of Daisyfield.

A wife at the theatre and a mistress in the suburbs was not enough for Tree, who soon introduced a third woman into his life, the actress Constance Collier. She was quite different from the others, both of whom shared similar middle-class back-grounds. Maud was at first a priggish and slightly pious young woman, then a liberated and independent actress; May was a more broad-minded, quiet daughter of a clergyman. By con-trast, Constance, a Gaiety girl who performed in music halls around London, had not yet found fame or financial security. Although she appeared on stage as a well-dressed, fun-loving woman, she returned home to her mother who lived in poverty off the Kennington Road in Vauxhall.

Meeting Herbert Tree was to transform her life. She was to become a sought-after actress and she became rich – rich enough to buy her mother a comfortable home. She became Tree's lover when he cast her in his production of Stephen Phillips's *Ulysses*.

Constance was twenty-four in 1901 when she was taken to see Tree in the dome room of Her Majesty's, but she told him she was twenty (Herbert was forty-eight). Their first meeting must have made a lasting impression upon him. She was a tall, strikingly good looking, part-Portuguese woman, with dark features and large, prominent eyes. She was wearing a hat which was crowned with a large, green, stuffed bird. Accord-ing to Constance, during the course of the short interview, she seated, he standing, he gently stroked the bird's feathers. The forwardness of Tree's caresses proved too much for her and she walked out of the room in some embarrassment and without a job. Tree did not forget her, however, though it took a whole year before he began to subject her to a most formal, contrived and cruelly extended game of seduction by casting couch.

He first sent a note to the theatre in which she was working, the Comedy, asking that she meet him at Her Majesty's the following morning. Constance arrived in good time. When she was shown up to the dome room, Tree was sitting at his desk working. He looked up and said: 'Where's that bird?' His eyes raked her up and down for some time, now and then he muttered 'Yes,' then he asked her whether she had ever spoken blank verse on the stage before. She said she had not. 'Then it's impossible. Good morning, Miss Collier.'

A week later she was sent for again and again he asked her the same question. Again she replied no and again she was told it was 'impossible'.

At the third 'audition' she was again dismissed, but she begged Tree to allow her to try reading for the part. After his performance that evening she read for him and he told her to report to the theatre the following day. She stood on the stage and read Calypso's lines from *Ulysses*, was deemed by Phillips to have the right profile and was given the role. In rehearsals, which mostly took place after midnight, Tree told her: 'I want you to play this part with a *mauve* voice.' Following her success in *Ulysses*, Constance was given a three-year contract and became Tree's lover. The affair did not last for long. Constance had more sense than to wish to be merely the third woman in an actor's life.

For as long as they shared the same stage, Constance accompanied Tree in public, except on semi-official occasions when Maud reappeared. Maud continued to preside over first-night parties and evidently enjoyed herself in her public role as Lady Tree, wife of the great Sir Herbert. Tree was happy to have Maud by him at such moments, and not only because she was his wife and propriety expected her presence. But May and the children were also welcome at the theatre and attended each dress rehearsal in lieu of the first nights, which were forbidden them. Even Tree could not defy convention enough to parade his mistress and their illegitimate children in front of the great and good who assembled to see his new productions.

Maud also proved a fine partner in the one-line witticisms which Tree enjoyed so much. They used to hold parties in the banqueting room of Her Majesty's, which Maud dubbed 'Herbert Tree at Dome', and she was noted for her amusing remarks at them. 'Life is very disappointing,' she once said. 'Nothing comes off except buttons.' When a hostess greeted Maud, wearing a hairpiece, with the compliment, 'How charmingly you've done your hair, Maud!' she instantly replied, 'Sweet of you to call it my hair.' The American who suggested to her that England was an island off France was met with the rejoinder, 'America is a continent off colour.'

The combination of Tree and Constance Collier on stage was highly profitable for Tree. In a succession of Shakespeare's plays he established with her a partnership at His Majesty's aping if not rivalling that of Henry Irving and Ellen Terry at the Lyceum. Nor did they restrict themselves to Shakespeare. One of their most popular pairings was presented on the last day of the 1904 season when Tree played Fagin to Constance's Nancy in Comyns Carr's adaptation of Dickens's *Oliver Twist*. Tree was nervous of the script but was convinced that it should be staged when Constance took an option on it with her own money. He was still reluctant, but agreed to a one-night trial, his solution to many awkward decisions. The public's response would decide.

When it came to the key scene of the murder of Nancy, Tree decided that it should take place off-stage, and the audience would be left with the sight of Fagin, staring into the moonlight, the sound of Sikes's club beating down and their own imaginations. Tree compounded the effect by forbidding Constance to take a curtain call. Fagin became one of Tree's most popular roles and the production, planned for just one night, lasted a year.

Olivia Truman, drawn to His Majesty's – renamed in 1901 in honour of the new king, Edward VII – in the hope of glimpsing her hero, caught sight of Tree and Constance in the Carlton restaurant. 'We "teaed" at the Carlton,' she wrote, 'and I saw – H! He came with Constance Collier (looking wonderful) at whom he gazed as if he could eat her – with rapture!' In fact the affair between Tree and Constance did not last for long. In 1902 she befriended Herbert's brother Max and, after a romantic seaside holiday in Dieppe, they became engaged in 1903, although it came to nothing. In the meantime, Tree was looking elsewhere.

Olivia was only twelve when she first wrote to Tree and offered him her devotion. In 1900 she had been to Her Majesty's Theatre to see *A Midsummer Night's Dream* in which Tree appeared as, of all parts, Bottom. It is a tribute to the young Olivia's imagination that she was immediately struck by Tree's handsome looks and charm, for they were buried beneath the most extraordinary make-up. Pictures of him in the role show him with wild, short-cropped hair, draped in a short toga tied at the waist, and wearing Roman sandals. Despite his disguise, Olivia wrote to him declaring her love, although she took the precaution of adopting a pseudonym and borrowing a friend's address in case her passionate outburst evoked a reply. Parents in 1900 did not approve of daughters who wrote to actors. Out of politeness, Tree wrote back, though what he said we shall never know, for Olivia's friend was on holiday when Tree's letter arrived and the family's servants, not recognising Olivia's false name, gave it back to the postman.

Adolescent passion is not so easily put off. Inspired by seeing Tree in *Rip van Winkle* and a revival of *Julius Caesar*, Olivia wrote again: 'I am thirteen and never loved so passionately before.' This time there was no response. So she wrote a more moderate letter, asking Tree for a donation to the Society for Soldiers' and Sailors' Families, a fund set up to support widows and orphans of the Boer War. Tree wrote back in his own hand, enclosing a cheque for two guineas.

To give him his due, Tree did attempt to dampen Olivia's passion. The following month, having received several further letters, he wrote to her from Gruenes Kreuz, Marienbad: 'I think you ought at once to tell your mother that you had written to me and that I had responded to your request. I do not think it would be becoming, were I to write to you without her knowledge, and I am sure you will agree with me in this, and not think me churlish or priggish.' But the put-down also contained a come-on. He added not one but two postscripts, the second of which said: 'It is rather lonely here as I am almost the solitary Englishman and my family are at home.'

Tree was a compulsive philanderer who could not resist teasing even an immature thirteen-year-old in hot pursuit.

Olivia continued to stalk him. She made her way to the front door of the Tree residence at 77 Sloane Street and wiped a handkerchief, decorated with blue-and-white clover leaves, over the spot below the lock where his hand would rest each time he used his key. This holy handkerchief she then encased in an enamel reliquary.

Tree followed his letter to Olivia with another, to Olivia's mother, asking whether she would visit Her Majesty's Theatre and speak with him. This she did, taking Olivia with her. The trembling daughter remembered: 'My emotion and excitement were so great that I could hardly contain them. . . . Within a minute or two of my mother leaving me he came down the stairs leading to the foyer and dress circle with the quick light step I was to know so well. He wore the frock-coat and top hat that was then generally worn by men in London. Again I beheld the rounded pale face, the brilliant blue eyes, and the mobile mouth drooping to the left corner, of . . . the reality behind Bottom, Rip, Mark Antony, Herod, Malvolio.' She was summoned out of the cab to meet her hero. They shook hands. 'My tongue was cleaving to the roof of my mouth, my knees nearly giving way under me. He stood regarding me, I expect rather embarrassed himself in the presence of a third party.' Five years were to pass before they next met.

Tree had tried to avoid meeting her again, at one time consenting only if her mother were to accompany her. In 1905 he wrote to her: 'It would not be right – there is no other reason – that we should meet. Please, please, think of me only as one who deeply appreciates your goodness, you would only spoil your life if I were to intrude into it.' Yet intrude he did, later that year, in the dome room above His Majesty's.

She visited him during the interval of a performance, accompanied by a friend. Then, pretending she had lost her bracelet, she returned to him briefly at the end of the play. They made love almost at once. 'Everything I had to offer of body, soul and spirit, I gave him then.' He was aged fifty-two; she was just seventeen.

He made a rendezvous for the following day at the theatre, and they spent the afternoon driving around London in a hansom cab. She had worried that when they finally met he would be paternal, but instead he put his head on her shoulder.

Her description of their meeting was candid in the extreme. 'He made love quite beautifully and just like a boy. I have nowhere seen such amazing vitality. He is a simple mass of inconsistency and so wayward – that it is I who guide him and not he me.' She was surprised by his youthful looks. 'His skin instead of being yellow and freckled as I had always fancied is fine and fresh – and I am in a position to judge!!!' She told him that even if she were eventually to marry a more suitable man, she would still visit Tree and beg him to continue their affair. She asked him how he would react. His inability to say categorically that nothing would occur caused her to deliberate that 'all thoughts on matrimony must be at an end' and that she was 'fully resigned to thick boots and good works'.

Their friendship, which lasted for the rest of Tree's life, remained largely based on sex. Olivia did not find this a cause for shame. 'That I never became his mistress in the accepted sense of the word is true,' she wrote, 'and there are people who seem to think that such a thing is of importance, marking the line between what is "moral" and what is "immoral", as if a mere physical act, taken by itself, can have any significance other than legal.'

Within two months of Tree meeting Olivia, they were so intimate and Tree was so trusting that he explained to her the complications of his life. He took her to the Temple, where he was to see Sir George Lewis, the most eminent divorce lawyer of the time and, when he emerged from the meeting, told her everything about his tangled domestic arrangements.

It was plain to Tree that divorce from Maud was out of the question. It was inevitable that in any proceedings the existence of his second household in Putney would be exposed. He would not only have his private affairs splashed over the gossip-hungry newspapers, but, in such scandalous circumstances, his wife would gain sole custody of his three daughters. To be distanced from them was more than he could bear. He was therefore obliged to remain married to Maud. It was plain to Olivia Truman that Tree was devoted to May and she to him. Olivia was despondent. 'Here indeed was a barrier between us which all my tenacity would never break down.'

On the long carriage journey to Putney, Tree told Olivia the story of how he had come to meet May and made her his mistress. It was to be the first of many journeys to Daisyfield which Olivia would share. 'How often I drove there,' she later wrote, 'but half a log was better than no Tree.' The cab pulled up at a gateway to a long drive, at the end of which was a grand bungalow. Tree told the driver to take his young lover back to London, paid him off and walked to the house, where he took out his latchkey, opened the front door and disappeared from view.

Olivia sobbed all the way home, 'sitting huddled up in the corner, a miserable little black-clothed figure, feeling tragically lonely, in face of my first big encounter with the fire of life'. She determined that May's existence would not overshadow her love for Tree and that she would bear her no jealousy.

On the day that Carol Reed was born, Sunday 30 December 1906, *The Observer* published a typical notice of Tree's most recent production, as Antony to Constance's Cleopatra, which reveals Tree's status as an actor-manager at the time. It read: 'Mr Tree has never lacked the courage of his managerial convictions. He certainly showed it when, in choosing the evening after Boxing night for a Shakespearian production of the order of his *Antony and Cleopatra*, he braved the cheap sneer about belated pantomime that was sure to go round the house. Such comment, although ungracious and to some extent unfair, was inevitable, since there can be no doubt that the chief impression upon the mind of the audience was left by the spectacle rather than by the acting, by the frame rather than by the picture, by the mounting rather than by the tragedy.'

It would be some years before Carol and his brothers and sister came to understand how well known a public figure their father was. From the inside, the Reed family appeared as Herbert and May had intended it to appear: an ordinary Edwardian gentleman's family. Those who lived close by, however, knew Tree's parallel family for what it was. May's neighbours saw Tree's regular appearances at Daisyfield. He was a conspicuous figure, tall and striking, with pale blue eyes which could not be mistaken. Although neighbours knew that the 'Reeds' were not married, it was not known by the Reed children, nor by children who came to play with them.

Tree was a good father to both his Tree and his Reed families. A description of Tree at home has been left by his daughter Viola. 'We always heard his voice before we saw him, for he never came into the room, or, in Hampstead and Chiswick days,

into the garden, without calling out loudly and penetratingly
from where he was, "Viola!" or "Children!" This had the effect of
a flourish of trumpets; we all dropped our game or our lesson
and ran to find him. I remember him best standing on the stairs
or in the hall, always leaning on something; sometimes he
leaned on my head – always with his hat on, and wearing a big
flamboyant coat, and carrying some very tall walking-stick (he
had a succession of sticks) in his hand – he had really beautiful
white disproportionately small hands.' She remembered Tree
scolding her for accepting pennies from an actress visiting their
home. He glared at his daughter and asked her: 'You didn't ask
for them, did you?'

At Daisyfield, Tree enjoyed a similarly warm family life. At
the heart of it was May Reed. She was a strikingly handsome
woman, with bright eyes and a fresh complexion, highlighted
by sparingly used make-up. Her dark hair was done up in a
French pleat. One friend of the family described her as 'statuesque. It was her perfect deportment. She carried herself
magnificently.' She wore ankle-length dresses, as was the style,
and had a bold taste in hats, often worn in the Tyrolean fashion,
with a lone feather. She was gentle and kind to children,
particularly young ones. Yet she could be stern when dealing
with Tree. After the birth of Claude, there had been a disagreement between them which caused him to return to Maud,
during which time Viola and Felicity Tree were born.

At the end of January 1907, three weeks after Carol was born,
Olivia Truman wrote to her aunt Judy about the first night of
Tree's *Nero* and of trouble at Daisyfield. 'His other woman is
behaving so badly that he is beginning to fall in love with me!!!!
She is such a devil! is furious he succeeded and she calls herself
in love with him.' A couple of months later she reports, 'Putney
has been behaving better to him latterly – and he runs off from
me to her with avidity – an extraordinary man!' And in June of
the same year Olivia was telling her aunt, 'Remember his
mistress cannot become his wife – come what may I must have
that supreme advantage over Putney should Maud die.' Exactly
what May's disqualification for marriage was is not explained. It
would have been unconventional for a widower to marry his
mistress, but no more so than the lack of conventional behaviour
which Tree already displayed. Had Olivia been told of a legal

impediment, such as an undisclosed marriage? It remains a mystery.

By September even Olivia had become scandalised by the literal state of affairs in which she found herself. Her mother had been told that Tree had even more lovers running concurrently than Olivia knew about. Olivia wrote a sharp letter to him which elicited from Tree one of the most heartfelt descriptions of May and the troubled conscience that not being able to marry her caused him. He wrote: ' I have for many years had a friendship with a *lady* – and I think you know of this – to this lady I have been attached by the strongest ties – you are right in assuming that I have not been guilty of dishonourable conduct and I may tell you that the lady in question said to me not very long ago that she thought I "could not do a mean thing if I tried". That of course is only her opinion, but I thought that, coming from this woman, it was the highest compliment that had ever been paid me.'

In October, Maud and Lewis Waller were injured in a car accident. Her jaw was severely broken and, although treated and mended, she was left horribly disfigured. Tree seriously considered divorce. Maud had been with Waller despite his express order that the affair should cease. She had behaved recklessly and had put the welfare of their daughters in jeopardy. This would have been a good time for pressing a divorce suit against Maud, citing Weller as co-respondent, if he was to keep custody of his daughters. He consulted George Lewis, but concluded that the case would still expose May and the children.

Olivia proved a perceptive commentator on the event. 'Personally I think it would have been the sheerest hypocrisy for him, with May and her children in the background, to have brought an action.' She concluded that, if Tree did not divorce Maud in these circumstances, he would never divorce her and that therefore all her hopes of eventually marrying him were hopeless. 'So my matrimonial project receded,' she wrote. 'In any case, it was an absurd idea, at his age and with his commitments, nor can I imagine a less satisfactory husband. His theatre was his home, and he had no leisure or inclination for anything else. What time he did spend with his family, or families, he must have been tired, and probably irritable, as are all highly strung people when fatigued.'

This last remark was far from the truth. Childhood friends of Carol Reed and his brothers and sister testify to Tree's good humour and fondness for children. Claude, his first child with May, was much older than the rest of his brothers and sisters and played little part in family life at Daisyfield. He followed Tree onto the stage and openly exploited his father's position, acting with his father and with Constance, even being taken on an American tour with Tree. He was, however, a weak-willed young man who took to drink and caused embarrassment to May and the younger children. In later life, it was Carol who kept Claude's wayward behaviour out of sight and paid for his upkeep in a nursing home.

The other children, however, enjoyed a warm home life, and Tree was a good father, taking an interest in each of them. He liked performing for them, drawing screams of laughter from them as he pretended to be in turn a short-sighted man, a drunken man, a tired man and an absent-minded man. He would lift the children onto his shoulders, so that they towered over eight feet from the ground, as he ran around, weaving in and out of the branches of a cedar tree in the middle of the garden.

The Reed children were all quite different. Robin was out-going and flamboyant, a reaction, perhaps, to a congenital deformation of his right hand. His fingers stopped short at the end of his palm and he had nail-less stumps instead of digits. This handicap, which was to reappear in a different form in Carol's son Max, did not slow him down. Robin was immensely sporting and noisy and enjoyed practical jokes.

He was quite the opposite of Carol and Guy, who were more sedate, more introverted and unsporty. Carol was always bookish, happier inside the house reading than outside playing cricket. He was interested in his father and eldest brother's trade and used to study books about stagecraft and newspaper and magazine articles about theatrical productions. He was also a keen keeper of pet animals, such as rabbits and guinea pigs, a hobby which was to reappear in later life.

Guy was similar to Carol but slightly more chatty. Peter, the youngest boy, was a friendly child, although capable of occasional outbursts of surliness. And Juliet, always known as Judy, was a good-looking girl, with long chestnut hair. As she reached her teens she took a keen interest in clothes and fashion. She grew to become tall, with a shapely figure and an aloof manner. She and Robin went to dances together.

During the early years of Carol Reed's life, his father remained highly successful. When Carol was three, Tree was knighted, much to the pleasure of his followers. By chance, he was appearing as Malvolio in *Twelfth Night* when the honour was announced and, when he came to the line, 'Some have greatness thrust upon them', the audience at His Majesty's rose to their feet. Although Carol was too young to appreciate fully his father's productions, he attended the dress rehearsals of many of them and lingered around His Majesty's when some of the most interesting were in preparation. One production which he might have remembered, as he was eight when it reached the stage, was Bernard Shaw's *Pygmalion*.

Tree had for many years been trying to encourage Shaw to write something for him, and Shaw had consistently refused. *Pygmalion* had been written in 1911 with Mrs Patrick Campbell intended to play Eliza Doolittle, but because of a taxi crash in which she was injured she had not been able to appear. Shaw waited for her to recover, and would not allow anyone else in London to produce it – although it had been presented in Vienna and in Berlin. Mrs Campbell had not wished Tree to have anything to do with the play, but by the end of 1913 and an enforced convalescence, she was very short of money. Against Shaw's advice, she approached Tree.

Tree had at first hoped to play Eliza's father, the dustman Alfred Doolittle, but he was persuaded by Maud, who thought the part too obvious for him, and by Shaw, who thought it demeaning for Tree to play a minor role in his own theatre, that he should play the elocutionist Professor Henry Higgins. Shaw decided to direct the play himself, not least because both Mrs Campbell and Tree were capable of desecrating a play to make it work in their favour. Rehearsals began in February 1914. Shaw described his problem: 'One must confess bluntly at the outset that Tree was the despair of authors. His attitude towards a play was one of whole-hearted anxiety to solve the problem of how to make it please and interest the audience.' The business of attracting and holding an audience was for Shaw a problem for the author, not the actor. Actors were mere cyphers. Tree disagreed with Shaw on the relationship between actor and text and took liberties without thought or guilt, even when Shaw was sitting in the stalls during rehearsals, watching his play disintegrate in front of him.

According to Shaw, Tree 'with his restless imagination, felt that he needed nothing from an author but a literary scaffold on which to exhibit his own creations . . . the notion that a play could succeed without any further help from the actor than a simple impersonation of his part never occurred to Tree. The author, whether Shakespear [sic] or Shaw, was a lame dog to be helped over the stile by the ingenuity and inventiveness of the actor-producer.' At the opening rehearsals of *Pygmalion*, Shaw found that 'instead of having to discover how to make an effective histrionic entertainment on the basis of such scraps of my dialogue as might prove useful, he had only to fit himself into a jig-saw puzzle cut out by me, and just to act the part as well as he could, he could [not] grasp the situation'. Shaw and Tree held a crisis luncheon at the Royal Automobile Club in Pall Mall and agreed that they must find a way of working with each other.

The truce lasted until Tree remarked during a rehearsal, 'I seem to have heard or read somewhere that plays have actually been produced, and performances given, in this theatre, under its present management, before you came. According to you, that couldn't have happened. How do you account for it?' 'I can't account for it,' Shaw replied. 'I suppose you put a notice in the papers that a performance will take place at half-past eight, and take the money at the doors. Then you have to do the play somehow. There is no other way of accounting for it.' Eventually Shaw came to the conclusion that the only way to take control of the anarchy on stage was to widen his ambition. 'I very soon gave up all expectation of being treated otherwise than as a friend who had dropped in; so, finding myself as free to interfere in the proceedings as anyone else who dropped in would apparently have been, I interfered not only in my proper department but in every other as well; and nobody gainsaid me.'

Shaw became a cautious admirer of Tree's craft: 'Tree always seemed to have heard the lines of the other performers for the first time, and even to be a little taken aback by them.' He cited, as an example, the scene where Eliza, in a rage, throws

Higgins's slippers into his face. 'When we rehearsed this for the first time,' Shaw remembered, 'I had taken care to have a very soft pair of velvet slippers provided; for I knew that Mrs Patrick Campbell was very dextrous, very strong and a dead shot. And, sure enough, when we reached this passage, Tree got the slippers well and truly delivered with unerring aim bang in his face.' The effect was appalling. 'He had totally forgotten that there was any such incident in the play; and it seemed to him that Mrs Campbell, suddenly giving way to an impulse of diabolical wrath and hatred, had committed an unprovoked and brutal assault on him. The physical impact was nothing; but the wound to his feelings was terrible.' Tree collapsed in his chair, amazed, while his loyal theatre staff crowded around to offer him comfort. 'The worst of it was that as it was quite evident that he would be just as surprised and wounded next time, Mrs Campbell took care that the slippers should never hit him again, and the incident was consequently one of the least convincing in the performance.'

Tree was not the only one to present Bernard Shaw with problems. Mrs Campbell spent so much time moving the furniture so that she could upstage Tree that Shaw had everything screwed down except the grand piano, remarking: 'She can move that if she likes.'

Twice Shaw walked out of the theatre in disgust. Each time Tree nonchalantly waved him goodbye as casually as if he were simply passing through; and each time Shaw's return to rehearsals, following urgent appeals from other members of the cast, was greeted by Tree as if a friend had dropped in to witness the great man at work. As Shaw put it: 'I had to fight my way through to a sort of production in the face of an unresisting, amusing, friendly, but heart-breakingly obstructive principal.' Shaw having resisted Tree's requests to play the dustman, he was instead forced to play 'a sort of man he had never met and of whom he had no conception'. Shaw left Tree little room for interpretation, but Tree was determined to make Higgins a romantic lover in his own mould. 'He was quite baffled,' remembered Shaw, 'until he lit on the happy thought of throwing flowers to Eliza in the very brief interval between the end of the play and the fall of the curtain.'

Shaw became so resigned to despair at the final outcome of the rehearsals that he refused to attend the first night, telling Tree that he would happily attend the hundredth, adding that he therefore expected never to see the production at all. In fact *Pygmalion* proved to be his most commercially successful play yet, and he did attend the hundredth night, though it shocked and displeased him that Tree had added to the second act 'a stroke of comic business so outrageously irrelevant that I solemnly cursed the whole enterprise, and bade the delinquents farewell for ever'.

In the winter of 1915 Tree and his daughter Iris set out for the United States to make a film of *Macbeth* with Constance Collier in Hollywood. Two of his stage productions had already been filmed, but this was to be the first film in which he would learn a script specially adapted for the screen. He had cast himself in a stage production of *Macbeth* four years earlier. Before he set off for Los Angeles he had been giving some thought to the cinema, which he considered the coming medium. 'New and vigorous impulses seem to me to be at work in it,' he wrote, 'and doubtless before long it will drop all slavish copying of the stage and strike out along fresh paths.' He jotted down a number of projects in which he had been engaged which he thought might make suitable film projects, among them *Richard II*, *The Merchant of Venice* and *Othello*, Sheridan's *School for Scandal*, Tolstoy's *Resurrection* and his adaptations of Dickens, *David Copperfield* and *Oliver Twist*.

Tree arrived in New York on 24 November and set off for the west coast on 21 December, arriving six days later. As the *Christian Science Monitor* reported at the beginning of January 1916: 'Sir Herbert was entering a new and strange artistic world.'

Constance was well established in Hollywood, having made two films already that year, D. W. Griffith's extraordinary epic on the history of love, *Intolerance*, and *The Code of Marcia Gray*. She had rented a bungalow for Tree near her home and introduced him to the film people she knew. These included Griffith, the silent star Lillian Gish and Charles Chaplin, who turned out to be a great admirer of Tree. Chaplin told Constance that he had often sat in the gallery of His Majesty's, and had happily spent the shilling or so price of his supper on a ticket to watch Tree.

Tree and Chaplin became friends and went on walks along Venice Beach. 'Contrary to expectations', Tree found Chaplin to be 'a young man of a serious and sensitive disposition, who has artistic ambitions of a kind not suggested by his public records and who in private life is thoughtful as well as versatile and entertaining.' But in one way Tree did misjudge him, and the medium of the cinema. He wrote: 'I shall be more than a little surprised if he had not a very brilliant future before him upon the legitimate stage, after his vogue in pictures is done.'

As for his own film of *Macbeth*, the production was in some disarray. Work was started under the direction of John Emerson, the husband of the humorous writer Anita Loos, who had written the title-cards for *Intolerance*. Tree was reputed to have been paid a fee of £2000, a fabulous sum, for his appearance, but he soon discovered that the movie business expects total commitment for the duration of shooting. Los Angeles was experiencing torrential rain and flooding when Tree arrived, and outdoor shooting had to be accomplished with flares to compensate for the poor light. The shooting schedule was so behindhand that Tree and Constance found themselves working eighteen-hour days, finishing in the early hours of the morning. As the *New York Times* reported: 'The distinguished star was hustled out of bed at daybreak and kept on the move till after sundown.' In the middle of one night, between 3 and 4 a.m., they discovered that their drivers had been sent home early. Too tired to take off their costumes, they set out on foot along Sunset Boulevard in the pouring rain, she in flowing robes and a crown, he as Macbeth, with false beard, a wig and a primitive kilt.

The film-makers became very fond of the master of the art of stage acting from London and gave him a suitably Hollywood send-off. Tree had particularly amused the actors in the silent westerns, and the train on which he was to depart was surrounded by cowboys in full fancy-dress, rearing their horses up on their hind legs and firing blanks from their revolvers. Constance noticed a look of some relief on Tree's face as the train finally pulled out of Los Angeles station.

He returned to New York where, before long, a print of *Macbeth* arrived and a preview was arranged. Constance was in New York for some stage work, and accompanied him to the screening, which was filled with people from the motion picture industry eager to discover what the great man thought of their investment in his talents. By the time the lights went up at the end of the film, Tree was sound asleep.

In June 1916 *Macbeth* went on public release at the Rialto Cinema, New York. The critics were positive, particularly about Tree's performance, which was, they considered, far more athletic than might have been expected from a man in his sixties.

Another important event took place in New York at that time. Tree met another young actress, Muriel Ridley, who had done well on the London stage before leaving for New York in 1914, at the age of thirty. He must have met her when passing through New York on his way west, for by June 1916 she was pregnant by him.

Tree returned to London and, after discussing the war with the Prime Minister, Herbert Asquith, agreed to undertake a public speaking tour of the United States and Canada, explaining the importance of American involvement in the war. He arrived in New York on 1 October 1916 and set out on a tour of American cities, returning to New York in the New Year of 1917. He was receiving telegrams of congratulation on the effectiveness of his speaking engagements when Muriel Ridley gave birth to Paul Ridley-Tree.

On his return to London in May he first went down to Sutton Courtney to see Maud, who was staying with Asquith and his family for the Whitsun parliamentary recess. Then Tree took May on holiday to Kent. They stayed in the old coastguard's cottage Constance had bought as a summer home at 7 Ethel Bay, Birchington. Although it was primitive, with a hand-drawn well for the water and a domineering local woman who kept house for visitors, Tree was always happy there.

Climbing the steep staircase, on the evening of 16 June, he missed his footing and fell. When May went to help him, he told her, 'This is the end.' He was, as usual, being overdramatic. She helped him to a sofa, where he gave the opinion that he had broken his leg. While May went to telephone for a doctor, Tree tried to walk and again fell over. He was lying on the floor when she returned to him. The doctor arrived, diagnosed a ruptured tendon above the knee and recommended an operation.

Tree and May returned to London by car the following day and he was admitted to a nursing home in Henrietta Street, Covent Garden, as the patient of Sir Alfred Fripp, the surgeon who had mended Maud Tree's jaw and also tended Mrs Patrick Campbell after her near-fatal taxi crash outside the Albert Hall in

1913. The following day Fripp examined Tree and declared that he would operate the next day.

Tree was an impossible patient, refusing anaesthetic until he had watched all the preliminaries to the operation. As he slipped into sleep he murmured, 'Nirvana!' and said, 'I shall see you again.' And he did.

The operation was successful and Tree regained his good humour. Olivia went to see him, bearing delphiniums and lilies, and he was very lively, revising the proofs of a collection of thoughts and witticisms, appropriately entitled *Nothing Matters*, and talking about film projects he was planning. He was considering the sale of His Majesty's and had broached with Bernard Shaw the prospect of reviving *Pygmalion*, as Shaw later recorded, 'as if it promised to be a renewal of the most delightful experience of our lives'. Shaw, then aged sixty, recorded that Tree looked 'incredibly young and sanguine, and made me feel hopelessly old and grumpy'. Olivia wrote: 'I have seen him once since he has been in hospital – looking very squelchy – with his hair on end – and quite unattractive pyjamas – Poor old darling!' She described him as 'looking too comic bless him, with his hair brushed forward a la Romaine – a yellow scarf round his neck – and a purple and gold bed cover'. He wrote to his daughter Viola from his bed: 'All goes miraculously with me – Fripp is overjoyed – and I am thankful.'

He was eager to get up and get on with his next project, a play called, appropriately, *The Great Lover*. Fripp and he exchanged jocular insults about when he should be allowed to return to normal life. The stitches were removed from his knee and the wound had healed perfectly. Tree demanded that he should leave his hospital bed; Fripp ordered him to rest. It was the rest which killed him. Staying in bed caused blood clots to form, which led to a thrombosis.

On the evening of 2 July 1917, May visited him. He told his nurse, 'She is a wonderful woman,' and 'She is a marvellous mother. She is a noble woman. She makes one feel – happy!' Half an hour later the nurse peeled a peach for him and, feeling short of breath, Tree asked her, 'Would you open the window?' When she turned round his head slumped and he was dead. His death made front-page news the following morning. He was sixty-five years old.

The funeral was a semi-public occasion. Lady Tree was dressed all in black, in a costume which many thought a little too extravagant for the occasion. Tree was cremated at Golders Green crematorium and his ashes taken for burial to Hampstead, where the press photographers were waiting to record the final farewell to a great actor. Maud was genuinely distraught, but her performance at the graveside, draped in the pall from the coffin, invited criticism. Olivia, admittedly a partial witness, records: 'Lady Tree has behaved with inconceivable vulgarity – No doubt you saw the picture of her in exaggerated weeds sprawling over his grave.' Worse was to come. Maud went home and, still wearing the pall, took to her bed, giving audiences to friends who were concerned at her distraught condition.

A memorial service for Tree was arranged at St Martin-in-the-Fields, Trafalgar Square, just around the corner from His Majesty's. It was a showy affair. The church was filled with prominent figures from the stage and literature, and a handful of senior politicians. As Olivia observed: 'The large congregation of celebrities, experts at memorial services, sighed the sighs proper to the occasion.' Olivia sat with the box-office manager of His Majesty's. During the service, Clara Butt sang a valedictory and the Bishop of Birmingham delivered a sermon in which he praised Tree, while pointing out that 'his treatment of Shakespeare on the stage has been questioned'. The bishop told Tree's assembled friends and colleagues that his brain had been fully active until the moment 'his clogged heart stopped'.

One important person missing from all the funereal celebrations was, of course, May. Even after Tree's death her existence had to be concealed. She had been closer to him than anyone else in his final days, but Lady Tree was the one whom convention dictated should play the weeping widow. For May it must have been a relief. Olivia paid tribute to her: 'I cannot tell you how fine and brave and dignified she is – I admire her infinitely.' May had never been allowed to enjoy the entertainments and jollity of the public life surrounding Tree. Such duties had been monopolised by Maud and, briefly, Constance Collier. But she could take comfort from the tribute Tree paid to her and her children in his will.

It was a masterful document, drawn up by Tree's solicitor, William Webb, and dealing in lengthy and complicated detail with arrangements for the income of a trust fund to be paid to Maud and her daughters. Maud received a tenth of the income of the trust for life, and the three Tree daughters also received a tenth each. A further tenth fell to Tree's stepmother, his sisters and his brother Max. Then, after giving one hundred pounds to a 'Mrs Browning now in my service', he left a full half of his fortune, without strings, to 'my faithful friend of many years May Pinney. . . . for her use absolutely.'

It was the end of the Tree company's tenure of His Majesty's Theatre. The trustees of the will, who included Max, decided that the enterprise was too intimately related to Tree to be carried on without him. While the Chinese musical *Chu Chin Chow* ran and ran, providing steady funds, it was decided that the theatre and all Tree's effects should be sold by auction. Viola Tree and Olivia Truman attended one of the sales, 'sat in a grief too deep for tears.' There were pictures of Tree in various poses. The furniture from the dome room was sold. Even the small presents given to him by lovers were sold. Olivia watched as 'the brick from Nero's statue I had brought him from Rome when he was acting the play of that name, and had had mounted with a piece of Antony's rostrum as an antique lamp; the fold-mounted notebook he carried; the very frame that used to hold my photo' were put under the gavel.

The total of Tree's estate was £140,000, of which the theatre raised £105,000, £35,000 more than he had paid for it. May's half produced an income of about £2,000 a year.

Carol Reed was never to remember much about his father, being only ten and a half years old when Tree died. There was no mistaking the fact that he was his father's son. He closely resembled Tree, growing to be tall and strikingly handsome, with his father's clear blue eyes. Those who knew them both commented on their similarity. They walked in the same way.

The success of Tree was awesome for Reed, and like the children of other successful parents, he grew up with a father whose achievements could be admired, perhaps emulated, never ignored. Reed's abilities also led him into the theatre, into acting and theatre production and, like Tree, finally into films. Like his father, and certainly because of him, Reed adored actors, with all their egotism, vanity and constant need for attention. In particular he enjoyed the actors of Tree's generation. He knew many of them well and made it his business in later life to flatter them by casting them in his films.

Importantly, most people who knew Carol Reed knew who his father was. Tree was a rampant self-promoter and a colourful public personality whose witticisms and actions on the public as well as the theatrical stage were widely reported. Reed attempted to ignore his link with Tree throughout his life, and even went to great lengths to try to disguise the connection. But his father provided an invisible thread through Reed's life which he could not deny. Of all Tree's children, Carol was the closest in character, in looks and in achievement.

3

The Wallace Connection

The three Reed boys, dressed in grey flannel trousers, grey pullovers and grey blazers, were first sent to the Greycoat School in St John's Road, Putney, off the Upper Richmond Road, a small private school presided over by a Mr Chote. In February 1917, however, all three were despatched in a cluster to King's School, Canterbury, to begin their studies in the Lent term. By the end of the year their father was dead.

Tree's family had a weekend house in Thurham Court in Kent, and he married Maud there. He and his two brothers had started their education in Kent, at Mrs Adams's dame school at Frant, near Tunbridge Wells, and many of their contemporaries at that underschool made their way to King's. King's was therefore a school with which he was familiar and which he knew not to be punishingly oppressive. Tree's own schooldays had been blighted by the experience of following in his father's steps to a spartan Prussian school, and he had no wish to see his sons endure the same miserable experience. He also rejected sending his sons to the secondary school he had attended, run by Dr Stone in King's Square, Bristol, concluding that the place had taught him nothing from which his own three boys would benefit.

King's was a good, well-established school, which in the 1880s, according to a contemporary cyclopaedia, ranked as seventh among the English public schools. It had taught Christopher Marlowe and later Somerset Maugham and Hugh Walpole, and was set in the cloisters of Canterbury Cathedral. It had the look of an ancient public school yet it felt homely. A detailed description of King's has been provided by Michael Powell, the British film-maker who arrived as a new boy, known at King's as a 'Parrot', at the junior school in the year before the Reed brothers. Oddly, he cannot remember any of them, perhaps because, as his family lived nearby, Powell began life at King's as a day-boy, while the Reeds were of necessity boarders.

In Powell's words, 'the vast shadow of Bell Harry Tower falls across the quadrangle as the sun sinks. The buildings of the school are half monastic and half-modern.' The school could be approached in two ways: around the side, through its front gate; or, on foot only, via the transept of the cathedral, part of the cloisters of the old monastery. At night, access to the school was through a long, dark passage, lit only be flickering gas flares. The boys thought it haunted and believed their echoing steps to be ghosts in hot pursuit, and were grateful to emerge, 'usually at a panic-stricken run', into the Green Court, whose large, comfortable houses around a great square of lawn were home for both the masters of the school and the leading lights of the cathedral. The school quad was a gravelled square and the main buildings were of red brick and Kentish flint.

In addition to its obvious physical appeal, so important to Tree and his romantic notions of the surroundings in which his three young Englishmen should be educated, the school's headmaster, Algernon Latter, was thought to be discreet and the school was a considerable distance from London. May and Herbert Tree were, after all, choosing a place in which to hide their sons from the public gaze while they gained an education. Where better than Canterbury, so convenient for them to visit when they were staying close by, as they did so often, in the privacy of Constance Collier's holiday cottage near Broadstairs? Indeed, Herbert and May were taking a brief holiday at the cottage when Tree had the fall which was to lead to his death.

(Tree's will allowed May to continue to send her sons to King's. Muriel Ridley was not so lucky. Tree had drawn up his will in 1911, five years before he met Muriel. She and Tree's last son, Paul, were therefore not provided for. Paul Ridley-Tree was happily acknowleged by Tree as his lawful son, yet his will was not amended to take account of this change.)

The headmaster, Latter, according to Powell 'tall, dark, ferociously moustached', knew the true parentage of the Reed boys and was helpful enough to disguise the name of their father in the school register. They arrived on 24 February 1917; Robin, Vivian, Guy and Carol. In the column marked 'Father's Name' the school secretary has discreetly written 'Herbert I', the whole

name placed in quotation marks to signify that it is a
pseudonym. The 'I' appears to be an error rather than a
subterfuge, perhaps the beginning of a 'T' which was left
incomplete. Under 'Father's Profession' the entry reads 'of
independent means', the words again placed in knowing pairs
of inverted commas. The place and date of birth of each boy are
accurately recorded.

But it was impossible for a boy to keep the name of his father a
secret in a confined community like King's. The other pupils
knew that the Reeds were Tree's children. According to
P. R. H. Elliott, a King's schoolfriend who came to know most
of May's children, the secret was so open that one of the Reed
brothers had a prayer book inscribed with Viola Tree's name.
Reed later said that when he first arrived at the school he was
unconstrained about his father's identity. Indeed, it was a fact
worth boasting about, that his father was none other than
England's leading actor, Sir Herbert Beerbohm Tree.

Reed's bragging was so extensive, however, that it came to the
notice of Latter, who was not happy that a boy should be so open
about being the illegitimate son of a famous actor. He therefore
summoned May to the school to ask her son to desist. There was
little point in the discretion being provided by the school if one
of the very children to be protected from scandal was openly
discussing his strange parentage. The young Reed took his
mother's reprimand, however gentle, very badly. Its seriousness and urgency were betrayed by the fact that she had to
travel all the way to Canterbury to deliver it. He later said that
after that moment his schooldays were thoroughly miserable.
To have had to deny the existence of his father at such a sensitive
age appears to have caused Reed's lifelong secretiveness about
Tree. He was proud of being Tree's son, but could not bring
himself to publicly acknowledge the fact. From the moment of
his mother's reprimand Reed reserved discussion of his father to
conversations with his mother and his brothers and sister. The
sole exception to this rule was to be his second wife, Pempie.

If Tree and May had investigated the reputation of King's they
would have found that it was by no means good. Alaric Jacob,
who later became a distinguished foreign correspondent,
spending time in Russia during the early years of the Revolution, was a pupil at the same time as the Reeds. His Soviet

experience led him to a sympathy for Communism, so he is perhaps an unreliable witness to the qualities of a conventional English public school. He certainly had little good to say of the place. 'In September 1918, just before the conclusion of the war' (and eighteen months after the Reed boys arrived), Jacob wrote, 'the staff of masters was, with three exceptions, deplorably inefficient; all sorts of queer creatures, whose academic distinctions were in some cases as shady as their morals, were in charge. Few of them could teach; few of them could keep order.'

Carol Reed first fell into the hands of the Reverend H. B. Tower, the Headmaster of the Junior School, known as 'The Parrots', which Carol was to attend, wearing a cap with a blue stripe and red badge, for two years. Or, rather, he fell into the hands of Tower's domineering wife. Tower had been the Chaplain to the Bishop of St Edmonston and Ipswich, and had married the Bishop's bossy daughter, Stella Hodgson. He remained in her grip for the rest of his life. Christopher Worsfold, a contemporary of Carol's, remembered: 'Her motto seemed to be: "Don't you dare forget that I am a Bishop's daughter". She was extremely arrogant and treated the boys like dirt and was equally rude and discourteous to parents. She was, not surprisingly, cordially loathed by the boys for her rudeness and general unpleasantness. She also behaved badly to the masters.' Michael Powell thought otherwise, though, as a day-boy, he could hardly know the full horrors of living with the Towers. To him, Mrs Tower was 'a pretty wife' who 'had auburn curls and invited selected small boys to tea with French conversation'. As for Tower himself, Powell remembered him as 'quick, sturdy, clean-shaven' and a classical scholar. Worsfold's more caustic judgement was that he 'could be pleasant if he chose, although he was not generally liked very much'.

Powell recalled Tower as an inspiring teacher of the classics, who 'taught us Latin and made it a living language. He made us hear and see the bustle of the Roman marketplace. He introduced us to to Roman slang and proverbs and supplied us with racy equivalents in English (*Carpe diem* – "Make hay while the sun shines").' From Tower, Reed learnt about Julius Caesar, the Gallic Wars, the Roman invasion of Britain and the Roman walls of Canterbury.

The senior school of King's was ruled over by the spirit of

Latter, who had lived so long in the confines of the school that he had become blind to its many shortcomings. He had spent ten years at King's as a schoolboy, then, eight years later, having won a sporting blue at Oxford and spent two years teaching at Felsted, returned to the school as a teacher, eventually succeeding the Reverend C. R. L. McDowall as headmaster. According to W. d'A. Maycock, a King's pupil in the 1920s, Latter was 'a tall, rather gaunt, impressive man, with sunken eyes which seemed to pierce one from below heavy eyebrows'. He preached a conventional public-school creed, describing his ambition at his first speech day as being to produce 'clean, straight, self-reliant characters'. Jacob's view was that, 'left to himself he would have been happy to breed a race of Indian Policemen and Malayan rubber-planters'. Indeed, one boy of the time who did end up in Malaya, Sir Roland Braddell, believed: '"Algy" was the idol of every boy in the school. He was the model of the gentleman and sportsman, and his every action, particularly on the cricket or rugby field, left one knowing exactly what was expected of one.'

What was plainly not expected was an attempt to acquire academic qualifications. As Jacob saw it, during Latter's time 'the school sat very lightly to any sort of learning. It was "not done" to work.' Tree had chosen to place his boys in the hands of a man whose attitude 'was almost completely that of the caricature of what is regarded as the "public-school" type. He was a bad teacher, impatient and sarcastic, and never got the best out of people in consequence. As a man he was charming and profoundly kind, and to his personal generosity the school, always a poor one, owed its survival.' During the years around the Great War, according to Jacob, 'only one open Scholarship was gained at the Universities. This was a Musical Scholarship and was treated with the contempt with which in those days, generally speaking, the Arts were regarded. The boy who gained the musical Scholarship was clearly slightly abnormal and moreover, being no good, much, at games, the abnormality appeared conclusive.' When the scholarship was announced, with due pomp from the second step of the school's Memorial Court, the crowd of boys greeted the news with a roar of laughter. The scholarship was a rare enough event to cause Latter to grant a half-day holiday.

The school's lack of academic aspirations was not to perturb Carol too much. His marked lack of sporting prowess was to prove much more awkward. According to Jacob: 'Academic distinction was definitely a liability, so that the few who acquired it did their best to hide it. Ability to play games opened any door. Failing this, you could be "a bit of a lad".' Leslie Mitchell, later to become a pioneer of radio and cinema news-reading, remembered: 'Carol was noticeably unmuscular and much more interested in discussion than athletics. We had a common interest in books – not school books so much as what we regarded as "literature", though some history turned out to be equally interesting. We both thought cricket a bit of a bore but were careful not to say so.'

Carol and his brothers found themselves at a hearty school where, like all such places, the games played were tough, the boys were mostly dull and uncreative and the staff incompetent and intimidating. Each morning began with a compulsory cold bath. 'We lined up in the main bathroom which contained two baths half-full of what I estimated to be ice-water drawn direct from the North Pole,' remembered Mitchell. 'Each member of two shivering queues had to dive headlong over the sloping end and, artfully avoiding the taps at the far end, jump out and seize a minute towel on which to dry himself.' Had Tree taken a little more care with his choice of school he might have found one which would not, like King's, subject his sons to the full horrors of cross-country running. J. W. B. Laine, who arrived at the school as the Reeds were leaving, has testified: 'Throughout the school there was a great emphasis on being tough. For example, the senior steeplechases in the Easter term covered four and a quarter miles. From just beyond St Stephen's church the course ran to the Blean woods and then over fields to St Edmund's School, to Harbledown, and to the main railway, crossed by "Jacob's Ladder". In the marshy land beyond, we had to plough waist deep through the dykes and then plod over waterlogged fields.'

Running across the countryside may have had its hazards, but it also brought the boys at King's close to the drama of the Great War. Canterbury was the county town of Kent, which was closer to the action than any other part of Britain. The War might have caused shortages, particularly of food, but it also caused the boys to become intimately involved in a huge adventure. The whole of Kent had become a landing-stage for troops waiting to be posted to the front. Hoath Farm, from where Michael Powell set out for school each day on pony-back, was soon submerged in soldiery. 'Within a week the Camp in the meadow was as orderly as a busy village where everything is regulated by the bugle calls. We boys soon knew most of the Regiment by sight and rode our ponies over to the horse-lines as if we had been used all our lives to be part of an active professional community. A big Union Jack hung from a staff on the wall of Hoath Farm, and an armed sentry marched up and down challenging intruders with "Who Goes There?".' As Powell was happy to admit: 'I was soldier mad.'

No wonder that so many King's boys signed up for the trenches of France as soon as they were old enough. C. E. A. Pullan, who left King's in 1913, was one among many. Commissioned in the Durham Light Infantry as soon as the War started, in September 1914, he was sent to the front after training in November 1915, and was killed in Flanders sixty-one days later. Such deaths tempered the romance of the countryside around Canterbury, which was teeming with soldiers biding their time before being summoned to the front or recovering from their wounds before being despatched back across the Channel.

Nevertheless, the War fuelled the imaginations of all the boys at King's. They read adventure, military and mystery stories avidly. Michael Powell consumed everything that came his way. 'If anyone thinks that a nine-year-old boy couldn't have known all this and had no vivid picture in his mind of what was going on in these days before radio and television, he only had to look at the stout, green-bound volumes of The Bystander 1914–18 which are on my shelves today. There in photographs, articles, reports and cartoons – especially cartoons – today's reader can follow week by week, year by year, England's surprise turning to horror, horror to contempt, contempt to fear, fear to hatred, hatred to intolerance, intolerance to cruelty and revenge. We children never looked at the daily newspapers, but we read The Bystander and Punch . . . And we read The War Illustrated in fortnightly parts, and other periodicals. We knew what was going on: but it seems to me that it was the naivete of glossy mags like *The Bystander*, with their photographs and chit-chat and desperate attempts to keep peacetime pleasure alive, that was most informing to an observant little boy.'

Stories of the War in France and adventure stories set in the War were supplemented by other ripping yarns. The classical myths were, of course, the staple diet during classtime, but in dormitory or sprawled in the grass during interminable games of cricket there were more up-to-date diversions. Michael Powell's taste in books reflected the preferences of Carol and his brothers and their whole generation. There was Jules Verne, Rudyard Kipling, G. A. Henty, Edgar Jepson, E. F. Benson and Rider Haggard, and Edgar Wallace's 'Sanders of the River' stories in *The Windsor Magazine*; the monthly episodes of Arthur Conan Doyle's 'The Adventures of Sherlock Holmes' in *The Strand Magazine*, which spawned many imitators, like *Pearson's Mag*, with its yellow cover; and more gentle tales like Captain Marryat's *The Children of the New Forest*. In 1921 Reed's Christmas holiday reading list included Marryat's *Mr Midshipman Easy*. Thirteen years later, the first film Reed was to direct was an adaptation of the novel.

The War also brought hardships for the boys. By 1916 the German U-boat campaign had started to bite. Food rationing began and 'bread and scrape', thin bread with a slim layer of margarine, became part of their regular diet. There were two 'meatless days' a week, and when meat was served it was, as like as not, boiled mutton. Desserts were steamed pudding, often without jam or any other redeeming sweetness. Tea was served without sugar and with condensed milk. For farm boys like Michael Powell, there could hardly have been a less appetising diet. School food, always the most memorable and miserable aspect of school life, became unbearable at King's.

Boys could supplement the school diet with food from the tuck shop, presided over by Mrs Benn, which they were able to cook in their studies. But even this did not prevent the protest among the boys over the serving of a rancid pumpkin pie for lunch one Sunday. 'This unusual delicacy when it appeared was most revolting to look at and to taste,' according to Jacob, 'and a hundred plates piled high with the yellow mess, reeking of the unmistakeable odour of decaying vegetation, garnished the mid-day lunch table. Algy was furious; his housekeeper in tears.

Boys and masters hurried away from the scene with averted gaze.' The ensuing row lasted a fortnight as Latter, incapable of understanding the nature of the problem, began a lengthy investigation, the upshot of which was that two monitors toured the dining room for a week, taking down complaints about the food.

This deprivation affected the Reed boys less than some of their classmates. Each week May sent them a hamper from the food hall of Harrods, which contained eggs, jam, biscuits and even butter, so scarce in wartime Britain. It is against this background that the only certain story of Carol Reed at King's must be set. It concerns the theft of a tin of chocolate biscuits, and is a sorry incident from which Reed comes out well, but permanently scarred; an event almost as traumatic as his mother's strictures never to mention his father. The mystery of the missing biscuits is the stuff of a Saki short story, and it also formed a key influence on Carol Reed's choice of cinematic topic. He was to return time and again to stories about small boys fearless in their strident denial of a crime or cruelly embroiled in the criminal activities of adults.

All the boys at King's had lockers in which they kept their letters from home, their most precious toys and trophies and, most important of all in a closed community where the food was both scarce and barely edible, their tuck. One day the word buzzed around the boys that a whole tin of chocolate biscuits had gone missing. The theft became a *cause célèbre* because of its audacity and because of the administrative methods of Algernon Latter. His horror that a King's boy should be guilty of so heinous an act led to a contrived crisis. He announced that unless the culprit owned up, the whole school would be kept in the following Saturday. Carol Reed had been the primary suspect all along, despite testimony from a friend, P. R. H. Elliott, that he could not have stolen the biscuits because he was temperamentally incapable of such a crime, was not greedy by nature and, in any case, was the beneficiary of a weekly food hamper from his mother.

In face of the collective punishment threatened by Latter, the pressure mounted not so much on the anonymous thief, who had merely to keep his head down, but on Reed. When Friday came, Reed went to Latter's study to 'confess'. He protested to his friends at the time that he was not guilty, but wished to save the rest of the school from the tedium of a Saturday incarceration. Latter welcomed him with the words: 'Aha. I knew it was you all along. I won't punish you, but I will let the other boys know you did it. That should prevent you ever doing anything like this again.'

Latter was right at least in his assessment of the beastliness of young boys. Although Reed protested his innocence, arguing that it was a tactical false confession, he was treated by the vast majority of boys as if he were not only a thief but one who had nearly caused them all to suffer from his dishonesty. It was a hard lesson for Reed, and the whole experience appeared to hound him for years afterwards. He was not remembered as a thief, as few of his contemporaries could recall the incident. But he was haunted by the spectre of a stainless reputation unjustly blemished, and used to greet old friends from King's until the end of his days with assertions of his innocence. P. R. H. Elliott's recollection of the affair sixty-five years later was this: 'He had no reason whatever to steal, nor was he the boy who would stoop to it in any case. My guess was that somebody stole the biscuits from him, he discovered who did it and recovered the box in his own way. That boy reported the loss of the goods he had stolen and Carol's code was not to sneak on anyone, which he would have to do to prove his innocence. But I'm sure he would refrain from discussing the matter even with his brothers.'

The Reed brothers were not so intimidated by the fact that their parents were not married that they did not invite friends home for the holidays. One was Elliott, who remembered going to Daisyfield and being greeted warmly by the Reed boys' mother, known by him, for some reason, as 'Madame Reed', 'a woman with a fine personality'. His memory of Daisyfield is that it 'was built like a spider, with an entrance hall as its head leading into a reception chamber, furnished as such, which again led into an octagonal room out of which came Mme Reed's private suite, a library, a dining room, private bedrooms and then a passage down to the many family rooms. The whole was pivoted together by a full sized portrait of Sir Herbert Tree, dressed as "Hamlet" (?) and holding in his right hand a cup from which he is about to toast.' Elliott confirmed that 'it was then common knowledge that the family who lived in the bungalow were there as the second family of Sir Herbert who were on close terms with his widow and daughter'.

The eldest of the Reed children was Claude Beerbohm, whom Elliott believed had been educated at Cheltenham College. By the time of Elliott's visit Claude was about thirty, and well known for his work 'on the halls'. Carol, much chastened by his own boasting about Tree, came to despise Claude's bragging. After Claude came Robin, Guy and Carol – according to Elliott, 'none of them with stage or film aspirations'. Elliott considered Robin 'by far the most brilliant of them all in art and other respects and in features very like his distinguished father . . . Robin did not come to face the prospect of becoming an actor as it was not easy for him to hide the permanent deformity of his right hand.'

Guy was 'a very different character. He was quieter, more gentle, without the mischief which flowed from the other two. I enjoyed a friendship with him which was deeper and more sincere.' And, unlike his brothers and sister, Guy was a Roman Catholic, his road to conversion lined with hospital beds. According to Elliott's account, 'He, being born at Hillingdon when the Reed family lived there, was, when very young, struck down by serious illness and sent to Hillingdon Convent where the nuns nursed him back to health and in gratitude he was then put into the R. C. faith.' Judy was remembered as 'an entrancing ballet dancer for her age, but it was sincerely hoped by her mother that she would always remain an amateur'.

As for Carol, he was quieter than the others and merely observed what was going on. The school records barely mention his progress through King's. Michael Powell did not remember him or even know that they had shared the same schooldays. Alaric Jacob, ever caustic, dismissed Carol as 'a nonentity while at school' and compounded the insult by misspelling his name 'Reid' – a mistake committed by King's itself when Carol's departure was noted in the school magazine, *The Cantuarian*. The three Reed brothers were unlucky to discover that they shared their lives at King's with a family of three Read brothers, from Whitstable, so misunderstandings were commonplace.

Even P. R. H. Elliott's memory of Carol was so dim that he was not sure whether, in a 'Rag Concert' held at the end of the summer term of 1922, he shared the stage with Robin or Carol. He and

Robin Reed certainly constructed a humorous duologue entitled 'A Sister to Assist Her', 'a two-character comedy from French's' which included the line 'You do nothing but work, think and dream of work all day and night,' at which Latter gave a loud derisive snort. Elliott's dim memory was, however, of Carol stepping in for Robin at the last moment because of his brother's sudden illness. If so, this is the first recorded time that Reed translated his evident interest in the stage into an active involvement.

'A Sister to Assist Her' transferred later that year to the annual Christmas entertainments at Daisyfield, with Robin and Elliott sharing the makeshift stage created from the entrance hall. The library contained an audience of 'twenty-five to thirty mostly currently distinguished stage folk'. Among the other players was John Boddington, another contemporary at King's, who the following year went to RADA, which had been founded by Herbert Tree.

Carol's contribution to the evening goes unrecorded, as did any participation in the King's Debating Society meeting two and a half years previously, in July 1920, when the motion 'Kinemas do more harm than good' was hotly contested. Boddington led the anti-cinema side, arguing that films were good only for amusement, 'and that of a very low type'. He blamed the cinema for encouraging juvenile crime, for spreading disease and infection and for causing eye-strain. He summed up by saying that the stage had suffered at the hands of the cinema, because actors were now capable of earning large sums for performing in front of a camera. Boddington might have looked for support from Carol and his brothers. If they intervened in the debate at all, their words were not considered newsworthy to the reporter from *The Cantuarian*. The motion that the 'kinema' did more harm than good was lost by thirty-nine votes to thirty.

Almost exactly five years after arriving at King's, Carol Reed left the school, aged fifteen, in December 1922, Robin having left the previous March and Guy in July of the same year. Robin was the most academically successful of the brothers, winning a place at Emmanuel, Cambridge, where he was an active sportsman, running in relay races for the university against Oxford in 1925, 1926 and 1927. In the 1931 King's register, neither Carol nor Guy was credited with having achieved any distinctions after they had left the school.

On leaving, Carol was convinced that if he wanted to be anything, it was to be an actor. When Tree died, May had moved away from Daisyfield, with its memories of happier times, to Wimbledon, and that, perhaps, is the basis of the semi-fictional account of his first steps on the road towards film-making which Reed, constantly covering up the truth of his early life, gave an interviewer. 'My parents had a house with a big garden on Wimbledon Common and because I used to bring the eggs in from the chicken coop, and look after the vegetables, they said: "He will be a farmer," but when my two elder brothers left school I asked to be allowed to leave also and go on the stage. My mother said I must go farming with one of my brothers in Maine, U.S.A., but that if after a few months I still wanted to be an actor, I could come back to London.'

Having fallen in love with an actor, and knowing the problems of the stage, first from Tree and then Claude, May wished at least to provide Carol with another source of income. There was no evidence that Carol would be a good enough actor to earn an easy living. She therefore insisted that he try something else first. As he was a keen keeper of pet animals at Daisyfield, she suggested that he might try his hand at farming. Carol's brother Guy was working as a farmer in the United States, and an alternative to acting so far from the London stage appealed to May.

Carol set sail on his own on the *Berengaria*. After a week stuck on Ellis Island, waiting for the immigration officials to check his credentials, he arrived at Tewkesbury near Andover's Ballardvale, Massachusetts, where Guy was working for a family called Lord. He was remembered as 'a tall lanky boy. He was a big eater and he seemed to enjoy life.' Reed's memory of his experience was unenthusiastic, 'I didn't care a great deal for chickens. There were about sixty hen-houses. We had to get up early, Guy and I, to stoke the fires. Eventually we worked out a system by which we would take turns getting up at dawn. It was wonderful to stay in bed on these alternate mornings. We lived in a little shack we built for ourselves out of odds and ends. I think I got about $21 a week. After about six weeks I started thinking seriously about acting. But I stuck it out for six months. Then I wrote to my mother and said, "I don't care for chickens any more."'

He was soon back in London, looking for a job as an actor. It is quite likely that May wished to keep him from the stage. One actor son, Claude, was quite enough, particularly as he was growing increasingly rowdy and dependent upon alcohol. May had certainly discouraged Judy from believing that life as a professional dancer would be a sensible career. Robin was too busy being successful at Cambridge to bother about the stage. Carol had always been interested in his father's business: 'During holidays from school, I was always at the theatre. Why does a boy get an idea into his head?' But he did not appear obviously cut out to become an actor. He was too reserved, too restrained a personality to do well. But he was persistent, and determined to make his own way.

Claude Beerbohm gave a helping hand and, thanks to the generally fond memories of Tree, the whole theatrical community was sympathetic. But there is little evidence that Reed pulled any strings to make his way in the theatrical world, although he once let slip that his mother had contacted Sybil Thorndike, asking if she could help. Thorndike said she had nothing to offer, but put him in touch with Bruce Winston, who was looking for an actor to appear in a play of his which was running matinees only.

And so in 1924, three years after leaving King's, Carol Reed, aged eighteen, walked on stage in his first small acting part, as Constantine in *Heraclius*, by Lord Howard de Walden, at the Holborn Empire. Then Sybil Thorndike's company found room for him to appear in Bernard Shaw's *St Joan*, starring Thorndike herself. Another young actor in the production was Laurence Olivier, and he and Reed met again in *Henry VIII*, with Thorndike and Lewis Casson, at the Empire Theatre in Leicester Square. In 1937 Reed remembered: 'I was playing in one scene with Cardinal Wolsey. I had a long and complicated speech – you know, thirty lines with inversions and no full-stops – which wasn't to be looked forward to on the first night, especially since I had the stage-direction to look after too. However, I made my entrance and got through it all right. But to my horror Wolsey dropped his cue. Luckily for himself he was a real old trouper and rose to the occasion. Looking at me sternly, he said: "Say once again, what is it you would tell me of?" and I had to go through the whole speech again.'

Another actor who encountered the young Reed was Jack Hawkins, who left a memory of him which revealed the extent of Reed's love for animals and what little regard he had for conventions. He was entirely of his age, a rather dashing young man who cared little for the stuffy generation above him. He was extravagantly relaxed, wearing the most casual of clothes, jumpers with well-cut pale tweed suits and suede shoes, and lolled around with an air of casualness which bordered on the insolent, always with his hands firmly pressed in the pockets of his wide-bottomed trousers. Outdoors he wore a striking, sumptuous overcoat, an indulgence which he was to retain throughout his career.

In Hawkins's autobiography, Reed is remembered for 'a crazy exotic frolic' with a fox. 'I think we were in Liverpool and in a street market he suddenly spotted a caged fox for sale. This was more than he could bear, and he bought it and took it back to his digs. It was all very laudable, but a little tricky, to say the least. He let it loose with some water and some mince, locked his room and went to the theatre. On his return he was met by a furious landlady complaining of the smell on the landing. He made some excuse, and went to his room. To his dismay there was no sign of the wretched animal, but presently there was reynard perched on top of the wardrobe. From his description, I would not recommend teetering on a rickety bedroom chair, trying to prise a wild fox off the top of a wardrobe. With some difficulty he managed it, however, got it back to its cage and set it free in the country next morning.' Hawkins thought that episode explained in some way Reed's later gentle approach to directing actors.

Certainly Reed maintained a lifelong devotion to the acting profession. Fifty years later he confessed: 'You know, I wasn't a good actor. I began as a spear-carrier and then appeared through the countryside in repertory, but though I got decent parts and so on, I was never very good. Yet I'm glad that I did it for seven years or so because it helped me subsequently in understanding the actor's problems.'

In the next three years Reed worked with a number of companies. His brother Claude, who was producing and directing plays, offered him work in a production of Peter

Garland's *The Eternal Spring* which opened at the Royalty in London before playing Croydon, Coventry, Northampton, Sheffield, Glasgow, Colwyn Bay and Torquay. Reed played a callow poet called Pat in the main production and a cockney in the accompanying play, *Swank*. A photograph from the production shows Reed lying back on a sofa and a cartoon from the *Evening News* has him sitting on the same sofa with his collar undone, shrieking: 'I want revenge!'

T. R. Coxou, a friend of the family who had been given a pair of tickets by Claude, wrote to Reed on 19 February 1925, 'Your mother had led me to expect a good deal, but I'd really no idea I should see such a perfect piece of acting.' Her (or his) judgement had been backed by 'the girl I went with, who is above the average in intelligence and much better up in theatrical knowledge than I am, who thought just the same'. The play's leading actor, Basil Gill, wrote at the end of the run that 'one of the brightest spots has been Carol who I am more than pleased with. He is so *keen* and *conscientious* and loves nothing more than to be at work. In my opinion he has the strongest natural aptitude for the stage. And his performance for a first one is the most promising I can remember. I would not be at all surprised one day to see him in a fine position. He is too a Dear Charming boy and we are all very fond of him.' Gill thought enough of Reed to help him into the cast of Channing Pollock's *The Fool* at the Apollo, in which he played a character called Mack.

In April 1926 he appeared in a matinee 'Birthday Celebration' production of *The Merchant of Venice* presented by The British Empire Shakespeare Society, whose vice-presidents included Sybil Thorndike. Reed was playing Philostrate in an Italia Conti production of *A Midsummer Night's Dream* at the Winter Garden Theatre, Drury Lane, when Ion Swinley, playing Oberon, fell ill. Reed stepped into his part and, in the true theatrical tradition, the understudy who took the stage was spotted by a producer in the audience, in this case Dennis Neilson-Terry, a relative of Ellen Terry. He did not guarantee a part, merely the prospect of another understudying position, but Reed decided to take up the invitation. It was a turning point in his life, bringing him into contact with the man who would hurl him into making pictures, Edgar Wallace.

Reed was to appear in a number of productions during 1927, including *The Corvan Conspiracy* by Bertha N. Graham and W. E. B. Henderson in February and The Fellowship of Players' *The Winter's Tale* in October, but none had as important an effect upon his career as his two parts for the company Neilson-Terry had asked him to join in Wallace's *The Terror* at the Lyceum. The play was a highly entertaining piece of frightening nonsense about a group of suspicious characters all waiting to be murdered while staying at a haunted priory. Reed was surprised to find that the part he was offered was so small that he was asked to act another in the same play. When he had finished as Stein, he was expected to change costumes and, importantly, make-up and wig in order to play the part of Detective Constable Katman. It was all part of the assembly-line approach to the theatre adopted by Wallace.

Wallace, an extraordinarily successful war and foreign correspondent, most notably for the *Daily Mail*, had harnessed his prodigious writing talent into a one-man industry through which he hoped to fill all of London's theatres with his plays and every bedside table with his thrillers. He had begun his popular crime cycle with *The Four Just Men*, which, as a publicity gimmick, he had harnessed to a £500 competition, daring the public to guess the solution to the mystery he was unravelling. Discouraged by publishers, he founded his own publishing house, Tallis Press, and reaped an enormous profit (admittedly not before some hair-raising brushes with insolvency).

Wallace set out to write one best-seller after another, dictating his words to a Mr Wood, his shorthand typist. Even Wallace became suspicious of the ease with which he was able to rattle off a good story. In 1926 he wrote to his publisher: 'If I had my way I would give up writing books. I write them much too quickly for the comfort of any publisher. That is the only way I can write them . . . If I can only get my plays to go, I will give up writing books. That is my solemn promise to you. God knows how many more you will get before Christmas!' Success followed success until Wallace extended his success to stage plays and, eventually, films. He was a master of delegation, and it was as a Wallace functionary that Reed was to move towards the world of cinema.

At the time Reed first encountered Wallace, the master story-teller was still reeling from the triumph of his play *The Ringer*. He owed its success – a year of full houses and about £7,000 in royalties – to Gerald du Maurier, an expert on theatrical techniques who was able to take Wallace's raw play and craft it into an efficient piece of popular entertainment. It had been Gerald's father George, the writer and *Punch* cartoonist, who had written the novel *Trilby*, on which one of Herbert Tree's most profitable successes was based. While in the United States in 1894, Tree had asked his half-brother Max Beerbohm to see Paul M. Potter's stage adaptation of du Maurier's novel, with a view to buying the British rights. Beerbohm saw the play and came back with the verdict that it was nonsensical and would be a huge flop on the London stage. Tree trusted Max's opinion and would have left the matter there had he not had a spare evening before sailing back to London. Instead of going to Niagara Falls as planned, he went to see *Trilby* for himself, immediately spotted the play's money-making potential and signed up the rights during the interval.

On his return to Britain, Tree met George du Maurier in Folkestone and persuaded him that various amendments should be made to the text for his own purposes, including two new episodes. Bernard Shaw noticed the changes and up-braided du Maurier for allowing Tree to take such liberties. He wrote: 'If I were Mr Du Maurier, I should ask whether the theatre is really in such an abject condition that all daintiness and seriousness of thought and feeling must be struck out of a book, and replaced by vulgar nonsense before it can be accepted on the stage.' The play opened at the Haymarket Theatre on 30 October 1895, ran for six months and remained in the Tree repertory for years, becoming the biggest financial success of his career.

Wallace enjoyed a similarly profitable experience when he began to employ Gerald du Maurier's extraordinary theatrical skills. Gerald had played the small part of Dodor in Tree's production of *Trilby*, and stayed with him as an actor for over four years, steadily perfecting a nonchalant acting style. A series of successful collaborations with J. M. Barrie followed, beginning with his appearance in *The Admirable Crichton* and including the first performances of *Peter Pan* in which du Maurier created the dual parts of Mr Darling and Captain Hook. At the same time he began a series of stage productions which were both efficient and profitable.

In 1926, Wallace, aged fifty-one, despaired of ever being capable of writing a successful play. After the spectacular failure of his sentimental play *M'Lady*, a celebrated theatrical fiasco, Wallace had written a number of plays and sent them to theatre managers, but none had shown much interest. Then, in the early summer of 1926 he conceived the plot of what was to become *The Ringer* and interested Gerald du Maurier in it – a triumph in itself, for du Maurier now had more lucrative work offered to him than time available. He had met Wallace in unusual circumstances. Wallace had written an article in the *London Mall* entitled 'The Canker in our Midst' which sharply condemned homosexuality and, worse, hinted at the homosexuality of a number of leading figures of the stage. The intolerant tone of the piece had scandalised the enlightened artistic community and drove Gerald du Maurier to telephone Wallace in rage. Wallace disarmed his opponent with the words: 'I hoped you'd ring up. Of course, you've had my letter.' Du Maurier had not, but agreed to have lunch to sort out Wallace on a number of matters. At the lunch Wallace proposed to du Maurier, who had been completely won over by his charm, that he should stage his new play, *The Gaunt Stranger*, and perhaps even act in it. Du Maurier, who was intrigued by the possibilities of the plot, said that the lead part, the criminal in disguise whose true identity is revealed in a suitably dramatic *dénouement*, could not be played by him as his face and profile were too well known to theatregoers and would undermine the surprise ending. Wallace then suggested an alternate title for the mystery: *The Ringer*. Du Maurier thought the play would work, if Wallace were to follow his advice, and they shook hands on a deal.

Wallace's biographer, Margaret Lane, gives full credit to du Maurier for the success of *The Ringer*. 'No amount of sitting through rehearsals, listening to actors and counting laughs, could teach [Wallace] the essential secrets of economy, pungency, and logical construction; but with du Maurier as mentor he developed rapidly from untutored experimentalist into playwright. Du Maurier was a skilful "play doctor", and the final script of *The Ringer* bore only a family resemblance to the drama which Edgar had written at top speed after their first conversation.' The success of the play was to transform the finances of the du Maurier family. When Gerald's daughter Daphne bought Ferryside, her home in Bodinnick, near Fowey in Cornwall, with money given to her by her parents, her mother pointed out that 'none of this would have been possible but for *The Ringer* and the generosity of Edgar Wallace in sharing the royalties with D. [her father]'. Wallace and du Maurier shared the £7,000 royalties equally. The play was also to transform Wallace's life. Margaret Lane points out: '*The Ringer* cannot be said to have made his financial fortune; but it paved the way for that fortune more surely and rapidly than anything else had done. His book sales boomed, and managers who before the production of *The Ringer* had returned the scripts of his plays with polite regrets now regarded him with a fresh and speculative eye and were more than willing to listen to his suggestions. Film companies began to woo him and actors to regard him as a man to be flattered and cajoled. His life changed, gilded for the first time by appreciable prosperity and coloured by the flattering promise of future success.' In the next six years, no less than seventeen of Wallace's plays were presented on the London stage.

By the Christmas of 1926, after nine successful months of *The Ringer*, Wallace had prepared a sequel, dreamt up during his traditional annual winter holiday at Caux-sur-Montreux in Switzerland. It took him five days to write, and the result, *The Terror*, was to be Reed's springboard to the cinema. The plot closely resembled those of Wallace's best mystery novels. A group of guests arrive at Monkshall Priory and one by one they are lured to the dungeons to be murdered by an unknown hand. The play contained two favourite Wallace devices: the killer turns out to be a mild-mannered character; and the detective has witnessed everything, disguised as a drunk.

When the play opened at the Lyceum early in 1927, *The Times* reviewed it without a mention of the young Carol Reed in his two minor parts. It was the first time that Reed had been on the receiving end of a master stage director's instructions, and the experience was important for him. 'To watch Gerald du Maurier producing a play,' he said later, 'was the most wonderful thing in the world. I learnt such a lot from him. It was tremendously exciting. At the first rehearsal he would introduce everybody and talk about nothing in particular. Then he would tell us about the play and say: "I don't know if it's any good. I don't suppose so, but anyway it will be lots of fun doing it." At the second rehearsal he might suddenly turn round and say: "That line's not much good, but don't let's worry about it now." The third day, there was no more joking.'

During the run of *The Terror* Reed moved from being an actor towards becoming a director, taking on stage managing duties as well as acting. Working backstage, he became acquainted with Wallace, who closely monitored the staging of his plays. Reed remembered: 'I was engaged to play a small part in *The Terror* by Edgar Wallace and then they asked me to be assistant stage manager. Wallace used to come to the prompt corner to watch, rather like a schoolboy, how everything was done, and he was so crazy about the stage that sometimes he would ask what a certain button was for, and I would say: "That's for the trapdoor." When the time came for the trapdoor to be opened, he would turn to me and whisper: "Please let me push the button!" Then he would push it and there would be a terrified expression on his face, followed by such ecstatic relief to see that he had made it work, that we must have looked like two conspirators. After the performance, he would say to me: "Let's go and have dinner and talk about more plays." He would take me to supper at Ciro's and one evening he announced he was going to launch into the theatre in a big way, adding: "What are you going to do at the end of *The Terror*?" I said I had no plans. Then he asked me to join him in a film venture called British Lion of which he was to be chairman. The company was going to make his books into films and each would require three or four weeks to make.'

At the end of the run of *The Terror*, which made £35,000 for Wallace and his backers and ran for seven months, Reed was asked to join the cast and become the stage director of another Wallace police thriller, *The Flying Squad*. It opened at a suburban theatre before taking its place at the Lyceum as one of three Wallace thrillers playing in the West End simultaneously. Reed and Wallace kept in close touch. After the first night, Wallace cabled Reed from Epsom racecourse with his observations and remarks for the cast: 'Congratulations on fine performance. Tell Annie Hughes keep her performance down Cut out piano organ last act Tell Sternroyd he was a little inaudible Wallace.'

Wallace was revelling in his success, and invited the casts of all three of his plays to a party at the Carlton Hotel. Reed had scarcely improved his position on the cast list, playing a character named 'John Smith' in as unanonymous way as actors' good manners allowed, but he developed a good working relationship with Wallace. At Wallace's party Reed had the opportunity to watch the great man at close quarters, a charming, lively, larger-than-life fellow whose character resembled that of Tree.

Wallace was a warmhearted man who treated his work, particularly his new theatrical career, as an extension of his family life. Reed became a regular guest, along with other members of the casts of Wallace plays, to days at the races, watching one of Wallace's stable of horses run, and to Wallace's family home at Bourne End, near Henley. Wallace's house overlooked the lush Thames Valley in Oxfordshire, conveniently close to Beacons-field studios and to London. The Wallace nanny, who looked after Penelope, his daughter by his second marriage, remem-bered the house in those days full of actors, theatre people and those in the film business. It was at Bourne End that Reed met Wallace's daughter Pat and her close friend, Daphne du Maurier, the first woman with whom he fell in love – an infatuation which was to last the whole of Reed's lifetime.

Reed continued to act in Wallace's plays as well as direct them. He said many years later that he became a director 'because I was disappointed as an actor. I became a stage manager because I always enjoyed the entertainment business. I joined Edgar Wallace, the writer, who, in the late twenties sometimes had two or three plays running in London at the same time. I would appear in one, supervise the others and then direct the touring companies.' In 1919 he took a small role in Wallace's racing play *The Calendar* at Wyndham's Theatre, which was followed by the chance to co-direct *On the Spot*, a play about an Italian gangster which Wallace had written, in Reed's presence, in an extraordin-ary fit of writing and dictation over four days. Charles Laughton was cast as the hero, Tony Perelli, and Emlyn Williams played his sidekick.

Reed enjoyed directing, but was now coming to the conclusion that an actor's life was not for him. As evidence of his lack of confidence on the stage, on one evening some of his Putney Hill neighbours came to Wyndham's to see him perform, taking with them their 'darling old antique retainer' Nellie, who had become very fond of the Reed boys over the years. Carol was playing one of Perelli's nervous henchmen, and everyone commented politely on his fine performance. When the party arrived home, however, old Nellie, incapable of artifice, quietly commiserated with Reed. 'Never mind, dear, I don't think anybody noticed how nervous you were. I think you were wonderful.' Reed, who thought he had perfected the art of hiding his nervousness on stage, was shattered. It was time for him to give up acting.

Emlyn Williams, who had been called to audition for *On the Spot* at the New Theatre, St Martin's Lane, remembered: 'A tall, gangling young man bustled in from the stage door. "Sorry Charles [Laughton], it was Edgar on the phone." He was hurrying past when he saw me. "Mr Williams is it? I'm Carol Reed, stage director." He looked younger than me; I had read that Wallace swore by him and it was not hard to see why, his enthusiastic charm was infallible.'

Reed spoke to him: 'Sorry this is so sudden – you know? – I'm afraid all the scripts are out but here's the part; you've time to get the hang of it.' Reed was plainly close to Wallace, for he called him by his Christian name. And he was a big enough noise to call the awesome Charles Laughton 'Charles'. He may have been just one of the gaggle who followed one step behind the man Williams described as 'the King of the Jungle, the long cigarette-holder trailing a cloud of Staff', but he was the most influential and the most powerful.

He held the position by a quite natural combination of effortless charm and calm efficiency. Wallace had enormous admiration for Reed's relentless energy. He told a reporter: 'Reed's the best stage director in this or any other country – amazingly efficient. He rehearses several touring companies at once, and he never sleeps. I've had him down to my house to make sure, but I never found him asleep. At 4 a.m. he is singing the latest blues from America. At 6 a.m. he is on the tennis court. So far as I know, Reed doesn't eat. I once saw him drinking a bottle of ginger beer, but only once.'

A mark of the awkwardness of Reed's tasks and the diplomatic skill with which he performed them can be judged by Emlyn Williams's account of his audition. Reed whispered to him: 'The position is this. Mr Wallace had pictured Angelo [the part for which Williams was auditioning] as a big, older, Middle Western thug – you know – and cast Roy Emerton. But Charles got to feel he was too like the other gangsters and sees Angelo as a different type, young, dark – you know? – so he's been switched to a small part, you know how these things can happen.'

Wallace was using Reed as a junior version of Gerald du Maurier, relying heavily upon his theatrical expertise. They became close friends and developed a father and son relationship of which the Wallace household was acutely aware. Wallace had two sons, Bryan and Michael, by his first wife Ivy, and it was telling that he should so obviously favour Reed, a tall, slim, athletic young man who, although still living with his mother, led a very fast life.

Wallace knew who Reed's father was, though whether they spoke about the matter is not recorded. The fact that Reed was illegitimate was a bond between them, for Wallace was uncertain of the identity of his father, had been deserted by his actress mother, and was brought up by the family of a Billingsgate fish porter. This lack of natural parents encouraged Wallace to adopt a wider family, and his home was always full of people he worked with invited at short notice. His annual winter holiday to the skiing resort of Caux-sur-Montreux in Switzerland also became a much wider party of people, all paid for by Wallace himself.

It was inevitable that sooner or later Reed should be asked to join a Wallace party to Caux-sur-Montreux. He had formed a friendship with Wallace's daughter Patricia, always known as Pat, and was a useful commodity on such carefree holidays: a young, handsome, single man. It was inevitable, too, that he should meet sooner or later one of Pat Wallace's best friends, Gerald du Maurier's daughter Daphne.

Perhaps it was surprising that they had not met before, for Daphne's closest friend was Reed's half-sister Viola Tree. Gerald du Maurier had depended upon Viola to keep the young Daphne, his second child and a broody girl who preferred the company of adults, out of trouble by sending them off on trips together, to Cambridge to mix with the undergraduates and once for a week together in Berlin. Daphne was small, not beautiful but with spirited good looks and an extraordinary dynamism for life, enjoying a dangerous mixture of adventure and romance. She had been to finishing school in France, was already writing short stories and had danced with the Prince of Wales – 'Nice, but rather a pathetic figure,' was the entry in her diary.

She was a regular member of the Wallace household parties, going to Ascot, where Edgar took advantage of his sporting knowledge from his days as a racing journalist, and to the first-night party of *The Ringer*, also attended by Reed. There is little doubt that they had not already met, because Daphne's intimate diaries would have revealed it. She committed everything to paper, including an awkwardness with her cousin, the actor Geoffrey du Maurier, twenty-two years her senior, who continually made advances to her. She handled him with extraordinary ease, allowing him to maintain his dignity while ensuring that his passion came to nothing.

Daphne was fourteen and Geoffrey thirty-six when, on a summer holiday at Thurleston in 1921 he smiled at her and 'My heart missed a beat.' She knew from the beginning that their friendship was special and, most importantly, illicit. Geoffrey was a tall, strikingly handsome actor who had been marrried twice. When Daphne lay out on the lawn in the chilly sunshine with a rug over her knees, he would lie next to her and they would hold hands out of sight. As Daphne du Maurier described that first subsexual contact in her old age: 'Nothing, in a life of seventy years, has ever surpassed that first awakening of an instinct within myself. The touch of that hand on mine. And the instinctive knowledge that nobody must know.' The simple affair continued: 'The dancing, from time to time, and the holding of hands under the rug. No whispers. No kisses. No fumblings in the dark.' Daphne became infatuated. Whether her father suspected what was going on is not certain, but, having found a part for Geoffrey in his latest success at Wyndham's, *Bulldog Drummond*, there was an American tour to keep the couple well apart. On the day the cast set off across the Atlantic, Daphne wrote in her diary: 'Geoffrey sails for America. We see him off. Oh, I am terribly miserable. When shall I see him again?'

Daphne also came close to Constance Collier when, in a flight of her father's fancy, she screen-tested for the part of Tessa in the film of the stage hit *The Constant Nymph*. Basil Dean, the director, auditioned her at Gainsborough studios in Islington, and liked her 'piquant charm, well caught by the cameras' but the producer Michael Balcon thought otherwise. The test was retrieved some time later when Viola Tree and Ivor Novello hoped to make a film in Budapest with Daphne in the cast. Everyone was keen, including her father, but Daphne, then preoccupied with her home in Fowey and writing stories, ruled out the film and an acting career once and for all.

Daphne and her sister Angela had first joined a Wallace party for skiing in the winter of 1926, when she had been invited at the request of Gerald, who was increasingly concerned that Daphne was not mixing enough with people of her own age. The holiday was a great success and encouraged her to join another similar bout of 'skating, luging, skiing' when invited by the Wallaces in January 1929. Among the fellow guests was Reed.

Unlike her previous trip to Caux, when Daphne remained aloof from the teenage love affairs going on about her, this time, 'for the first time in my life I found the young men flocking. L'amour physique? Well, hardly. But dancing cheek-to-cheek, kisses in the bar, tottering up to bed at four a.m., where Pat [Wallace] and I boasted of our conquests until we fell asleep.' She wrote to one of the tutors at her Paris finishing school: 'I was kissed by two young men at the same time and another man, married, kissed me outside in the snow.'

Daphne's tutor was scandalised that such licentious behaviour should be allowed in respectable company, and wrote to her godmother. Wallace got to hear a version of the events. Daphne believed 'the story had been exaggerated to such an extent that it appeared to be the general belief that I had cast my favours amongst every available male in the hotel. Dear Edgar's affection for me, and his confidence in my behaviour, were considerably shaken, and despite the vehement denials of his daughter Pat that anything serious had ever occurred I was, for several months, no longer persona grata in their family circle.' There was some cause. One Frenchman pursued her to the home of her finishing-school tutor. Daphne wrote in her diary: 'Disappointing. Fred wore a dreary suit and talked to us about big game in Africa. How different from Caux, where he looked so attractive in a dinner-jacket.'

A more welcome suitor pursued her back to London. Carol

Reed, 'the young man I secretly liked the best', telephoned to ask her out for dinner. He was 'tall, slim-hipped and twenty-two'. She confided to her diary: 'I don't know what there is about that boy, but I can't help loving him a bit.' They got on very well and were soon seeing each other two or three times a week, depending on Reed's commitments at the film studio. Reed offered unusual entertainments for his first girlfriend: 'Dinner first, a film afterwards, and then supper of eggs and bacon in the gallery of the Kit-Kat, and a zig-zag drive round London in his battered Morris before I was dropped at home. Never the conventional outing. No dancing, no evening clothes. And if we gave the Kit-Kat a miss, then it would be a pavement coffee-stall and a ham sandwich apiece.'

The affair was unconventional in all respects. One entry from Daphne's diary recalls: 'We drive crazily along the Watford by-pass. We climb the scaffolding up the roof to a half-built house, clinging to each other, laughing. We played, and fought, and fooled. Oh it's fun being young sometimes.' She had fallen for his blue eyes and his bold good looks and, above all, his sense of adventure.

Already Gerald du Maurier was beginning to worry about the blossoming relationship between his young daughter and the illegitimate son of Edwardian London's most notorious woman-iser. Daphne was kept on a short leash and told to be in by a certain time. Still Carol pursued her, even after she had been despatched to bed. She wrote in her diary: 'I opened the window of the loft and talked to Carol after I'd let myself in. He wanted to do a Douglas Fairbanks and climb up to me, but hadn't the courage of his ideas! It would have been awful, I suppose, if he'd been seen. As it is, my going out with him in the evenings like this is causing much discussion in the family. Honestly! They might have been born centuries ago. They treat me like a Victorian miss of sixteen, instead of being nearly twenty-two.'

Her father cross-questioned her about Carol's intentions. Was she in love with him? 'He's a dear, I'm fond of him.' Was he serious about her? 'I don't know what you mean by serious.' Where did they go when the restaurants were closed? 'We . . . sort of drive around.' It was hardly a wooing which Gerald du Maurier would understand. One night they drove down to Limehouse and the London docks, then a dubious area, especially after dark. They walked along the beach, where a Thames barge was anchored. Carol was exploring, combining romance with observations about ordinary life. Daphne was spinning tales in her mind, in which Carol was the hero, running away to sea. The du Maurier parents became increasingly anxious about the affair, not least because it was taking place in odd parts of London, at the dead of night. They imposed a midnight curfew and cross-questioned their daughter each morning over breakfast. Daphne asked herself: 'Why does there have to be such a drama?'

There was one last night of motoring around the East India docks, a frantic drive home to allow for five minutes' hectic kissing before the bells of Christ Church, Hampstead, struck twelve. Gerald, home from the theatre early, was at a window, peeking from behind the curtains. The following morning, to the du Mauriers' great relief, Daphne set off to her beloved ferry-house at Fowey and the closest that Carol could get to her was safely at the end of a telephone, or a rather scrappy love letter asking: 'Darling Daph, how are you, when are you coming back?'

Daphne's departure at least gave Reed time to pay more attention to the responsibilities placed on him by Wallace, who was spending increasing amounts of time on film work since becoming chairman of the new British Lion Film Corporation in 1927. It was, to an extent, an honorary post, for Wallace was not expected to take any part in the running of the studio. His name was good for instilling confidence in investors, however, and there was an added financial reward. He was to receive an immediate payment of £10,000 for the exclusive rights to his books and plays. In addition he was to receive £1,000 for every picture made and £500 as a notional director's fee.

British Lion set up at the ramshackle, outdated former George Clark Studios at Beaconsfield, and within eight months had made eight hectic silent versions of Wallace stories. Wallace recruited Reed to help him. During the day Reed assisted Wallace on the films *The Valley of Ghosts*, *Alias* and *Chick*, and even acted in *The Flying Squad*, directed by Arthur Maude, and *Red Aces*, the only film directed by Wallace himself; in the evenings at the theatre Reed found himself helping to direct *Persons Unknown*, *The Calendar*, *On the Spot*, *Smoke Cell* and

Charles the Third, with Peggy Ashcroft in the cast. Reed remembered: 'I would keep [Wallace] informed about how things were going, and in the evening I would rush back to London to act in his plays and be assistant stage manager. We never minded how long we worked in those days. Everything was such tremendous fun.'

Reed travelled to and from his many widespread tasks by fast car. After a time, Wallace became concerned that he might be arrested for speeding when he was due at the theatre. In August 1929 Wallace wrote to Reed, who was touring with a play and had arrived at the Palladium, Llandudno: 'I intended writing this before to tell you how pleased I was with the work you have done in regard to the production and also to tell you how satisfied I am with your acting. I think you have a great career before you and I am terribly pleased if I had anything to do with launching you on it. As a stage manager you are completely satisfactory and as an actor I think you have the makings of a really great actor. You must keep down any mannerism that you find is creeping into your work and especially you must go slow outside the theatre for the next year. I don't want that damned car of yours to get you into any trouble. You will never forgive yourself if you find yourself pinched and missing a performance. I don't think we want that kind of shop.' Reed was so associated with speed in Wallace's mind that he named one of his stable of racehorses after him as a mark of affection.

Meanwhile, Daphne was celebrating her twenty-second birthday alone in Cornwall and spending a great deal of time thinking of Carol, snipping out amusing things from the newspapers to send to him. She was still being wooed by Geoffrey, now aged forty-three, who had left his second wife and was living in rooms, with no job and no prospect of one. At this time her first short story was published in *The Bystander*, for a fee of ten pounds. She returned to Hampstead and found herself beset by the same problems she had gone to Fowey to escape.

Geoffrey was staying, hoping to restart their special relationship, but her friendship with Carol had changed everything, although she felt her new lover might be too young for her. On her first day home she had lunch with Geoffrey and dinner with Carol. She returned to confide to her diary her latest thoughts about Carol: 'He's looking very thin and pale, but is such a darling, what shall I do? We talk and talk for ages, and of course it got too late and we had to dash home in case M[other] was cross. I think I do love him, but not a "swept off my feet" thing, more a sort of tugging maternal feeling. Whereas Geoffrey, whom I saw for lunch, and who is looking well and fit, is still a brother. Brother and son. Such a muddle.' Although Carol was not quite right for her, she found her writing interrupted by thoughts of him.

They would meet each evening, and her diary tells of the confusion in her mind. 'What is there about him that crumples me up? His extreme youth, I suppose, though he is five months older than me. I sat in his room during the matinee, and he kept leaping up there from the stage to kiss me, and then dashing down again. So lovable and childish. But he's so good to talk to as well. We can discuss everything, or else just drive along in his car without speaking a word. It's something about being together.' Whatever Daphne's doubts, Carol was deeply in love. But the affair was not to last for much longer.

One night they had supper at the Café Anglais and Carol drove Daphne home to Hampstead as usual. It was one in the morning by the time they reached the du Maurier house in Channon Place. The following morning Muriel du Maurier was determined that the episode would not be repeated. She wrote to Carol making it plain that there was no future in his friendship with Daphne and that his latest breaking of the curfew would be his last. Carol wrote back promising never to deliver Daphne home late again. As he was working in the theatre until late every evening, this would leave very little time for anything. His solution was to propose marriage – the first of many proposals to Daphne during the course of their lives. Daphne told him it was impossible. They had nowhere to live, and she was too fond of Fowey to give it up. He did not earn enough money to keep them both while she was trying to start a writing career. Marriage was out of the question.

Gerald du Maurier decided to take action. His solution, as before, was to recruit Viola Tree to take Daphne away from the influence of her half-brother. An invitation was summoned up from a Rudolf Kommer, whom Viola and Daphne had met in Berlin in 1927, to cruise around the Norwegian fjords on a steam-yacht owned by the millionaire Otto Khan. At first Daphne refused, but to her parents' relief she was eventually persuaded to go.

Although the enforced holiday did not break the spell Carol held over Daphne, circumstances now worked against the affair continuing much longer. On her return Daphne visited him at the Shaftesbury and watched him take off his make-up. He asked her whether she had enjoyed herself. 'Yes, in a way. But not like this.' He 'just smiled boyishly, in his inimitable way'. But the affair was drawing to an end. He was due to go on tour with *The Calendar*, and she was off to Paris for a holiday which would last for several weeks.

Back from Paris, she spent a bare day in London before setting off for Fowey to work on her first novel. Carol wrote to her every day. He was in London for the opening of *The Calendar* at Wyndham's, and was missing her. She told him that she must work, just as he must. They would be together again before long, she said. But during those months in Fowey, working obsessively on *The Loving Spirit*, she decided that she wished to live permanently in Cornwall. 'What have I to do in London? I shall live and die in Cornwall.' Before she returned to Hampstead that November her mother wrote to her. She was determined to stamp out the affair with Carol. 'I hope when you come home you won't start that practice of going out again in the evenings, which was so worrying,' she wrote. This made Daphne feel 'like a maid receiving reproof from the mistress of the house'.

On her first full day home she lunched with Geoffrey, looking 'pale and tired', before a 5 o'clock date with Carol at the Park Lane Hotel, where he was living. 'Oh it was lovely to see him again,' she reported in her diary. 'We sat in the lounge and drank orangeades, and talked for an hour. Then he drove me home, for me to be in time for dinner, and we stopped in Regent's Park for ten minutes because we simply had to kiss each other!' They kept the same rendezvous and the same surreptitious kissing four days a week until Christmas. She bought him a Christmas present and stole into the hotel to deliver it in his absence. 'I'd known for months what to give him. I went to Hay's and bought him a gramophone – Columbia portable – with eight records in the lid. Then I went to the Park

Lane Hotel, knowing he was out, and went up to his room and arranged it there, all open and ready, with a record on it.' While she was there she looked around. 'I looked at his things in the wardrobe. Poor sweet, he had no buttons on anything, nobody looks after his clothes. It's these sort of touches that makes me love him,' she wrote in her diary.

Christmas Day was spent in Hampstead, but on Boxing Day she went to the hotel to see him. They played 'Am I Blue' again and again on the gramophone. Carol was 'absolutely thrilled'. 'I've never seen anyone so pleased. He was just like a little boy, all red in the face and smiling. We went upstairs and played it, when I sat with him while he had dinner before the evening show. But I think I shall have the song of "Am I Blue" in my head till my dying day.' Carol gave Daphne a cigarette lighter and a matching fountain pen and pencil.

They continued to see each other almost daily into the New Year, but the strain was beginning to tell on Daphne. She returned to Fowey to finish her novel, and when the writing was finished she rushed back to London to take advantage of the few days' grace left by her parents, who had gone on a sudden holiday to Capri. That meant several days and nights with Carol without restrictions. But Carol had a heavy cold and was deeply involved in rehearsals. When her parents returned from Italy, Daphne decided that everything was hopeless, and made plans to go to Paris.

She went to the Park Lane Hotel to tell Carol. 'He didn't want me to go at first, but afterwards agreed that anyway the next month will be hopeless as regards "us".' In Paris she started thinking about her next novel, which she gave the title *I'll Never Be Young Again*. It was to be a romantic fictional record of her love for Carol.

4

Action Stations

Daphne du Maurier began work on her new novel in May 1930. Her first, *The Loving Spirit*, had just been delivered to the publishers Heinemann, and she started planning the plot of the second while in Paris awaiting their verdict. She spent a day on the rive gauche and had tea at the Café du Dôme at Montparnasse, writing in her diary: 'Somewhere there is a story singing in my ears, "I'll Never Be Young Again" . . . "I'll Never Be Young Again".' This was to be the final version of the romantic story she had been turning over in her mind while she and Carol had wandered along the banks of the Thames during those long, dark, adventurous nights which had since been forbidden by her parents.

She decided that the novel would be about a boy who ran away to sea, and that the young, present-day hero, 'the same age as Carol and myself', would eventually come to live in the rue de Cherche Midi in Paris. She had written *The Loving Spirit* in far-off Fowey, but for this her second novel she took a room in Orchard Street, in the centre of London. This would allow her to lunch each day with Carol at the Café Anglais. Their liaison was still frowned upon by her parents, but lunchtime assignations were permissible. As she wrote: 'No one could object to that.'

With Carol about to set off to the United States for Wallace, Daphne made once more for Cornwall for two months of solid writing. Wallace so trusted Reed by this stage that he asked him to co-direct *On the Spot* in New York with Lee Ephraim. At an out-of-town preview, Reed was pleased to discover that the stage-hands thought that the play would certainly be a 'turkey', an expression which meant the opposite of what he imagined. 'I remember how I beamed and how I strode all around, proudly proclaiming to everybody who'd listen: "What do you think! We've got a turkey! Isn't that fine!" Nobody put me wise. I thought a turkey was a great big smash.

So we brought it into New York and it wasn't a turkey at all but had a very decent run.'

While Carol was on the other side of the Atlantic, Daphne wrote her story of their love affair. It is a hectic account of young, unbridled love, written in the first person and, as so often with du Maurier, from the male point of view. In the central love affair between Dick and Hesta, the whole story of Carol's attempts to make love to the young Daphne is told.

'Of course, people make the most absurd fuss about sex,' I was saying; 'they go on as if it was the only thing in the world that mattered. And it's nothing really, it's just a little phase in life that scarcely counts. Men and women ought to make love like they play a game of tennis; they ought to consider it a healthy, physical necessity, and no more.'

She expressed the feeling of both of them that being young and in love was an enjoyable, frenzied state.

There was the fun of nonsense, of pointing up at the sky above her head and saying, 'See that patch of blue, the square bit, between the two clouds, you can have that . . .' and she sucking her lemonade through a straw, . . . And knowing we were fools, and other people could not hear, and reaching for her hand, and kicking at her ankle, and, anyway, that man who went out of the café leaning on a stick was old, old . . .

And sometimes they even spoke about their work, in this case Dick (Daphne) was a writer and Hesta (Carol) a musician.

'It's no good waiting until ideas come,' I said softly, 'otherwise I'd just sit around and wait all day. I have to force myself, as much as a bricklayer forces himself to lay bricks. And I dare say it's the same with your music, you have to work your fingers at scales and arpeggios, you don't wait until some melody comes floating out of the air. You hammer away . . .'

Christmas 1930 was to be Daphne's last with Carol. They snatched a few moments with each other in the few days before Christmas Eve and exchanged presents. His gift to her was a cigarette case in which he had had inscribed: 'Daph from Carol'. The stifled affair continued at a halting pace. The displeasure of her parents, which might once have added spice to their meetings, now cast a shadow. It became increasingly evident to Daphne that their romance had no future.

While in New York, Reed had seen Spencer Tracy in *The Last Mile*, a prison drama which he attempted to transfer to the London stage. He was frustrated by the first of his many encounters with the censors, in this case the Lord Chamberlain's department, who considered the play 'too rugged' for public consumption. Not to be stopped, Reed promptly put on a production in a private club, thereby dodging the Lord Chamberlain's grasp, followed in January 1931 by an opening at the Phoenix Theatre. By February Carol was in Berlin, arranging for a Wallace play to be presented there, and Daphne set off once more for Fowey.

The affair was over. Daphne was not to return until the autumn. By then everything had changed. First, she had become entirely financially independent. The advance on royalties for her first novel was £67 and soon more was added by her American publishers. *I'll Never Be Young Again* earned her a larger sum, and by November she had sold her third novel.

But much more important to the end of the affair between Carol and Daphne was an unexpected encounter which took place in Fowey in the late summer of 1931. Daphne's sister Angela was staying with her and noticed 'a most attractive man going up and down the harbour in a white motor-boat'. Daphne agreed that he was very attractive. She watched him during the remaining weeks of the summer, sailing the stretch of water between Fowey and Polruan, and learned that his name was Browning and that he was the youngest major in the British Army.

They did not meet, however, until the following April. Major Browning sent her a note. 'Dear Miss du Maurier, I believe my late father, Freddie Browning, used to know yours, as fellow-members of the Garrick Club . . . I wondered if you would care to come out in my boat? How about tomorrow afternoon?' She accepted the invitation at once, and her diary tells everything: 'His friends call him Boy, but he told me to call him Tommy, which is what his family call him. He's the most amazing person to be with, no effort at all, and I feel I've known him for years. I showed him all over Marie-Louise [her boat] and then we came back, sat over a roaring fire which I lit, talked about everything in the world, and it was the most extraordinary evening I've ever spent.' She was, at last, truly in love.

That June they became engaged. They composed letters to their parents and 'I also had to break the news to Carol.' The wedding was held in Fowey in July. Cousin Geoffrey was the best man. As Daphne remembered in old age: 'Henceforth I would come to know what it was to love a man who was my husband, not a son, not a brother.'

Carol never gave up his quest for the love of Daphne, and for the rest of his life he would visit her in Cornwall when Boy Browning was away, repeatedly raising the subject of their love affair. He even proposed marriage twice.

Four years after their affair came to an end, Reed was asked which subject he would most like to direct. He chose, without hesitation, Daphne's autobiographical account of her love affair with him, *I'll Never Be Young Again*. He told J. Danvers Williams of the *London Film Weekly*: 'Of course, under existing conditions I should never be allowed to embark on this picture, for it has an unhappy ending.'

1932 was a bitter year for Carol Reed. The loss of Daphne followed another heavy blow, the death of his friend and mentor Edgar Wallace. In November 1931 Reed produced a one-night only performance of Emlyn Williams's short play *Port Said* at Wyndham's Theatre. Wallace set sail the same month for New York en route to Hollywood, where he had been offered a contract with R K O to write screenplays. Before he left he told Reed that talking pictures were the coming thing and that Reed should see as many films as he could before he returned. As well as the money on offer, Wallace considered it right that his effortless talent for story-telling should be exploited by the largest motion picture industry in the world, and he was confident that he could amuse a worldwide audience as well as he amused the British public.

Despite his brimming confidence, however, Wallace was oddly reluctant to leave Britain, and tried a number of excuses to put off his trip across the Atlantic, the most extravagant of which was his participation in the 1931 general election as the Liberal Party candidate for Blackpool. To have been elected a Member of Parliament would certainly have given him a cast-iron alibi, but the electors of Blackpool declined to fall in with his plans, chosing the Conservative candidate after a highly entertaining, expensive, self-indulgent and bitter campaign. Disappointed but hardly surprised at his failure, Wallace reluctantly set off for the United States.

Nothing ever slowed Wallace's relentless output. Even on the journey to New York on the *Empress of India*, he boasted to his wife Jim in a letter: 'My record since last Monday week . . . is one novel length story, one 20,000 word story, one 3-act play (*The Green Pack*), one scenario rewritten, 16 articles, one broadcast (there is something else which I can't remember).'

He arrived in Los Angeles by train on a Friday evening, and booked in to the Beverly-Wilshire Hotel. Despite his public show of confidence, he was nervous about working in Hollywood, for he knew it would be the ultimate test of his ability as a story-teller. He was worried that the executives at RKO might consider the speed of his writing unnerving. 'I shall make lots of money,' he wrote, 'always providing they don't get scared by the very rapidity of the work.'

His first task was to write a 'horror picture'. This he did, with his usual speed, but he was to discover that the working methods of Hollywood were arcane and Byzantine, and that the writer was considered a mere drudge in a business directed simply towards making money. His work entered the labyrinth of RKO's executive structure and disappeared from sight. He despaired at being unable to discover how his screenplays were being received by his employers. 'In some ways,' he wrote, 'it is rather like living in a madhouse.'

He was, however, learning from the experience, and thought that it was sharpening his ability to tickle the popular palate. He promised that when he returned home he would be able to offer British Lion 'a real rip-snorter'.

Wallace was working on a script with Merion Cooper which was to become *King Kong*, but before the screenplay was completed to the studio's satisfaction he fell seriously ill. His domineering personality had prevented him from listening to his staff's sound advice about his health, and he had persistently gone out in the bitter Californian winter with inadequate clothing. He contracted double pneumonia and was also diagnosed as having sugar diabetes.

By the time *The Green Pack* opened at Wyndham's, Wallace

was falling in and out of a coma. There was a pall of gloom over the theatre as the newspaper headlines reminded the first-night audience that he was 'Gravely Ill'. His sensational plan to broadcast live from California to the audience before curtain-up was abandoned. Wallace's temporary home on North Maple Drive, Beverly Hills, was crowded but silent, with the actor Walter Huston leading the vigil. Wallace died on 10 February 1932.

The death was a particular blow to Reed, who had learned a great deal from the master of suspense and intrigue. And Wallace's death brought Reed an immediate practical problem: he needed a job. His flattering elevation to chief sidekick to Wallace had given him extraordinary opportunities to watch at first hand the workings of the theatre and the cinema at its most commercial. Having a licence from Wallace to fix deals and admonish those to whom his boss had delegated work had familiarised him with the intricacies of theatrical and, most importantly, cinematic production.

The cinema is an industry like few others. It demands an organisation of resources equivalent to the building of an ocean liner. A film producer finds the money for a director to assemble all the ingredients of the production, from the casting of the characters to the lighting of the set, and then to orchestrate the efforts of the immense team to perform their duties competently, within budget and on time. Wallace had given Reed not only the means to see how a complex team was brought together and set to work, but also how to make such a team run smoothly. These were to be essential lessons for his subsequent film-making career.

In February 1932 everyone working for Wallace had to look to their qualifications, for they were very swiftly out of work. Wallace's extravagance had led him to live considerably beyond his means, and at his death his whole empire crashed amid the clamour of creditors. His assets were nil, except for the rights to his works, many of which had in any case been sold for a single one-off fee. He owed £140,000. In order to meet his debts, the managers of his estate began winding up his business affairs. Emlyn Williams, acting at the time in a Wallace play, described how those dependent upon Wallace felt when they heard that their master was ill: 'We were like a family with father away and in danger.'

Reed was not to be unemployed for long. He tried his hand at directing plays without Wallace, presenting *Poet's Secret* at the Ambassador's in 1933, followed by a season of Shakespeare at the Open Air Theatre in Regent's Park. But it was a fond memory of Reed's father that was the key to his next employment. Twenty years before, Tree had been generous to Basil Dean, a young theatre producer. Hearing that Reed was looking for work, Dean felt obliged to give the son of his mentor the chance Tree had once given him.

Dean had also found himself suddenly without employment when, in 1913, he was working at the Liverpool Repertory Theatre and fell out with the theatre's chairman. By coincidence, on the day that Dean left the company, a letter arrived from the manager of His Majesty's Theatre asking him whether he would join Sir Herbert Beerbohm Tree's staff. After a typically strange interview in the dome, throughout which Tree doodled on the back of an envelope, Dean was hired as 'assistant producer', which meant assistant to Tree himself.

Although on his first day at the theatre Dean was taken by Tree to lunch at All Soul's Place with Lady Tree and their three daughters, where Viola told him, 'Daddy is out of touch with new things in the theatre. You must give him new ideas and all that,' he soon discovered that the last thing Tree expected from him was ideas. In his early days at His Majesty's Dean made suggestions about staging to Tree, which were all entirely ignored. He was taken aside by the stage management and told: 'Better keep your ideas to yourself; the Chief knows best.'

'The Chief' used to take Dean off to the Garrick late at night, to talk about the latest production and to gossip with the likes of Pinero, Bancroft, John Hare and others. As Dean put it: 'I might be dog-tired and anxious to go to bed, but it was useless to protest, for a major planet in the theatrical firmament naturally expects to be accompanied by satellites.' It was a frustrating period for Dean, who felt that his time was being wasted running around after Tree when he would be better off producing plays of his own.

After an amusing and instructive time as representative for Tree to Mrs Patrick Campbell and Bernard Shaw during the open warfare which passed as rehearsals for *Pygmalion*, Dean left Tree's employment. The Great War was just beginning and he enlisted in the army. By the time the war ended, Tree was dead.

Dean remained a great friend of Viola Tree's, and knew exactly who Carol Reed was when he heard that Reed needed a job. Although Dean had kicked his heels at His Majesty's and was largely ignored by 'the Chief', his admiration for Tree remained. By 1932 Basil Dean had founded Associated Talking Pictures and was head of the film studios at Ealing, which were about to embark upon a string of musical successes starring George Formby and Gracie Fields. It was immediately clear to him that Carol shared many of his father's qualities, which would be of great use to him in making talking pictures.

Reed's experience of the stage and his knowledge of the ways of actors meant that he was well trusted by Dean and his studio colleagues. One of his first tasks was to attend the graduating performance of the Webber-Douglas School of Acting and assess the talents of Victoria Hopper, a young Canadian actress. He was sent to audition the young woman by Sydney Carroll, the casting director of the studio who had been involved in the production of *The Poet's Secret*. Dean had fallen in love with Victoria Hopper and wanted to make her a film star. Reed tactfully returned with the answer Dean wished to hear and Hopper was immediately placed under contract to ATP.

The next job Reed was to perform for Dean was that of dialogue director, a relatively new position in film-making caused by the arrival of sound. Silent-film directors usually had little experience of the theatre or spoken-word entertainment. When, in 1927, Al Jolson was heard to talk and sing in *The Jazz Singer*, the whole of the cinema industry took fright. Before the evolution of directors who could both select the pictures and direct the actors in their lines, silent directors had to depend on dialogue coaches. Reed, with his knowledge of the theatre and of actors, was one of the first of this new breed.

Dialogue directors were not needed for long, for the brightest directors quickly dispensed with their services. Alfred Hitchcock was the first British silent director to use sound, dubbing a few words and sound-effects onto *Blackmail*, and he was one of the few directors adept enough to make the awkward passage from silent to sound films successfully. Soon all the skills of silent film-making were purged from the studios, and the silent directors with them.

The only film on which Carol Reed is known to have worked as a dialogue director was Basil Dean's *Nine Till Six*. Reed described his job as 'giving the actors instruction in intonation and voice projection, but I had nothing to do with shooting films'. Like most film directors, he began as an assistant director, to Dean himself.

The first film in which Reed was to direct scenes was Dean's *Autumn Crocus* (1934), based on Dodie Smith's successful West End hit play about a Manchester schoolteacher who dreams she is holidaying in great style in the Austrian Tyrol. It was to star Fay Compton and Ivor Novello. Although written as a stage play, Dean saw that there were great possibilities in opening up the action by shooting all the Tyrolean scenes on location. However, Dean had a timing problem. The good summer light which was essential for filming was rapidly running out as autumn approached. He was already in the Tyrol filming *The Constant Nymph*, and 'I could not be expected to direct two films in the Tyrol simultaneously.' The solution was to send Reed off to the location in Medratz to film less important scenes for *Autumn Crocus* while Dean finished *The Constant Nymph* in nearby Pertisau.

As it happened, for several days the weather in Medratz was too wet for filming and Basil Dean remembered: 'Carol, who was already showing signs of that single-minded devotion to film-making that was to bring him to fame, was in despair, sitting day after day by an open casement, watching the rain drip, drip from the overhanging wooden eaves . . . This, I fancy, was Carol's first modest assignment as a film director.'

Dean joined Reed when location filming on *The Constant Nymph* was completed and they worked together for four or five days, mostly taking 'atmosphere shots', among them a peasant wedding with members of the Vienna Boys' Choir to record the singing. After Dean left to complete studio filming of *The Constant Nymph*, Reed continued shooting more background shots.

On his return to Ealing, Reed began work on Dean's next picture, *Java Head*, adapted from the novel by Joseph Hergesheimer. The film had an extraordinary cast, led by Anna

May Wong, with Elizabeth Allan and Edmund Gwenn. In the minor parts were Ralph Richardson and John Loder. David Lean was the editor. According to Basil Dean, the charm and patience with which Reed repeatedly brought Richardson and Loder's attention to the job in hand was essential to the success of the picture.

Next, Reed was to assist Dean with *Sing As We Go*, a musical vehicle for Gracie Fields with a distinguished screenplay by J. B. Priestley. One of Reed's tasks was to marshal the large Blackpool crowds, who had come to gawp at 'Our Gracie' filming, and make use of them as extras. It was the classic assistant director's job, bellowing at a crowd of amateur actors through a megaphone, reminding them not to look straight at the camera. A newspaper reported that: 'the man who has won all film-struck girlish hearts in the town is Mr Carol Reed, who is personal assistant to Mr Dean, and whose tall, athletic figure in the immaculate flannel trousers and yellow golfing jacket is so often striding across the set, as much in the picture as the stars themselves. But Mr Reed has no time for anything but real hard work. His job never finishes. He seems to be at it all the time, good tempered in spite of a busy and sometimes harassing responsibility.'

Reed spent three years as dialogue coach and assistant director, shooting minor scenes and location footage, on *Nine Till Six*, *The Sign of Four*, *Three Men in a Boat*, *Loyalties*, *Autumn Crocus*, *Love, Life and Laughter*, *Looking on the Bright Side* and *Lorna Doone*. Then he was given his first chance to direct a film, *It Happened in Paris*, adapted from Yves Mirande's play *L'Arpète* by John Huston, the American scriptwriter who went on to direct such masterpieces as *The Maltese Falcon*. Reed shared direction with another young director, Robert Wyler. Nothing remains of the film, but contemporary reports describe it as the story of a wealthy American who studies painting in Paris and poses as a poor man. It was released on 9 December 1935, and must have been at least a satisfactory debut, for Dean handed Reed a script of *Midshipman Easy* and told him to direct the picture himself. So Reed began his directing career.

In these early days, Reed was in no position to choose the material he was to direct. He was merely grateful to Dean for being given the chance. His feelings were revealed in a lecture to film students many years later: 'It did not occur to me to wonder if the script was good or bad. I accepted it with gratitude. One can try to pick and choose too much before one has established oneself. I have seen many people fail because they have not realised they were being given an opportunity which would probably never come their way again. Don't wait, therefore, for the ideal thing, but take the chance that comes and make sure that you do everything to make a success of it.'

With *Midshipman Easy* Reed set out on a succession of apprentice works in which he would be given the chance to try his hand at a great number of different subjects in disparate styles. During those years he consolidated his knowledge of the film-making trade. The special talent he offered was a gentle touch with human subjects and a lightness with comedy. Reed made a point of using stage actors in minor parts, to magnify the drama around the edges of the main action. He did not deliberately develop a personal cinematic style, instead allowing his cameramen to dictate the look of his pictures. His attraction for film producers was his ability to finish a film on budget and on time, and he prided himself on the achievement. Before long, Reed was happy only when directing, and would work for anyone who offered him a budget to make a film.

Britain in the thirties was a hostile and competitive place for film-makers, one reason why Reed's skill at keeping costs to a minimum proved so valuable. Elizabeth Coxhead, writing in 1939, estimated that 70 per cent of British film technicians were unemployed and that only Hitchcock could count on making any film he wished. 'Each of the others has a dozen ready-made ideas, scenarios, all typed out, stories he wants to do – and must wait until someone comes along with the £20,000 which would let him make one.' Robert F. Moss described the situation succinctly: 'For a young film director, working in England in the 1930s was precarious and demanding. Regardless of the so-called "boom" on Wardour Street, most directors found the pressures enormous, the compensation meagre and the future uncertain. It was in this daunting atmosphere that Reed earned his stripes as a film-maker. He was a transient, ever on the move from one film company that had no more work for him to another that did need his services. For him, the experiences of the period combined a cram course in movie-making, a form of survival training and a baptism of fire.'

Reed was certainly conscious of the pressures on him to succeed, and the first thing he learned was to act confidently and to improvise. 'I was indefinite and indecisive,' he remembered. 'I thought I had picked up a lot about cutting and camera angles, but now, when I had to make all the decisions myself and was not just mentally approving or criticising what somebody else decided, I was pretty well lost. Fortunately I realised that this was the only way to learn – by making mistakes.'

From the first film Reed learned how to handle his budget and keep strictly to the shooting schedule. 'You were handed a script and told you had to shoot so many scenes a day,' he recalled. 'And you got on with it. If you hadn't finished by 6 o'clock you broke for supper and went back to work until the day's job was done. It was a six-day week and you were seldom through before eight any night. If, at the end of the first week of production, you were a day behind schedule you were told to pull your socks up. If you were, say, two days behind at the end of the second week, you were very unpopular indeed. As your schedule was probably a month, things were getting a bit strained. If you didn't make up your lost time you were liable to be taken off the picture and somebody put in who *could* push it through on time.'

These early days of film-making left Reed with little private life of any sort. He found his friends among those with whom he was working. He had stopped living at the Hyde Park Hotel and for a short time stayed at his mother's home at Lingfield Road, Wimbledon, before taking a small service flat at 20 Grosvenor Gardens in Mayfair, where he arrived home each night too tired to do anything much except sleep. He was well suited to this permanent bachelor existence, as he had little longing for the comforts of conventional domestic life. How he managed to stay alive was a mystery even to those who were close to him. He never ate at the studio, nor did he cook at home, and he was only rarely to be found at a restaurant. Usually he satisfied his hunger alone in workers' snack-bars. Nor was he a great partygoer or socialiser. Although he was always happy to watch others enjoying themselves, he saw little point in conversation for its own sake, preferring to discuss specific elements of the work at hand. He justly gained the reputation of being a workaholic.

This made him a difficult young man for others to decipher. He was well liked, and his diffident charm was appealing to both men and women, but he always appeared preoccupied. He was shy among strangers, and even with those he knew he affected a certain diffidence which was often unnerving. When he was about to speak he would raise himself to his full height, gesticulate vaguely with his arms and hands, purse his lips as if in preparation to say something interesting, even profound, then he would stumble out the words: 'You wouldn't have a cigarette, would you?'

At the end of 1936, his first year as a director, having made his first two films, Reed was asked what he considered to be the best thing to have happened to the British film industry in that year. During 1936 Charles Laughton had appeared in Alexander Korda's *Rembrandt* and there had been the science fiction epic *Things to Come*, Michael Powell's *The Edge of the World* and Basil Wright and Harry Watt's *Night Mail*. Reed's reply was that of a technician, not an artist: 'In my opinion the best thing that happened to the industry in 1936 is the fact that more preparation is being given to pictures prior to the shooting date. And I am certain the best thing that can happen in 1937 is still more preparation which will improve production and greatly reduce costs.'

It was such prudence, in a trade which rarely discovered a director aware of the virtue, which Reed was to display from the beginning of his career. He was determined to make a success of *Midshipman Easy* and, as it happened, his preparations had begun very early. Captain Marryat's book had been part of his holiday reading in the year he left school. It was a swashbuckling adventure story set on the Spanish-infested high seas of the eighteenth century.

Mr Midshipman Easy, the young naval hero of Marryat's adventure yarn, was to be played by the sixteen-year-old Hughie Green. The plot was straightforward, a series of episodes in which Easy fights a duel, captures a pirate, saves his ship, the HMS *Harpy*, during a storm and flirts with a Spanish girl, played by Margaret Lockwood. The cast also included stalwarts of the British stage. According to Basil Dean, Esme Church and Harry Tate 'still struggled to remember a line or two'.

A great deal has been made of the fact that Reed's films often concentrate upon the life of a young boy in an adult world, and it is therefore notable that his first picture should contain such a hero, even if the project was assigned to him by chance. Reed's adoption of the viewpoint of a young man heightens the scale of the drama and also reflects upon his own early life, surrounded as he was by the larger-than-life figures of the London theatre. He went on to people his productions with child actors to whom he extended a special friendship, drawing from them some of the most appealing performances of juvenile leads in the British cinema.

Reed identified with child-actors, surrounded by actors with their extraordinary ways. He understood them and their worries because of his days at Daisyfield, when his glamorous father would return from the theatre full of stories about his colourful friends from the stage. And he remembered being backstage at His Majesty's when, as a small boy in the school holidays he was engulfed by the magical world of grown-ups who lived their lives peddling make-believe.

He approached *Midshipman Easy* in a rigidly no-nonsense way. Unlike the American system of shooting films, in which endless takes were finally edited into a tight narrative, British film-makers were encouraged to edit as they went along, keeping wasted footage to a minimum. Reed's apparent vagueness and the confusion of his bachelor home and his private life disguised a highly ordered mind when it came to work. He quickly established a system by which his final shooting script, which divides the screenplay into small care-fully-plotted sections, would be scrupulously adhered to. His personal copy of the script became an impeccable record of the filming, each shot marked out then struck off by him in pencil until all of the scenes were complete. Pace between the various shots was ensured later by sharp editing.

Reed treated the script as, literally, a textbook to making the film. He told the film critic Dilys Powell: 'The really essential thing is a good script. With that, the rest is easy.' It was this which was to attract him to writers who understood the importance of a good, literate script.

For all Reed's close links with the theatre, he brought almost none of his stagecraft with him to the screen. Nor at the outset of his career was he considered proficient enough by Dean to be the dialogue director on his own films. Instead the grand not-so-old man of the British stage, Tyrone Guthrie, joined the *Midshipman Easy* crew to advise the actors. However, throughout his life Reed remained devoted to the talent and expertise of British actors. He wrote many years later: 'We cannot make or train actors in the studios; that is done on the stage. All we can do is to select the most suitable for the screen and exploit their gifts to the full; and our flourishing theatre, with its great wealth of actors and actresses, is one of the greatest assets of British film production.' And he was more sensitive than other directors to actors' problems. 'All actors, particularly men, are nervous in the first weeks of shooting. Either they overact or they underact in their anxiety to show they can really do it. It comes out first in the hands – nervous movements and fiddling with their fingers. I always give them something to hold – a book to turn over – furniture to push about or lean against – until they've got the feel of the thing. That's one reason why I like to shoot the beginning of a story straight in sequence. After a few weeks the actors know where they are, and what the parts mean, and you can afford to dodge about a bit.'

Reed proved himself to be a pure film-maker from the start. In *Midshipman Easy* he went out of his way to use locations which would reduce the unavoidable artificiality of studio work. He chose Portland, a rugged stretch of the English coastline, to stand in for the Sicilian coast around Palermo, and he also took the cameras and crew out to Basil Dean's home, Easton Manor.

Sidney Cole, the editor of *Midshipman Easy*, remembered Reed at the end of production, when the studio was demanding finished prints to be sent abroad. There was a gruelling eighteen-hour sound re-recording session, which involved the whole cast and the consumption of a great deal of whisky. 'For Carol Reed it must have been torture,' said Cole. 'Not physically, but sitting there for hours while the soundmen and editor did incredible things to his first-born . . . Till he must have despaired of ever seeing his film whole and healthy again.'

Cole paid tribute to Reed's lack of ego, describing him as 'no performer on the trumpet. Which, if he doesn't realise it already, is why technicians like working for him.' And he remembered

Reed talking about a story of his own which he wished to make into a film and whose plot he tried out on the actors and technicians on the *Midshipman Easy* set.

In August 1935, when the film was completed and roughly edited, Basil Dean wrote to Reed: 'I saw the rough cut of this film last night, and I must give you my heartiest congratulations on a most excellent job of work. The film is buoyant, well directed and photographed, and well acted, with the possible exception of Hughie Green, who is rather a disappointment. The latter is, of course, not your responsibility. I have great hopes that the film will do extremely well at the Box Office. We shall have to be very careful that the fights are not considered so brutal as to rob us of a "U" certificate.' On the night of the film's premiere, Dean sent Reed a telegram: 'Wishing You Every Success With Your Film Tonight.'

According to the British Film Institute's *Monthly Film Bulletin* the film displayed 'humour, plenty of fighting, a very small feminine element, and an engaging air of youthfulness throughout'. And in the *Spectator* of 3 January 1936 there appeared this review by the magazine's film critic and Reed's subsequent collaborator, Graham Greene, which Reed pasted into his almost full cuttings book:

> *Midshipman Easy* can be unreservedly recommended to children. It is the first film of a new English director, Mr Carol Reed, who has more sense of the cinema than most veteran British directors, certainly than Mr Wilcox or Mr Basil Dean. It is simply and dramatically cut, it contains the best fight I can remember on the screen and I can imagine no child too sophisticated to be excited and amused. Hugh Green gives an excellent performance as the courageous, argumentative and rather absurd Easy whose father has brought him up, on the principles of Godwin, to belive in human equality, and Mr Harry Tate's boatswain is deliciously mellow.

Greene's admiration for Reed was evident, and he was astute enough to notice through the miasma of such frail material as *Midshipman Easy* an instinctually good story-teller on film. The clarity of the action and the ability to heighten excitement were two skills which he as a writer had also mastered.

Greene's review was to some extent embarrassing for Reed, for it praised him above Basil Dean, his boss, and Herbert Wilcox, who had adapted British stage hits for the silent screen, including in 1923 the long-running musical success from His Majesty's, *Chu Chin Chow*. Greene's objection to Wilcox was what he saw as the lazy pillaging of the theatrical hits of Shaftesbury Avenue in plays-turned-films like Ben Travers's *Rookery Nook*, *Goodnight Vienna*, *Carnival* and Noël Coward's *Bitter Sweet*. There is no doubt that, compared to the stagebound work of Dean and Wilcox, Reed's approach to the screen appeared entirely cinematic. But having it pointed out in print when Reed relied upon Dean for his next film might have proved uncomfortable. Ironically, Reed's next film was to be an adaptation of a successful play.

If Dean noticed Greene's unflattering comparison, he did not blame it on Reed. The film was, after all, in Dean's words, 'a rip-roaring success' on its London release at Christmas 1935. Reed had little time to consider what success at the first attempt would mean. As he explained: 'Everybody was very kind and the first performance [of *Midshipman Easy*] was well received, but by that time I was in the middle of another picture – Priestley's *Laburnum Grove* – so I was too preoccupied to enjoy any praise that may have been given to me. After that it was one picture after another.'

Laburnum Grove was one of Priestley's most successful sub-Shavian morality teasers intended to discomfort bourgeois theatregoers. It concerns an upright suburban family man who shocks his relations by revealing that he has lived his comfortable life through the proceeds of counterfeiting money. The play had been Priestley's sequel to a similar morality play, *Dangerous Corner*, and it opened at the Duchess Theatre in November 1933, settling in for a run of many months before touring the provinces and, eventually, opening in the United States.

The play was obvious material for Basil Dean to plunder, and Reed, with his stage experience and his knowledge of Wallace thrillers, was an obvious choice to direct. The script was adapted into a screenplay by the actor Anthony Kimmins and Gordon Wellesley. The film was generally thought by reviewers to be too stagey for comfort, with the anonymous *Monthly Film Bulletin* notice saying: 'The direction is here and there rather uncertain and the photography is undistinguished. Altogether it is more a substitute for a stage play than a real piece of cinema art.' Andrew Sarris wrote some years later that the sets contained 'overstuffed gardens encroaching on cluttered interiors'. Reed used many of the actors from the original stage production, including Victoria Hopper, now Dean's wife, Edmund Gwenn as the crooked businessman and Sir Cedric Hardwicke, who stole the film as his dependent brother-in-law.

Leading the praise for Reed once more was Graham Greene, who began his *Spectator* review: 'Here at last is an English film one can unreservedly praise.' He went on:

> *Laburnum Grove* maintains the promise of [Reed's] first picture. Both films are thoroughly workmanlike and unpretentious, with just the hint of a personal manner which makes one believe that Mr Reed, when he gets the right script, will prove far more than efficient. *Laburnum Grove* set him and Mr Anthony Kimmins, the author of the screenplay, a difficult problem for it is much harder to adapt a play to the screen than a novel. Mr Priestley's suburban fairy-tale of the respectable amateur gardener of Ferndale, who confesses cheerfully over the supper-table to his family that he was really a successful counterfeiter wanted by the Yard, was admirably suited to the three acts of the stage. Nine directors out of ten would simply have canned the play for mass consumption: Mr Reed has made a film of it. One remembered the opening sequence of *Midshipman Easy*, the camera sailing with the motion of a frigate before the wind down the hedge and the country lane to Easy's home, when the camera in Mr Reed's new film led us remorselessly down Laburnum Grove up to the threshold of the tall grim granite church at the bottom. Mr Priestley has been allowed to tell his agreeable and amusing story in much the same order and the same words as on the stage; but Mr Reed's camera has gone behind the dialogue, has picked out far more of the suburban background than Mr Priestley could convey in dialogue or the stage illustrate between its three walls: the hideous variegated Grove itself, the bottled beer and the cold suppers, the crowded ferny glass-house, the little stuffy bedrooms with thin walls, and the stale cigarette smoke and

Bertie's half-consumed bananas. Suburbia, one of the newest suburbias, where the gravel lies lightly still over what was grass and clover, insinuates itself into every shot. There isn't a wasted foot . . . Mr Reed's camera acts with a kind of quick shrewd independence of the dialogue, and presents its own equally dramatic commentary, so that the picture of suburbia seems to be drawn simultaneously from two angles – which is as near as the screen can come as yet to stereoscopy.

Greene's review is a useful insight into his thinking at the time. For a writer of substance who had, somewhat reluctantly, turned to the construction of 'entertainments', the thought of writing for the cinema was plainly in his mind. Greene was reviewing from the perspective of a potential practitioner of the art of film-making and, although he had never met Reed, it is evident that he thought his directing method admirable. His phrase 'when he gets the right script' reads like a hint. Although impatient with the British film industry's pillaging of the London stage, Greene recognised a director who remained true to the text and yet was truly cinematic.

Greene's review also reveals Reed's acute sense of perception. What he observed on the long nights he spent driving around with Daphne du Maurier among the building sites of suburban London is portrayed on screen. Although a stranger to the lower middle class he was presenting, Reed had accurately reproduced their cosy, stifling lifestyle.

Laburnum Grove was a moderate success and, like *Midshipman Easy*, warranted an American release. However, Reed did not stay with Basil Dean and ATP but worked next for Herbert Wilcox's company, British & Dominions, under the producer Jack Raymond and with R. Norton as 'executive director'. Reed had been working on a story of his own during the shooting of *Midshipman Easy*, and perhaps Basil Dean was not prepared to take a risk on the project. Wilcox, however, was, so Reed left Dean to become a freelance director.

Reed's complex thriller, which he had called 'The Man With Your Voice', was translated into a screenplay by Reed himself along with Anthony Kimmins, who had co-written the *Laburnum Grove* script, and George Barraud. In his first attempt to write for the screen, Reed kept close to the style of the mystery stories of Edgar Wallace.

The plot was somewhat over-elaborate, as this outline in the *Monthly Film Bulletin* suggests: 'John Findlay, managing director of a ship-building firm, has a scapegrace half-brother Stephen, and a charming ward, Ann Marlow. Ann is engaged to Ray Allen, who has a gift for imitating other people's voices, and who by this means unwittingly enables Stephen to obtain some confidential information about a shipbuilding contract, which Stephen uses for his own profit. As a result John Findlay feels compelled to resign, and commits suicide. The police suspect that Ann has poisoned him. Stephen, knowing that Ray is about to denounce him to the police, attempts to drown him; but Ray escapes and confronts the villain, forces him to shoot himself, marries Ann, and they live happily ever after.'

As the *MFB* rightly comments, 'The plot takes some swallowing.' In fact the germ of the story had come to Reed when he found that if he imitated Basil Dean's voice down the telephone to others in the studio, things got done at remarkable speed.

The film depends for a great deal of its effect upon the substitution of the mimic's voice with those of the characters he was meant to be imitating, a complex process which involved the actors overdubbing by reading their lines from subtitles, a new technique for which the cast and much of the technical crew had to travel to France. By November 1936 the title had been changed from 'The Man With Your Voice' to the more commercial *Talk of the Devil*, and the film was scheduled for release at the New Gallery cinema in February 1937. No print of *Talk of the Devil* has survived.

Wilcox was aiming the film at the American market, so the cast was led by the American romantic actor Ricardo Cortez, playing the impersonator, the American actress Sally Eilers as Ann and the British stage actor Basil Sydney as the villainous brother-in-law.

The Times's reviewer stabbed close to Reed's heart when he dismissed the plot device of a man who could adopt other people's voices as something that would be better suited to a Marx Brothers comedy, then turned the knife by saying the film 'resembles a collaboration, or perhaps it would be better to say a conflict, between Galsworthy and Edgar Wallace', and continuing that the wicked brother 'is perhaps a little too uniformly bad even for Wallace'. As for the expensive complication of taking the principals to France to perfect the dubbing trick, he wrote glibly that 'in a film it is obviously easy to graft one person's voice on to another'. It was altogether 'a rather solemn but efficiently told story'.

Basil Wright, the distinguished documentarist and film historian, commenting on the film in the fifties, sees in it a quality which was to resurface in Reed's films later in the decade: its empathy with working-class heroes. 'The motivation of the thriller-plot,' he wrote, 'arises from a real situation – unemployment. It arises too from the singlemindedness of Findlay, who is represented as a man who has risen from the ranks of the workers and has never forgotten them. Throughout the film the scenes in which he appears are in quality markedly superior in feeling to all the others.' Two boardroom scenes, in particular, contained 'assurance in direction and in the pacing and movement of his camera [which] will stand up to comparison with much of his later work'. Wright also commended the film's original ending, as it used no play-out music. 'Instead we hear only the roar of the rivetters as the shipyard swings back to life.'

An anonymous review, pasted into Carol Reed's book of cuttings, tells more about *Talk of the Devil* and Reed's reputation at the beginning of 1937. 'Last year Carol Reed directed a picture entitled *Midshipman Easy* which had much to commend it. Later he made *Laburnum Grove* which was too much like a photographed stage play to create a great deal of interest in the director. Now he has made *Talk of the Devil* and I would class him, on account of his work in it, as one of the most likely British directors.'

As 'one of the most likely British directors', Reed set off to Hollywood, to look about him and see what prospects there were for him there. While making *Talk of the Devil* at Pinewood he had enjoyed his first taste of Hollywood glamour when Jack Warner, Ben Lyon, Bebe Daniels and Edward G. Robinson visited the set. Reed had no wife or family to keep him in Britain and, with three films now under his belt, the American film industry might offer him more opportunities. He made a tour of the largest studios, MGM, Fox, Wallace's old studio RKO,

Warners and Paramount. If he was looking for a job, he didn't find one.

Within ten days he was home, and later in the year he was playing down the importance of the trip. 'I had a month to spare between pictures and had always wanted to get a glimpse of how they did things there so I went. There seemed to be plenty of enthusiasm and lots of competition for jobs.' He admired many of Hollywood's working practices. 'What impressed me was the scale of their industry, which enables them to specialise departments in a way which our necessarily smaller studios can't. Back-projection, for example. Director tells them what sort of plates he wants and the action he's going to play in front of them. The specialists shoot the plates, then shoot tests of them with doubles going through the foreground action. On the schedule day, the director walks on the floor and directs his action. And their preparation seemed to be very thorough.'

But, he declared, he had decided to stay in Britain. 'By and large, studio operation is much the same as it is here. And, I don't know, perhaps the future holds even more for us.' The decision was to last his lifetime; he never did work in a Hollywood studio and he maintained a lifelong suspicion of their ways. Edgar Wallace's experience was instructive and his own visit confirmed his suspicions. As a quiet, unassuming, diffident character, the naked competition of Hollywood didn't suit him.

Even in 1937, with one shared credit and three further films to his name, one film about to come out and another one about to begin shooting, he was reluctant to talk about himself. Aged thirty-one, he was a strikingly handsome young man, with a broad, beaming smile and pale blue, slightly staring eyes like his father. He dressed fashionably, with a trilby hat worn cocked on one side and a wide-lapelled coat. He was still protective of his private life. The truth was that there was little to say, for his life hardly existed outside the studio and he was not prepared to invent a glamorous fictional lifestyle for the purposes of publicity.

On his return from the United States he set to work for Martin Sabine, a producer for Dorian Films, on a film adaptation of a German stage hit, *Who's Your Lady Friend?*, again scripted by Anthony Kimmins, from a story by Julius Hoest. The musical comedy had already been filmed by E. W. Emo in Germany in 1934 as *Der Herr ohne Wohnung*, the title of the original play, and it included music by Robert Stolz, the composer of *White Horse Inn*.

In Reed's film, the dance-band leader Vic Oliver plays a beauty specialist who, expecting an important French woman client, sends his male secretary to meet her at the station. He mistakenly returns with a cabaret star (Frances Day), but not before his girlfriend spots them together. The cast included Margaret Lockwood, Frederick Ranalow as a cabby, and Vic Oliver's wife Sarah Churchill, the red-haired, dancing daughter of Winston Churchill. For Reed, it was another film on which he could experiment with new techniques. A musical was quite different from anything he had yet attempted, and offered a particular challenge.

The film also tested his ability to deal with difficulties, as the shooting was riddled with accidents; the chief electrician, Jack Ford, fell, causing himself serious injuries, and the chief cameraman, Jan Stallich, was admitted to hospital with acute appendicitis. Margaret Lockwood had domestic problems and turned in a lacklustre performance which showed on the daily rushes. Reed and the rest of the cast and crew were very grateful when, after considerable overtime, shooting was completed.

In September 1937 Reed began work on a film which was to significantly enhance his reputation. The press had followed his early efforts with interest and Greene's reviews were a great help. But what he did not yet have was a big popular success. *Bank Holiday* (titled *Three on a Weekend* in the U.S.) entailed a change of studio. He was loaned by ATP, which was based at Ealing, to the producer Ted Black, whose Gainsborough company made films at studios in Islington. The screenplay was written by Rodney Ackland and Hans Wilhelm, the cast included John Lodge and, again, Margaret Lockwood, and the storyline depicted a national half-day holiday at the fictional seaside resort of Besborough, from various points of view.

Reed decided to open with a montage of shots showing London preparing itself for a bank holiday. He took his cameraman, Arthur Crabtree, to the Hastings carnival to take exterior shots of crowds on the front, and other stock shots were taken of crowds setting off from Waterloo Station. A beach was built at Islington Studios, with twenty-five men hired to shovel one hundred tons of sand and sixty-five tons of shingle, and a set was constructed representing seaside boarding houses and a large part of Waterloo.

The film offered Margaret Lockwood her largest part to date and she was cast early on, but some of the key scenes, including a large-scale ballroom set-piece, were shot before it was confirmed that the American actor John Lodge had agreed to play the male lead. The smaller roles were filled with a string of character actors. Wally Patch, a former music hall entertainer, was teamed with Kathleen Harrison, another stage actress, to play the Cockney parents of a gaggle of children on a day-trip. Wilfrid Lawson's portrayal of a Sussex policeman with a nonchalant investigative style was to steal the picture.

The plot was split between a variety of characters of various social classes and the action was little more than a succession of often unconnected incidents, yet Reed skilfully brought the threads together. By trusting his actors, and coaxing from them some extraordinary performances, he was able to present the variety of British life without appearing to patronise his working-class characters. This keen observation betrays an eavesdropper at work, unaffected by class prejudice and therefore, a rarity in British films, able to make a film which would appeal to a wide range of audiences. Reed handles the gentle humour with certainty, and affectionately depicts the futility of stage life with his sympathetic portrayal of an end-of-the-pier show undermined by atypically good British weather.

The film's sexual frankness was unusual for the time. The plot opens with a nurse (Lockwood) who falls in love with a widower (Lodge) on the day that his wife dies in childbirth. This sudden infatuation upsets the nurse, who is reluctantly setting out on her first dirty weekend with her boyfriend (Hugh Williams). The sexual content of the plot is further revealed in the rivalry between beauty contest competitors, with 'Miss Mayfair' not only making it her business to seduce the most senior judge, but also wearing no knickers – a fact revealed as she walks arm in arm with her latest conquest over the lattice-grid floor of the pier, to the indignation of the jealous 'Miss Fulham' and her plain friend sitting below. And on the beach the crowds unable

to find or afford a hotel room indulge in surreptitious nocturnal
sexual adventures.

Bank Holiday was a great success and showed that Reed could
sympathetically translate his broad understanding of the human
condition onto the screen. Although he still had no obvious
personal cinematic style – he relied for the most part on the
cameraman Arthur Crabtree to frame the shots – there was a
generosity of spirit and an ability to draw good, natural
performances from his actors which few other British directors
could achieve.

Reed's efforts brought almost universal praise. The *Sunday
Express* critic called it 'one of the ablest pieces of picture-making
to come out of a British studio'. The *London Evening News* said of
him, 'Even if new directors were not so scarce he would be a
treasure in British studios.'

Reed was regarded by the cinema trade press at the time as
one of a new generation of British directors whose approach was
fresher and less hidebound than the generation before them.
But there was anxiety too (then as now) that there might not be a
British film industry to employ them. At the beginning of 1937
an unattributed newspaper cutting in Carol Reed's scrapbook
contained this appeal: 'What is concerning me, and should
concern all who have the progress of native production at heart,
is the fact that the future of such men as Walter Forde, Maurice
Elvey, Milton Rosmer, Robert Stevenson, Carol Reed, Albert de
Courville, Norman Walker and Tom Walls seems curiously
unsettled.'

The reason for the anxiety was the dominance of the industry
by foreign, mostly American, money. As the piece went on: 'The
spending of nearly all the big money is in the hands of non-
British chiefs. Brilliant as some of them may be, it is not
reasonable to expect a thoroughly British outlook.'

C. A. Lejeune, the distinguished film critic of the *Observer*,
wrote at much the same time: 'I should like to see the British
industry combining without jealousy to give newcomers like
Carol Reed and Brian Desmond Hurst the best facilities that cast
and studio can offer.'

Of all the bright talents working in British films in the mid-
thirties, Reed was the most successful. Michael Powell and
David Lean would watch him, tall and confident and evidently

in command, on his set. Although in the business themselves, they were too nervous of Reed and his reputation to approach him to talk about their shared trade. Reed's reputation as the golden boy of British films and the impression of effortlessness he gave attracted an unhealthy envy among many of his contemporaries. His aloofness was unintentional, for Reed never gave himself airs about his success, which he attributed to a combination of good luck and hard work. He was not conscious of the awe in which he was held by those slightly younger than him, and certainly did nothing to encourage it. Yet he did not find it easy to mix and had no small-talk, unless it concerned the technicalities of film-making.

In the same year Reed also enjoyed some success as a screenwriter, selling a script treatment called 'The Little Fellow' which, as the title suggests, owes a great deal to Charles Chaplin's hero, the tramp. Reed's tramp lived on a building site in Park Lane and had only one ambition, to be a parking attendant. One evening, when opening cab doors outside the Dorchester in the hope of earning a few pence, a letter falls at his feet. It is the reference for a job and a fellow tramp encourages him to take it to the address on the envelope and offer his services. Here Reed introduces the tramp to the world of Edgar Wallace's thrillers, for the innocent finds himself among jewel thieves and the job on offer that of getaway driver. The story becomes a comedy adventure, with 'the little fellow' unwittingly slipping into crime. The treatment includes a spectacular car chase through the streets of Mayfair and ends on an absurdly happy note, with the tramp made a car park attendant for his honesty.

The story was closely based on successful screen formulae and contained, despite its criminal background, a great deal of mawkishness. Herbert Wilcox, however, thought that with some alterations – the getaway driver becoming a gunman; the letter to be found in a suit of clothes 'borrowed' from the hotel – a profitable film might come of it for his British Lion company. He commissioned Gerald Elliott to write a full script and the screenplay was filmed at Beaconsfield by Jack Raymond under the title *No Parking*, with Gordon Harker as the tramp, Frank Stanmore as his pal and Irene Ware as the moll. Geraldo and his Orchestra also appeared. Reed was already familiar with Harker as he had played one cockney after another on the stage for Wallace.

No Parking was completed by February 1938 and shown to the trade in June. The inspiration for Reed's story appears to have been an incident which happened to him on the way to Denham Studios when, visiting a roadside café one evening, he pulled his car across the right-hand side of the road and parked. He was charged by one Police Constable Heathfield, who testified that Reed's action had 'caused considerable confusion to approaching drivers and danger through narrowing the road, especially to bus drivers'. The magistrate, although conceding that it was not illegal to park on the wrong side of the road, determined that 'the practice can be dangerous to other drivers and is liable to conviction'. Reed was fined.

Reed was due in November 1937 to film a screen adaptation of Gene Markey's *The Sporting Peer* starring Edmund Gwenn, the first film of a new contract with ATP. The production was announced in the trade press, a scenario was begun and Reed confirmed that, after *Bank Holiday*, he would start work on the film, but the project came to nothing.

Bank Holiday was shown to the trade at the end of January 1938, by which time Reed was preparing a return to ATP for his next picture, 'Penny Wise', renamed *Penny Paradise*, about a football pools winner who belatedly discovers that his coupon has not been sent. Studio work began at Ealing in May 1938, a number of location scenes having already been shot in Liverpool and the Merseyside docks. The screenplay was adapted from an idea by Basil Dean himself by a Lancashire writer, Thomas Thompson. Gwenn, who had played a leading part in *Laburnum Grove*, this time played the tug captain who thinks he has won a fortune, with Betty Driver as his daughter, who was to sing a couple of musical numbers. Again Reed showed that he was able to portray ordinary people in a way that audiences found realistic and dignified.

He told Freda Bruce Lockhart, who thought him 'quite disarmingly diffident, quiet and almost tender with his actors', that the secret of film-making was to win over the cast. 'If you can get them enthusiastic, you've got half your picture,' he said. 'When I see that, I know I'm getting something real and good.'

The *Manchester Guardian* thought the film 'a model of what an unpretentious, genial comedy ought to be. For once (and how rare this is in British films!) the characters are homely folk who work for their living in shabby clothes and live in shabby houses and yet are not music hall figures of fun.' The film 'is one of the few made here that has captured what it is that makes most American films lively and entertaining'.

Dean was very pleased with the completed film. 'My dear Carol Reed,' he wrote from the head office of ATP at 169/171 Oxford Street, 'I have now been through the Rough Cut of this picture with Jack, and want to tell you that I am very pleased with it. Any slight hesitancies that may have been in the film due to the inexperience of some of the artists with whom you had to deal, have now been removed, and the picture moves along very well indeed.' He felt sure it would do well and thanked Reed for all his hard work.

The letter reveals Dean's working methods, typical of the whole of British film-making at the time. The art of editing the final screen print, so essential for a creative director, was the responsibility of the studio executives, who snipped the rough version of the print into shape, ensuring that its final form would be thoroughly commercial. It was an affront to a director's dignity, but even at this stage of his career, when he was heralded as the most distinguished of a new generation of British directors, Reed had to accept it.

As he complained later: 'It was such a different business then. Bob Dearing [chief editor at Gainsborough] was inclined to resent directors. Very often I wasn't even invited to see the editing. But a director must work with his editor. Directing is conveying to actors what you had in mind while working with the author. After that, the editor must understand not only what you did on the floor, but what the author had in mind – a man the editor has never met.'

Although by this time Reed was mentioned as often in newspaper reports as the actors he directed, he was given no special treatment by the studio, as was demonstrated by the next task they awarded him. Never could a 'contract film' have been so aptly named. Jessie Matthews, the singing and dancing musical star, was under contract to Gaumont-British. Work was due to begin in April 1938 on her latest picture, *Asking for Trouble*, under the direction of her husband, the actor-producer Sonnie Hale, who described the film to his wife as 'a big one. A musical extravaganza. We'll put British films back on the map.' Hale and Lesser Samuels wrote the script and Matthews began rehearsing the dance sequences with Buddy Bradley. As Matthews explained, 'the music was composed, the recordings made and the production was ready to go on the floor'. But the start of shooting was delayed by a shortage of finance, a fact covered up by the studio, which announced to the press that Matthews was unwell. Eventually production started, only to be halted almost immediately.

After six weeks, with the studio still scrabbling around for cash, two American actors, Kent Taylor and Noel Madison, who had been cast to improve the chance of selling the picture to the United States, were laid off. After three months, by which time filming should have been completed, George Lewis of Gaumont-British began new negotiations with Hale and Matthews.

Matthews's contract was about to expire and she still owed the studio two films. Hale's contract had lapsed before *Asking for Trouble* had reached the shooting stage and the studio bosses made it clear that they had no further use for him. Hale was indignant. 'Who do they think I am? An office boy? I've slaved my guts out on this script and now they say they don't want me.' He tried to persuade Matthews to pull out of the picture unless he were to continue as director, but she remained clear-headed, reasoning that there was little point in them both being out of work at the same time. After rancorous negotiations, an agreement was reached. In order to wrest from Matthews one of the two remaining films in her contract, she agreed to extend her existing contract by three months, on condition that she would act but would neither dance nor sing.

Matthews was given director approval by Maurice Ostrer, and was shown three reels by different directors. She chose the reel by Carol Reed, about whom Ostrer remarked: 'He's one of our contract directors. Rather young, and he's never done a musical.' Reed was embarrassed at being given a task which was little more than cinematic debt-collection, mopping up the tail-end of an awkward contract with an awkward actress. 'I don't know anything about musicals,' he told Maurice Ostrer. 'Don't worry,' the producer replied, 'we're just doing the book.' As an economy measure, all the song-and-dance numbers had been cut, although Hale's screenplay was still to be used. Reed protested, 'How can you make a film of a musical comedy book without the music? The situation won't be strong enough to hold on its own.' He was proved right.

In June 1938 it was announced that work on the film, retitled *Climbing High*, would resume at Pinewood. Joining the cast was Michael Redgrave, a young Shakespearean actor whose film work already included being directed by Alfred Hitchcock in *The Lady Vanishes* and appearing alongside Elisabeth Bergner in *A Stolen Life*. It had been announced that he would join Reed and Margaret Lockwood in a film of Sir Walter Scott's *Rob Roy*, but like Reed he was switched at short notice to attempt to save *Climbing High*. *Rob Roy* was to have been the first of Reed's films in his new Gainsborough contract, and it offered extensive location work in the Trossachs mountains in Scotland and in Jamaica. It would also have been his first chance to work in colour, but that would have to wait. In the same month it was announced that Reed would direct Redgrave and Lockwood in an adaptation of Henry de Vere Stacpoole's novel *The Blue Lagoon*, with a screenplay by Frank Launder and Sidney Gilliat. This proved to be another project which Reed would not be given the opportunity of starting.

Climbing High was to be a slapstick comedy, with a script by Sonnie Hale, Lesser Samuel, Stephen Clarkson and Marian Dix, in which a rich young man (Redgrave) knocks down in his car a poor advertising model (Matthews), falls in love with her and ends up escaping to the Alps with her to avoid the wrath of her Canadian brother (Noel Madison). Highlights of the film included a scene in an advertising agency in which a wind machine sprays everyone with custard pies; an appearance by Alastair Sim as the 'before' model for a patent medicine advertisement; and a reluctant song dragged from Miss Matthews, a piece of mock-opera sung to a lunatic (a character in dubious taste, played by Francis L. Sullivan) from the end of a rope high in the Alps. Among the supporting players was Basil Radford.

For Reed, the whole experience was unedifying, but he was glad to have the chance of working with Redgrave, whose stage work he admired. Their friendship would lead to three pictures together. Redgrave admired Reed's way with actors, which he

described in his autobiography: 'He was the gentlest of directors, so quiet that his "Action!" was almost inaudible. Yet
underneath that gentle touch was an iron will which eleven
times out of twelve would have its own way. I found that
admirable. With Reed I learned for the first time how subtle the
relationship between an actor and a director could be. The
theatre and acting were in his blood and he was able, with
infinite pains and care, to bestow on his actors the feeling that
everything was up to them and that all he was doing was to
make sure that they were seen to their best advantage.'

Jessie Matthews's relationship with Reed was more stormy.
She described him as 'a very large young man, unusually tall
and broad shouldered, nice looking with strong features. But a
completely new breed of director to me. All the other directors
I'd known looked as if they'd been born in the business. There
was no slickness about this young man. He was calm and
gentle.' First she fought with Redgrave, who had the ill-
judgement to say in her hearing, 'Must I say these dreadful
lines? Such ghastly musical comedy dialogue.' According to her
account, 'I surveyed the wonder boy. He'd made three films in
rapid succession and behaved as if he'd invented the medium.
"My husband wrote that ghastly dialogue." You could have
scraped the ice off my voice.' She returned home to tell her
husband, 'Those two young know-alls. They're still wet behind
the ears and yet they act as if they'd just made *The Birth of a
Nation*.'

Before long she also fell foul of Reed. One morning she arrived
at the studio and strode across the set dressed in a pink chiffon
gown by Norman Hartnell with matching turban. The men in
the gantry began wolf-whistling. Reed was anxious to restore
his authority and said to her sharply, 'Matthews, when you take
off that "I'm so beautiful" look we might start shooting.'
Matthews paused before letting forth. 'How dare you? It took
Victor Saville five years to get that look on my face. I used to sidle
onto the set looking like a half-drowned cat until I learned not to
be frightened of people like you. That look, as you call it, is on!
And it bloody well stays on!' Reed looked at her and slowly
began laughing. 'Keep it,' he said. 'Keep it, but not the hat. Not
the hat, please. You don't need all these trimmings. You've got
enough without them.'

The encounter broke down any further barriers between them and, much to each other's surprise, they began to like each other a great deal. Both were about thirty, yet they had very different approaches to show-business. He told her, 'I have to be in love with my picture to make it work.' She thought that 'Carol Reed was an unusual man to work with. There was none of the brisk camaraderie that would be gone just as soon as the last shot was in the can. He lived with the picture. He had a habit of walking up and down, his head bent, worrying, working out the next scene.' He told her, 'I'm not critical of what you're doing. I'm just thinking. I admire those directors who can sit around and have cups of tea and laugh and joke and tell stories, but I cannot.' He was worried about directing his first film with a star 'personality'.

At the end of shooting the big slapstick scene, in which the whole cast and set were drenched with custard pies and paint, Matthews went off to her dressing room to wash and returned to the sound stage to find Reed sitting in the chair with his name on the back, engrossed in the script. She picked up a left-over custard pie, tiptoed up behind him and pushed it into his face. He leapt up, chased after her and finally gave her a boisterous slapping. Matthews recognised Reed's act for what it was. 'The reason for the chase was as old as Adam and Eve. He might be the most promising young director, I might be the most modern of actresses, but our instincts were suddenly as old-fashioned as a Victorian Valentine.'

A love affair ensued. Matthews was not inhibited by the existence of her husband Sonnie Hale, for he was a philanderer and their marriage was 'peeling a little at one corner. Sonnie wandered now and then. But never too far and never enough to really hurt. When he brought me a lovely gift or a new piece of jewellery, I guessed that Sonnie and some lady in the film business might be holding hands. But he was always discreet and it never lasted long. I knew the dangers we had around us, we were young and well-off, but most of the time we worked too hard to have time to play.'

Her description of Reed is revealing. 'Carol's ideas were bohemian for those days. He didn't want a large home with servants. A hotel room or a rented flat while the film was shooting was enough. Then on to the next film. He showed me a new kind of freedom, and I was very tempted.' One afternoon, when shooting finished early, he had time to go to her lavish home, a farmhouse by the Thames at Hampton. He told her, 'It's all too much, Matthews, it is all too much. It's a very grand house. Too grand for me.' As Matthews remembered, 'He'd told me often enough that possessions bored him. He didn't want to be tied to any place, any town, or, I thought sadly, any woman. He didn't want marriage.'

The affair lasted no longer than the shooting of the film. Once they met at Madame Tussaud's, went for a drive around Regent's Park, then parked outside Cumberland Terrace. 'I'll buy you a house like this one day,' he told her, but she realised that their affair had reached its end. She thought Reed was a puritan at heart and that he would marry one day. He said to her, 'I wish I could have done more for you, Matthews. I wish the picture could have been better.' She said to him, 'It doesn't matter. I met you. That's enough.' Her affection for him was to last. 'For years afterwards every time I heard his name mentioned and they talked of the new girl he had on his arm, I felt I had suffered a loss. Would I have been happier had I gone with him? I don't know.'

Climbing High completed shooting in October 1938 and, after a sneak preview in Croydon following which some alterations were made, it was released in May 1939, attracting tepid reviews. The *Observer* was particularly scathing. 'Miss Jessie Matthews, who can sing and dance, is scarcely ever called upon to sing or dance. Mr Michael Redgrave, who can act, is never noticeably stimulated to act. Mr Carol Reed, who can direct – but why go on with this chapter of misadventures?'

Reed set to work on his long contract at Gainsborough in Islington with a similar comedy, *A Girl Must Live*, which borrowed some of the themes of *Climbing High*. The plot concerned ambitious young dancers who hoped to make their fortunes by displaying their sex appeal on stage, and it seems that Reed must have taken note of what Jessie Matthews had told him about backstage life. The screenplay was by Frank Launder, Austin Melford and an uncredited Michael Pertwee and was adapted from Emery Bonet's novel *Gold Diggers of Bloomsbury*, which Reed had admired. The plot owes almost everything to American backstage musical models, such as

Busby Berkeley's *42nd Street*, the 'Gold Diggers' series and, above all, George S. Kaufman and Edna Ferber's play *Stage Door*, which had been made into a film by RKO in 1937.

Margaret Lockwood led the cast as an upper-class young English girl who absconds from her Swiss finishing school to become a dancer. Asked many years later why he had so often used Lockwood, Reed replied: 'She was under contract to Ealing when I was a dialogue director there. When I moved to Gainsborough, she also went as a sort of resident ingenue. I thought she was very good.' As in *Bank Holiday* and *Climbing High*, the action was seen from the point of view of a penniless young woman trying to make her way in the world who shuns the easy option of marrying money or slipping it from the wallet of a gullible old man (played here by George Robey). This time, however, there was greater emphasis on girls who were less scrupulous with their favours (Renee Houston and Lilli Palmer) and the ne'er-do-well young men who help them in their fleecing (Naunton Wayne). Further comic scenes were set in a Bloomsbury theatrical boarding house, meticulously appointed by the Gainsborough designer Vetchinsky. Mary Clare, an old stage actress, played a theatrical landlady surrounded by would-be chorines and various theatre types, which provided a great chance to smuggle in some old stage comedians. There were some rather wooden musical numbers, which Reed directed himself.

The film is a highly entertaining comedy, which is more than can be said for most British attempts to tackle a genre which American film-makers made so well. Still, when it was released the following year, critics had some harsh things to say. The *Monthly Film Bulletin* pronounced: 'This sordid story exploits sex in situation and dialogue. The latter is full of double entendres, and while admittedly amusing at times, is frequently vulgar.' Filming at Islington was delayed for six weeks, along with everything else at the studio, while Gainsborough negotiated a new distribution deal, switching from Metro-Goldwyn-Mayer to Twentieth-Century, and was completed by December 1938. After Christmas Reed was again due to start on *Rob Roy*, but still nothing came of the project.

A Girl Must Live was previewed on 19 April 1939 and released later that month. It received both acclaim and moral reprimands.

To-day's Cinema was the most euphemistic in its warning to the film's would-be renters. Describing the film bluntly as a 'sex comedy', it continues: 'The exploitation of sex in situation and patter will doubtless be voted highly piquant by the generality of popular patrons . . . unabashed sex warfare put over in terms of unmaidenly sloshings with brush-backs, whirling legs and hair-tuggings . . . a departure from the more conventional British effort in screen entertainment.' *Variety* in New York was hardly more encouraging: 'This picture has an unsavory subject and generally needs speeding up.' It is little wonder that America had to wait until 1942 before the film was released there.

At the end of the year Reed was asked what new developments in pictures might be as momentous as the arrival of the talkies. His answer was telling. He said: 'In time I believe we shall get away from the eternal happy ending – it is difficult to get an audience really interested in the problems of the two main characters of a story when they know in the end it will work out all right, however difficult it may seem. The French have done it. Why shouldn't we?' He had complained before about this obligation: 'The work of any director making pictures in this country is conditioned absolutely by the happy ending. I am sure that this is a wrong-minded policy and keeps many intelligent people out of the cinemas, for whatever the circumstances of a story, the end is inevitably the same, boy gets girl.'

Reed was not alone in wishing to see an end to the obligatory optimistic ending. Early in 1939 the New York critics voted King Vidor's screen version of A. J. Cronin's *The Citadel* the best film of 1938. This was extraordinary, because the picture was made and set in Britain and concerned the primitive health care endured by the British working class.

Cronin had written *The Citadel*, his second novel based upon personal experience, the previous year. The first, *The Stars Look Down*, the story of a mining disaster, was taken from his life between 1921 and 1924 when he was first a doctor in a mining area of south Wales, then a medical inspector of mines. *The Citadel* was closely based on his researches into the danger of miners inhaling coal-dust, then his experience as a Harley Street specialist.

After the success of *The Citadel* it was commonly assumed among film people that whoever bought the film rights for *The Stars Look Down* would undoubtedly score a hit. Anthony Asquith had declared his interest, believing that the film would be most effective if real miners were employed instead of actors.

Towards the end of 1938 a new film company, Grand National, was created with money from, among others, Billy Butlin, the holiday-camp proprietor. It boasted £500,000 to invest in British films, which it would make at studios in Twickenham and Highbury. Grand National bought the rights to *The Stars Look Down* from a German producer and announced that Reed, on loan from Gainsborough, would direct the picture with a budget of £100,000 – an enormous sum at the time. The film would star the popular acting team of Redgrave and Lockwood.

Reed remembered the nervousness with which Gainsborough agreed to loan out their best director and their two most valuable stars: 'She [Lockwood], Redgrave and I all wanted to be released from our contracts in order to do the film. I remember telling Gainsborough how valuable this would be because, as there was nothing for us to do at the time, releasing us would save money. But when they received the script they said she couldn't play the part; it would ruin her reputation to play a bad woman.' Lockwood, in Hollywood making *Susannah and the Mounties* with Shirley Temple and *Rulers of the Sea* with Douglas Fairbanks Junior, balked at first when offered the part of the shallow, materialistic former girlfriend of a miner who ditches him in favour of a richer man. But Reed charmed her and suggested that such a serious turn would be good for her career and would broaden her attraction. She agreed to do the film at the end of June, and was never to regret her decision.

The Stars Look Down deals with the fate of coal miners from the north of England who work for a pit-owner whose greed leads to men being buried alive. At last, Reed was to make a film without a happy ending. But he later denied that he had any intention of making a polemical film, despite a stirring moral commentary added without his knowledge to the final credits on the American print. 'I simply took the novel by

Cronin; I didn't feel particularly about his subject, the nationalisation of mines. One could just as easily make a picture on the opposite side.'

Reed's intention was to make *The Stars Look Down* as realistic as possible. He would make extensive use of actual locations, real miners would appear as extras, and the mining disaster would require extensive studio work. As the film was the jewel in Grand National's opening programme, Reed was to be denied nothing. He was thrilled with the prospect of the most important film yet of his fast-moving career. The film's pedigree was impressive before a single frame was shot. Reed had already worked with Redgrave and Lockwood, and he would amplify the minor parts, as he had done before, with established character actors from the London stage.

The story was broad and dramatic and, helped by J. P. Williams, Cronin had adapted his own rich novel for the screen. If anything, the plot was too rich. 'The trouble with the book is that it has ten film stories, not one,' Reed told a reporter. The generosity of the budget meant that Reed was able to extend his field of operation very wide. He decided to use as much outside location shooting as possible, matched to meticulously accurate studio sets.

Filming began in Cumberland at the beginning of March 1939. Reed took a small team – scriptwriter, production manager and a technical expert – to a pit at Ashby de la Zouch in Leicestershire to see underground conditions in a coalmine at first hand. Reed needed to reproduce the atmosphere down a pit and the technicians needed to assess how exactly to replicate the tunnels of a coal mine.

Michael Redgrave, a socialist, was eager to play David Fenwick, a young, idealistic miner's son who goes to university but returns to the pit village to support his father's strike. Redgrave was pleased to act in a film which showed working men in such a sympathetic light. 'It's a remarkable opportunity,' he told a reporter. 'You might wait all your life for a part like this, saying "Why don't they let me play this?" without any result. And here it has fallen in my lap. No wonder I'm excited.' He dyed his hair red for the part.

By May, Emlyn Williams had been cast as Joe Gowlan, a miner's son who leaves his local community to become a bookie in the nearby town, and Nancy Price was signed to play Martha Fenwick, Redgrave's screen mother, a proud, hard-bitten miner's wife, crushed by the poverty and disappointment of her existence. The evident bitterness with which Price played the part was later attributed to her own experiences as a Staffordshire pit-owner's daughter. At the end of June, Mutz Greenbaum joined the team as cinematographer.

Reed set off on 13 June with Redgrave and a small number of actors and technicians to film on location at St Helen's Siddick Colliery, Workington. He had made a tour of a number of villages before deciding that the miners' cottages at Great Clifton outside Workington gave the right feeling of an enclosed urban community. The dignity of the miners impressed him, as did the way their wives kept their modest homes clean despite a mean living and harsh conditions. It was a world unlike anything Reed had seen before.

He had hoped to use as many real locations as possible, but there was a problem with sound recording. Tests were made in Workington to see whether filming could take place against the authentic background of the colliery, but the noise proved too great.

The unit filmed crowd scenes, panoramic pitscapes to be projected behind studio sets, and a specially staged soccer match between miners at the Borough Park ground of Workington Football Club. Redgrave also visited a colliery and travelled down the thousand-foot shaft dressed in a miner's rough-cloth suit and hobnailed boots. He was walked miles along the shafts and at the coalface was escorted for a hundred yards along a tunnel no more than twenty inches from floor to ceiling. He was even allowed to use a pneumatic drill for ten minutes.

Up on the surface, the weather was dull and there was insufficient light for filming. Each day without sunshine meant a hundred pounds wasted, but Reed was unperturbed, believing that the strength of the film would be in the studio work. He wanted to spend his vast budget on building the most realistic sets possible. If all the set-building deadlines were met and he scheduled the order of scenes so that the actors remained fresh, he saw no reason why the film should not be completed on time and within the costs laid down. In fact his Cumberland trip took only six days, less than expected, and studio work began a week early.

At Twickenham Studios the film's art director, Jim Carter, had taken a month to build, at a cost of £6,000, the largest interior set ever constructed at the studio, described by one trade paper as 'the most ambitious ever fashioned for a British film'. It was Carter's five hundredth set and consisted of a huge coalmine, two rows of miners' cottages based on houses in Great Clifton, and a street with a butcher's shop. There were also three large watertanks to simulate the flooding of the pit, using a scale model and a section of a shaft in which actors would be subjected to a huge torrent.

To ensure that the pits looked authentic, Archie Gordon, a former mining inspector who had advised on *The Citadel*, was hired to check the detail. Fifty tons of coal were brought to the studio, and used first as moulds for canvas coal piles, then ground into fine dust and sprinkled on the studio floor. Pit ponies were brought from Cumberland and caused a great diversion among the studio staff. Carter's men bought pitmen's clothes from Cumberland instead of having the studio costume department simulate the ragged suits and leather pads worn by miners. Stanley Ratcliffe, a dialogue coach, attended each day's shooting to ensure the accents were credible. Students were employed to check the university debate scenes for inaccuracies in style or behaviour.

At the end of June, between his trip to Cumberland and starting work at Twickenham, Redgrave took a short holiday in Paris. By mid-August, having worked twelve hours a day for six uninterrupted weeks, he was showing signs of exhaustion. His doctor ordered him to rest for four days. Redgrave was quoted as saying that filming had become 'a nightmare'. Reed was supportive and kindly, though he was anxious that the delay should be kept to a minimum. Redgrave felt warm-hearted enough towards Reed to say, 'Maybe I'll go fishing or something. I hate to let the unit down like this. Everybody has been splendid about it, especially Carol Reed. My only regret is that he can't come fishing with me.'

Filming on the final death scenes continued for three days without Redgrave, then the cast and crew relocated to Sound City at Shepperton, recreating the set of the minehead for the crowd scenes on the surface. On the first day Redgrave returned to work, the sun was shining so strongly that the cameras had to be fitted with filters to make the scene appear more northern and murky. There were other tricks. A bonfire was kept going off-camera to darken the sky, and two machines belched steam to add to the industrial gloom. Reed shot with three cameras, calmly ordering the takes and mouthing the actors' lines as they spoke them.

As shooting drew to a close the European political situation was becoming increasingly unsettled. Hitler had marched into Prague and was threatening to invade Poland. I. Goldsmith, the managing director of Grafton, the producers of the film, became worried about whether filming would be completed before war broke out. If not, it might have to be abandoned. As it was, all filming was complete by 29 September, the day Hitler's troops reached Warsaw and Britain declared war on Germany. From now on, Carol Reed would become part of the war effort.

5

Officers and Gentlemen

At the outbreak of war Margaret Lockwood considered becoming a nurse, to the horror of her agent who told her to do nothing drastic until the exact nature of the war was clear. Carol Reed was committed to film work. Extricating himself from his contracts and volunteering for the army would have been possible but awkward. His only useful skill was film-making, and if motion pictures were to be part of the war effort, he hoped he might be used in that way.

A month before war was declared, Reed had been assigned a topical wartime project, tentatively titled *Report on a Fugitive*, based on a story by Gordon Wellesley. On the day war broke out, all filming ceased. Studios were requisitioned by the government for other uses. Korda's old studios at Denham were converted into a sugar store and Pinewood's sound stages were submerged beneath stockpiles of flour. The studio at Islington was also closed. Reed was left as he had been when Edgar Wallace died, nervously biding his time, waiting for something to turn up.

He was not the only one to find the war interfering with his career. For two gruelling years Rex Harrison had been developing his suave stage persona at the theatre by night while working by day under a punishing film contract for Alexander Korda. As war approached he was appearing in Noël Coward's *Design for Living* at the Haymarket. It was playing to full houses when war was declared and, in accordance with the contingency plans in the event of war and the beginning of German bombing, all the West End theatres were closed. Harrison was jobless, but not for long. Theatres were still open outside London and a tour of *Design for Living* was swiftly arranged, with the original cast.

Neither the London theatres nor the film studios remained closed for long. Michael Balcon and Edward Black, two of the film industry's most forceful producers, persuaded the Board of

Trade, which was responsible for the suspension of film-making, that the cinema would be a useful means of maintaining morale, educating the public and inspiring them to endure the stringencies of war. When film production was resumed, Reed started work on *Report on a Fugitive*, quickly renamed *Gestapo*, at the studios in Lime Grove, as the Islington studios were to remain closed. Changing the title to *Gestapo* was part of the propaganda war, allowing long press releases to be adapted from Foreign Office briefs, describing in great detail the history and operation of Himmler's squads of secret police and their special powers.

The production of *Design for Living* had reached Newcastle upon Tyne by early December, and Reed travelled from London to ask Harrison whether he would appear in the film. Harrison accepted Reed's offer. Shooting was about to begin, but Harrison would not be needed until mid-January, by which time the play would have returned to London's reopened theatres for a final short run. The journey north was to prove momentous for Reed. While in Newcastle he met Diana Wynyard, a member of the *Design for Living* cast, with whom he was to fall deeply in love. She was the first woman he was to consider marrying since he had been rebuffed by Daphne du Maurier.

With her ethereal grace and large, intense eyes, Diana was an exquisite looking woman, described by *Picture Post* as 'the personification of statuesque English beauty'. The critic James Agate had written that she was so 'beautific' that Raphael himself would have fallen for her. She was blonde, graceful to the point of regality, and always wore gloves. She took care to look her best at all times, and her handbag always contained a spare pair of stockings, just in case she were to ladder the ones she was wearing.

Diana was a light, forceful stage actress who, like her closest friend in those days, Peggy Ashcroft, had a strong personality. Rex Harrison, who was very fond of her, described her as 'a bit of a sergeant-major, in the nicest possible way, a very pretty sergeant-major'. She was 'wonderful to be with in the theatre . . . invariably unruffled and calm'. He remembered: 'When I was off for a week with an inner-ear infection she used to ring up regularly and shout at me, "Rex – get up!" which did nothing to aid my recovery.'

'Diana Wynyard' was a pseudonym. She had been born Dorothy Isobel Cox in Croydon in 1905, and was eleven months older than Reed. At school she met Peggy Ashcroft and they remained close friends. She studied for the stage under two notable teachers, Gwen Lally and Ket Emil Behnke, and made her debut at the Globe in 1925 in a walk-on part in *The Grand Duchess*. After touring with Hamilton Deane's players, in 1927 she joined the Liverpool Repertory company at the Liverpool Playhouse, where she met Rex Harrison. On her return to the London stage in 1929, she quickly achieved success, first as Lady Sheridan in *Sorry You've Been Troubled* at the St Martin's, then more notably as Charlotte Brontë in *Wild Decembers* at the Apollo in 1933. She had a reputation in the acting trade as a first-class leading lady of the pre-war sort, not only the principal woman actress but the core of a company's morale. Her close association with her fellow actors meant that she attracted fierce personal loyalty.

But the London theatre could not contain her, and in the early thirties she left first for New York, then Hollywood, appearing in a number of films, starting with Richard Boleslawski's *Rasputin and the Empress* in 1932, with Edward Arnold and the Barrymores, John, Ethel and Lionel. In her next film, Frank Lloyd's adaptation of Noël Coward's *Cavalcade*, she played the central part of the brave upper-class English mother watching over the progress of her family in the years between the Boer War and the First World War. Having signed a long contract with MGM she changed her mind about film acting in Hollywood and returned to London and the stage. After a five-year break from films, she returned to the screen in 1939 in Brian Desmond Hurst's film version of F. L. Green's *On the Night of the Fire*, a grim story of blackmail in which she starred opposite Ralph Richardson.

Reed pursued her around the country while *Design for Living* was on tour, ringing her up and planning how they should spend their time together when she finally returned to London. But when *Design for Living* returned to the reopened Haymarket, they found that they both had full working schedules. Reed was working on *Gestapo* from six in the morning until eight in the evening, and Diana's life was even more hectic.

Stage performances took place in the afternoons to avoid the danger of the night-time bombing raids. Diana also had filming work of her own, appearing in Anthony Asquith's *Freedom Radio* as a Nazi actress whose husband transmits information to the Allies, and Thorold Dickinson's *Gaslight*, as the wronged wife of a womanising murderer.

On 14 December 1939, a week before shooting began on *Gestapo*, *The Stars Look Down* was shown to the press. With London waiting each night for German bombs to fall, a sombre film about a mining disaster with an unhappy ending was not exactly what cinema managers wanted. Something more light and escapist would have had more obvious appeal. To cater for this sudden sensitivity, some of the grimmest pit disaster scenes were removed from the film at the last moment to lessen the effect of the tragic ending. It was impossible to pass the story off as light-hearted, however, and Reed and Redgrave awaited the public's verdict with trepidation.

Convinced that the war had changed everything, including the public's taste, Reed had asked a reviewer what films people now wanted. He was given the reply 'Comedies'. Reed looked sombre and said: 'I have just made a gloomy little piece called *The Stars Look Down*.' He need not have worried. The film was greeted with enormous enthusiasm. The arrival of the war had altered perceptions among film critics and the fact that *The Stars Look Down* made few compromises to commercial demands and unashamedly told a decent, humane story about the conditions of ordinary people was appropriate to the new egalitarianism of the times.

This feeling was reflected in the reviews. C. A. Lejeune led the praise. 'If the British studios have ever made a more moving or bone-honest picture . . . I should be glad to see it.' The *Daily Herald* described it as 'imaginative, forcible and deeply moving' and declared, 'This production puts 33-year-old Carol Reed at the top of British directors.' The *Daily Telegraph* considered it 'probably the finest British picture ever made', and the *Sunday Pictorial* also thought it 'the finest film ever to have come out of a British studio'. The *London Evening News* announced that Reed was 'our most able movie-maker, since Alfred Hitchcock is now working in Hollywood'.

The film was even praised by William Joyce, the Nazi propaganda broadcaster known to British audiences as Lord Haw-Haw, who pronounced it 'magnificent'.

More than one critic compared Reed's picture to

G. W. Pabst's *Kameradschaft*, in which a mine disaster on the French-German border breaks down xenophobic resentment between the two sides. Graham Greene was among them.

Dr Cronin's mining novel has made a very good film – I doubt whether in England we have ever produced a better. Mr Carol Reed, who began some years ago so impressively with *Midshipman Easy* and then became involved in the cheap little second features that were regularly churned out by the smaller English studios, has at last had his chance and magnificently taken it. Since this is the story of a mine disaster his work will inevitably be compared with Pabst's in *Kameradschaft*: he can bear the comparison. When the miners who are on strike advance against the butcher who has refused meat to a sick woman, and when the siren blows for the accident and the children rush across the cement school playground to the rails, and when we listen to the condemned imprisoned men – the youth who was to have played in a football trial on Saturday and who refuses to believe that Saturday has ever come and gone in their darkness: the old miner feeding the new young hand with cough lozenges: the man with religious mania and the boozer's muttered confession – we are aware of direction which is every bit as good as Pabst's. If the film – constructed authentically though it is of grit and slagheap, back-to-back cottages, and little scrubby railway stations – fails to remain in the memory as long as *Kameradschaft*, it will be because there is too much story drowning the theme: the particular is an uneasy ally in literature of the general. The theme is the dangers of private ownership. Michael Redgrave plays a miner who gets a scholarship and leaves the pits, and he expresses this theme in two speeches – at a college debating society and a meeting of union representatives: the theme that there will always be owners ready to take a gamble sometimes, while the miner takes a gamble always. It isn't so dramatically effective a theme as Pabst's, and the punch is a little pulled. The owner responsible for the disaster has a stroke, repents and dies – this, I imagine, is pure Cronin. Once before Mr Reed tried his hand at a documentary story – *Bank Holiday*. It was highly praised and was full of 'characters', but it smelt of the studio.

Here one forgets the casting altogether: he handles his players like a master, so that one remembers them only as people. Miss Lockwood alone as the studious miner's disaster of a wife remains an actress to the bitter end.

On the film's first Saturday night the Odeon, Leicester Square, London's largest cinema, took more than £1,000, and in its first week *The Stars Look Down* attracted 27,700 people, a record for the house since the war had begun.

Gestapo was one of the first British films to be an integral part of the war effort, a picture designed to feed a public appetite for knowledge about their new enemies, the Nazis. Politicians and newspapers had personified the German threat by ridiculing and abusing Hitler himself, leaving the public largely unaware of what life was like in Germany and the German-occupied territories. With Britain now threatened with invasion, films were seen as a quick means of explaining to the public what Nazi tyranny entailed.

The plot of *Gestapo* concerned a distinguished scientist and his daughter who escape to Britain from Czechoslovakia ahead of the Nazi invasion, only to be kidnapped by the Germans and smuggled back to work for the Reich. Although the war had begun, there was still a hesitation about painting too grim a picture of the Nazi menace, for fear of causing unnecessary panic. *Gestapo* was therefore to be a comedy thriller starring light actors, Margaret Lockwood and Rex Harrison, and reflecting little of the horror of war. When filming began in January 1940, Reed said: 'The time for serious war pictures will be after the war.' *Gestapo* was an odd mixture; one of the first films to portray the true face of Nazism, yet essentially a comedy thriller closely following Hitchcock's *The Lady Vanishes*, which, like *The Stars Look Down*, starred Lockwood and Redgrave.

The Lady Vanishes was Hitchcock's penultimate British picture before leaving for the United States. Seven years older than Reed, and with considerable experience in British films from the early silent days, he was the brightest and most successful of the young British directors of the thirties. Thanks to the success of *The Man Who Knew Too Much* in 1934, he had been wooed by Hollywood, but had resisted repeated offers. However, while shooting *The Lady Vanishes* in 1937 he was approached by the producer David O. Selznick to make a film about the sinking of the *Titanic*. Hitchcock sailed for New York that year, his first visit to the United States, and signed a contract for four films, starting in April 1939. By the time Britain declared war on Germany Hitchcock was in Hollywood directing a film version of Daphne du Maurier's *Rebecca*. He remained in the United States for the rest of his life, and in his absence Carol Reed became Britain's most distinguished film-maker.

In fairness, Reed could hardly compare with Hitchcock, either in fame or singleness of vision. Hitchcock was by far the most indulged of British directors and had chosen his work well, dodging a tempting offer to work with Korda in favour of working with Gainsborough and Gaumont-British, where he kept close control of his own work. His personality and highly idiosyncratic directing style travelled well, and he became a celebrated screen personality, not least through a series of conspicuous but uncredited portly appearances in each of his films.

He achieved a solid string of successes, including Britain's first sound picture, *Blackmail*, in 1929, then *The Thirty-Nine Steps* in 1935 and *Sabotage* in 1937. He had intuitively made 'American' pictures in Britain, and was greeted on his first visit to the United States in 1937 by a crowd of admirers bearing portraits of him to autograph.

Reed trailed a long way behind Hitchcock, yet after the success of *The Stars Look Down* he might also have expected an approach from America. Then the war intervened. With two films already planned, he was committed to remaining in Britain. Those British directors and actors who were living in the United States before war was declared were put under pressure to return to help Britain's war effort, and many did. For Reed to have left for Hollywood so shortly after war had been declared would have been unthinkable, and his decision to remain in Britain completely altered the future of his career. Although he was, both during and after the war, encouraged to work in the United States for an American studio, he resisted all offers and made a virtue of his decision.

Reed was linked to Britain in ways in which Hitchcock was not. His roots ran deep into the British theatrical world and his sensitivities, too, were very English. He understood the nuances of class and education which created the wide variety of British characters, and delighted in reproducing them on the screen. The 'democratic' dimension of American pictures, with their classless homogeneity, which Hitchcock so effortlessly adopted, would not have allowed Reed to display one of his most important gifts. His skills were primarily those of observation and subtle replication. The American cinema demanded something more clear-cut, less meticulous, to lure its enormous audience to the cinema.

By the time the war was over, Reed's reputation was high on both sides of the Atlantic and he concluded that he could enjoy the best of both worlds by making British films for an American market in Britain.

Hitchcock's *The Lady Vanishes* was set in an unnamed country which the audience assumed to be Nazi Germany, and had proved a popular means of informing people of the horrors of living in a police state where anyone, even an innocent old lady, could disappear without trace. *Gestapo* was to be a deliberate sequel to Hitchcock's film, with a similar cast: Lockwood again; Harrison in place of Redgrave, who was singing Macheath in John Gielgud's Glyndebourne production of *The Beggar's Opera* at the Haymarket; a script by Frank Launder and Sidney Gilliat; and the reappearance of the comic duo Charters and Caldicott, played by Basil Radford and Naunton Wayne.

Great prominence was to be given to a glimpse of Hitler, played by Billy Russell, who had appeared in Reed's *Penny Paradise* and, since the rise of Hitler, had exploited his remarkable similarity to the dictator. Paul von Henreid, who was to drop the 'von' and become the epitome of anti-Nazi resistance in Michael Curtiz's *Casablanca*, made in Hollywood the following year, was to be the principal Gestapo officer. He had become a voluntary air raid warden in Hampstead and could be seen on the *Gestapo* set studying his Air Raid Precautions manual.

Filming began on 21 December 1939 in Shepherd's Bush with Otto Kanturek behind the camera and Lockwood and von Henreid talking through barbed wire in a Nazi internment camp, the authenticity of which was checked by a real-life camp victim. Location footage was taken by J. Perry in Glencoe, posing as the Swiss–German border.

Gestapo, which was retitled *Night Train to Munich* by the time it was released at the end of June 1940, was the first film on which Harrison and Reed had worked together, and they became fast friends. Harrison admired the way Reed deliberately set out to establish on the set a feeling of relaxation, coupled with an intensity which ensured good work from everyone. His assessment of Reed at the time was: 'He's careful, he's technical, he's a perfectionist.'

Harrison's memories of Reed include his generosity to an old English stage actor, Charlie France, who plays an ageing German admiral in the film. Although he appeared only in a brief scene, the old man continually forgot his lines, to the point that there was general embarrassment on the set and France became distraught. Reed took Harrison aside and suggested, 'Rex, you forget your lines in this take. Before Charlie has his, you forget yours.' Harrison repeatedly pretended to fluff his lines until the old actor had recovered his composure; filming continued without a hitch.

Shooting was scheduled to take ten weeks and, like most Reed productions, went exactly according to plan, even when key members of the production went missing through illness. Widespread influenza among the cast and crew was followed by chicken-pox, which delayed Naunton Wayne's appearance. A large mirror which fell over, just missing Margaret Lockwood and Rex Harrison, added to the dramas.

Ill-health continued at the studio throughout Reed's next project, *The Girl in the News*, a cheap sequel to the popular pair of *This Man . . .* films about a reporter-turned-detective played in both films by Barry K. Barnes. In May 1938 Gainsborough had announced that Alfred Hitchcock would direct the picture, with Lockwood and Redgrave in the star parts, but Hitch had left for Hollywood in the meantime. It was not flattering for Reed to be drafted in at short notice, even if it could be justified by the difficulties the war was causing. Once again he was reminded that he was undervalued by the studio and treated merely as a contract director.

In the picture, Lockwood plays an innocent nurse framed for murder, who is rescued by the amateur detective-work of a reporter, played by Barnes. The film offered nothing for Reed and was little more than a production-line effort for a popular market. But with so many studios closed, Reed considered any film work welcome.

The project may have been demeaning, but Reed could take solace in the fact that the rest of the cast and crew were in the same position as him. He surrounded himself with old friends, keeping together as many as possible of the *Night Train* team. As well as Lockwood there was Emlyn Williams, Roger Livesey, Kathleen Harrison, Basil Radford, Felix Aylmer, Irene Handl and the writer Sidney Gilliat, who adapted the screenplay from Roy Vickers's novel. Some distinction to the look of the film was again provided by cameraman Otto Kanturek and the designer Alec Vetchinsky.

Reed decided to at least make the best of a humdrum job and spent some time in the Old Bailey, trying to discover the true atmosphere of a courtroom for the trial scene which would dominate the picture. He told Dilys Powell that his most valuable observation was that in a place of high drama, where people's lives were on the line, all the principal protagonists kept straight faces. The emotions inside them, which must have been running as high as at any time in their lives, remained concealed. He told her that he would try to reproduce this disguising of emotion in order to heighten the reality and therefore the tension of his film's central scene.

Progress on *The Girl in the News* was constantly interrupted. Barnes fell ill with 'flu and Lockwood caught chicken-pox, but again Reed kept everyone on a tight schedule and brought the picture in on time.

After five films without a break, Reed promised himself a long holiday, although he knew full well that he was incapable of taking a holiday if there was another film to be made. First, though, he and Harrison decided to volunteer for the war effort, hoping not so much to be drafted into active service immediately as to have something useful to do until it had been determined what part the entertainment industry was to play in the war. In June 1940 they made inquiries at one of the Guards regiments and just avoided being signed up on the spot, then they drove out to a Royal Air Force aerodrome to see one of Reed's friends, a wing-commander, who suggested that they become Air Force policemen guarding airfields.

Finally they both joined the Chelsea branch of the Home

Guard, under the ultimate direction of Sir Herbert Gough, an epitome of David Low's cartoon character Colonel Blimp. Neither Reed nor Harrison were considered a great success as part-time soldiers. As young, educated men they were appointed officers, but their theatrical manner and general diffidence made giving orders to men much older than them very difficult. On being asked by one of the veterans whether he would like help, Harrison replied, 'I'd love you to', which brought the sharp reply, 'Don't love me to – tell me to!' It was a strange summer for the two of them, guarding Chelsea Bridge from Nazi attack.

The notices for *Night Train to Munich*, released in Britain on 24 June 1940, were disappointing for Reed, mainly concentrating on the return of Radford and Wayne as the successful comedy duo they had established in *The Lady Vanishes*. Reed took solace in the knowledge that the war was changing attitudes very quickly and it was not always easy to keep up with public taste. 'There are several snags to war films,' he told the magazine *Picturegoer*. 'The principal one is that they deal with an all-important topical subject which is always changing in aspect. While the film was in production and being got ready for showing, the whole aspect of the war changed. There are still some lines in the dialogue which reflect the mood of pre-Dunkirk days rather than of the present time. Fortunately, filmgoers seemed to have thought it was a pretty amusing comedy anyway and it has been a great success. But you can see how another film with a war background might have been outdated and rendered completely useless by the speed with which the war itself had changed.'

If memories of *The Lady Vanishes* overshadowed the opening of *Night Train* in Britain, it may be argued that in some respects Reed's film is superior to Hitchcock's. It deals head-on with the Germans as Nazis, where *The Lady Vanishes* merely hints at a sinister regime, and it generates a furious pace towards the end as the Gestapo chase their quarries, disguised in S.S. uniforms, across Germany to the Swiss border. Reed's film was also more sexually sophisticated than Hitchcock's, with Harrison playing on his seductive appeal, sharpened in a score of West End drawing-room comedies, to convince the Germans that he has an erotic influence over Lockwood as the scientist's daughter.

Prior to the film's American release on 18 October 1940, where it was renamed (for the third time) simply *Night Train*, *Variety* summed it up as 'Thrill packed, suspenseful and spiced with hokum right where it helps, this film is a nifty surprise.' It lasted ninety-five minutes, which the showbiz bible considered a little long for American audiences, and Reed could not have enjoyed *Variety*'s suggested solution: 'U.S. bookers may wince at its running time, but it could do with cutting, and once that surplus stowed away, film should make a swell supporting feature.' Still, with *Night Train* following *The Stars Look Down* to America, Reed was proving to British producers that he could make films which would easily cross the Atlantic.

In July 1940 Reed began work on a screen version of H. G. Wells's *Kipps* for Twentieth Century Productions, to be made at Shepherd's Bush Studios, a 'very large figure' having been paid for the film rights. *Kipps* had been filmed before, as a silent picture in 1921, with George K. Arthur in the lead, but Wells confided to Michael Redgrave, who was to play the title role in Reed's remake, that he was 'more interested in this than in any previous film version of his novels'.

As well as Redgrave, the cast included Reed's usual assembly of stage actors. He cast Phyllis Calvert, Helen Haye, Hermione Baddeley, Betty Jardine and Michael Wilding and found a special cameo role for his friend Lord Castlerosse, the fat gossip columnist of the *Daily Express*. Sidney Gilliat again wrote the screenplay, edited by the studio scenario editor, Frank Launder. Vetchinsky was to design the sets, lavish reconstructions of Edwardian interiors and the Folkestone promenade, and the costumes were to be designed by Cecil Beaton.

Although it was apparently a light-hearted film, set in the nostalgic, halcyon days of Edwardian England, both Reed and Redgrave believed that Wells's message about the hatefulness of class snobbery was worth delivering to wartime audiences. Reed was adamant that *Kipps* was not merely an escapist film: 'I'm sure filmgoers don't want a string of comedies or musical farces one after another. I believe that they are just as ready to see serious stuff in wartime as at any other time. In fact, I think they would be bored and annoyed by a series of farces.'

A sense of purpose united the cast as if they were, in their way, contributing to the war effort, if only by lifting public morale. As Redgrave explained: 'There is probably only a short time before we are called up and he [Reed] ceases to be a director while I cease to be an actor. There is a feeling of urgency. There is no time to waste.' Reed agreed. Making pictures in wartime was more exciting than in peacetime. 'There's more bite in it. People seem to be more helpful, more anxious to get on with the job.'

Reed felt a particular affection for Wells's novel, as one of its characters, a would-be dramatist, Chitterlow, was based on Sidney Bowkett, a dubious stage producer and former schoolfriend of Herbert Tree. When Tree was enjoying success with George du Maurier's *Trilby*, Bowkett had visited the Haymarket Theatre and taken a shorthand note of the play and its staging in order to mount a replica production, without permission or payment, which he took on a tour of provincial theatres. Tree took Bowkett to court for plagiarism and a notable case ensued, which Bowkett not surprisingly lost. Reed's fondness for his father, and perhaps an inherited sense of the fun of it all, meant that he relished the character of Chitterlow and awarded the part to Arthur Riscoe, a Yorkshire stage comic, giving him a series of hilarious scenes in which he was allowed to flagrantly upstage Redgrave.

Another important piece of casting was that of Diana Wynyard as Helen Walsingham, the upper-class woman with whom Kipps falls in love and to whom he proposes. Reed was by now madly in love with Diana and they were spending every available moment together. The only thing keeping them apart was their work. Then came the chance to cast her in *Kipps* at short notice. He had asked Margaret Lockwood to play Ann Pornick, the servant girl Kipps abandons in favour of Helen Walsingham, who was to be played by Phyllis Calvert, but Lockwood declined, allowing him to switch Calvert to the Pornick role and give the part of Helen to Diana.

The film became an expression of Reed's love for Diana. As Helen Walsingham, the aloof, suburban beauty, always a little out of reach of the cumbersome, socially awkward Kipps, Diana appeared much as Reed saw her in life. She was slightly unreal, an ideal woman, desirable but somehow too good to be true. As with Daphne du Maurier, Reed had once more chosen an unattainable beauty with whom to fall in love.

Reed was a strikingly good-looking man at this time, and he wore his clothes with a romantic insouciance. He dressed in an expensive suit or a lumberjacket around the studio and an ever-present duffle coat and scarf on location. A reporter described him during the making of *Kipps*: 'He has a deceptively casual approach. Lolling his prodigious height against the camera, he munches a bun, maintaining through cups of strong tea that direction is not all: that, with the evolution of movies, script-writing has come to occupy a more important place, and that given a good script, a director is sitting pretty. But not sitting back, it seems, for his quizzical glance has observed some trifling imperfection. Reed lopes lankily off across the set, supervising every aspect of the scene, rehearsing the players with that meticulous, searching care which is a legacy from play-acting and stage managing. Above the cosy din Carol Reed dominates, without domineering. Oddly, he gives me the impression that he is not yet quite sure about Carol Reed – though very sure about his job.'

From September 1940 onwards, during the filming of *Kipps*, Carol and Diana were able to share the whole of each other's lives. By day they were at the studio; at night they would have dinner together and go to the cinema. Their choice of pictures was suitably romantic. They saw Greta Garbo laughing for the first time on screen in Ernst Lubitsch's *Ninotchka* and, a more ironic choice, the cuckolded baker Raimu in Marcel Pagnol's *La Femme du Boulanger*. Their liaison was kept secret from the rest of the cast, and they went about their affair with the utmost discretion. While the blitz raged, Reed continued to live in his small flat at 20 Grosvenor Gardens while Diana remained in her top-floor flat in Pall Mall, retiring each evening to a basement air-raid shelter where the lights were put out at 9 p.m. Each morning at 5.45 she would drive herself to the studio, picking up her hairdresser, Francis, en route.

One reason for their secrecy, at least during the two months it took to film *Kipps*, was that Reed and Michael Redgrave were living in the same block of flats. Some evenings the two men would discuss the progress of the film and the state of the world long into the night, and they would travel to Lime Grove together at 6 a.m. to start shooting at 8. Redgrave wrote; 'We could meet in the evenings and talk; a time I remember above all because of its utter divorce from any reality except that of imaginative work. For to face the cameras each morning as a younger man I was obliged to take heavy sleeping pills each night in order to sleep through the noise of the bombardment. No question then of retiring to a shelter . . . In the evenings we left the studio ten minutes before the blackout and as we drove home in the dusk the sirens would start. If they did not, I remember, we were faintly worried. No wonder that my memory of the blitz is largely a picture of a fictitious Folkestone in Edwardian dress.'

Redgrave's affection for his director stemmed from Reed's total devotion to his work. In the first volume of his auto-biography Redgrave gave a glowing tribute to Reed which reveals his working methods and the effect that his devoted commitment to making films had on those around him.

Reed is one of those dedicated beings, the artist who is completely absorbed by his dream. He eats, drinks and sleeps cinema. You might hear him carrying on an eager con-versation with a farmer, a chemist or a nuclear physicist, but that would not mean he is even for a moment interested in farming, chemistry or nuclear physics. It would be more likely that he was studying the farmer's way of scratching his head to punctuate his conversation, the chemist's tone of voice or the particular physicist's calm way of letting drop horrendous statistics. He would not be purposely observing these. It is his habit. If he had nothing else to observe he would watch a flea. He has a very friendly and charming way of asking a lot of gentle questions and watching you as you give the answers with his big blue eyes as wide as a child's when listening to a story. The wide ingenuousness is almost too good to be true and his repeated exclamations of surprise or incredulity: 'Do you really?' 'That's fascinating!' 'How true!' would strike one as naive to the point of absurdity if after a short time one did not become aware that these simple, direct questions are not so simple nor so direct as they seem. Unwittingly you have supplied him with an answer or clue to some quite different question. He would, I think, disclaim this and he seldom, I am sure, consciously lays traps. He is not an intellectual man and like most intuitive artists he mistrusts analysis. He is not startlingly original, nor particularly daring. Being schooled in the hard school of commercial cinema under such experts as the late Ted Black, and of success by his early master, Edgar Wallace, one of his big blue eyes always has at least an oblique squint in the direction of the box office. This, I would have you understand, is not intended as criticism of Reed's achievement.

Reed reported for a medical inspection by the military authorities in September 1940 and was classed Grade One. He was registered number SHP 20105, and was reminded in the process that his fame had not reached every part of Britain, as his name was mis-spelled on the form as 'Carrol'.

Work on *Kipps* began the same month, with Arthur Crabtree, the cameraman, travelling with assistant director Bertie Mason to Lacock in Wiltshire to film location shots. Studio work began at the end of the month and on the first day was delayed by an air raid. Another three raids followed that day, but Reed, as well-ordered as ever, ensured that only thirty minutes of valuable filming time was lost.

The persistence of the British film industry despite the German aerial raids became an important propaganda story, and in the first week of filming British Movietone News and the press arrived on the set to show Reed and his cast and crew demonstrating their stiff British upper lips. During a raid, Redgrave played cards with members of the crew and others napped while Reed discussed the progress of the schedule with the producer, Edward Black. Many of the crew now lived and slept in the basements of the studios, to avoid the heavier air raids in central and east London. Phyllis Calvert joined them, having been bombed out of her mother's home, and converted the studio waiting room into a bed-sit.

Despite the constant threat of air raids and the many personal dramas endured by cast and crew, Reed kept up his tight schedule. On the first day, a scene was shot between Redgrave and Wynyard in which Kipps daydreams about proposing to her. In the second week, a scene on the Folkestone promenade set was shot, involving an enormous effort from the props and costume departments, not least from Cecil Beaton, the painter, caricaturist, journalist, satirist, photographer and designer.

Beaton's intimate knowledge of the interiors of the homes of the fallen gentility and the high fashion of the Edwardian seaside dandies and their ladies was brilliantly marshalled to reproduce an age which had been lost but was not forgotten by cinema audiences. Vetchinsky and Beaton between them toyed with the memories of the wartime public, who longed for even the recent past to be restored to them. In one scene an especially potent symbol of an age gone by, the Crystal Palace, which had burnt down in 1936, was recreated as a backdrop.

Beaton had confided to his diary in September 1939 that he liked Reed 'more than anyone I've met through films', and the precision and ingenuity of the art direction in *Kipps* was so effective that it was to become the model for three later films celebrated for the quality of their art direction and costumes. Redgrave reappeared in similar Edwardian striped blazer and flannels to those he wore in *Kipps* in Anthony Asquith's film of *The Importance of Being Earnest* ten years later. Beaton won an Oscar in 1958 for his reworking, in colour, of his *Kipps* costumes for Vincente Minnelli's film musical *Gigi*, and he developed them still further in 1964 for George Cukor's *My Fair Lady*, starring not Redgrave but Reed's other favourite leading man, Rex Harrison.

By the seventh week of filming, Reed was shooting a scene inside a draper's shop, again magnificently depicted by Vetchinsky, then the cast and crew went on location to Barmouth in North Wales. In the ninth week Reed shot Kipps and his new wife being interrupted in their bedroom by a triumphant Arthur Riscoe. Despite the constant diving into shelters to escape from German bombing, *Kipps* ended on schedule at the end of October 1940. One final idea came to nothing: H. G. Wells could not be persuaded to appear in a filmed introduction to the picture.

Once again Reed had demonstrated his extraordinary versatility and efficiency, but in *Kipps* he also showed his brilliance with child actors. The first quarter of the picture concerns the early life of Kipps and his roots among the modest shopkeepers of his mother's family. Phillip Frost, who played Kipps as a boy, and Diana Calderwood, as his young girlfriend, were encouraged to act in a realistic way, providing a foundation for Wells's commentary on social manners. Reed exhaustively auditioned child actors for the two parts, rejecting most of them because they had acting-school accents unsuitable for the characters. Having made his choices, he coaxed good performances from the young actors by being relaxed and understanding with them on the set.

The end of filming meant that Reed and Diana were once again separated by work. While he prepared his next projects, she continued to be in great demand, both on the stage and at the film studios. Their busy and conflicting working lives, combined with the disruptions and inconveniences of wartime, meant that they had little time to pursue their love affair. They despaired at being apart, but neither could avoid their commitments.

The Fox producers were planning two films to which Reed's name was linked, *Spitfire*, a blatant propaganda piece to star John Mills, and *Pitt the Younger*, later called *The Young Mr Pitt*, a more subtle contribution to the war effort which, with Britain blockaded and under daily threat of invasion, was intended to conjure up an earlier age when the country was under similar threat. The idea had evolved after a lunch at Claridge's between Reed and Lord Castlerosse, who volunteered to write a screenplay full of the amusing and entertaining aspects of William Pitt.

Diana was already engaged in a similarly patriotic project at the Teddington studios, *An Empire is Built*, Thorold Dickinson's life of Disraeli, later to be retitled *The Prime Minister*, with John Gielgud as Disraeli and Diana as his wife. By December 1940 she had joined Rex Harrison in a stage production of S. N. Behrman's *No Time for Comedy* and had once again set off on tour around the country. A part had also been found for Harrison's girlfriend of the time, Lilli Palmer, who had appeared in Reed's 1939 film *A Girl Must Live*. The tour lasted until March 1941, and each night without fail Carol and Diana would talk to each other on the telephone.

In March the play arrived at the Haymarket Theatre with a peculiar schedule of morning and afternoon matinees so that the audience could get home before the blackout. It was a unique time for the actors, who for once found their evenings free. For the first time since *Kipps*, Carol and Diana had a reasonable amount of time together each day in which to strengthen their fragile love affair. This temporarily normal life for two such busy theatrical people continued until the play closed in January 1942.

The Young Mr Pitt was to be an extraordinarily lavish affair, with sets, again by Vetchinsky, reproducing the House of Commons, the Bastille and many of the streets of eighteenth-century London. The film had an enormous cast of 128 speaking parts, all to be costumed by Beaton. Building the sets at Lime Grove and making the costumes would take months, so Reed agreed to do some war-work to fill in the time.

There was a well-ordered campaign to try to persuade the United States to enter the war, mostly taking the form of radio broadcasts by well known British actors and actresses explaining to American audiences the bravery of the British people in the face of aerial bombardment and the deprivations of life on an island cut off by German U-boats. The British government wished to put pressure on American public opinion to make it easier for President Roosevelt to defy Congress and bring his country into the war. Reed was to make a short film to be added to existing American cinema programmes, which would show the difficulties of life in Britain.

The seventeen-minute-long film, to be called *A Letter From Home*, was to be made under the auspices of the British Ministry of Information, and all concerned gave their services free and uncredited. The script was written by Rodney Ackland, and focused on a day in the life of a young woman played by Celia Johnson, in her first cinema role. The film opens on her two daughters, who have been evacuated across the Atlantic to stay with their aunt, played by Joyce Grenfell. She reads them a letter from their mother and, as they are put to bed, Celia Johnson is shown queuing for a bus, exchanging news about the previous night's bombing with a neighbour, shopping for eggs and unexpectedly being given two, then going to fire-bomb practice and home to write to her children from the safety of the cellar. During the filming Reed met a young actress, Penelope Dudley Ward, and she was instantly charmed by him. The feeling was mutual.

Penelope Dudley Ward, always known as 'Pempie', shared a flat in Devonshire Street, Mayfair, with an actress friend of Reed's, Judy Campbell. When she returned home from the first day of filming, she said to Judy Campbell, 'I have met the most wonderful person, Carol Reed.' Pempie was well known on the London stage as an actress of gentle talent. She was also familiar

in London society because she was the daughter of Freda
Dudley Ward, the separated wife of a Liberal Member of
Parliament, who for sixteen years had been the mistress of
Edward, Prince of Wales, later Edward VIII, the timid, reluct-
ant king who was to abdicate in 1936 for 'the woman I love'.

Freda Dudley Ward had met the heir to the throne quite by
chance, when, walking through Belgrave Square one evening
during the First World War, the maroons went up announcing
an air raid. She made for the open front door of a house in the
square and was invited down to the basement for shelter. In the
semi-darkness Freda met and spoke to a man who, it transpired,
was the Prince of Wales. He asked Freda to stay for the rest of the
party which had been interrupted by the bombing. They danced
until the early hours and their intimate friendship lasted for the
next sixteen years, until she was frozen out of the prince's life by
Wallis Simpson.

The love affair between Freda and Edward, known to her and
the royal family as 'David', was never kept very secret, but
somehow it never became public knowledge. It was conducted
with discretion on both sides, but there was little moderation in
their affection for each other. As Frances Donaldson described it
in her biography of Edward VIII, 'he was madly, passionately,
abjectly in love with her'. He telephoned her each morning in
what the Dudley Ward household came to know as 'the baker's
call' – 'Has the baker called yet?' – and each day he would meet
her, usually at 5 o'clock, and would go on to dine with her,
public duties permitting.

Between 1919 and 1934 Freda Dudley Ward became the most
important influence in the prince's life, and this intimacy with
the heir to the throne had its effect on her two daughters,
Penelope and Angela, who both came to know him very well.
They called him 'Little Prince'. Angela in particular became close
friends with him, playing truant from school in order to take tea
at St James's Palace or to play golf with him at Combe Hill.
Pempie was four years old when the affair began.

Pempie and Carol had fallen in love with each other every bit
as quickly as her mother and the Prince of Wales. Reed had little
appetite for royal gossip, and he was never much impressed by
titles, so the importance of Pempie's mother's association rather
passed him by. But he found that he shared with Pempie a

complicated family background which caused them to feel close to each other. At the time Reed met her, she was married to Anthony Pelissier, the son of the actress Fay Compton, and they had a baby daughter, Tracy, but the marriage was almost over. Pelissier was in the merchant navy, stationed in the north of Scotland. Although Reed and Diana were soon to become engaged, he began to have an affair with Pempie, who was nine years younger than him. Neither of them expected anything to come of it, yet it soon became clear that they had discovered something neither of them had experienced before: true love without doubts or reservations.

Diana had no idea that Carol had fallen in love with another woman. They were now living together in his flat in Grosvenor Gardens and Pempie and Judy Campbell were close neighbours who regularly called in for a drink. Judy, who knew what was going on, remembers a particularly awkward dinner with Carol, Diana, Pempie and herself, just as matters were coming to a head. Reed had to choose between one woman with whom he was in love, and another of whom he was very fond but who offered a life which was already beginning to make him feel anxious and restricted. He was in his mid-thirties and was confronting the most profound personal decision of his life.

As he waited to start work in earnest on *The Young Mr Pitt*, Reed received some good news from the United States. Despite the initial coolness of the American distributors to *Night Train* and its unpromising release in New York, the film had slowly taken off and had been redefined, in Hollywood terms, as a 'sleeper'. Suddenly the small theatres on both coasts which were showing *Night Train* found that they were attracting celebrities. Hedda Hopper, the influential Hollywood gossip columnist, wrote: 'At a neighborhood theater where it was showing the other night I saw six of our prominent directors and Bing Crosby, Spencer Tracy, Walter Pidgeon and Claudette Colbert in the audience. You know, this is the picture of which Winston Churchill asked to have a special showing. If you miss it, don't say.' Marlene Dietrich, Joe Pasternak and Alfred Hitchcock were reported sneaking in to see it. And Walter Winchell, one of America's most widely syndicated columnists, described the film as 'a dazzler . . . the ice it puts on your spine is brand new'.

Paul von Henreid, still an Austrian citizen, was instantly wooed by Hollywood, where he was put to work on *Now Voyager* with Bette Davis and *Casablanca* with Ingrid Bergman and Humphrey Bogart. Hollywood offers were sent to Reed, too, as studio chiefs clamoured to sign up the latest hot British director. But it was too late. Nothing could seduce him to Hollywood until the war was over.

There could have been no more urgent reminder that Britain was at war than the gala opening of *Kipps*, which took place not in central London but in Folkestone, where the novel and film were set. Folkestone, on the south coast of England, was at the front line of the Battle of Britain just twenty-five miles from the coast of France, where the Germans sat in Calais and Cap Gris Nez with their big guns, capable of firing across the Channel. On 12 May 1941, Carol and Diana, accompanied by Michael Redgrave, Phyllis Calvert and the producer, Edward Black, set off for the Central Theatre, Folkestone, for a most unlikely world premiere. It was an inventive act of bravado, good for public morale on the south coast and for publicity.

What brought home to Reed and his colleagues the nature of active service life was the reception the public gave to six Royal Air Force pilots who attended the opening. They had brought down five German aircraft the previous Saturday night, and a further three the following morning, and had become local heroes, greeted with whoops and cheers far louder than those which welcomed the film stars.

Kipps was given a respectful reception. The combination of Reed, the distinguished cast, H. G. Wells – who had seen the film and approved it – and the extravagance of the sets and costumes appeared to disarm the critics. The general view was that this was the sort of film wartime audiences wished to see. It was British and light-hearted, containing a worthwhile moral, some enjoyable performances and a great deal of nostalgia for the Edwardian days of plenty. It was, in a word, 'charming'.

Some, however, could not bear to drop their critical guard. James Agate, writing in the *Tatler*, was as sharp as ever, particularly about the sets and costumes by Beaton. The film, he said, appeared to be set in the eighties and nineties, not the nineteen hundreds of Wells's novel. The clothes were wrong, the music was wrong, the style of singing was wrong. The costumes in general were too early and the ladies' costumes, in particular, were overdone. He declared: 'Shop-girls out for an evening walk at Folkestone as anywhere else in 1905 did not look as though they were going to be photographed by Mr Cecil Beaton.' The Walsingham women were both 'over-gowned and over-hatted' and their outfits far too new for the straitened circumstances into which they were meant to have fallen. Then there were the actors. 'Mr Redgrave is not right for Kipps, being too tall and too wide-awake . . . Mr Carol Reed, the director, would have done better to go to the nearest draper's, abduct a junior assistant and coach him.' As for the women: 'Helen Haye plays Mrs Walsingham like a duchess and Diana Wynyard suggests that Helen is training to be the consort of a reigning monarch.' In conclusion he felt: 'Kipps is not any kind of version of Wells's saga of faded gentility and dingy shop parlours. It is an entirely delightful bit of romanticism a la Hans Andersen.'

The socialist newspaper Tribune also spotted some discrepancies. 'The dresses of the lady shop-assistants out "on the mash" are far too elaborate for the wages they could draw at Shalford's Emporium. They could not afford them, Mr Reed.' And Harold Hobson had some important reservations. 'Miss Wynyard's natural style of acting is bred so high that it would not merely chill Kipps, but freeze him beyond hope of thawing. Miss Wynyard's bearing is, in fact, such as would make Chatsworth seem suburban and a duchess self-conscious . . . Kipps himself is Michael Redgrave, who is physically far too distinguished for Mr Wells's diffident and insignificant hero.' Most other critics shied away from finding anything wrong with the picture at all.

The exact order of the appearance of Reed's work on both sides of the Atlantic at this time is rather confusing. Kipps had just been released in Britain, yet Night Train was attracting all the attention in the United States. Several of his films, including The Stars Look Down and A Girl Must Live, had yet to be released across the Atlantic, but American distributors were demanding the very latest Reed film, The Girl in the News, which had not yet been released in Britain. Although it was not the ideal film on which to build on Reed's new reputation in America as a thriller director based on the success of Night

Train, *The Girl in the News* was rush-released in the United States at the end of May 1941.

Despite the fact that *The Girl in the News*, although efficient and at times powerful, had a run-of-the-mill plot and some indifferent acting, the film was well received in America. The notice in the *New Republic* was typical: 'Carol Reed, who directed *Night Train*, has hit the jackpot again.' Reed also benefited from a desire among journalists, particularly on the east coast, to bolster Britain's war effort. Reviews were spattered with 'plucky little Englishman' quotes. In Britain *The Girl in the News* was seen as little more than a solid piece of film-making, and Reed was credited with doing his best with a rather static, courtroom-bound plot. Comment was made, however, on a personal touch by Reed, the opening scene in which the camera concentrates on a cat stalking its mistress as she takes an overdose of pills; a device which was reproduced with chilling effect with another cat in *The Third Man* seven years later.

In July 1941 MGM released *The Stars Look Down* in America. At first the company had been nervous about releasing the film at all. Although it had cost a great deal to make, there did not seem to be much of a market for a sombre film about a mining disaster. But suddenly there was an appetite for Reed films, and there were several in stock. Another reason for MGM releasing *The Stars* so quickly was the fact that John Ford was at work in the rival Fox studios in Hollywood on *How Green Was My Valley*, also set among Welsh miners. The films were to be so similar in tone that Ford had bought 6,000 feet of Reed's shots of mining scenes to be used as backdrops to his studio action and as references for his scene-painters. MGM mounted an American publicity campaign to anticipate the public demand for Ford's picture with the slogan 'The stars look up to *The Stars Look Down*', and MGM contract stars such as Clark Gable, Hedy Lamarr, Robert Taylor and Norma Shearer were wheeled out to praise it. Still, the studio had little faith in the film and expected it to close soon after it opened at the Criterion, New York, in late July 1941.

Like *Night Train*, the film was a surprise success with the American public. In its first week at the Criterion, which had 1600 seats, the film grossed $13,000. Even MGM's premier cinema, the 4500-seat Capital, was only expected to gross $10,000 per week. Again the critics were enthusiastic. The *New*

York Post described it as 'surely one of the greatest pictures England has ever sent us'. John Ford could hardly complain for, if anything, *The Stars Look Down* acted as a trailer for his own mining film, which did even better business and won four Oscars, including Best Picture and Best Director. What might have been more irritating to Ford was the fact that the title of Reed's *The Young Mr Pitt* was an intentional echo of his own 1939 hit, *Young Mr Lincoln*.

Reed achieved a cinematic coup by luring Robert Donat back to the screen for *The Young Mr Pitt*. Donat's mild manners and ordinary looks had had an electrifying effect on cinema audiences on both sides of the Atlantic before the war. After a substantial stage career, he had slipped into film acting, working at one time for Alexander Korda, then attracting international attention with his performance as Richard Hannay in Hitchcock's *The Thirty-Nine Steps*. After taking the lead in the film of A. J. Cronin's *The Citadel*, it seemed natural for him to be cast as the schoolmaster Mr Chipping in *Goodbye Mr Chips*, for which he received an Oscar for Best Actor.

Donat was devoted to stage acting, however, and he saw films merely as a means to underwrite his work in the theatre. After *Chips*, therefore, and with the permission of Louis B. Mayer, the boss of MGM, to whom he was contracted, he joined the Old Vic company at the Opera House, Buxton, Derbyshire, where he acted in a wide range of plays, from Shakespeare to Shaw, and turned down persistent offers of film parts from both Britain and the States.

When war was declared, Donat had attempted to join the armed forces but was turned down as medically unfit. He had expected as much as he suffered from crippling asthma. Yet the army doctors found his chest 'perfect' and ruled him out instead because of the flatness of his feet. Donat, a fierce patriot, announced that under no circumstances would he leave Britain, although his wife and children were sent to the safety of the United States. His decision to stay behind brought him into sharp conflict with Mayer, who was not best pleased that his expensive asset was unavailable for work.

When Reed approached Donat to star as the young William Pitt, Donat applied to Mayer for permission to break his contract, believing the film to be part of the war effort. Far from understanding Donat's sentiments, Mayer was angry to discover that one of his most popular stars, who had made no films for MGM for a number of years, was offering his services to a rival company, Twentieth Century Fox British. Mayer cabled an abrupt 'No' across the Atlantic, to which Donat replied with indignant patriotism: 'You offer me freedom to continue working in theatre but absolutely refuse me work in film studios for third parties thus depriving hundreds of people of work in the most difficult period in Britain's history . . . Frankly cannot believe that in this period in this island's history when she needs every man including actors you personally cannot see my point of view and will definitely refuse me the right to earn my living on stage and screen until war is over.' Mayer, against his better judgement, eventually relented.

In *The Young Mr Pitt* Donat could make a statement about his commitment to the war and to Britain. He was a stalwart broadcaster to America and Australia, constantly encouraging his audiences to sympathise with the besieged British. The film would be an important means of winning over Americans to the British way of seeing things. It was no accident that the opening scene showed Robert Donat as the Earl of Chatham, denouncing in the House of Lords those who advocated war against the Americans with the words, 'You cannot conquer America!' Francis L. Harley, the head of Twentieth Century Fox in Britain, intended *The Young Mr Pitt* to be a long, reasoned plea to the Americans to join Britain in defending their common heritage against an expansionist dictator.

The film was to be an epic, taking Pitt from boyhood to death, allowing Donat to age on the screen as he had in *Chips*. Reed's filming schedule was also to be epic by conventional standards. The Shepherd's Bush studios, where Donat had made *The Thirty-Nine Steps*, had allocated three months for the film's completion, and the budget was to be £250,000. The cast included almost every British character actor available for work, among them Robert Morley as Charles James Fox and John Mills as William Wilberforce. Although Arthur Crabtree had been billed as the cinematographer, Reed took on Freddie Young, who had shot *Goodbye Mr Chips* for Sam Wood. The screenplay was written by Launder and Gilliat and Cecil Beaton designed the costumes and some of the decor. Filming began in the last days of July 1941.

Six months later the film was completed, having taken three months longer than at first estimated. The complications of the sets, the large cast, the succession of short scenes and the epic nature of the project meant that it took nearly twelve months from the film being given the go-ahead to the shooting of the final scene. And still there was a long period of post-production work to come.

Reed was used to working quickly and effectively, and had never been tied to a single project for so long. Some of the delay was caused by inefficiency, though not on his part. The screenwriters upset Donat by not providing a completed script on time. He wrote to Tyrone Guthrie: 'So far they have sent me twenty pages of script. The rough idea is extremely good, but when will these people learn that scripts take a long time to prepare? Both my MGM scripts were in my pocket three months before the film started.' The British film industry had never been as organised as Hollywood and, after all, there was a war on. Everything took place against a background of bombing, fire-fighting, rationing, queuing and mourning. Donat, a nervous character at the best of times, found the working conditions intolerable. 'The awful length of the studio hours, the waiting, waiting, waiting, worsened by raids. You don't know what I'm like at the end of a day's filming. I'm not fit for human society.' The whole cast and crew shared the same plight, and Donat's lordly ways were quickly defused. One day, while he was sitting in his costume and waiting for the make-up girl to dust his face with a powder-puff, an anonymous voice from the gantry rang out: 'Donat! He takes as much looking after as a Borzoi!'

By the time the film was complete, the Japanese surprise attack on Pearl Harbor had already given Roosevelt the public backing he needed to join the Allies. The film was still perceived, however, as a skilful appeal to the common ground shared by the English-speaking world and an obvious homage to Winston Churchill's leadership in adversity. As soon as the film was cut to Reed's approval, Churchill was invited to see it. Unsurprisingly, he approved. The magazine *Cinema* commented: 'Never has any film more perfectly expressed the feeling and temper of the British people in times of stress and trouble such as we are passing through today.' Reed 'impresses us that William

Pitt was the leader of the people and not merely the head of the government and that liberty is a treasure for which we must make a continuous fight'.

The film inadvertently raised a political debate about Churchill's leadership. The magazine *Truth*, a regular wartime critic of the prime minister, thought it a little too early to conclude that Churchill was a second Pitt. 'Before we raise Winston Churchill, however, to the pedestal occupied by William Pitt, the aspirant must prove his mettle. Britain is not yet saved, Hitler not yet defeated. Our prime minister would, surely, be the last man to encourage us to holloa before we are out of the wood. Comparison between Pitt and Churchill can only serve a useful purpose if it stirs the latter to emulate the former. We want our Churchill to become more and more Pitt-like; we do not want him – under the influence of uncritical adulation – to sit back complacently as though he were already worthy to wear Pitt's mantle.'

With the considerable post-production work which such a complex film entailed, *Pitt* was not released until July 1942, by which time Reed had made two important decisions which would guide his life for the next few years. He signed a film-making contract with Alexander Korda and took a commission in the army. As a member of the Army Officers' Emergency Reserve, which he joined with Rex Harrison, he was made an acting captain in the Royal Army Ordnance Corps (RAOC) on 12 June 1942. Two days later his papers arrived ordering him to report to the Royal Army Ordnance Corps depot at Wembley. The RAOC included the Army Kinematograph Service, which was based at the old Fox British studios, now known as Central Depot, Empire Way, Wembley. The AKS came under ADAK, or Assistant Director of Army Kinematography, a lieutenant colonel sitting at a desk in the War Office building in Curzon Street, Mayfair. An attempt on 22 September 1942 to have Reed transferred to the Royal Air Force Volunteer Reserve in Padgate was an error stemming from his visit with Harrison to an old RAF chum at the beginning of the war.

Captain Carol Reed's call-up precipitated another decision: he became engaged to Diana Wynyard. This act can only be regarded as short-sighted and ultimately cruel, betraying a profound lack of judgement. During the course of a long Sunday afternoon walk with Judy Campbell in Hyde Park earlier that summer, Reed had confessed that he could not bear the prospect of being incarcerated in a suffocating marriage. He was very fond of Diana, but, despite her success as an actress and her experience in films on both sides of the Atlantic, she remained a conventional woman in many ways. Even her real name, Dorothy Cox, was so humdrum that it seemed to betray the true Diana Wynyard beneath the stage personality. Reed's love for her was already fading. There was something too suburban about her, too ordinary. He imagined life with her as a traditional, middle-class existence in a semi-detached house, a prospect he could not countenance.

In fact Reed's fears were absurd. Although not as unconventional in her attitudes to marriage as Reed, Diana was a mature thirty-six-year-old woman, hardly likely to demand that they settle down to the sort of cloying married bliss Reed so dreaded. The most obvious reason for Reed's hesitation was that he had fallen in love with another woman. It would have been difficult and painful to break off his engagement to Diana, and he chose to follow a path which he already knew was unlikely to lead to happiness, believing that he was behaving dutifully.

He later insisted to close friends that he felt he had little choice but to do the honourable thing and marry Diana, as he had promised. He could not humiliate her by breaking off their engagement. He was committed to her, felt loyal to her and had promised to marry her, but then he had begun to have doubts. Since he had met Pempie he had realised that he was no longer in love with Diana. His solution would have done credit to the memory of Sir Herbert Beerbohm Tree: he could not prevent himself from making love to Pempie, yet he resolved that he must stand by Diana and marry her.

6

Captain Carol Reed

Carol Reed had confided his worries about Diana to very few people. He was an intensely private man, but one evening in the flat at 20 Grosvenor Gardens at the beginning of February 1943, while waiting for the bombing to start, he did open his heart to Michael Redgrave. Their conversation reveals Reed as a complicated, even devious man in his relationships with women.

Reed told Redgrave that Diana was 'at the height of her mature beauty'. He then made a proposition. 'Carol maintained that she had yet to come to terms with her looks, that she was at arm's length from her beauty. "She needs some man to wake her to the realisation of her glorious self. You could help her do that. Why don't you have a shot, Michael? Go on, wake her up, wake her up!" The next day Diana casually informed me that she and Carol had been married a few days before. It was not I who woke her up, if indeed such a thing was necessary.' Reed apparently wished to continue his affair with Pempie after his marriage by encouraging his new wife to take a lover of his own choosing.

The marriage of Reed and Diana came as a surprise not only to Redgrave but to almost everyone, even those working most closely with him. Eric Ambler remembers visiting Reed in a suite he had taken in the Hyde Park Hotel – a favourite haunt since the days when he wooed Daphne du Maurier there. It was 3 February 1943 and Ambler stayed behind to work on a screenplay for an army training film while Reed and Diana, who was appearing at the time in *Watch on the Rhine* at the Aldwych Theatre, went for lunch. They returned as man and wife, having married at Caxton Hall register office, Westminster, in the company of members of Diana's family. Reed was in uniform and Diana wore a sable coat over a black two-piece suit.

On their return to the hotel, they announced their news to Ambler, saying that they had ruled out a big, noisy wedding to avoid disrupting their work. Diana said that she thought at least a little disruption was in order, however, and she telephoned room service for a bottle of champagne and three glasses. Although the wedding had been a private ceremony, photographs of the couple appeared in the popular papers the following day. The headlines 'Diana Wynyard Marries' suggested how much a background figure Carol still was. As a mention of their marriage in the American *Time* magazine proved, they were both by now as well known in the States as in Britain.

Reed made a very strange soldier, as his brief time in the Home Guard with Rex Harrison had already shown. Peter Ustinov accompanied Reed to Savile Row to be fitted out in his captain's uniform and remembered his casual approach to military form. 'I must say, as an officer he had perhaps even less natural aptitude than I did as a private. He wore his clothes with an exemplary elegance, but had an unfortunate tendency, perhaps as a result of having directed one or two historical films, of raising his cap to those who saluted him.' Reed did not appear to Ustinov to be linked to any form of reality, and most certainly not to the absurdity of army life. 'Carol was a captain who behaved as though the war was a superb invention of Evelyn Waugh's. He had a tendency to daydream which was most engaging and blissfully unmilitary, and his mind was tremulous with tender mischief.'

As a captain specifically commissioned to make films, Reed was excused all normal duties of his rank, although he was once obliged as a practical joke to spend an evening as Orderly Officer by some fellow officers who thought his role was a comfortable sinecure. Eric Ambler remembered: 'With great dignity, Carol went to the studio and watched a guard mounting, said that it seemed to have been well rehearsed and asked what else the boys had lined up for his entertainment. That was the end of the matter. None of the uniformed technicians there really wanted to make an enemy of Carol Reed. The joke was not repeated.'

Reed's task was to make training films, the first of which was intended for would-be beachmasters as part of the Combined Operations effort preparing the joint Anglo-American invasion force to open the Second Front. After three weeks' preparation, Reed was assigned scriptwriters, in the shape of Eric Ambler and Peter Ustinov, and was despatched to Troon in Scotland to report to Thorold Dickinson, the director of *Gaslight*. Dickinson had also directed Diana Wynyard in *The Prime Minister*, at the time Reed had been directing *The Young Mr Pitt*. He was now a major and effectively the producer of Reed's film.

Dickinson, Reed, Ambler and Ustinov were billeted on the sea-front at Troon, and worked with two liaison officers, one British and one American, who gave technical advice on how commandoes landed on a hostile beach and what each soldier needed to know about the organisation of a beach landing. The British Royal Navy officer had been on the St-Nazaire raid and gave details of the conventional army tactics for a beach landing which were soon to be put to the test in the ultrasecret invasion of the north French coast at Dieppe. The American was a major in the Wisconsin National Guard, who made it clear that his appointment to the team was an absurdity as he had no knowledge of beach landings. The material on which the film was to be based was unpromising, consisting of little more than pages of training instructions. Animation techniques were out of the question and the army authorities resisted any attempt to make the film entertaining. 'It doesn't have to be entertaining, you know. The film'll be part of the course. The buggers will have to see it and pay attention,' was the official line.

Reed despaired at ever being able to make a film at all, but encouraged Ambler and Ustinov to write a screenplay which might get some of the most important points across. They became alarmed at some of the facts they were discovering about the army's plans for beach landings, not least the number of casualties to be expected. 'If I may pose a rather delicate question,' Reed asked a British colonel, 'what would the average casualties be on one of your commando raids?' The colonel replied: 'On the contrary, damn good question. Got to be asked sooner or later.' He paused. 'Of course, you have to realise that most of your casualties are not caused by the Hun at all, but by your own covering fire.' Reed looked at Ambler with appalled incredulity. The colonel went on: '80 per cent. But I don't think we ought to frighten the public. Say 70 per cent.'

Although the team was now depressed as well as professionally cramped, great effort went into writing a massive script. Eventually they were put in touch with soldiers from No. 6 Commando, with a view to shooting some trial scenes.

Suddenly the project was cancelled. The reason was not at first evident, but Reed's speculation was confirmed by news which began trickling through about the tragic debacle of the Dieppe landings. There had been a massacre of British soldiers following inappropriate orders, and the whole strategy of beach landings had to be rethought before another invasion could take place. All existing procedures were to be cancelled forthwith and the training film abandoned pending further instructions. Reed, Ambler and Ustinov returned to London.

With the abandonment of the project the trio might well have been broken up, but they were attached to the Directorate of Army Psychiatry, with a view to making a morale-boosting film for new recruits. The problem that the army had by the middle of 1943 was that they had run out of the most suitable men, aged between twenty and thirty, and had now moved to the under-twenties and over-thirties, who were often mixed together in a demographically unhappy platoon. Many of them had quite justifiable grievances against their call-up, and their combined discontent could lead to indiscipline.

The Director of Army Psychiatry was Brigadier J. R. Rees, who had taken personal charge of the debriefing of the mentally disorientated Rudolf Hess, Hitler's deputy, who had parachuted into Britain in the mistaken, not to say crackpot, belief that he could persuade the Scottish landowners to rise against Churchill. Rees gave his blessing to a film which would be useful in raising morale among the new recruits, if Reed and his writers could come up with a plausible idea. All three of them feared that they would be assigned less congenial war work unless they proposed an attractive film treatment.

It was Peter Ustinov who suggested a film which would deal with a fictional group of new recruits, showing their initial attitudes to army life and suggesting ways of overcoming some of the worst hardships. Ustinov, in his early twenties, was a private soldier and he and Ambler, in his thirties, had first-hand knowledge of a new recruit's life and the miserable early weeks of training. Reed and the psychiatrists, Ronald Hargreaves and Tommy Wilson, both lieutenant colonels, had no such experience and were impressed by Ustinov's proposal. The psychiatrists referred Reed and his men to *Disenchantment* by C. E. Montague, an account of the demoralisation of troops in the

1914–18 war, as a guide to the states of mind the film should depict and to which it should suggest solutions.

It was decided that the film should be entitled *The New Lot*. It was to be made at Wembley, where Thorold Dickinson had assembled a talented team of film-makers, including the writer Jack House, the film editor Reggie Mills and Freddie Young, Reed's lighting cameraman on *The Young Mr Pitt*. Reed assembled a cast which included Stanley Holloway, Raymond Huntley, James Hanley and William Hartnell, all of whom gave their services free. Robert Donat also agreed to appear as an officer in a training film within the film whose archaic military advice on screen causes Reed's new recruits to burst into laughter. The scoffing at Donat's old-soldier image was in keeping with the tone of the film, which was to speak directly to new recruits by being modern in approach and candid about outdated military bull.

The main potential stumbling-block to the film was the attitude of the army chiefs. The bungled raid at Dieppe had caused an outcry in the War Cabinet and Churchill was determined that the old guard who were responsible should be removed. The army had become hypersensitive to criticism and Reed's proposed film was hardly a ringing endorsement of the traditional way of doing things. At the same time Michael Powell and Emeric Pressburger, working outside the army and therefore with a much freer hand, were in trouble over their plan to make a film based on the cartoonist David Low's stuffy old-fashioned military type, Colonel Blimp. The army had vetoed *The Life and Death of Colonel Blimp* and, unable to ban it, had declared that no War Office co-operation would be extended to Powell and Pressburger. They went ahead with the film regardless, finally running into trouble with Churchill.

When Reed's forty-minute film was completed, it was shown to a committee of generals in a War Office screening room. As the lights went up, one of them went over to Reed and spluttered: 'You can't call these men soldiers; they do nothing but grumble. Real soldiers never grumble.' The film was branded unhelpful and possibly subversive and was banned from being shown not only to new recruits, but to anyone not directly concerned with army films within the War Office. Reed was distressed but hardly surprised. Making films for the army was a thankless task and it seemed inevitable that he would now be dismissed from the AKS and sent God knew where.

He was saved from this ignominy by a smart rearguard action mounted by psychiatrists within the DAP, members of the Adjutant General's office, the Public Relations Directorate and above all by Brendan Bracken, the Minister of Information. Bracken agreed with the army that they were losing the propaganda war between the services. Both the navy and air force had benefited greatly from films featuring their men which had been popular successes at the cinemas. The navy had had *In Which We Serve*, a commercial film made by Noël Coward and David Lean about the survivors of a torpedoed destroyer, and the Royal Air Force had *One of Our Aircraft is Missing*, Powell and Pressburger's film of a bomber crew brought down in Nazi-occupied Holland.

The army had no such picture, and needed a film to increase morale among new recruits. David Niven, technically a major in the Rifle Brigade, was asked to fix something up. He enjoyed a unique position as a go-between linking the services to commercial film studios like Two Cities, which had made *In Which We Serve*. First Niven turned to Coward, asking him to make a similar film for the army. Coward politely declined. Niven was then shown *The New Lot*, which he liked a great deal. It was decided that a successor to *The New Lot* should be commissioned by Two Cities from Carol Reed, the final go-ahead dependent upon the quality of the script proposal by Eric Ambler. Although closely based on the original short, it would be more positive and broader in appeal.

At first the plan was kept from Reed. Ustinov had appeared before an officer selection board and had upset them by a misguided, irreverent interview and been sent back to the AKS at Wembley. Ambler was given a desk in the War Office building in Curzon Street and ordered to start work on the script, but not to mention anything about the film to Captain Reed, who was to direct the film. The army hoped that by keeping both Reed and Ustinov away from the original draft of the screenplay, it would be a more serious, purposeful film, devoid of mischief. Inevitably, however, Ambler and Reed arranged to meet and, with Reed living at the Park Lane Hotel, it was easy for Ambler to walk from Curzon Street, through Shepherd Market to the rear entrance of the hotel to discuss progress on the script treatment. Niven kept Reed in touch with the thinking of what he referred to as 'the brigadier belt', the very senior army officers who would give final approval for the picture.

With Niven's help, Reed also managed to negotiate his way out of the army. The deputy director of the Films Division of the Ministry of Information, R. Nunn May, had been leant upon by Filippo del Giudice, the head of Two Cities, who said that his studio had urgent need of both Thorold Dickinson and Reed to make 'films of national importance'. As his was a commercial company, it would be inappropriate for them to remain in uniform, thereby avoiding complications about rank. Nunn May agreed on the strict understanding that, before they signed future contracts, they would offer their services to the Ministry of Information. Nunn May duly wrote to Reed on 11 September, in familiar terms, relaying the happy news that the War Office and the Ministry of Labour and National Service had finally agreed to the Ministry of Information's request to have him released from military service. He confirmed the bargain, struck at an earlier conversation, that before signing a commercial contract Reed would offer his services to the Film Division. This was more than a cynical pact on Reed's part, for in his letter to Nunn May he goes out of his way to bind himself to his promise. 'I might mention that I had hoped, immediately on the completion of *The Way Ahead*, to make a short film for the Ministry on some subject to be mutually agreed.'

Reed was now free to apply himself to the extended version of *The New Lot*, optimistically titled *The Way Ahead*. Ambler's treatment was, by film industry convention, written as a short story, breaking every so often into dialogue. When the army top brass read it, there was by no means universal agreement that the film should go ahead. One of them had scrawled all over the treatment: 'Tripe! Why can't we have a full-blooded story by a full-blooded soldier?' They finally gave the go-ahead only after Niven had countered their anxieties about the portrayal of the soldiers – they had complained that the troops in *The New Lot* were neither smart nor respectable enough – by agreeing to play the officer in charge of the conscripts. The army agreed that the film would be made as a commercial feature at the Two Cities studios at Denham under del Giudice.

Del Giudice was also relieved by Niven's decision to star in the film, for, as he pointed out to him, if it was to stand any chance of gaining an American release and therefore covering its costs it would have to feature an international star, and Niven was the only one available. Many of the original cast – Holloway, Huntley, Hartnell – were recalled, and Peter Ustinov was to play a cameo part as an Italian café owner in North Africa.

Reed paid particular attention to the casting of the small parts, and contributed to several successful careers by his decisions, *The Way Ahead* providing a blueprint for a number of post-war projects which fondly looked back at the war and the camaraderie enjoyed by those who fought. William, billed as 'Billy', Hartnell was to enjoy a long post-war career of sergeant roles, including the first 'Carry On' film, *Carry On Sergeant*, and a very similar role in a television series based on National Service, *The Army Game*. John Laurie, the carping Scotsman, resumed a similar role in BBC Television's long-running *Dad's Army* in the 1960s and 1970s.

Another member of the cast, Trevor Howard, came to Reed's attention in an unusual way. Eager to become a film actor, Howard sent Reed a copy of his identity card picture and landed himself a role. Reed believed that there were certain actors whose faces were right for the cinema, and he always looked first at an actor's face to see how it would appear on a screen. *The Way Ahead* was Howard's first screen part, as a competent merchant navy officer.

A significant addition to the cast was a small part awarded to Penelope Dudley Ward. She was to play David Niven's wife, a role to which her elegant, easy, upper-class manner and sweet looks suited her, and would appear in a number of romantic scenes with Niven, including one with her real-life daughter Tracy as their screen child. Clare Tracy Compton Pelissier remembered that after five takes she said: 'Tracy will do it once more and no more.'

Script conferences began in earnest in a room in the Ritz Hotel in Piccadilly, with Reed, Niven, Ambler and Ustinov. Ustinov, still a private, was made Niven's batman in order to allow him free access to the officers in the team. It was an enjoyable time for them all, with extensive use made of the Ritz's ration-free room service and bar. Shooting began in Denham in early summer

1943, followed by location work in the British countryside. As the person in charge of production, Niven laid down the guidelines for how the film should be perceived. He wrote a memorandum:

1) The film must have one object only, and that is to make everyone who sees it say either, 'There, that's what our Bert is doing: isn't it wonderful?' or 'See, we old-timers started something in the last lot' or, in the case of an American audience, 'The British Army is OK.'

2) In order to accomplish the above, the film must be on a really important scale and must certainly not be just a small propaganda short.

3) The movie-going public, which in this country, the Dominions and the US numbers nearly 200 million, after three years of war can smell pure propaganda a mile off.

4) Therefore the film must be of first-class entertainment value, with the benefit to army prestige coming as a natural result of the story.

The script for *The Way Ahead* was the first in which Reed collaborated as an equal with his screenwriters. He had always believed that the preparation of the screenplay was the key to a competent film, and although of course every eventuality could not be worked out behind a desk, he was happiest when a film was so tightly scripted that shooting became almost a form of painting by numbers. He had depended on the brilliant screenwriting talents of Frank Launder and Sidney Gilliat for his last three pictures, and they were such masters of the well-formed and succinctly worded script that to an extent he had merely to follow their lead. When *The Way Ahead* was released, he remarked that the script was so tight and so perfect that he had little option but to produce a fine film, although he did not reveal how intimately he had been involved with the writing.

Reed, Niven, Ambler and Ustinov had a certain amount of fun at the army's expense with the script for *The Way Ahead*, reflecting the irritation and annoyance each of them felt about the service's over-formal, unimaginative approach to their work. They created a scene in which the new recruits would be invited to Sunday tea by a good-looking young woman. When they arrive they discover that she is just about to go out to the cinema with an airman – who wore a collar and tie with his uniform, in a civilised way – and they were going to see 'that merchant navy film, where they don't wear uniforms at all', a reference to *San Demetrio London*, which had just been released.

There was a good deal of British location work to be done, with the cast enduring the indignities of a genuine training assault course, before the news came that they would be allowed to film on location in North Africa. In September the cast and crew set off for Libya on *The Monarch of Bermuda*. Again Ustinov discovered the penalties of being a private. His rank could not be forgotten when dealing with the two army advisers, a captain and a full colonel. And on the ship, which contained reinforcements for the North Africa regiments as well as a team of American sportsmen on a morale-boosting tour, Ustinov was to be separated from Reed and Niven, who were entitled to the facilities extended to officers only. The War Office could still not bear to promote Ustinov, so he was made an honorary civilian for the duration of the shooting. As they put it to David Niven: 'Tell Ustinov he can reach for his bowler.'

The Libyan location work went without a hitch. The U.S. Army provided explosions on demand and locals were recruited as extras for a café scene. Reed spent a great deal of time and care on two scenes which he decided should have the feeling of newsreel films, a sharp documentary approach with camera positions which emphasised the drama: one was a fire on board the troopship; the second was the military action. If a film with a fair share of propagandist lines was to maintain the interest of its audience, it needed to be as realistic as possible. On time and within budget, as usual, Reed returned to Britain for post-production work in January 1944.

While Reed was shooting in North Africa, Pempie Dudley Ward had decided that it would not be fair on anyone for her to continue living so close to Reed and within sight of Diana. The decision to marry Diana had been Reed's and she respected him for it, and had no wish to break up a marriage. Her own marriage to Anthony Pelissier had already fallen apart (it was to be formally dissolved in December 1944), and she had no wish to see anyone else suffer in a similar way. Carol had behaved honourably towards Diana, so Pempie was determined to behave honourably herself, although she was deeply in love with him. When she had first met Reed she was also being wooed by a much more conventional man. She went to a fortune-teller for advice, who read the tea-leaves in her cup, and said: 'There are two men in your life; one is solid tea-leaves; the other like a prince in a pantomime.' She chose the prince in the pantomime, but she now decided that if she could not marry Reed, she would make herself scarce before living in the same city as Mr and Mrs Carol Reed began to depress her.

Pempie had been offered a leading role in *Lady Windermere's Fan* on Broadway, which would provide a convenient escape, but she could not find a way of flying to the United States in wartime until an old friend came to her aid. Alexander Korda was close to Pempie and a great admirer of her beauty. He had left for the United States on the outbreak of war, but, as a close friend of Churchill and after some savage criticism of his departure, had recently begun visiting Britain to do what he could for the war effort. He arranged for Pempie's flight, and she set off for New York with Tracy. *Lady Windermere's Fan* was a great success and her career blossomed as never before.

On its release in Britain in June 1944, *The Way Ahead* was welcomed as a refreshing means of bringing home to those in and out of uniform what life was like for a new army recruit. The trade press laughingly described it as 'a he-man picture of obvious feminine appeal', but went on to call it 'an outstanding general booking; a war film that all will want to see . . . It is box office in battle dress.' One critic thought it rather demeaning for Reed to deal with such a humdrum subject. 'Carol Reed's direction is so assured that employing his talent on army and Ministry of Information shorts is rather like giving Constable the job of painting farmhouse doors.' Reed himself felt rather the same, but he was not above corniness. Instead of the final titles finishing with the words 'The End', he twisted convention and ended with 'The Beginning'. A moderate success in Britain, *The Way Ahead* turned out to have little appeal to the Americans, and the film marked the end of Reed's association with the Army Kinematograph Service.

As soon as he returned from North Africa, Reed began working on his next project, a film commissioned by General Dwight D. Eisenhower, the chief of the Allied expeditionary force which was assembling in the south of England to invade

the north coast of France. Working for the army had been a
nightmare for Reed. He was happy with how *The Way Ahead* had
turned out, but the delays, bureaucracy and military vanities
involved had irritated him. He looked forward to a time when he
could stop being a soldier directing films and return to commercial film-making. In December 1943 he allowed his name to be
linked with the announcement of Alexander Korda's return to
Britain. Korda had decided that it was not too early to plan the
post-war British film industry, and assembled a list of talented
directors and writers who would lend their names to his
audacious plan to make his studios in Britain a true rival to the
Hollywood studios once the war had ended. Reed was not
under contract, but he had agreed to put himself at the
government's disposal on completion of *The Way Ahead*. Korda
would therefore have to wait.

Reed's next project had been conceived at the beginning of
1943 when the Supreme Headquarters Allied Expeditionary
Force (SHAEF) in London, under Eisenhower's command,
began finalising its top-secret plans for the invasion of France.
Robert E. Sherwood, the American dramatist, who was on the
staff of SHAEF, suggested that there should be a proper
documentary film account of this great historical event, the
invasion of the European mainland by sea. Eisenhower agreed
to the plan, but insisted that there should be one single, official
record, a joint Anglo-American production, with the direction
shared between a British and an American film-maker.
Sherwood proposed Captain Garson Kanin as the American
director and the British chose Carol Reed. Eisenhower appointed himself producer of the film.

Reed met Kanin in London and they spent several days
discussing the difficulties of working so closely together. They
both wanted to be sure that their initial friendship would be able
to stand what might be years of close collaboration, as it was
impossible to guess how long the invading force might take to
reach Paris, which was scheduled to be the end of the film. They
were both wary about making a film with two directors, which
Kanin described as 'like expecting to have a baby be born and
have two fathers', but they agreed that as Eisenhower was
determined that the film should be a collaboration, it might as
well be them.

Kanin described his relationship with Reed as 'a kind of love affair from the start. I simply adored Carol Reed and I took pains to see that he responded in kind – I did everything I possibly could. I dripped charm and we got along very well.' Reed, for his part, returned the compliment and used his considerable charm to ensure that the film, which both he and Kanin regarded as of the utmost importance, would be successful. They reported to the Anglo-American Film Planning Committee that they would accept the assignment.

The committee sent them to see Eisenhower. This was the first of many visits to Eisenhower's headquarters, which after the invasion became increasingly close to Berlin, during which Reed and Kanin would report their progress and show some of their footage for Eisenhower to comment on and criticise. One particular meeting, when Eisenhower's HQ was in Rheims, illustrated to Reed and Kanin the extent of his commitment to ensuring that the whole of the Allied invasion should be a united effort between all the countries involved. Walking through an outer office, Reed, Kanin and Eisenhower overheard one half of a heated telephone conversation in which an American major referred to a British colleague as a 'Limey son of a bitch'. They began their conference about progress on the film, but Eisenhower interrupted the meeting and asked that the major be brought before him. He appeared and was dismissed from Eisenhower's command. 'You can call anybody you want a son of a bitch, if that's your opinion – that's all right with me,' Eisenhower told the surprised major, 'and you can call anybody a Limey if you want to. But when you call a man a Limey son of a bitch, then I don't want you in this command.'

Eisenhower was no easier to work for than any other producer and, said Garson Kanin, 'got to be quite a pain in the neck after a while', but there were advantages in having a friend in such a high place. First, there were no budgetary constraints because there was no budget. According to Kanin: 'I suppose it may be the most expensive film in history. You couldn't possibly estimate the cost and we were never given any figure. We had permission to commandeer any units that were available. We flew people everywhere.' Second, red tape was minimised by Eisenhower's single order commanding Reed and Kanin to make the film: the directive for the making of the film was a letter on small notepaper in Eisenhower's own handwriting, ordering the film to be made. Reed and Kanin used it as a passport to get everything they needed. The film remained top secret until four months after D-Day.

The two directors agreed very quickly on the basic principles of the film. Theirs would not be a heroic story of fighting men but a deglamourised record of a military campaign. It would be called *The True Glory*, a title taken from a prayer by Sir Francis Drake before defeating the Spanish Armada. The film would show no bias towards the fighting troops of any one country or of any one service. They would depend for footage on seven hundred cameramen following as many different military companies as possible. In no circumstances would any of the action be staged. This was to be as truthful an account as possible. They had both taken a dim view of the British documentary account of the North African campaign, *Desert Victory*, which had supplemented genuine footage with fictional studio scenes.

They also considered John Ford's instructions to his cameramen on *Why We Fight* and his other wartime documentaries to shake their cameras now and then to give the film added 'authenticity' to be deceitful. Much of Reed and Kanin's footage would, in any case, be rough-and-ready, for many of the camera operators had little or no experience of their trade under any conditions, let alone on active service under fire. The pair of them were conscious that this film would be the first and perhaps the only time that the public would be able to understand what the invasion of Nazi-occupied France was really like, for news of the war only reached people through radio broadcasts and the delayed, censored cinema newsreels.

Reed and Kanin were given five dates on which the invasion of France, codenamed 'Operation Overlord', might take place. The date was, in fact, fixed for 5 June 1944, but bad weather over the Channel caused Eisenhower to delay the invasion by one day, to 6 June. The invasion force was accompanied by 440 combat cameramen. Before long an avalanche of raw footage was being sent back to London, from the build-up of troops on the south coast of England to fighting on the Normandy beaches and at Caen, St Lo, Falaise, Avranches and Cherbourg, the liberation of Paris, Arnhem and Remagen. Teams of film-makers edited it as they went along, with no idea whether the campaign would last weeks, months or years. A method for assessing the footage was determined: it would be sifted and sorted by Reed and Kanin themselves, assisted by a team of viewers, then selected lengths of footage would be handed to editors, cutters and soundmen. Those who agreed to sift the material included Peter Ustinov, Eric Ambler, Eric Maschwitz, the scenarist of *Goodbye Mr Chips*, and Claude Dauphin from France.

Ustinov remembers going to the office of military censorship in Davies Street, London, to view the latest batch of footage from the front and seeing, without warning, film of the capture by American officers of Hermann Goering, the German air force minister. His American captors were relaxed and jokey and could be seen taking turns to have themselves photographed with the once-fat and now ill-looking Nazi chief. They asked for his autograph and offered him chewing gum. Those in the London viewing room were agog at the gentle treatment Goering received, and when that section of film was drawn to the attention of Eisenhower – not by Ustinov – he went into a rare rage and sent back to the States all of the U.S. officers who could be recognised.

Other film arrived from unconventional sources; some was German news footage bought in Lisbon, some was stolen. An American poet, Harry Brown, was commissioned to write blank verse in a mock-heroic style to describe the progress of the campaign. Kanin suggested that the film of actual events should be matched with a commentary by the servicemen and women themselves, but telling the story of units other than their own. Reed was hesitant but agreed to try out the technique on one reel. Four months were spent editing a single reel of image to its soundtrack and both directors agreed that the idea worked. Teams of sound recordists began a tour of hospitals, fighting units, air force bases and ships, interviewing thousands of troops about their experiences. One hundred and thirty voices are heard in the final film. One of the interviewers was the American screenwriter Paddy Chayevsky, whom Kanin sprang from hospital where he was recovering from a wound.

The mass of film footage, some $6\frac{1}{2}$ million feet, was made manageable by breaking the story into sections and assigning each to a small team of three or four editors to produce a coherent and economic episode.

Difficult choices had to be made about the subjects to be shown. In particular there was great discussion about the portrayal of black American servicemen who, in the early forties, were still mostly segregated from their white colleagues and were given the lowliest jobs, such as truck-driving and cooking. There were very few black fighting units, and Reed and Kanin were determined that these should be given some prominence. Looking back on the film with the benefit of more than forty years' hindsight, Kanin regretted that more was not made of the role of women in the campaign.

How much of the concentration camp footage should be shown also caused arguments among the film-makers and in the Anglo-American Planning Committee. Peter Ustinov remembers the arrival of the footage of British soldiers entering Belsen for the first time. The film was silent, which added to its poignancy. 'A sergeant came out of the gates, and even on the black and white screen, his face had gained an expression over which he had no control. It was of extraordinary complexity, at once earnest, furious, resolved and glacial.' The sergeant ordered his men to slow march into the camp. 'The long line of soldiers marched slowly through the gates into the stench, and came face to face with the obscene evidence of genocide, the mountains of bones, linked by a webbing of flesh; the expressionless eyes of the fittest, the survivors; the miserable human garbage scattered on the soil. One after the other, individual soldiers fell out, vomiting helplessly on all fours. The sergeant could threaten and bluster, it made no difference. The shock had felled these men with a blow to the stomach, and there was nothing discipline could do. Suddenly one soldier went berserk. He broke ranks for no visible reason. Eyes wild, he ran, and the camera followed him.' There was a view among some of the film-makers and the committee that Belsen was no part of the fighting, merely an incident along the way, and that their film was an account of 'Operation Overlord' and should be nothing more. After months of debate, it was decided to include footage of the concentration camps.

As the film neared completion, music was commissioned. The first composer, Marc Blitztein, fell ill and a score was ultimately written by William Walton. Reed encouraged Kanin to ask Eisenhower whether he would introduce the film himself, in a recorded address to the camera. The general agreed, and Kanin wrote a script, heavily edited by Reed, which Eisenhower learned and spoke to camera without notes in a single take, with a second take to allow close-ups. The introduction was to be swiftly followed by action aboard a landing vessel, with a regimental sergeant major telling his troops: 'Men who want to take their anti-seasick tablets should take 'em now.'

Of the 1400 cameramen whose work was used, thirty-two had been killed in action, a further sixteen reported missing and over a hundred wounded. Carol Reed had avoided danger, for the most part, but he had sacrificed a great deal of time. Although grateful to be out of the clutches of the Army Kinematograph Service, he had no idea that the film would take so long. At first the plan was to complete the film when the Allied troops liberated Paris. Then it was to be when the Rhine was crossed, then when the Allies reached Berlin. By June 1945, nearly two years after it was first conceived, Reed and Kanin approved the final version of the film. The end of the war in Europe had been celebrated in the middle of May. All that remained was obtaining Eisenhower's final approval.

The difficulty was finding the general in one place long enough to screen the film, as he was constantly on the move, directing the final stages of the war. When he did finally grant Reed and Kanin enough time to show him their work he stared at the screen silently before marching out of the room without giving his verdict. Shortly afterwards, in a room crowded with press eager to hear Eisenhower's opinion, Reed telephoned the general's car. It was a very bad line and Eisenhower's assistant answered. Reed asked what Ike thought of the film. Then, between long bouts of crackle, came resounding praise, which Reed repeated to the assembled reporters. It was most moving, a considerable achievement, the most effective use of the footage available. At the end of the superlatives came a pause, before the assistant said, 'Of course, that is only my opinion.' As the press were leaving to file their stories, Reed could not bring himself to explain that everything he had told them had not been Eisenhower's opinion at all.

Although SHAEF officials estimated that it would be the most widely distributed film in history, with translations commissioned in nineteen languages, *The True Glory* was not seen as a likely commercial success, nor anything but a patriotic chore to distribute. According to Harry Cohn, the boss of Columbia Pictures, who finally distributed the picture in the United States, 'All the major companies drew lots to see who would distribute this picture, *The True Glory*. And what can I tell you? Columbia lost.'

The film was first screened simultaneously in London and Paris on 2 August 1945. British critics heaped praise upon it, although the blank-verse commentary came in for some sharp remarks. 'It sounds wrong and high-falutin',' wrote one. The complexity of the film's maps and graphics also came in for criticism. Dilys Powell took a wider view: 'The war films of the Western democracies are sometimes compared to their disadvantage with the Russian war films: they lack, it is said (often truly), the drive and savage magnificence of the Eastern Front records. Well, nobody can say that of *The True Glory*. Here is a film which has a dreadful size and haste, which is deafening as battle is deafening: here is war.' Queen Mary went to see the film at the Odeon, Leicester Square, before the month was out.

It was not until 21 August that the film was shown in America, premiered simultaneously at the Plaza Theater in Abilene, Kansas, the home town of General Eisenhower, and at the Victoria Theater, Broadway, with searchlights stabbing Manhattan's night sky and a military parade led by an army band.

The film took some time to be screened to the American public because it fell foul of the Hays Office, the film censors, who disliked the bad language such as 'hell' and 'damn' which some soldiers used in the film. After unanimous press uproar against Hays and his moral guardians for daring to criticise soldiers who cursed when liberating Europe from tyranny, the Hays Office went out of its way to deny reports that it had made such complaints. As it turned out, *The True Glory* was screened without recourse to Hays and his watchdogs because it was a government film, and therefore not subject to the film industry's production code.

The film was greeted as a masterpiece by the Mayor of New York, Fiorello H. La Guardia, who declared that it should be screened free of charge each day for the benefit of families of servicemen. La Guardia said: 'Every American ought to see this picture and, after he sees it, will pay his taxes with a smile and pray with tears in his eyes.' At the gala Washington preview at the end of September, American and British government officials were joined by Lord Halifax, the British Foreign Secretary at the start of the war, and Maynard Keynes, the brilliant British economist who was to be the architect of the West's economic prosperity. At the Oscar ceremony in Hollywood the following March, *The True Glory* was awarded an Oscar for 'distinctive achievement in documentary production', an honour which Reed and Kanin refused out of respect for those who had shot the footage and those who had died in action.

For Reed it was time for a rest. At the beginning of August 1945 he went off to the races at Windsor with his brother Robin, David Niven and a number of friends. Like everyone else who had survived the war, he needed to take stock of how he could best live and work in peacetime. He had had a relatively peaceful war, although he had suffered the worst of the Blitz and had lived throughout in the centre of London, despite the danger. But he had seen no military action himself and had lived a life of comfort, drifting around the hotels of Mayfair, with their contempt for rationing, free of the tedious military regulations which most conscripts had to endure. He had had a 'good' war and had avoided its worst discomforts. Wartime had brought marriage to Diana, then growing estrangement, and love for Pempie. Peacetime would bring great opportunities, but it was by no means clear to Reed what they would be.

7
Korda Classics

Alexander Korda, a Hungarian by birth, had made repeated attempts to become the saviour of the British film industry. Each was an ambitious, extravagant, unlikely, self-indulgent, financially risky venture, yet each succeeded. British films were made, which was in itself something of a miracle.

Of all the British studio bosses, only Korda appeared to enjoy himself. Since 1909 he had directed an average of two films a year in Paris, Berlin and Hollywood – in one year, 1916, he made nine – before leaving for Britain in 1932. In his new country he directed *The Private Life of Henry VIII* and *The Girl from Maxim's* in 1933, then *Rembrandt* in 1936, before restricting himself to producing the films of others. His ideas were always highly commercial and often vulgar, and he was extremely imaginative when it came to money. The raising of risk capital is always a confidence trick above all, and Korda whisked his would-be backers into a world of glamour, make-believe and fun.

Sometimes the bubble burst. London Films, his pre-war empire at Denham Studios, collapsed in 1939 and Korda decamped for Hollywood, where he joined United Artists as a partner. He still felt however that his future lay in Britain and, much to the annoyance of his wife Merle Oberon, he spent much of the war flying across the Atlantic in the empty bomb-bays of new American aircraft.

He had been criticised for leaving Britain when it seemed on the point of being invaded, but he remained faithful to his adopted country. In 1940 Winston Churchill encouraged him to make *Lady Hamilton* in Hollywood, with Laurence Olivier as Lord Nelson and Vivien Leigh as Emma Hamilton. It was an unabashed piece of pre-Pearl Harbor British propaganda, encouraging Americans to join the fight against Hitler. Korda also made his rented Hollywood facilities available as a base for

British intelligence officers. His commitment to Britain was genuine and he mollified many of his sternest critics, who considered his flight to the States disloyal, by inviting them to dinner with him when he was in London. The penthouse of Claridge's Hotel in the centre of the West End was an uncomfortable place in which to relax when the bombs were falling, but Korda maintained a stiff upper lip which many of his British guests could not match.

In 1942 Churchill recommended Korda for a knighthood for his services to the war effort, the first British cinema personality to be so honoured, and Sir Alex announced his plans to set up new film-making facilities in Britain. He left United Artists to become Louis B. Mayer's independent arm of the MGM empire in London and arrived in Britain in May 1943, immediately attempting to bring under contract as many as possible of the best British film-makers currently free of commitments, no easy task in the middle of the war.

In December 1943 Reed, technically a civilian and with no commercial contractual obligations, allowed his name to become associated with the enormous £5 million package put together by Korda to make between sixteen and twenty pictures for MGM-British-London Films in Britain. Korda had assembled a galaxy of British talent with which to make his announcement. He had tentatively secured the services of the actors Robert Donat, Ralph Richardson, Vivien Leigh, Deborah Kerr, Glynis Johns, Greer Garson and Walter Pidgeon, his own wife Merle Oberon, and Penelope Dudley Ward. His list of writers was, if anything, even more distinguished: Enid Bagnold, H. E. Bates, Clemence Dane, Robert Graves, James Hilton, Geoffrey Household, Eric Linklater, A. E. W. Mason, Nevil Shute, Evelyn Waugh and Graham Greene. Freddie Young was engaged as a cameraman.

Among the projects announced were *War and Peace*, to star and be directed by Orson Welles, a sequel to *Goodbye Mr Chips* and two projects attached to Reed's name, John Buchan's *Greenmantle* and a life of Robert Louis Stevenson, which would star Donat and Oberon. The announcement was a typical piece of hyperbole by Korda, declaring yet again that the biggest, the best and, important to him, the most creative British talents had been brought together at last. Korda had little hope of making all the films he had announced, or of employing the names he had assembled. Reed, for one, was unavailable and, before long, engaged on *The True Glory*.

By the time *The True Glory* was completed in July 1945 Korda's circumstances had drastically changed. His arrangement with MGM had not worked out. During his two years as head of MGM-British-London Films, the company had produced only one film, *Perfect Strangers*, starring Deborah Kerr and Robert Donat. Although the picture had been a success in both Britain and America, Korda's new company had lost MGM over a million pounds, and in October 1945 Korda resigned from MGM amid rumours that this time he would abandon his film-making dreams for good. Within a month he was back in business. But Korda's third coming was too late for Reed. He had happily allowed his name to be associated with Korda's plans in the middle of the war, but now British MGM was under different management and Reed could not wait around to discover what Korda would be doing next.

The end of the war brought many opportunities for Reed. Already a civilian and released from his obligations to the army after his work on *The True Glory*, he was a free agent, at the top of his trade and ready to take advantage of the chances which he had forgone during the war years. The war had interrupted his career and removed the option of going to Hollywood, but he had gained from his wartime films. Each was quite different and he had enjoyed displaying his versatility. He was now known on both sides of the Atlantic as a master of the thriller, the costume comedy, the costume drama, the action picture and the documentary. He was so much in demand that he could pick a subject and know that a producer would find the money for his film to be made.

Korda was still gathering his resources and was unable to back Reed financially. Reed therefore agreed to make a second film for Filippo del Giudice, the producer of *The Way Ahead*, and his choice was an unusual one, more sombre in tone than any of his previous pictures. The nearest he had come to undiluted tragedy was *The Stars Look Down*, but A. J. Cronin's novel had allowed some light into the plot through the love interest between Michael Redgrave and Margaret Lockwood. Reed had always been unhappy about such material, and he decided that now he would make a picture which was unrelenting in its seriousness.

Reed believed that the war had changed the public's perceptions of films and that good film-makers must adjust to the new audience. People had endured so much unwelcome excitement in their lives that they would not return easily to the artificial, candy-floss world of pre-war British pictures. 'Today,' he commented, 'audiences the world over are more conscious of the phoney and stock film situations than they were pre-war. People who were plunged into war were so immersed in reality that nowadays they expect it in both the living theatre and pictures. It is a natural reaction.' What people wanted was realism, and that was best achieved by strict authenticity of set design, costume and accent. This was a common perception of film-makers throughout the world, leading to the 'neo-realist' movement whose champion was Roberto Rossellini.

During the final days of production on *The True Glory*, Reed had been looking for a subject which would suit more serious audiences. He was a compulsive reader of new novels, hoping always to come across the perfect story to be turned into a film, and he went to the theatre as often as possible, also with the hope of finding suitable properties for film treatment. One day in April 1945 he stumbled across a review of F. L. Green's novel *Odd Man Out* in an evening paper. He bought a copy, read it and promptly bought a month's option on the film rights. Green's story told of an IRA terrorist limping fatally wounded across Belfast, shunned by his friends and co-conspirators. Reed 'liked the theme of someone who had done something wrong for the right reasons – and the incidental characters'. He was already familiar with F. L. Green, for Diana had appeared in a film based on a Green novel, *On the Night of the Fire*, released at the beginning of the war.

Odd Man Out had been published by Michael Joseph in London in April 1945 and was given a great popular boost the following July by being published in paperback by Penguin Books. Green was four years older than Reed and came from Portsmouth. In 1934 his first novel was published and he moved to Belfast with his Irish wife. *On the Night of the Fire*, published in 1939, had made his name, and this achievement was confirmed when Josef Somlo bought the rights to make a film, directed by the Irishman Brian Desmond Hurst.

Reed's first task was to visit Green in Belfast and ask him whether he would write a screenplay from *Odd Man Out*. Reed had come to the conclusion that, in the absence of the talented screenwriters who could be found in American studios, British authors must translate their own works into film scripts. Green was pleased, but hesitated. Reed therefore proposed that R. C. Sherriff, who had written *Journey's End*, scripted *Goodbye Mr Chips* and co-written Korda's *Lady Hamilton*, should be recruited to help in the writing, but that the most important thing was that Green should be intimately involved. Reed explained that he too would assist with the script, for he had developed a method in which he would prepare a detailed script to ensure that there were no expensive surprises once filming had begun.

It was Reed's close involvement in all aspects of his films, from scriptwriting to set design, cutting and editing, which had caused him to hesitate about working in Hollywood. Only in Britain and France were directors expected to be able to perform every job on a set; in America things were organised very differently. First, producers often regarded themselves as creative artists, and considered directors merely technicians who translated their ideas into pictures. Second, directors were expected to administer shooting the picture and be concerned with how the action was recorded, but were not encouraged to involve themselves in the work of other departments. Sets, costumes, lighting, editing and all the other technical aspects of films were the responsibility of others in the studio hierarchy.

As soon as the rights to *Odd Man Out* had been bought and Green had been persuaded to assist with the script, Reed began three months of preparations. The author moved into Reed's flat in Grosvenor Street and sat with him through a month of daily script conferences in which the structure of the film was discussed and the dialogue written. Green could only work with music playing, and set himself up in Reed's flat with his own gramophone, which played constantly for four weeks. Reed wanted to ensure that every element of Belfast portrayed in the film was accurate, in particular the accents, which differed a great deal from those in the rest of Ireland.

Reed had come to believe that it was absurd for British films to chase an imaginary 'international' – by which most film producers meant American – audience. His success in the United States with *Night Train* and *The Stars Look Down* had taught him that Americans would happily watch British films, despite the British accents and the unfamiliar customs, as long as they were of good quality. He explained: 'A good picture is a good picture, regardless of its origin and that's still the only box office test.' What audiences throughout the world wished to see was something sincere and authentic. In the past the British film industry's hunt for an 'international' audience had caused it to make films which could not be enjoyed on either side of the Atlantic. Reed commented: 'The films were not genuine and did not ring true and the American public realised it. Instead of trying to make pictures for a country we don't understand, we must make pictures our way.' He therefore demanded that everything about *Odd Man Out* should ring true, not least to Irishmen. The details of Belfast city, the religious conflict between the Catholics and the majority Protestants and the accuracy of the slang used on the streets were all important to him. If those were accurate, the rest of the film could not help but appear genuine.

Reed then turned his attention to casting. It was inevitable for the commercial success of the film that the principal part of the IRA man on the run, Johnny MacQueen, should be an actor of international standing. As Michael Redgrave has pointed out, Reed always kept at least one eye on the box office. His choice for Johnny was James Mason, whose many performances in British costume dramas had made him an international heart-throb. *Odd Man Out* was to be a considerable change of mood for him. Mason had few lines to speak, but he had to maintain the audience's interest in Johnny's plight as the main thread which drives the narrative through a procession of highly coloured cameo roles.

Mason was thrilled to be approached by Reed. He believed that in Britain there were only as many good pictures a year as there were good directors – and that was not many. He counted them to be Reed, David Lean, Michael Powell and Emeric Pressburger, Launder and Gilliat, Anthony Asquith, plus one annual fluke. Mason had come to the conclusion that as long as he remained in Britain he needed to work with those directors to be sure of appearing in a good film and therefore furthering his career, and he was considering a permanent move to Holly-wood. As he put it: 'Since of those directors I had worked only with Anthony Asquith, who, I was sure, would prefer Trevor Howard any day, I thought it more than likely that I might have to go on knocking myself out in an unbroken line of banalities, whereas the Hollywood people were liable to be much more impressed by my highly touted popularity; I would extend my range, have a wider choice.'

Of his named directors, Reed was his favourite. 'Before *Odd Man Out* I had never worked with him, but in every one of his films that I had seen there was great warmth and understand-ing . . . the only common ingredient had been an affectionate sense of humour.' The approach from Reed came as a great surprise. 'I had admired Carol Reed only from a distance. Though he was the director with whom of all the directors in the world I was most keen to work, I never thought of this as a target within my range. And then suddenly out of the mouth of Al Parker [a leading theatrical agent] came casually the all-important news flash that Carol was to make a film of F. L. Green's book *Odd Man Out* and that he wished to have me playing the leading part.'

Having cast Mason, Reed turned his attention to the other parts. He considered smaller parts just as important as the large ones, for a number of reasons. His love of actors meant that he was always eager to allow each of them their contribution, and his indulgence of them had earned him the reputation of being an 'actors' director'. He was also convinced that each part, however small, was important for the whole film to be perfect, an obsession with detail which he extended to sets, costumes and all the other elements which would be visible to the audience.

For a rich supply of Irish actors he turned to the Abbey Theatre, Dublin, a company whose hallmark was highly col-oured characterisation and, above all, a history of good troup-ing. Although the soft southern Irish accents were a long way from those of Belfast, the tradition of character acting at the Abbey convinced Reed that northern accents were within their range. He chose William George Fay to play the Catholic priest to whom Johnny's friends turn for help. Fay had founded the Abbey with W. B. Yeats in 1904, and managed the company as well as acting in it. He had appeared in the first production of J. M. Synge's *The Playboy of the Western World* in 1907, when the angry audience was only prevented from storming the stage by a call-boy wielding an axe.

Reed was more anxious about picking Kathleen Ryan, the twenty-three-year-old wife of a Limerick doctor and daughter of an Irish senator, as Mason's girlfriend. She had only had a short career on the stage before breaking off to have a child, but had left a great reputation. She was summoned by telegram and reported to the Denham Studio, where she was given exhaustive screen tests, auditions and coaching by Reed himself. After three months' gruelling appraisal, she was pronounced suitable.

F. J. McCormick, a fine Irish character actor who had played four hundred stage roles in thirty years, was chosen to play the old villain Shell, who tries to sell the wounded Johnny to the authorities and whose scene-stealing performance was later described as 'not theft; it is grand larceny on the grandest scale'. Cyril Cusack, who had been much praised as the hero of *The Playboy of the Western World* at the Abbey, was chosen for his ability to perfectly intone the difficult Belfast accent of the nervous, guilty driver of the get-away car, and his wife Maureen was also in the cast.

British players included Robert Newton, who was to be much criticised for his extravagant performance as the artist who wishes to paint the glint in the dying Johnny's eyes. During the filming, Newton had to pick up two quart bottles of beer, his change and a walking-stick from a bar, while being hustled by William Hartnell, one of the discoveries of *The Way Ahead*. After several bungled attempts, Newton appealed to Reed, 'I've got so many things to pick up.' Reed suggested he should keep this as his line. There was a part, too, for Fay Compton, Pempie's former mother-in-law.

To further ensure authenticity, two priests were employed on the set, and two advisers. Joseph Tomelty, of the Group Theatre, Belfast, described Reed's exhausting interview, in which he made clear the sort of detail which he required his experts to know. 'Describe an armoured car. Do the letters GPO appear on Belfast pillar-boxes? Is a police car a Ford, Vauxhall or Morris? What is the uniform of a prison warder in Northern Ireland?' Everything was done to ensure authenticity. At one stage on location Mason, running across a bomb site, was followed by a stray dog, which Reed kept in the final footage.

The filming at Denham took twenty weeks, three times as long as Reed's pre-war films, and ended in January 1946, when he took the cast and crew on location to Belfast. Location work continued in Shoreditch and Islington, whose Georgian and early Victorian terraces matched those of Belfast. The music, as with *The Way Ahead*, was composed by William Alwyn under the direction of Muir Mathieson.

Robert Krasker was the photographer. He had never shot such a literally dark film before, and he followed Reed's descriptions of the atmosphere of gloom which should pervade each scene. Krasker was among the best lighting cameramen working in Britain. An Australian of French and Austrian parents, he had studied art in Paris, abandoned painting in favour of photography and went to Germany to study optics. This German period of his life not only gave him the foundations of his technical knowledge but also introduced him to the heightened lighting techniques which were practised between 1903 and 1933 in Germany and which came to be known as German expressionism. This movement introduced psycho-logical shapes and highly artificial sets, as in Robert Wiene's *The Cabinet of Dr Caligari* (1919), but its most lasting effect was its dramatic lighting, heavy with long shadows and few light sources.

Krasker returned from Germany to work at Paramount's Joinville studios in Paris, working with the American maestro Phil Tannura. In 1931 he left Paris to join Korda's London Films company at Elstree and worked as assistant cameraman on many of the studio's hits, including Korda's own *The Private Life of Henry VIII* and, a key influence on his lighting and camera-work with Reed, with Georges Périnal on *Things to Come*. His career took off and he was soon the principal cameraman on two of Leslie Howard's films, *The Gentle Sex* and *The Lamp Still Burns*, then *Henry V* in colour for Laurence Olivier, the pastel-lit *Caesar and Cleopatra* for Gabriel Pascal and the highly atmospheric *Brief Encounter* for David Lean.

Carol Reed

above left Herbert Beerbohm Tree in about 1885, *above right* May Reed in the 1930s
below left Reed the actor, in costume for *A Midsummer Night's Dream*, 1926
below right Edgar Wallace

above left The young Daphne du Maurier
above right Reed the novice director, on location for *Autumn Crocus*, 1934
below Reed with Jessie Matthews on the set of *Climbing High*, 1938

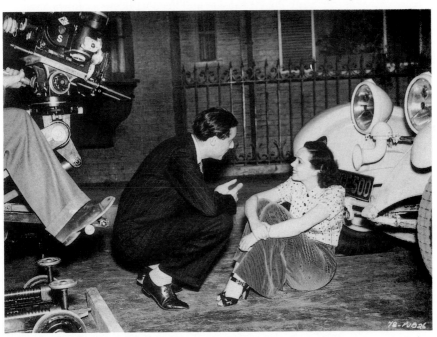

above left Diana Wynyard at the time of *Cavalcade*
above right Penelope Dudley Ward and Cecil Beaton
on the set of *Lady Windermere's Fan*, New York 1943
below Odd Man Out, 1946. Robert Krasker and Reed work out a camera angle

above left Reed and Pempie leave for their honeymoon, January 1947
above right Reed coaching Bobby Henrey on the set of *The Fallen Idol*, 1947
below Orson Welles and Reed in the sewers of Vienna for *The Third Man*, 1948

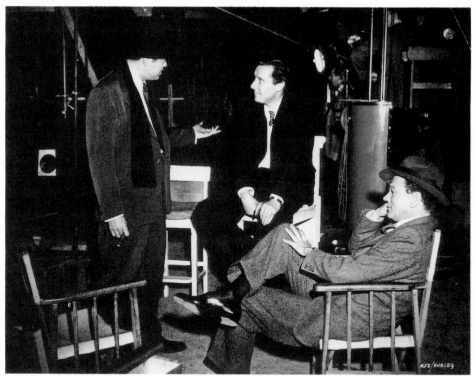

above Welles, Reed and Joseph Cotten on the *Third Man* set at Shepperton
below Reed and Ralph Richardson in Ceylon for *An Outcast of the Islands*, 1950

above Reed, Graham Greene and Alec Guinness on location for *Our Man in Havana*, 1959
below Fidel Castro visits the set

above Alex Korda and Reed on board Korda's yacht *Elsewhere*
below Ron Moody, Reed, Jack Wild and Oliver Reed during the filming of *Oliver!*, 1968

Krasker's most important contribution to the four films he made with Carol Reed was the power of the images he created by dramatic lighting, which came to be known as a Reed trademark. Reed enjoyed a reputation for versatility and competence, but he had established no identifiable style. According to Reed, this was because he preferred to treat each new subject in the most appropriate way, rather than shoe-horn it into his own mould. His main consideration, he declared, was to interpret the aims of the author of the original story, even when his own intentions began influencing the author. In *Odd Man Out* Krasker created such a distinctive 'look' that the dark, expressionist-lit scenes came to impose a style upon Reed, who denied any such personal intention.

Krasker's inventiveness is evident from the opening scene: the hold-up gang makes its way to the scene of the robbery, then drives furiously away. Close-ups of faces were intercut with sharp-angled shots taken through the windscreen, which established a disorientating urgency. As the gang makes its bungled escape, the hero Johnny, played by Mason, is left hanging to the side of the car. Again, close-ups of the driver and the men in the car trying to pull Johnny inside are alternated with Johnny's view, with the pavement spinning past just beneath him.

Sharpening an audience's perceptions by dramatic visual techniques was one thing, but encouraging them to sympathise with an IRA killer was quite another. In Johnny, Reed faced a difficult problem: how to ensure that the central anti-hero does not attract affection, but commands attention. Reed did not wish to take sides in the sectarian conflict, but for him to tell the story as something other than a straight gangster picture, MacQueen's idealistic motives had to be raised above those of a common criminal. Reed and Krasker decided on a subliminal device to elevate Johnny by shooting him from a low angle, thereby giving him the dignity of a public monument or a political orator.

A third device used to great effect is the wide-angle lens, which turns ordinary streets and alleys into long vistas, implying that Belfast is a maze in which Johnny can both hide and become lost as he tries to cross the city to safety. Krasker's mastery of these visual approaches, both dignifying the anti-hero and giving a city a character of its own, were also to be employed to enormous effect in *The Third Man*.

When the film was all but complete, Reed ran into trouble from the American film censors over the shooting of Johnny in the final scene. As Reed explained: 'Joe Breen [the successor to Will H. Hays, the principal American censor] was here on a goodwill tour, sort of instructing our own censorship people. He came to the studio one day and told me that the heroine couldn't shoot James Mason because that would be like murder in order to allow her lover to escape justice. He said, "Look, why not let the police shoot him while he's trying to escape." I agreed, but I got out of it. While the police are following them, she understands that Mason will never make it to the boat, so I had her turn around, fire at the police, and thus cause them to return fire and kill both. Everybody was satisfied. But I made her clearly fire toward the ground.'

Odd Man Out received unanimous praise from the London critics, who by now believed that Reed could do little wrong. The real test of Reed's success, however, was the Irish premiere at the Classic Cinema, Belfast, in March 1947. The following morning the *Belfast Telegraph* gave its verdict: 'It is difficult to view objectively a film which introduces so many familiar scenes of the city of Belfast and the occasional rather fanciful scene, too . . . The accents it would be unfair to fault. At times one feels the scene may have shifted to Dublin, so rich are the brogues, but for reassurance comes the unmistakable cry of a youngster, "Mister, give us a penny," and one is really back under the shadow of the clock. When you get F. J. McCormick in an attempt to reassure a suspicious police officer, flinging across the street "It's a hardy ould night, sergeant," you know it could be in only one particular area he walks.'

On the all-important question of whether Reed and his team had been too soft on the IRA, the paper concluded: 'It is natural to question the suggestion of sympathy with a terrorist organisation, but the direction of this film has been done so skilfully, and "politics" avoided so meticulously, that good taste is rarely offended.' To Reed's relief, the *Telegraph*'s final verdict was: 'It is a reckless, head-on attempt at greatness, and the attempt frequently succeeds.'

The *Irish News* in Belfast also commended Reed for getting so much right. 'The Belfast adviser of the company did a fine job. One remembers dozens of local touches that make one turn in one's seat with delight. Everything the children in the film did and said was dead right: their vicious fighting among themselves and their noisy begging for "pennies". Cyril Cusack's portrait of the wee Belfastman will stand forever as an example of the species homo Belfastensis. The policemen were just the right size – big enough to have to stoop warily through the door of the typical Belfast kitchenhouse, like horses going into a stable. A small point but it kept the whole thing dead on key.' But the *News* also had its criticisms, which were levelled more at Green and the Irish advisers than Reed. 'A Belfast Catholic does not usually quote the Bible, even when delirious, and when he does, he prefers the Douai to the Authorised version. He might remember, too, that when an Irish maiden is robbed of her man through a bit of shooting, she'd think it damned silly to go out and make a lone stand against the law. She'd merely remember the poor fellow in her prayers.'

Praise came, too, from south of the border. At the film's Dublin opening in March 1947, the Theatre Royal sold out within hours and the police had to be called to marshal the crowds. Among the opening audience were the Irish president, Sean T. O'Kelly and his wife, the minister for justice and the chief justice. The *Dublin Evening Mail* described the picture as 'the finest piece of cinema turned out in Britain since the British started making pictures'. The *Irish Press*, Dublin, also praised Reed, who, it said, had 'proven himself as the best director England has produced'.

But the Dublin papers did not agree with the Belfast critics that Reed had remained impartial about the morality of terrorism. The *Irish News* in Dublin wrote: 'There is no doubt that it is a really good film. There equally is no doubt that, in its essence, it amounts to a glorification of the IRA! If I had been a youth, emerging from the Theatre Royal on Sunday night and saw on the walls of Trinity College the slogan "Join the IRA" I have not the least doubt that I should have been sorely tempted to do so! All the romance is on the side of "the Organisation".'

On 10 February 1947, Reed passed through New York en route to Hollywood, where he was to meet David O. Selznick, Korda's American business partner. Korda had made an arrangement with Selznick for American distribution of all London Films releases, which meant that from now on all

Korda's films would also have to meet Selznick's demands. On the way back through New York, Reed had to battle with the American censors. All films released in the United States had to be submitted to the Motion Picture Association of America for censorship, although technically all suggested changes were made voluntarily, so that the United States constitution was not defied. Once again the censors objected to profanity on the screen. Reed was reluctant to allow American technicians to make the cuts demanded. As he explained: 'I've lived with the film. I know it better than anyone else. I know what substitute footage is available in case major changes are required. And I like to be around when deletions or additions are to be made.'

He used his spare time in New York to catch up on the latest American pictures. A reporter who went to interview him was told that he had gone to see the sights of the city. He tracked him from one cinema to another, nine in all, ending up in a Bowery 'flea-pit'. Typically, Reed was less interested in what was happening on the screen than on intently watching the down-and-outs' reactions to the film.

On 24 April *Odd Man Out* opened in the United States, to unanimous praise from the critics. In particular the Americans appreciated the film's technical brilliance. *American Cinematographer* magazine praised its photography, declaring: 'There has not been such lighting and imaginative use of the camera since Orson Welles's *Citizen Kane*,' which was quite a compliment.

While Reed's career flourished, his personal life was in tatters. His marriage with Diana was not working out. The war had precipitated the union, as it had so many other failed marriages, but there is little doubt that the true reason it foundered was the extraordinary circumstances in which it had begun, with Reed in love with Pempie Dudley Ward but feeling honour-bound to go through with his marriage to Diana. There was never much joy in the arrangement. Reed's professed anxiety that Diana would suffocate him in a conventional suburban marriage was not confirmed by events, because with both of them working so hard at their respective careers the marriage never really had a chance to become anything other than a loose arrangement. He confided to very few people exactly why he thought the marriage had not worked out. His son Max was only to discover that his mother Pempie was not his father's first wife when, at the age of about nine, he explored Reed's *Who's Who* entry. He confronted his father with his discovery, to be taken into Reed's bathroom and told: 'I was at the studio all day; she was on the stage every evening.' It was just one of those things. Diana's work was confined to the stage for most of the marriage, and she made no pictures between *Kipps* in 1941 and, ironically, *An Ideal Husband*, Alexander Korda's final film as director, in 1946. By that time the marriage was effectively ended.

Reed told friends later that he had tried to prevent Diana from being hurt by pressing on with a marriage which was doomed even before their informal engagement, but there is no doubt that her discovery that he was in love with Pempie and had continued their affair after the marriage was considerably more hurtful to her. Reed had behaved not so much as a cad as a man whose sense of responsibility to others was somehow fixed in a selfish period of adolescence. He was thirty-six when he married Diana, yet he behaved like a callow teenaged husband. Diana, who had always been a more vulnerable character, was profoundly distressed by the collapse of her marriage. There is little doubt that he did at first love her, particularly during the unreal circumstances at the time of *Kipps*. Until the end of March 1941, Carol and Diana were a genuine couple. During that summer Carol met Pempie and fell in love, yet in February 1943 he married Diana.

It is hard not to believe that Reed's upbringing had a great deal to do with his unhappy marriage and his fear that Diana would evolve into a conventional suburban wife. The Reed children had discovered early in their lives that their family was different from those of their friends, and not simply because their father was a famous actor. They learned that Beerbohm Tree had not one family, like everyone else's father, but two. Somewhere else in London there was a Lady Tree, whose daughters now and then visited the Reeds and played with them as if they were a single family. Tree's children appear to have taken all this in their stride, for it was plain that their mother, May Reed, was a happy woman, and their father was undoubtedly a happy man. However, what the Reed children were left with, like most children who are introduced early to the complications of adults' amorous lives, was a premature understanding that the conventions of marriage as enjoyed by everyone else's parents are not the only way to domestic bliss.

Pempie had exiled herself to New York for the duration of the war, but as soon as regular civilian air services to America were reinstated, Reed began regularly flying to see her to resume their affair. The forced separation had done anything but dampen his passion. Tracy Reed remembers that when Carol came to stay her nurse, Nanny Rosher, was told to take her for a walk. 'They would find any excuse to get me out of their way and I was showered with toys.'

By the time Pempie finally returned to live in London the marriage between Carol and Diana was at an end. Before long it became ugent for Carol to acquire a divorce as Pempie was pregnant. In July 1947 applications were made for divorce and it was granted the following month. The marriage had lasted less than four and a half years. On 24 January 1948 Carol and Pempie married in a civil ceremony at a registry office at Windsor, followed by a reception at The Old Vicarage, Winkfield, the home of Pempie's sister Angie and her husband General Bob Lacock. They then flew off for a quick honeymoon. Max was born within the year.

At first Carol, Pempie, Tracy, Max and Nanny Rosher lived in Pempie's flat in Albert Hall Mansions, where Pempie's mother also had an apartment, then Pempie started looking for a suitable house for their instant family. She showed the attention to detail and infinite care about pleasing Carol which was to typify their life together. Carol was now forty years old, and had not lived in a normal family household since he was a child. He was an independent spirit and could be moody, so what was needed was a big house – Carol was himself so large that a small home would cramp him physically – in which he could escape from the noise and interference of the children if necessary. Carol's only contribution to finding a house was to say that he wished to live as close to Piccadilly Circus as possible. He had once described his ideal home as Herbert Tree's dome room above His Majesty's. It was, of course, very difficult to find a family house so close to the heart of London. But Pempie bought from Michael Harrison the leasehold of a Church Commissioners' property, 213 King's Road, Chelsea. It was a grand Georgian house, set back from the road with a garden in front and another at the back. Pempie soon made it a home, with comfortable chairs and sofas in the large drawing room.

One of the advantages of the house was that it was linked via a vast studio to another house in adjoining Glebe Place. The Reed household would be a divided one. The King's Road house became home to Carol and Pempie, with their own cleaner and cook and, shortly, a secretary for Carol; the children, Tracy and Max, would live with their nurse, Nanny Rosher, and their own cook and cleaner, in their part of the house in Glebe Place. According to Judy Campbell, the reason for the division was 'so that Carol would never, ever be able to say to Pempie, "I can't work because of those children."' By coincidence, Herbert Tree had enjoyed a similar arrangement when Lady Tree bought them a house in Lord North Street, Westminster. It was so small that she bought a second home across the road in which the three Tree daughters and their nurse were billeted.

From the time that they moved into the house in the King's Road, Reed's private life took on a tranquillity which he had never before enjoyed. 213 King's Road became his headquarters and when not working he could be found there, relaxing with his family and preparing for his next film. The house became a second Daisyfield for him, a happy place and a warm, secure refuge from the irritations of outside life.

Pempie was entirely devoted to Reed, arranging everything so that he would not be troubled. She gave up acting as soon as she married him, found their home, arranged all his entertaining, helped choose his personal assistant, Dorli Percival, and followed him wherever in the world he was filming. Theirs was an exceptional love affair, although it appeared from the outside to be very one-sided. Pempie enjoyed the small formalities of domestic routine, while Carol was barely house-trained and kept to no plans whatever. Unless he was working, when he would rise at dawn and leave the house right away, he was incapable of rising early and would descend from the bedroom some time during the morning. Although he became increasingly overweight, it was hardly through eating. He ignored lunch and dinner, preferring to nibble at snacks or cook himself eggs and bacon at odd times. By the end of the evening, when Pempie was ready for bed, Carol would be wide awake and quite capable of noisily playing records to visiting friends like Judy

Campbell long into the night. Despite such provocative and inconsiderate behaviour, Pempie maintained a calm, patient composure. She remained deeply in love with Carol and was immune to the constant disruptions which sharing his life entailed.

There was, for instance, the menagerie of animals and birds which Reed bought at his favourite petshop in Camden Town, bringing them home as 'surprises' for Pempie and the children. He bought rabbits, guinea pigs and hamsters, a cockatoo and a minah bird which, irritatingly for everyone except Carol, was capable of whistling television theme tunes and, of course, the 'Harry Lime Theme'. Pempie had a standing arrangement with the shop that if she returned Reed's purchases within twenty-four hours she could obtain a refund.

There can never have been a sharper contrast between a man's domestic routine and his working habits, for when a film was in the making Reed operated with almost military precision, meticulously planning his schedule, leaving home on time to be at the studio or on location along with the first technicians. After a heavy morning's work, when the cast and crew would break for lunch, Reed would settle down in a viewing theatre to watch the rushes of the previous day's filming. He would happily work without a break well into the night, returning home exhausted and capable of little else but sleep.

Reed's next film, *The Fallen Idol*, provided almost ideal working conditions for the whole Reed family. Filming took place on location in Belgravia and in the studio at Shepperton, which meant that he could get home to Pempie very quickly. But above all he began working with two men who were to become close friends and colleagues, Graham Greene and Alexander Korda. The working friendship with Korda was the most personally significant. Not since he had left Basil Dean had Reed had such a reliable mentor. Reed could not be bothered with financial matters, and wished merely to be allowed to concentrate upon his film-making. Alex Korda provided those circumstances for him and also gave him encouragement and support, coaxing him to put the quality of his films above everything. Under Korda, Reed enjoyed a security and independence which allowed him to make some of the finest films ever made in Britain.

In January 1946, Korda resurrected London Film Productions as a private company and at the same time bought a controlling interest in British Lion Film Corporation, giving him a distribution company for his projected films. He subsequently bought a controlling interest in Shepperton Studios and Worton Hall Studios in Isleworth. Reed had been happy to leave Two Cities films, which was part of the J. Arthur Rank Organisation, after wrangles over the *Odd Man Out* budget and the final cut of the film.

Years later he told the American screenwriter Ben Hecht, while watching the film, that in his opinion it was still forty feet too long – little more than half a minute – and he offered the projectionist £100 there and then to cut the offending footage from the print. The projectionist declined, and there is no record of which thirty seconds Reed disliked.

Reed had always been immensely careful with his budgets, and resented the fact that Rank elevated tight-fistedness to a virtue. *Odd Man Out* was made in the immediate post-war period when money was tight, but Reed believed that a film as obviously international in appeal should not be subject to arguments over expense. He turned therefore to Korda, whose attitude to money verged on the profligate.

Reed joined Korda at the beginning of 1947, and it was Korda himself who suggested that Reed might be interested in making a film of Graham Greene's short story 'The Basement Room'. Greene's friendship with Alexander Korda had started on an unpromising note. As a fearless film critic for the *Spectator* in the years before the war, Greene had happily attacked Korda's efforts. He had dismissed two-thirds of *Things to Come* (1936), which Korda had himself suggested as a film idea to H. G. Wells, and had reacted to *Elephant Boy* (1937) with similar disdain.

Greene reserved his greatest vitriol, however, for *Rembrandt*, released in November 1936, which Korda had directed himself. Beginning with the words, 'Reverence and a good cameraman are not enough,' Greene continued, 'The film is ruined by lack of story and continuity: it has no drive. Like *The Private Life of Henry VIII* [which Korda had also directed], it is a series of unrelated tableaux . . . already I begin to forget how these unrelated scenes follow one another. From the dramatic point of view the first might just as well be the last and the last first. Nothing is led up to, nothing is led away from . . . I have called the film reverent, but pompous, I fear, would be nearer the mark.' The lesson of the picture, Greene suggested, was: 'No amount of money spent on expensive sets, no careful photography, will atone for the lack of a story "line", the continuity and drive of a well-constructed plot.'

When, not long afterwards, Greene received an invitation from Korda asking him and his agent to pay a visit to the studios at Denham, he assumed that 'perhaps he [Korda] became curious to meet his enemy'. Greene was left alone with Korda in his first-floor office and was asked whether he had any film story in mind. Greene had none but, bearing in mind that he had a wife and two children to support and that he was in debt to his publishers, he began to improvise the plot for a thriller. 'Early morning on Platform 1 at Paddington, the platform empty, except for one man who is waiting for the last train from Wales. From below his raincoat a trickle of blood forms a pool on the platform.' Greene stopped. 'Yes? And then?' asked Korda. 'It would take too long to tell you the whole plot – and the idea needs a lot more working out,' said Greene.

Half an hour later Greene left Denham having been commissioned 'on what seemed an extravagant salary' to write a film treatment of his plot. The result was *The Green Cockatoo*, released in 1937, about a man who takes revenge on the gangsters who killed his brother. It starred John Mills and Robert Newton and was directed by William Cameron Menzies, the maker of *Things to Come*, which Greene had dismissed as 'smug and sentimental'.

At much the same time that Korda was commissioning Greene to write *The Green Cockatoo*, he had been reading his short story 'The Basement Room', the plot of which he believed was suitable for film treatment. Ten years later he remembered the story when he was looking for a suitable film for Reed to direct, and invited Reed to his penthouse at Claridge's one afternoon. As Reed remembered: 'For a long time I had been looking for a story. Alex had been reading. I had been reading. One of us would suggest something half-heartedly. We would discuss it and throw it aside. On this particular afternoon in May [1947], Alex had an appalling cold, one of those running colds that grip one during the first fine days of spring.

'I had just read a story by Graham Greene called "England Made Me", which I thought quite good. Alex asked: "Have you read another one by him, 'The Basement Room' – a short story?" "No," I answered. "Very well," said Alex. "Here it is. Read it now." He gave me the book and I settled down in an armchair while Alex, who was feeling dreadful, went to bed in the next room. When I had finished the story, I went to see him. He was lying with his head propped up against a lot of pillows. I said to him: "This is a wonderful story, but I think what would really be exciting would be the continuation of it." "Perhaps," answered Alex. "Shall I try and get hold of the author?" "Yes, do that," I said, "If we could get him to work with us, I think it would be good."

'Alex stretched out an arm from under the blanket and caught the telephone. "Is 'The Basement Room' free?" "Yes." "Well, would you ask the author if he would lunch with Carol Reed and talk it over?" Ten minutes later the telephone rang. Graham Greene would be at the restaurant of Arlington House [Korda's headquarters] the following day at 1 o'clock.

'I had never met my guest before. On the other hand I had read quite a number of his stories and admired them. Many had been made into films. You must not therefore imagine that there was anything about my invitation to make Graham Greene particularly excited. Nor was I very excited myself, yet. It had been the same with so many other stories. I felt that "The Basement Room" was pretty good. Alex thought it was pretty good. Would Graham Greene work with us? That was the problem. I am not exactly sure of the words I used, but this was the sense of them: I had read "The Basement Room" and liked it. I had been thinking about the possibilities of making a film out of it. Would he be willing to work with us? As soon as he had come into the restaurant, I saw what sort of man he was – frightfully to-the-point and practical. There was no wasting of time with him, even to asking "How are you?" and that sort of thing. As soon as I had put my question to him, he answered: "How do you see it?" Then we talked things over.'

Greene had been surprised at Reed and Korda's suggestion because he considered the story, conceived to relieve the boredom on a cargo ship from Liberia to London, 'unfilmable' – as he put it, 'a murder committed by the most sympathetic character and an unhappy ending which would certainly have imperilled the £250,000 that films nowadays cost'. It was decided, despite Greene's scepticism, that work should go ahead and, according to Greene, 'in the conferences that ensued the story was quietly changed, so that the subject no longer concerned a small boy who unwittingly betrayed his best friend to the police, but dealt instead with a small boy who believed that his friend was a murderer and nearly procured his arrest by telling lies in his defence. I think this, especially with Reed's handling, was a good subject.'

Director and author began their partnership on a sound basis of mutual admiration. Greene had admired Reed's films since *Midshipman Easy*, as his reviews testified, but the thing which most attracted him to Reed was his approach to authors. In a 1959 interview Reed said: 'I think it is the director's job – as in the old theatre – to convey faithfully what the author had in mind. Unless you have worked with the author in the first place you cannot convey to the actors what he had in mind nor can you convey to the editor at the end the original idea. In making a picture you have got to go back to the first stage to see how important something may be in establishing this scene or that character.' Reed therefore offered Greene something which no other director could: collaboration on an even footing with a director who seriously wished to translate his intentions to the screen.

Reed and Greene set to work with a budget of £400,000. According to Greene, they evolved a system whereby they would take a suite of rooms in a Brighton hotel with interconnecting doors and a room with a secretary between them. Greene would write, Reed would revise and suggest, then Greene would write and counter Reed's suggestions. As Reed explained it: 'We typed the original story out but with the alterations necessary to make it lead up to the new portion. Then Graham Greene took it away and wrote ten more pages to introduce the agreed ending. All this took about ten days.' It was an amicable arrangement, cool and businesslike with a great deal of well-mannered friendliness on both sides. (It is worth noting that this system led to the First International Prize for Best Screenplay of the Year at the Venice Film Festival later that year.)

Greene was particularly satisfied with the arrangement, for it allowed him as much control over the finished film as any writer could have without directing the picture himself. His previous encounters with film-makers had been disillusioning, beginning with his experiences with Korda and *The Green Cockatoo*, but Reed's working method, which forged a near-perfect screenplay which would be faithfully translated into images, allowed a degree of confidence which few other film directors could offer.

The result, for Greene, was that the films he made with Reed were the closest to his intentions as an author. Even so, he believed that the film's eventual title, *The Fallen Idol*, chosen by the distributors, was 'a meaningless title for the original story, and even for the film it always reminded me of the problem paintings of John Collier'.

Greene did, however, agree to certain changes asked for by Reed. The location of the story was changed at Reed's sugges- tion from a large house to an embassy, 'since we both felt that the large Belgravia house was already in these post-war years a period piece, and we did not want to make an historical film. I fought the solution for a while and then wholeheartedly concurred.' Reed explained his reasons for the plot changes: 'Though Graham Greene and I were agreed about the main lines of the new script, there were certain difficulties to overcome. In the original story, the action took place in a private house in Belgrave Square, but "The Basement Room" was first published in 1936 and who now could afford to own a house large enough for a child to lose himself in, and who could employ sufficient servants to produce the right atmosphere for the film? To make the story modern it was necessary to turn the private house into an embassy where the man and his wife would be butler and housekeeper. The girl Julie would be one of the secretaries. Though it was not essential for the girl to be a foreigner there was much to be said for it, because at the end of the picture she had to disappear – to go home, preferably out of the country. So Emmy, as she was first called, became Julie.'

Greene himself proposed some changes to his original story. He thought that the girl should be cross-examined beside the bed she had shared with Baines, the butler. Reed suggested a man who wound the embassy clocks oblivious to the murder investigation going on about him; Greene added the boy's pet snake MacGregor after a period of 'sympathetic opposition' from Reed.

There was a single script conference with Korda, who otherwise allowed them a rare degree of artistic licence. Korda wanted the butler to be changed into a chauffeur 'because children are so interested in mechanics, and the parents are going away by plane and the little boy is very interested in the engine of the car'. Greene objected as it was a cliché to have a film beginning or ending with a plane taking off. Korda let Greene, backed by Reed, have his own way.

As for casting, Reed wanted Ralph Richardson, who was under contract to Korda, to play Baines, and he persuaded Korda to recruit the French actress Michèle Morgan as Julie. Sonia Dresdel was to play Mrs Baines.

Everything hinged, however, on finding a suitable child actor to play the central role. A boy was finally found in the most unlikely place: through his picture on the cover of a book, *A Village in Piccadilly*, written by his father Robert Henrey, who lived in Hertford Street, Mayfair, near to where Carol and Diana had lived when they were first married. Henrey's trilogy of books about the new London life enjoyed by French refugees from Nazism was based on his and his wife's experiences, and had been a popular success. On the cover of *A Village in Piccadilly* Henrey had placed a photograph of his eight-year-old son, Bobby.

The suggestion that Bobby Henrey would be right for *The Fallen Idol* came from Bill O'Bryen, Production Executive at London Films, although the credit was later given to Korda himself. O'Bryen wrote to Madeleine Henrey asking whether her son would be available for a screen test for a film starring Ralph Richardson. She was afraid that the attention of so many adults on the set would spoil him; her husband, however, thought it might add to his character. The boy was holidaying with his grandmother in Normandy at the time and, a typical piece of Korda flamboyance, was flown from Deauville to London and back for the initial screen test.

Reed was delighted. The boy was handsome and intelligent, spoke English with a hint of a French accent and, as the only child in a family of writers living in a small flat in central London, got on well and naturally with adults. Reed's only remark was that the boy had a black nail, caused by an accident with a hammer. He told Madeleine Henrey: 'Don't let him lose his accent. Don't let him play with any more hammers. And, whatever you do, don't let him grow any bigger.' She agreed to allow her son to become a film actor on condition that she could be present during the filming and supervise his work personally. A governess was appointed. Bobby Henrey was paid £1000 free of income tax, and if filming was not completed after ten weeks he was to be paid at the rate of £100 a week. He eventually earned a total of nearly £5000.

Filming began in September in a house at the north-east of Belgrave Square owned by the British Red Cross and St John organisation, who were happy to have the outside of the building painted and all the windows repaired. Other location filming was kept close to the house, with scenes shot in Kinnerton Street and Belgrave Square Mews, and there were also scenes in London Zoo. The cast was small and highly proficient. In the minor parts were Jack Hawkins, Dandy Nichols, Bernard Lee and Dora Bryan. Greene absented himself from the set and two writers, Lesley Storm and William Templeton, were hired for additional dialogue.

Reed turned to Georges Périnal, Robert Krasker's mentor, for the photography. He was a Korda favourite and had shot for him the highly atmospheric *The Private Life of Henry VIII*, and *Rembrandt*, and was also an expert in colour work, as he showed for Michael Powell in *The Thief of Baghdad* and *The Life and Death of Colonel Blimp*, although for Reed he would be working in monochrome. Reed repeatedly tried Périnal's patience, demanding shots which the cinematographer thought impossible. On one occasion he told Reed: 'You are crazy. You cannot photograph that. It is impossible,' to which Reed replied: 'Yes, yes, yes, yes. Impossible. Now, Georges, are you ready?' As in *Odd Man Out*, Reed paid particular attention to the sound, concentrating on the boy's view of events by muffling much of what the adults said as if it were barely overheard. The music was written once more by William Alwyn.

Madeleine Henrey, who at the last moment was asked by Reed to play Felipe's mother in the film, described Reed on the set:

The central figure was the director with his claret-coloured tie half out of his grey suit. Very much taller than the average man, he moved with a feline suppleness. His jacket was never quite unbuttoned, his tie never quite waving in the wind, his hair not quite dishevelled. His brown shoes were beautifully polished and his shirt-cuffs closed by elegant gold links. Clean-shaven, his skin was of a rosy texture and there was about his features an extraordinary openness which the child, quick to understand, exploited to the full, drawing without malice on his infinite patience. His authority was tremendous. Nobody ever questioned what Carol said, but there was no blowing through a megaphone or shouting angry words. Probably his strength was in part due to the fact that he was such an adept at hiding it. I seldom saw the director sitting down in the chair with his name marked on it. Generally he was exercising his long limbs gently in the wind, passing the fingers of his right hand through and through his hair, while his features became illuminated with satisfaction, for he had the uncommon gift of being quick and generous with praise.

What was evident from the very first scene, in which Bobby Henrey runs across the road in Belgrave Square, dodging the traffic, was the extraordinary relationship which quickly developed between Reed and the young boy. Reed described his method with child actors: 'A child of eight can't act. I wasn't looking for an exhibitionist. Adults have habitual features and defences. A good actor must take something away, lose a part of himself before he can create a role. But with the right sort of child such as Bobby, there is nothing in the way. There is absolutely no resistance. He will do everything you tell him.' Adults were too inhibited, even about the way they stood. 'Adults are controlled, they hold their arms and legs still, but if a boy is upset he twiddles a string, arches his back, twists his legs.'

Reed's model for Felipe, the boy in the film, was of course Bobby Henrey himself. 'I had planned certain scenes where Bobby would lean over the bannisters, but very soon I noticed that when left to himself he was always getting into the most graceful positions, curling up his hands, and this was so much more effective than anything I had imagined, so very much more natural, that I changed the scenes entirely to conform with his mannerisms. A director should plan in advance how a scene is to be played, but he should always be ready to put the camera here instead of there, and change everything at the last moment if he comes across a better way of doing it. That is why I never ceased watching Bobby when we were on location in Belgrave Square. It was my business to make him do on the screen what he did, without knowing it, in real life. When I had that miles-away look in my eyes, I was watching how he walked, and all his ways of laughing, and crossing the street. With children, it is much the same as with grown-ups. To be any good to a director, an actor or an actress must either be wonderful, or know absolutely nothing about acting. A little knowledge – that's what is bad!'

Reed discovered that a way of getting Bobby to act was to play the part himself and get the boy to imitate him. This coaching on top of the normal director's duties meant that Reed was working sixteen hours a day, constantly talking and living on a diet of studio sandwiches. It was little wonder that before long he caught laryngitis and lost his voice. He would run up and down the massive central staircase in Vincent Korda's magnificent set of the embassy entrance hall at Shepperton, then watch the boy do the same until his gestures were exactly as Reed wished. As Richardson, at six foot three, towered above the boy, all shots of Felipe walking alongside Baines showed the butler from the waist down only. Reed himself would be wearing the butler's trousers, giving instructions to Bobby from out of the camera's sight.

In one of the film's opening scenes there is a shot of the boy hanging over the landing railings looking at Baines. The facial expression Reed wanted was of warmth and admiration – the boy's hero-worship of Baines formed the key to the story. Unable to persuade Bobby to make the face he asked for, Reed had a children's conjuror perform at the bottom of the staircase while Bobby watched him delightedly from above. Felipe's lines were kept deliberately short so that Bobby could remember them and take and retake them until the inflection was correct. The longest line he had to say contained only fourteen words, albeit fourteen of the most telling words of the whole screen-play: 'Funny, Julie working at the embassy and all the time she was your niece.'

One of Reed's few problems with the boy was that he would persist in growing, encouraged by the studio tea-breaks, when a trolley loaded with tea and cakes would make its rounds. Reed was only half-joking when he told the boy's mother: 'Too much starch is fatal to a film star's line,' and he put Bobby on a diet.

The only disagreement Reed and Henrey's mother had on the set was over a haircut. A scene with the boy running up the staircase was half-complete on a Friday evening when the crew broke up, intending to resume where they had left off after the weekend. On Monday Bobby arrived on the set, having been taken for a haircut by his mother. The continuity department were horrified; between one stair and another the boy would appear to have lost two inches of hair. Shooting the scene would have to be abandoned until a solution was found and the delay would cost a great deal of money. The make-up department tried a number of absurd remedies, including sticking blond stage-hair onto Bobby's own. Reed was angry for the first time. 'It's the most expensive haircut in the world. Thousands of pounds! That's what it will cost! He can't have his hair cut between two steps climbing the stairs!' Reed's only course of action was to rearrange the shooting schedule and continue filming on the stairs when the boy's hair had grown. Apart from the delay caused by the haircut, the film made good time, completing on schedule.

By the time of the premiere, great public anticipation had been built up. To avoid disturbing the boy, his name had been kept from the press and no reporters had been allowed on the set when he was present. Rumours had started creeping out, however, that the boy's performance, inspired by Reed's masterful coaching, was exceptional. In a profile describing Reed's career so far, Dilys Powell wrote: 'His admirers have waited for *The Fallen Idol* with an eagerness for which impatience is too soft a word.'

For American release Selznick considered retitling the film *The Eye Witness*, but he finally settled on *The Lost Illusion*, the original working title. On 26 September Selznick send a telegram to Reed: 'Heartiest congrats on your brilliant directional job on *Fallen Idol*. You know how many years I have been a fan of yours and of your work but it has now reached a new high.'

The American release of the film was to be delayed until November 1949, partly because of demands from the American censors to cut various parts of the dialogue. The man with whom

Reed had to deal, with sometimes the help and sometimes the hindrance of Selznick's office, was Joseph I. Breen, a vice president of the Association, with whom he had tangled over the death of Johnny in *Odd Man Out*. Reed was anxious that the integrity of his film, Greene's dialogue and the actors' performances should be maintained, and that if there were to be any cutting or patching to remove offending material, the changes should be made by him in London, where he had a range of out-takes and other useful material to minimise the damage. Ultimately, however, he realised that the censors had the upper hand. As he wrote to Morris Helprin in the London Films office in New York, 'If it is a matter that we cannot show the picture unless it is cut, naturally I shall have to give in.'

Put briefly, the prudish Mr Breen was anxious that the prostitute Rose, who helps the police to identify Felipe when he wanders away from the embassy, should not be understood by American audiences to be a prostitute. And he objected to the cross-examination of Julie in her bedroom – a detail deliberately included by Greene – and her suggestion that at the time Mrs Baines died she had been in bed with Baines.

Breen demanded from the first scene 'elimination of whole opening scene about the arrest of Rose, and open sequence with the entry of the boy. From the point where the boy looks up and starts to move in direction of Rose, cut to sergeant on the telephone, eliminating all the first conversation between Rose and the boy and picking them up again only after Rose is seated and the boy is at her knee. In following conversation, Rose speaks with a much more natural voice without the falsetto effect and the toughness which went with her prostitute character. At the end eliminate her one sentence to the effect that she knew the ambassador . . . eliminating anything that indicates Rose is under arrest. Hopefully impression given that Rose is in some way connected to the police.'

The demands were ludicrous and, in retrospect, laughable. What Breen missed, and attempted therefore to remove, was the brilliance of Dora Bryan's performance and her humorous portrayal of that staple of English literature the tart with a heart of gold. In particular, Greene's line 'I think I know your father' is deliberately ambiguous for comic effect, its sexual innuendo softened by euphemism, and her tart-like greeting of the boy,

'Hello, dearie, where do you live?' which is instantly slapped down by the policeman, is simply funny. Reed gave some ground to the censors, but also took advantage of their naivety and banked on them not being confident enough in their knowledge of English inflection to argue with an Englishman.

He wrote to Morris Helprin, who was acting as a go-between, 'It is most discouraging to get this sort of censorship complication, since there was nothing in the scene that was in the slightest bad taste, it got enormous laughs which have nothing to do with vulgarity, but was in some small way to do with warmth and kindness. But this is an argument that I don't want to get into.' In suggesting some minimal cuts, he continued, 'There is no suggestion of Rose having been arrested, nor does she question the boy. With these cuts I see no reason why Rose should not be taken for somebody connected with the police: in which case surely there is no reason why she should not say "I know your daddy." Belgrave Square is a small place, and the police station is around the corner. All policemen of this district would know the people living in the area.'

As for the bedroom scene, Breen demanded a new dialogue track and 'elimination of footage which shows Julie looking shyly at the bed and pointing to it. Eliminate all in the questions and answers which has the idea that Julie was on the bed, and was undressed, and that she had to dress before she could leave the room and that she had been sexually intimate with Baines. Newly recorded dialogue must register definitely Julie's story that she and Baines were talking about breaking up their affair – no more . . . The piece showing Julie looking at and pointing at the bed to be cut so no reference or attention to bed.'

Selznick was, not surprisingly, eager only that the cuts be made and made quickly, for the picture was already doing good business in Britain. Eventually he agreed to put Reed's counter-suggestions to Breen, but he warned that 'Carol has merely had his first taste of it.' He was right; Reed would have a similar struggle with Breen over The Third Man.

When the film was eventually released in the United States, with a minimum of amendments, all administered by Reed, the critics unanimously commended his direction. The New York Post wrote: 'All that is so deeply satisfying in the best British pictures, the subtlety, intelligence, unforced humor and tragedy

free of theatrical posture is on view in *The Fallen Idol*. Here again
director-producer Carol Reed demonstrates why he is generally
regarded as Great Britain's best and one of the world's most
consistent makers of movie masterpieces.' The *Boston Globe*
agreed. 'The film is directed with skill and cunning by the
masterly Carol Reed, one of the great names of the film industry
and comparable to the best Europe has ever had.'

It had been announced that as soon as he had finished *The
Fallen Idol* Reed would fly to Hollywood to direct Joan Crawford
in a film for Jack Skirball and Bruce Manning, to be released
through Universal. The picture was to be based on the play
Portrait in Black, in which Diana had been playing in London. It
was to be a one-film contract, the first in a series which Reed
hoped would allow him to work alternately on both sides of the
Atlantic. He was still nervous of Hollywood and explained his
anxieties: 'I have no desire to stay there, purely for one reason.
When you have lived all your life in one country and grown
accustomed to the national traits and temperament, it is difficult
to do justice to your skill elsewhere. I have never yet seen it
succeed. In America, Renoir, for instance, never made such
brilliant pictures as he did in France. This applies equally to René
Clair – to almost everyone save Hitchcock, who, of course, keeps
to thrillers; these have an advantage over other types of plot
because they are richly spiced with incident from the start. In
contrast, the more delicate the story the greater the demands on
subtle treatment.' Reed did not think that in America he would
be able to make the sort of quiet, subtle films he now wished to
make in Britain. He did not rate Hitchcock as highly as others did
because Hitchcock chose to direct similar thrillers throughout
his career; Reed believed a great director should display his
range through filming a variety of subjects.

Although he visited the United States at the end of shooting
Odd Man Out, visiting New York en route for Los Angeles,
nothing came of his plan to direct a Hollywood picture. Instead
he remained with Korda and the British industry. Korda wanted
him to direct Cary Grant in a comedy called *The Devil and Mrs
Jones*, but this was one of many Korda plans for Reed which
came to nothing. Korda could be a nuisance, but Reed liked him
as a friend, he liked the sense of theatricality he shared with
Herbert Tree, and, above all, Korda allowed him to work in

Britain. Reed explained: 'The future of British films depends on how they are made; if the standard is high then the future is rosy. This achieved, there is no reason why the British film world should not become a big industry like its American counterpart. We have a wealth of good actors. The trouble here is that we do not make enough good pictures to keep them occupied. We must at least double our output – but not on the basis of twenty-five brilliant pictures and seventy-five bad ones.'

This was wishful thinking on Reed's part. As he was to discover, the quality of British films was actually dependent on the quality of the funding.

8

The Trouble With Harry

Alexander Korda had always thought that a story set in the bombed-out ruins of Vienna, once the capital of central Europe, would make a great film. He suggested the idea to Graham Greene over dinner when *The Fallen Idol* was reaching completion and appeared certain of success. Greene already had a story in mind and, just like fictional authors, had written a first paragraph on the back of an old envelope. His story began: 'I had paid my last farewell to Harry a week ago, when his coffin was lowered into the frozen February ground, so that it was with incredulity that I saw him pass by, without a sign of recognition, among the host of strangers in the Strand.'

Korda was insistent that the action must take place in Vienna, amid the confusion of the four-power occupation of the city by American, Russian, British and French troops. To Korda, such a complex situation would be a legitimate way of setting American stars in an exciting European setting, thus ensuring that his British film would be readily saleable in the United States. He saw it at first as a comedy thriller like *Night Train to Munich*, and even suggested reviving the Naunton and Wayne characters invented by Launder and Gilliat for Hitchcock's *The Lady Vanishes*, whom Reed had resurrected for *Night Train to Munich*.

In February 1948 Greene set off for two weeks in Vienna with 'Harry' in mind. Korda had used his contacts to book a room for him in Sacher's, which was otherwise reserved exclusively for officers of the occupation forces. Greene had little idea which way his plot might take him. His story began with Harry's false funeral, but the rest was blank.

He began by touring as much of Vienna as he could. As ever, he saw the seamy side of the city, visiting the enormous Central Cemetery ('the avenues of graves, each avenue numbered and lettered, stretched out like the spokes of an enormous wheel'), where the ground was so solidly frozen that gravediggers were resorting to electric drills to break the surface. He had a drink at the shabby Oriental nightclub and went backstage at the old Josefstadt Theatre. He visited the British officers in their temporary club at Sacher's, and toured Vienna's great amusement park. It was 'in the Russian zone where the Prater lay smashed and desolate and full of weeds, only the Great Wheel revolving slowly over the foundations of merry-go-rounds like abandoned millstones, the rusting iron of smashed tanks which nobody had cleared away, the frost-nipped weeds where the snow was thin'.

After ten days Greene was in despair, as he still had no story. The city, laden with snow, ice, atmosphere and colour, had merely provided a background. He was due to travel to Italy to meet a friend in three days' time and was intending to write the first story treatment there, but all he had was an opening sentence.

An old contact gave him a break. Greene had invited himself to lunch with a young British Intelligence officer, Charles Beauclerk. On beginning work in 1946 as Controller of Information Services, Allied Commission for Austria, Beauclerk had demanded from the Viennese authorities a full roll-call of their police officers. He was surprised to find listed a section termed 'Underground Police'. 'Get rid of these men,' he had told the Viennese, 'things have changed now.' A month later the police list revealed that the 'Underground Police' were still at their dubious work. He demanded an explanation and was told that he had jumped to the wrong conclusion. The 'Underground Police' were not secret policemen, but the police who patrolled Vienna's massive underground sewer network. Above ground the city was divided into four sections, each administered by one of the Allied powers; below ground there was no such division. The wide, brick-built sewers were reached from the street by staircases leading down from ventilation points disguised as advertising kiosks. The Russians, for reasons which Beauclerk had never discovered, refused to have these entrances locked. With a knowledge of the geography of the sewers it was possible to pass from one Allied zone to another without the need to pass through checkpoints.

This intrigued Greene and, when they had finished lunch, he asked Beauclerk to take him underground. Dressed in waders and mackintoshes, they explored Vienna's sewers. Greene was astonished. 'What a strange world unknown to most of us lies under our feet: we live above a cavernous land of waterfalls and rushing rivers, where tides ebb and flow as in the world above.' He discovered that the main sewer flowed like an underground river and that the air was quite sweet-smelling. 'The main sewer,' Greene recorded, 'half as wide as the Thames, rushes by under a huge arch, fed by tributary streams: these streams have fallen in waterfalls from higher levels and have been purified in their fall, so that only in the side channels is the air foul. The main stream smells sweet and fresh with a faint tang of ozone, and everywhere in the darkness is the sound of falling and rushing water.'

They also saw the Underground Police. 'One man had a small searchlight about half as big again as a car headlight strapped to his breast, and another man carried a brace of Roman candles.' Greene had discovered a key element of his story.

Beauclerk also told Greene about a sordid racket in penicillin, which was in short supply in Vienna as in the rest of Europe and was available only in military hospitals. No civilian doctor could obtain the drug by legal means, and some criminals attempted to match demand to supply by purchasing penicillin illegally from corrupt military hospital personnel, then reselling it on the thriving Viennese black market. They diluted the drug with coloured water, and sometimes powdered penicillin was spliced with sand to increase its bulk.

The results of the trade were tragic. Hospitals and doctors inevitably administered the penicillin in the wrong doses. Often the drug had been tainted by the impure additives. The victims were lying in hospital beds throughout the city. The lucky ones merely had their recoveries retarded. Others had to have arms and legs amputated. Some died. Worst affected were the children whose meningitis, treated with the doctored drug, had killed them or made them insane.

Now, with Vienna's web of underground passages and the vile trade in spliced penicillin, Greene had enough for a story. He wrote: 'The researches I had made into the functioning of the four-power occupation, my visit to an old servant of my mother's in the Russian zone, the long evenings of solitary drinking in the Oriental, none of them was wasted. I had my film.'

He described his working method: 'For me it is impossible to write a film play without first writing a story. A film depends on more than plot; it depends on a certain measure of character-isation, on mood and atmosphere, and these seem impossible to capture for the first time in the dull shorthand of a conventional treatment. I must have the sense of more material than I need to draw on (though the full-length novel usually contains too much). *The Third Man*, therefore, though never intended for publication, had to start as a story rather than as a treatment before I began working on what seemed the interminable transformations from one screenplay to another.'

Greene wrote the story of *The Third Man* in Ravello, went on to Capri, where he found a house he wished to buy in Anacapri, then returned to London to show Reed his work. His plot, written in short-story form, provided the key to the film. It is told through the words of Major Calloway, a British Army policeman whose discovery that Harry Lime, an Englishman, is running a penicillin racket makes him interested in Lime's friend Rollo Martins, an English writer of western novels, who arrives in Vienna at Lime's invitation only to discover his friend is dead. In his pursuit of Lime's 'killers', Martins falls in love with his friend's mistress, then discovers that Lime is alive after all and a vicious black-marketeer. He helps the army authorities trap Lime, who is shot dead trying to escape.

Greene's story was only partially original. A review of the film in the Oxford University magazine *Isis* pointed out that the plot of *The Third Man* bore a great resemblance to one of Greene's favourite films, Robert Montgomery's *Ride the Pink Horse*, released in 1947, which also concerns an ex-serviceman search-ing for the killer of his dead friend and which has a crucial meeting in a fairground and a notable unhappy ending. The notion of a friend who is presumed dead but emerges alive had also appeared in the film of Eric Ambler's novel *The Mask of Dimitrios*, released in 1944.

Greene had deliberately written crisp dialogue in his treatment, hoping that most of it would survive the inevitable rewriting when the story was translated into a screenplay. The story treatment was sent to David O. Selznick in Bermuda, who suggested a number of important changes which were incor-porated when Reed and Greene began work on the screenplay.

Apart from specific casting suggestions, Selznick thought that if Rollo Martins were to be played by an American, then so should Lime, otherwise 'what reason would they have for being such good friends?' Reed's view was that 'the whole story should be going at such a pace that nobody stops to figure that one out'. Reed knew the importance of casting and had always gone to great lengths to fill each part himself, down to the minor players. Korda, too, was keen on casting, for he believed that on it depended a film's success. American or international stars meant a profitable film; unknown British actors meant a loss. But the key to the casting was Selznick, who had struck a bargain with Korda that he would provide his contract stars and some valuable US dollars in exchange for the largest part of the distribution rights in the United States of any Korda–Selznick films. He could effectively veto any casting suggestion he did not like.

Selznick had wanted Reed to make a film of Thomas Hardy's *Tess of the D'Urbervilles* and had sent him a screenplay. Reed later explained: 'He had a script, which we both thought was pretty bad, so I asked him to have work done to it and meanwhile let me go ahead with *The Third Man*, since it was something we could knock off quick.'

The description of Harry Lime in Greene's treatment delineated the actor who might play him: 'Don't picture Harry Lime as a smooth scoundrel. He wasn't that. The picture I have of him on my files is an excellent one: he is caught by a street photographer with his stocky legs apart, big shoulders a little hunched, a belly that has known too much good food for too long, on his face a look of cheerful rascality, a geniality, a recognition that his happiness will make the world's day.' Selznick took the feed. He thought that Harry Lime should be played by either Orson Welles or Noël Coward, and that the part of his devoted friend Rollo Martins should be filled by either Cary Grant or James Stewart. Selznick's ideal pairing, he made it clear, would be Coward and Grant. Selznick was also 'very keen' on giving the part of Anna, Lime's mistress, to Alida Valli, whom he had 'discovered'.

Priority was to be given to the casting of Martins, who was on screen for most of the film. Once he was chosen, the rest of the cast would fall into place. Selznick knew that Korda had been trying to woo Cary Grant to return to Britain – he was born in Bristol – to make his sophisticated light romantic comedies for London Films. Korda suggested to Grant that he could work with Reed, the best director in his stable. But any hope of securing Grant for *The Third Man* disappeared with his decision to remain in Hollywood.

As for Selznick's suggestion of Noël Coward, the idea was given a great deal of consideration by Reed and Korda. Coward was forceful enough to play Lime, but for the suavely spoken entertainer to play a murderous black-marketeer would test the public's credulity. Coward's homosexuality would also make Lime's love affair with Anna rather unlikely. Reed did not want Coward, and the idea was never put to 'The Master' himself.

Selznick had made other casting suggestions: he was keen to use Erich von Stroheim as one of the Austrian characters; he wanted the author for whom Rollo Martins is repeatedly confused to be a distinguished writer, such as Ernest Hemingway, to make the mistaken identity more obvious; he was concerned about the importance of the Harry Lime part, for 'if you have a star actor to play the part of Rollo, it is very difficult in the last part of the picture for Harry Lime not to run away with it'; he thought that the importance of Anna should be built up; he was in particular anxious that the American and British military presence in Vienna should not be too one-sided and that more should be made of the four-power division of the city; and he felt that the ending should be downbeat, with Anna and Rollo not making up with each other.

When Reed and Greene travelled to Vienna in July to look for locations, Greene was appalled to find that so much renovation had already taken place that the world he had so vividly described was gone. The snow and ice had, of course, melted away. But the black-market restaurants which used to offer illegal, barely-nourishing food were now legally offering sparse but edible meals. The rubble in front of the Café Mozart had been cleared away. The city was gradually getting back to normal. Greene kept saying to Reed: 'But I assure you Vienna was really like that – three months ago.'

They returned to London to resume their script conferences, working out in close detail exactly what would be said by whom, how characters would move in each scene and how the episodes would link together, just as they had for *The Fallen Idol*, according to Greene 'covering miles of carpet a day, acting scenes at each other. (It's a curious fact that you cannot work out a continuity at a desk – you have to move with your characters.) No third ever joined our conferences, not even Korda himself; so much value lies in the cut and thrust of argument between two people.'

When the story 'The Third Man' was subsequently published in 1950, Greene was at pains to point out that, although changes were made, he was happy with the way that Reed and he had worked out the script together. 'To the novelist, of course, his novel is the best he can do with a particular subject; he cannot help resenting many of the changes necessary for turning it into a film play; but "The Third Man" was never intended to be more than the raw material for a picture. The reader will notice many differences between the story and the film, and he should not imagine these changes were forced on an unwilling author: as likely as not they were suggested by the author. The film in fact is better than the story because it is in this case the finished state of the story.'

Some of Greene's story did not survive – Rollo's drunken dream, in which he imagines he sees Lime alive; an American soldier running a racket in tyres; Lime's Roman Catholicism; a punch administered by Calloway to a Russian soldier. There were other more substantial changes. Both Harry Lime and Rollo Martins became Americans to accommodate the casting. Joseph Cotten, finally chosen to play Martins, was part of the Selznick–Korda deal; Orson Welles was selected by Reed to play Harry Lime. Bringing Cotten and Welles together again – Cotten had appeared in Welles's first triumphs, *Citizen Kane* and *The Magnificent Ambersons* – would be a coup for Reed. Cotten himself demanded one change. He objected to the name Rollo, which he said had homosexual connotations in the United States; oddly, he did not object to the name Holly, which might seem more obviously effeminate to some. The official kidnapping of Anna, Lime's girlfriend, was treated with fewer sexual undertones in the script than had appeared in Greene's original story.

Other, more minor elements were changed. Greene's recurring wariness of Americans was evident in his story. The American black-marketeer Colonel Cooler, constantly peddling the hypocrisy that 'a citizen has his duties' and that Europeans could not be expected to be 'good citizens', was replaced by a Romanian, and the remark in Major Calloway's commentary, 'American chivalry is always, it seems to me, carefully canalised – one still awaits the American saint who will kiss a leper's sores,' was excised.

Other original lines were removed. Anna's remark about Lime that 'When I have sex dreams, he's always the man,' was too saucy for the Americans. And a line with some personal relevance to Carol Reed, a passing reference to the literary merit of the work of Daphne du Maurier, did not reach the screenplay.

As with *The Fallen Idol*, the Breen office of the Motion Picture Association demanded changes for American audiences. In a letter to Selznick, in confirmation of a conference between Reed and Greene and two of Breen's representatives, the happily named Messrs Sherlock and Vizzard, Breen outlined his objections to the first draft of *The Third Man*. He declared that there should be 'no dialogue definitely pointing up illicit sex relationship between Anna and Harry'. The bedroom scene should be 'played without any emphasis on the bed, or other sex suggestive flavour to scene'. When Anna is arrested and has to dress 'she will at no time be shown in anything less than a slip and no suggestive reactions from soldiers present'. And the final shooting of Lime by Rollo 'will be on a direct shouted order from Calloway and there will be no flavor of either mercy killing or deliberate murder'. Americans should not be shown drunk and when the policeman Paine is killed, Reed should bear in mind the Association code stating: 'There must be no scenes, at any time, showing law-enforcing officers dying at the hands of criminals.'

Selznick was also approached directly by Breen to see if he could persuade Reed and Greene to amend their ideas. He too was told that there was 'too much drinking, drunkenness and talk about liquor in script', and that 'hero at no time to be shown drunk as he is two-thirds times in script – not good characterisation for American audiences and not necessary for plot or characterisation'. Selznick should 'check all references to the Catholic religion'.

Literary critics have described Graham Greene as a 'cinematic' writer, and that quality was evident from the first draft of *The Third Man*. It was Greene who invented the film's great *coup de cinéma*, the moment when Harry Lime, believed dead, reappears from the shadows. Greene wrote: 'A window curtain was drawn petulantly back by some sleeper he had awakened, and the light fell straight across the narrow street and lit up the features of Harry Lime.' Reed added the cat, a favourite device which had first been used in the opening scene of *The Girl in the News*.

Between the story and the film, the full dramatic potential of some scenes was realised. The scene in which Holly Martins is kidnapped began as an arrest by the British; the jeep collecting him for the lecture he had forgotten is flying the Union Jack. In the film the audience is led to believe that it is the black-marketeers, or maybe the Russians, who have kidnapped him. The conceit, however, of Martins, a pulp fiction writer, arriving not to meet his death but, perhaps worse, to lecture on the modern novel, is Greene's. It was an amusing inversion of Hitchcock's recurring plot device of the innocent man finding safety by thrusting himself into ridiculous public view, which made its first appearance in *The Thirty-Nine Steps*.

Similarly, a scene where a small boy speaking German accuses Martins of being a murderer, causing the crowd to chase him into a cinema, was made more dramatic. More, too, was made of Martins's reluctance to take part in the capture of Harry: in the story Martins happily obliges; in the film he must be shown children dying of meningitis in hospital before being persuaded of the right course.

The end of the film was a cause of disagreement between Reed and Greene. Greene had written: 'I watched [Martins] striding off on his overgrown legs after the girl. He caught her up and they walked side by side. I don't think he said a word to her: it was like the end of a story except that before they turned out of my sight her hand was through his arm – which is how a story usually begins.' Reed backed Selznick's view that a happy ending was inappropriate. Having just attended Lime's funeral, Anna would hardly take off with the man who had killed him. Reed argued that it would jar with the audience, who would consider it cynical of her and out of character. He preferred a pessimistic ending, in which Anna would reject Martins's effort at reconciliation. Greene was only half convinced. 'I was afraid few people would wait in their seats during the girl's long walk from the graveside towards Holly, and the others would leave

the cinema under the impression that the ending was still going
to be as conventional as my suggested ending of boy joining girl.
I had not given enough credit to the mastery of Reed's direction,
and at that stage, of course, we neither of us anticipated Reed's
discovery of Anton Karas, the zither player. All I had indicated
in my treatment was a kind of signature tune connected with
Lime.'

At the beginning of August 1948 Reed and Greene set off for
California and a face-to-face meeting with Selznick, who had
seen the latest draft of their screenplay. Selznick's agreement
with Korda meant that, sixty days before shooting began, Reed
had to consult him about the script. The series of late-night
encounters with Selznick was a revelation for Greene, who
learned for the first time 'what a director may have to endure at
the hands of a producer'.

They found Selznick not in Beverly Hills but at the seaside
resort of La Jolla, where Joseph Cotten and other Selznick stars
were encouraged to perform summer plays for the megalo-
maniac producer. It was Greene's first encounter with a producer on his home territory, and was so comic an experience
that, thirty years later, he wrote that 'the dialogue remains as
fresh in my mind as the day when it was spoken'.

Selznick got straight down to business: 'I don't like the title.'

Greene, taken aback, replied: 'No? We thought . . .'

Selznick steamed on. 'Listen, boys, who the hell is going to a
film called *The Third Man*. You can do better than that, Graham.
You are a writer. A good writer. I'm no writer, but you are. Now
what we want – it's not right, mind you, of course it's not right,
I'm not saying it's right, but then I'm no writer and you are, what
we want is something like *Night in Vienna*, a title which will bring
them in.'

Reed, who had worked for bombastic producers before,
intervened. 'Graham and I will think about it.'

Selznick had acquired an extraordinary view of the film's plot,
whether by misreading the screenplay or by an odd cast of mind
is not clear.

For instance, on the first day he surprised Reed and Greene by
telling them, 'It won't do, boys, it won't do. It's sheer buggery.'

'Buggery?' they asked.

'It's what you learn in your English schools.'

'I don't understand.'

'This guy comes to Vienna looking for his friend. He finds his friend's dead. Right? Why doesn't he go home then?' Selznick shook his head and repeated once more, 'It's just buggery, boy.'

Greene began to defend his story. Martins stays because he is beaten up by a military policeman then falls in love with Lime's girlfriend.

Selznick remained unimpressed.

'Why didn't he go home before that?'

At the end of the first, exhausting conference, Selznick went back to Hollywood and Reed and Greene made their way to a suite in Santa Monica which had once been the home of one of William Randolph Hearst's mistresses.

Selznick returned to Los Angeles and each evening at 10.30 p.m. Reed and Greene would make their way to his office and listen to his nightly assaults on the script, his remarks loyally being taken down in shorthand by a secretary and typed up overnight for Reed and Greene to consider before the next meeting. The conferences lasted until four in the morning, when Reed and Greene were dismissed. At the end of each sally by Selznick, Reed would quietly say: 'Graham and I will think about it.'

Over the next few days, Selznick came back to the title. His alternatives included 'The Claiming of the Body' and 'The Changing of the Chair'. He also proposed that Martins should by played with a southern drawl – 'Reminder for Mr Reed to joint meeting with Joe Cotten and writer of American dialogue, as to how far Cotten wants to go with characterisation of Southerner', the secretary noted. Selznick felt there should be a suggestion that Martins had gone to school with Lime in England, and that Martins should be portrayed as an American with an English mother. (By this time only Cotten had definitely been cast; the other male parts were still expected to be awarded to British actors.) Martins should speak in poor German, 'that is ordinary to non-linguist Americans, such as "Danke shon"'. Perhaps Martins should arrive by train and not by plane.

Selznick wanted the part of Anna to be built up, as he had indicated in an earlier memo. Anna should be a Czech, not a Hungarian, 'more topical', and she should work in a gymkhana, a circus or a nightclub, which were 'more pictorial and colourful' than the theatre. Perhaps she could be arrested in the wings of the theatre, with Martins looking on. She should have a more specific past, say her father was an active anti-Communist, killed by the Russians, while Anna escaped to Vienna. There should be a scene where Anna prays in a church with Martins looking on. Anna should have a brother whom the Russians would shoot trying to escape from the Russian zone. She should be woken at night by the tapping of the window-shade against a photograph of Lime. On the ferris-wheel Lime should suggest that Martins buy a car in which they could escape together. Also Lime could suggest another racket to top the penicillin trade and invite Martins to join. On leaving the wheel, Lime should be stopped by the police and asked for his papers, but bluff his way out of being arrested.

Some of Selznick's proposals were purely practical; he suggested omissions to avoid American censorship cuts. For instance, the censors would not allow the Army policemen to be referred to as 'crooked' or 'stupid'. The words 'bloody', 'bastard' and 'why the hell' should be omitted, as should a reference to the unmarried Anna and Lime hoping to have a child. Selznick was also quick to pick up any English expressions which would be misunderstood in the United States.

At the last conference before Reed and Greene returned to Britain, Selznick surprised them both by saying: 'There's something I don't understand in this script, Graham. Why the hell does Harry Lime . . . ?' and he described a scene which neither Reed nor Greene recognised.

'But he doesn't,' Greene said.

Selznick looked at Greene, amazed.

'Christ, boys, I'm thinking of another script.' Selznick then lay down on the sofa and chewed a benzedrine pill. According to Greene, 'In ten minutes he was as fresh as ever, unlike ourselves.'

Selznick continued his avalanche of suggestions even after Reed and Greene had returned to London. Korda sent Selznick the draft screenplay on 20 September, telling him that it was a great improvement over the previous draft. Selznick replied, by telegram on 16 October, that he believed the revised script to be good and 'in Reed's hands should make a very good picture'. He took the credit for the improvements himself. However, 'despite the improvements, it is not satisfactory from the standpoint of the price of the picture or its acceptability to American audiences'. Selznick asked Korda to stress to Reed the terms of the agreement between them. 'I am convinced that Reed has no familiarity whatsoever with our rights in the matter; and therefore has seen fit to take only those changes which suit him and Greene from the standpoints of English storytellers, making the picture for English audiences.' He demanded an American writer to smarten up the dialogue and make it more acceptable for Americans. 'Presently the dialogue is in many cases so ludicrous, from a standpoint of American characters being presented to American audiences, that the picture would be kidded to death by our gallery audiences.'

Selznick told Korda that he had assumed during their long Hollywood conferences that Reed and Greene had agreed to make changes, but this was plainly not the case. Although 'I am certainly not going to insist upon lots of little detailed things with a man of Reed's understanding and ability; but on the other hand, I certainly am going to insist upon certain basic things on which I spent many, many long hours of wrangling in order to get Reed's and Greene's agreement.'

He wanted more emphasis on the American contribution to the four-power agreement. At the moment it seemed as if the British were in charge, with a few Russians and Frenchmen wandering about. The only Americans were Martins and the crooks Lime and Tyler (the character originally named Cooler). He had gone through this problem 'at the greatest length and in the greatest detail with Reed and with Greene, and come hell or high water, I simply will not stand for it in its present form'. Selznick was certain that Korda had stressed to them that his suggestions would be 'intelligent and helpful', but Reed and Greene had only followed 'what they saw fit to follow'. His changes were 'absolutely essential to the film's acceptability and even a limited popular success'.

Reed took some of Selznick's suggestions seriously and incorporated them into his final shooting script. To give some context to the viewer, Selznick suggested that the opening of the picture should be a documentary treatment of life in Allied-occupied Vienna, with an act of violence and a body floating in the Danube among the opening shots, and three months after the completion of the rest of the film Reed added such an opening. Greene also wrote a short introduction, to be spoken by an unseen character, which explained how the occupied city was administered and how dangerous the black market could be. On the film's American release, the *New York Times* critic Bosley Crowther wrote: 'This voice, which belongs to nobody whom we later see in the film, is glib, shifty, cynical, sardonic – like the voice of a foxy tourist guide.' It was, in fact, the voice of Carol Reed. This uncredited contribution by the director was followed by a partial personal appearance. Welles was not available when the time came to film Lime's fingers appearing through the grating of the sewer, so Reed lowered himself into the culvert and lifted the manhole cover for the camera.

Selznick caused a number of other alterations. Reed's locating shot of the cemetery, panning over the graves of Schubert, Brahms and Beethoven, was lost. And Reed added, at Selznick's suggestion, a series of short scenes in which Colonel Calloway convinces Martins that Lime is a murderous criminal by taking him around children's hospitals. As for the rest, Reed and Greene stood their ground. Although Selznick later said that he had done 'a little work on the script', his claim that he 're-edited the film for this hemisphere' is an exaggeration.

The censors also caused changes. They objected to Martins shooting Lime in the final scene. Greene was obliged to write a new line for Trevor Howard, 'If you see him, shoot,' allowing Cotten to kill his friend in cold blood only because he was obeying army orders.

By the autumn of 1948, Reed was ready to start filming. As usual, he had filled the cast with actors of known ability. He went out of his way to hire Austrian stage actors, including Paul Hoerbiger as the witness to Lime's 'death', and eighty-year-old Hedwig Bleibtreu as the old woman who hauls herself up and down the staircase, harassing the soldiers who come to question Anna. The child of an Austrian film technician was employed as the boy who accuses Martins of murder. Wilfrid Hyde-White, the English character actor, was to play the British Council representative and Bernard Lee the sergeant accompanying Howard.

There was, however, one important decision still to be made: who to play the key part of Harry Lime, the story's amoral hero.

Reed wanted Orson Welles. As he later explained: 'I was having dinner one night with Orson. I'd just got the synopsis from Graham Greene, which I thought was all right, so I told Orson that there was a wonderful part in it for him. He asked to read it, but I said, "Look, the script's not ready yet, but I'm sure you'll like it even though you don't come in until halfway through."

'"I'd much rather come in two-thirds of the way through," he replied.'

Welles was an inspired choice. He was the ultimate actor-manager-director, the modern equivalent of Sir Herbert Tree. He was an accomplished actor, a natural showman, an ingenious publicist, a talented stage producer, and a master film director. He had achieved instant, mythical fame with his first film, *Citizen Kane*, released in 1941 when he was only twenty-six. In it Welles had directed himself as a cynical, domineering newspaper magnate, basing his story on the life of William Randolph Hearst, who had him blacklisted for his pains. The film's bravura acting performances, by Welles, Cotten and a repertory of former stage actors, and its dramatic lighting and camera-work had made Welles an instant cinematic legend. In the seven years following *Kane* Welles had confirmed his film-making genius while proving himself to be hopelessly extravagant with money and studio time.

He was the sort of larger-than-life genius whom Korda liked to have around him, and inevitably a number of putative films were discussed and announced. Their announcement, however, often had little to do with the likelihood of production. Both Korda and Welles enjoyed the publicity which such projects suggested about the scale of their ambitions. The Korda–Welles films, in which Welles would, of course, both act and direct, included *War and Peace*, *Salome*, with Vivien Leigh and Laurence Olivier, and *Cyrano de Bergerac*. Welles said of Korda: 'He cost me years of my life and I can't hold a minute against him, because every time he would start on a dream, he not only sold me, but I knew he'd sold himself.'

Cyrano was a case in point. Even Welles believed that the film would be made and he arrived in France in 1948 with an array of false noses. He had sets built in Italy and drew up a shooting schedule. But the film, like the others, was abandoned by Korda. As Welles remembered: 'My whole time with Alex was things like that. I kept doing projects for him, which I did not abandon but which he did. I didn't abandon one single project – in each case he said he didn't have the money or it wasn't the right time and why not do something else?' Korda still wished to employ Welles, but Welles was becoming increasingly wary of Korda.

Reed explained how he got his own way on the casting. He dealt directly with Selznick. 'I said I wanted Orson Welles and Cotten, who I knew was under contract to Selznick, as was Valli. "Cotten and Valli you can have," he said, "but you can't have Orson." I asked why, knowing very well that Orson wasn't under contract to him and that he preferred me to use someone who was. Selznick was very strong on Noël Coward's playing Harry, but of course that would have been disastrous. It went on and on. When I started the film, Selznick was still going on about Noël. Alexander Korda, the producer, didn't care, however, so in the end I got Orson.'

It was at a dinner party in Korda's luxurious eyrie above Claridge's Hotel in Brook Street, Mayfair, that it was finally decided that *The Third Man* would star Welles as Lime. Korda had invited a few close friends, some business acquaintances and, of course, some members of his family to a small dinner. The guest-list was as glamorous as the cast of any of his films, each of those invited both charming and accomplished, and it gives an idea of the glittering court which surrounded Korda. Reed was a reluctant member of this high-living, name-dropping, ultra-social circle and he had little time for partying, but this night he wanted the matter of Lime be settled once and for all.

Reed was an imposing figure. He stood well over six foot tall and, like his father, he had a lofty bearing and a hypnotic gaze. C. A. Lejeune described him at the time as 'a long streak of a man with a singularly stream-lined look. He has a weather-beaten, egg-shaped face, light brown hair brushed clean back from a high forehead, light blue eyes rather closely set on a strongly jutting nose, a slightly satanic tilt of the eyebrows, a nervous mouth and splendid teeth. He moves fast and very lightly on his feet; high shoulders add curiously to the impression of stature; he gives an odd impression of a man advancing steadily against a high wind; and in some way, however tall you are, you feel you are looking up to him.' He was accompanied by

Pempie, a particular favourite of Korda's, as were all beautiful women, and she accepted his flattering attentions with quiet, thoroughly English modesty.

One woman to be found at every Korda party was Moura Budberg, who had been Maxim Gorky's secretary in Russia before she emigrated to Britain, where she became a lively addition to H. G. Wells's long string of lovers. She had been a dark-eyed bohemian beauty, of whom Wells had said, 'I have rarely seen her in any room with other women in which she was not plainly – not merely in my eyes but to many others – the most attractive and interesting presence. Women fall in love with her at sight and men are compelled to come and ask about her and talk about her, with a certain insincere disinterestedness.' By the late forties her long hair was completely grey and her pleasant plumpness was turning to fat. 'Daahrling,' she said to Korda, dropping her weight onto a sofa, 'give me just a little vooodkah and a bit of caviar, just to restore an old lady who has had a terrible long taxi ride all the way from Kensington.'

Korda had also invited Brendan Bracken, Churchill's loyal disciple, the wartime Minister of Supply, owner of the *Financial Times* and a friend of the abdicated King Edward VIII. Evelyn Waugh caricatured him in *Brideshead Revisited* as Rex Mottram: 'His seniors thought him a pushful young cad, but Julia recognised the unmistakable chic – the flavour of "Max" and "F.E." and the Prince of Wales, of the big table in the Sporting Club, the second magnum, and the fourth cigar, of the chauffeur kept waiting hour after hour without compunction.' Once a red-haired dynamo who forced his way among the grandees of the Tory Party, he was now cruelly ill with throat cancer.

Alex's younger brother Vincent was also there. He was the brilliant art director of both Alex and Zoltan Korda's most important films, the designer of the sets for *The Private Life of Henry VIII* (1933), *Things to Come* (1936) and *The Thief of Baghdad* (1940). He had just designed the glorious embassy interiors for Reed's *The Fallen Idol*. He was a particular friend of Reed's and lived in The Vale, Chelsea, around the corner from the King's Road. Vincent arrived at his elder brother's party in a flurry, with pieces of tissue paper decorating the shaving cuts on his face. He had slipped with his razor because he was nervous that his second wife, Leila, who was compulsively unpunctual, would be late for one of Alex's parties yet again. He had flustered and blustered her to be on time and they had driven at enormous speed through the London streets to arrive, as usual, half an hour early.

Vivien Leigh was also expected at the party, as soon as she could tear herself away from the theatre. She had recently returned from a ten-month tour of Australia with her long-suffering husband Laurence Olivier, and they were about to transfer *The School for Scandal*, the first time the couple had shared a London stage. The publicity line was, 'For the first time together in London, the greatest actor in the world and his wife, one of the loveliest of women.' On-stage smiles, however, diguised the backstage tensions that had broken out in their marriage – always a stormy affair – during their Australian tour the previous November. Before the dinner party, Vincent and Leila had been told by Alex: 'For God's sake, don't mention Larry.' On tour in Sydney, Vivien Leigh had fallen in love with Peter Finch, aged twenty-four, and they had become lovers. He had followed her to London, but his arrival was not good for Vivien's frail state of mind. Once a dazzling beauty, the strain of her life was showing. Cecil Beaton confided to his diary the truth which few admitted, that 'she has lost her looks, very fat in the face'.

Without waiting for Vivien, Korda sat his guests for dinner. The conversation soon turned, as it inevitably did, to films. Reed spoke of his preparations for *The Third Man*, telling Korda of the difficulties he was experiencing in pinning down Welles. Reed knew that he wanted to play Lime, but he was in Italy filming his own production of *Othello*, with himself as the Moor. Welles had run out of money and needed the acting job Reed was offering to fund his next bout of filming, but he remained elusive. As Reed told Korda, 'Every once in a while he descends on Rome to scare up a little more capital, but when you talk to him about a part, he simply vanishes.'

Korda decided to take the matter into his own hands. After dinner, when the Havana cigars were being handed around to the gentlemen and to Moura Budberg, who took one and lit it with the remark, 'At my age, one is confined to the pleasures of taste,' Vivien Leigh arrived in a state of distress. Korda took her off to his study to allow her to compose herself and on his return spoke to his brother Vincent in the hall.

Vincent had his overcoat on, ready to make his customary early exit. Korda took him by the arm. 'I want you to go and get Orson. Find him. Bring him back somehow. Try not to let him know how much we need him, but get him back here and I'll persuade him to sign a contract.' Alex expected Vincent to set off at once, but his brother protested that it was impossible. He had no tickets and no foreign currency. He had things to do in London. Two days later, he set off to Rome to find Welles.

Vincent was mildly irritated to be sent on one of his big brother's errands, but he was used to it. It would, in any case, give him a break from London's relentless rationing, and he decided to take his teenage son Michael with him and to treat the task as a spontaneous holiday. He did not imagine that catching Orson would be easy, but he could not have expected what was to happen over the next week.

Arriving in Rome, Vincent took a suite at the Hassler Hotel. He assumed that Welles would be staying at the Grand Hotel. There was no hurry, so he took Michael out to dinner and passed by the Grand on the way back. They were out of luck. Mr Welles, they were told, had just left for Florence. Vincent telephoned his wife in London, cabled Alex about the change in plan, had the front counter book a suite at the Grand Hotel in Florence and two tickets on the late morning train, then went to sleep.

In Florence, booking into the Grand, Vincent was told by the concierge that he had just missed Mr Welles, who had left for Venice. Vincent knew immediately what Welles, a consummate practical joker, had in mind – a paper-chase across Italy. He had no option but to take part. Nothing could be done until the morning, so he cabled Alex in London, asked the Grand to make all the arrangements for Venice and went out to dinner.

When Vincent reached Venice, he found a note from Welles at the Danieli saying that he was sorry to miss him, but that he was needed urgently in Naples and was therefore heading south. By now, Alex Korda in London had worked out what was going on and was furiously sending cables to Vincent at the Danieli: chase him, find him, bring him back to London. Vincent was less bothered. Alex's dreary chore was turning into an adventure which was taking him on an enjoyable whistle-stop tour of Italy. He told Michael that he hoped that Orson would eventually make for Paris, his favourite city.

The next stop was Naples, which Vincent reached by plane. Welles had gone to Capri, so Vincent went to Capri. As the island ferry pulled up at the dock, Vincent caught a first sight of his mischievous quarry. Racing out of the harbour was a fast and noisy motorboat, heading back to Naples, and sitting at the stern on a huge pile of luggage was the unmistakable bulk of Orson Welles, extravagantly waving his condolences. He was headed for Nice.

Welles was enjoying himself. At the same time he knew he had no option but eventually to take the part being offered. It would be an interruption to his work on *Othello*, but that was halted anyway. He would take the part because Alex would pay him in cash and in that way he could restart his film. But he was determined to make Alex Korda pay for the time which, over the years, he had wasted on Korda's behalf. Welles explained: 'I knew I was going to do it, but I was going to make it just as unpleasant as possible.' The capture of Welles was inevitable. He was running out of ready money with which to continue his escape, and took a room at the Hotel Ruhl in Nice and waited to be apprehended.

Vincent knew all about Welles and his appetites. He was therefore certain that the actor would be found on the Côte d'Azur eating at an expensive restaurant. And so he was. It was fitting for a man about to play Harry Lime that Welles was betrayed by a woman, Madame Baudoin, the proprietress of the Bonne Auberge in Cagnes-sur-Mer, of which Vincent was an old customer. When Vincent marched up the restaurant towards him, Welles greeted him warmly with the good grace of a sportsman who has narrowly lost a game. But finding Welles turned out to be only half of Vincent's mission; getting him home would be more difficult.

The first job was to get him drunk and manageable and safely back to his hotel. Then, instead of risking a connecting flight through Paris, Vincent hired a private plane, saying to his son: 'There's less chance that he'll slip away from us. Otherwise we have to fly to Paris and change planes and he'll be gone at Orly the moment we let him go to the toilet.'

Welles took one last revenge on Alex Korda. In the cramped passenger compartment of the twin-engined plane which would fly them to London, he was asked to hold a large basket of fruit

Vincent had bought for his brother. No one in Britain had seen such an array of fruit since before the war. While Vincent daydreamed in the seat in front of him, Welles took a bite out of each piece of fruit in the basket, then fell sound asleep. As Welles explained: 'It was going to be offered as a great present . . . I knew Alex wouldn't touch any of it if it had been bitten into.'

Welles took a suite at Claridge's and began his negotiations with Alex Korda in the penthouse. He was not in the best of bargaining positions. Korda only needed Welles because Reed wanted him. It would be possible to make the film without him. Welles, on the other hand, had little option but to agree to take the part. The question was, how much money could be extracted from Korda? Korda's usual deal would be to offer a small fee with the promise of some of the profits if the film did well. This was a risky business at the best of times, but at this time, with *Othello* to be finished, Welles needed cash, not income in lieu.

He agreed to accept $100,000 for two sessions in front of the camera, one in Vienna, the other in the studios in London. It turned out to be a poor deal, which Welles was to regret for the rest of his life. He said later: 'I was given a choice between $100,000 or something like 20 per cent of the picture and I took the $100,000. Picture grossed, you know, something unbelievable. Because in America it was only a success, but in the rest of the world it was an absolute bombshell – it was *The Sound of Music*, you know. There never was such a hit in twenty-five years as there was in Europe. I could have retired on that.'

Welles did, however, wring out of Korda a valuable promise: in 1949 he would allow Welles to act in and direct a screen version of Pirandello's *The Emperor*. The film would of course never be made. Welles, however, kept his part of the bargain and arrived for work in Vienna in November, as planned. Reed was delighted.

The last important decision was the choice of lighting cameraman. Reed had little doubt it should be Robert Krasker, who had made *Odd Man Out* look so gloomily atmospheric. In *The Third Man* Krasker was to progress beyond the Belfast shadows to photographing Vienna, a once glorious city desolated by war. Many of the key scenes were to take place at night, others in the sewers. Krasker revelled in his task. He also heightened the drama by, at Reed's insistence, tilting each frame – a piece of conspicuous artistry which caused cartoonists to make fun of sloping tables and ceilings on the film's release. When the film was completed, William Wyler, a close friend of Reed's, sent him a spirit-level, with a note saying: 'Carol, next time you make a picture, just put it on top of the camera, will you?'

Reed later explained the thinking behind Krasker's photography: 'I shot most of the film with a wide-angle lens that distorted the buildings and emphasised the wet cobblestone streets (it cost a good deal to hose them down constantly). But the angle of vision was just to suggest that something crooked was going on. I don't think it's a very good idea. I haven't used it much since – only when I need to shoot someone standing behind another person who's sitting and I don't want to cut off his head.'

Even as Reed was about to set off for Vienna, Welles had still not been found and persuaded to play Lime, although the other casting had been settled. Selznick approved Cotten and Valli. Reed picked Trevor Howard, who had appeared briefly, without credit, in *The Way Ahead*, to play Calloway, but told him that he should be prepared to take the part of Lime at the last moment if Welles could not be found. By mid-November Welles had signed the contract and arrived in Vienna with Pempie, who spoke German as she had been to a finishing school in Austria. Reed took with him his favourite duffle-coat to protect him from the cold as he would be filming both night and day. He had said of directing: 'All I believe the director can do is to approach his subject with a meticulously prepared list of scenes to be shot with their general description and the dialogue entailed in each, and an absolutely clear idea of the effect he wants to achieve.' This he had done more thoroughly than ever before.

There was a great sense of anticipation among the cast and crew by the time Welles arrived. His reputation as an independent-minded, highly talented bully of an actor intimidated most actors and directors who had to work with him. Not so Cotten, who was too close a friend, nor Reed, who was confident in the face of even Welles's genius. Reed believed that his tight shooting script would prevent Welles from running amok. In Vienna, Welles had three key episodes to perform. Reed made a

great fuss of him, and for once he behaved impeccably. He liked
the part of Lime and was pleased that his scenes would take only
a short time. Reed knew what he was doing and gave clear
directions. For the most part Welles's work in Vienna was either
in action or standing in shadow.

Reed later described working with Welles. He was 'wonderful, marvellous. He was difficult only about the starting date,
telling me how busy he was with this and that. So I said, "Look,
we're going on location for five weeks. Any week – give us two
days' notice – we'll be ready for you. And give me one week out
of seven in the studio." He kept to it. He came straight off the
train in Vienna one morning, and we did his first shot by nine
o'clock. "Jeez," he said, "this is the way to make pictures." He
walked across the Prater, said two lines to Cotten, and then I
said, "Go back to the hotel, have breakfast; we're going into the
sewers and we'll send for you." "Great! Wonderful!"

'Comes down into the sewers and says, "Carol, I can't work in
a sewer, I come from California! My throat! I'm so cold!" I said,
"Look Orson, in the time it's taking us to talk about this, you can
do the shot. All you do is stand there, look off, see some police
after you, turn, and run away." "Carol," he said, "look, get
someone else to play this. I cannot work under such conditions!"
"Orson, Orson, we're lit for you. Just stand there." "All right,
but do it quick!" Then he looks off, turns away, and runs off into
the sewers. All of a sudden I hear a voice shouting, "Don't cut
the cameras! Don't cut the cameras! I'm coming back." He runs
back, through the whole river, stands underneath a cascade
over his head (all this out of camera range, mind you), and does
all sorts of things, so that he came away absolutely dripping.
"How was that?" he asks. "Wonderful! Marvellous!" I said.
"Okay. I'll be back at the hotel. Call me when you need me."
With Orson, you know, everything has to be a drama. But there
were no arguments of any sort at all.'

Other significant scenes were improvised on the set, including the cat which identifies Lime in the shadows. Reed explained how he decided upon the device. 'I just liked the idea of
a cat loving a villain – the charm of the man!' The cat also helped
to solve another problem. 'I was worried about finding Harry in
that doorway; I didn't want Cotten just to pass by and see him
because then audiences wouldn't know who the man in the

doorway was. When Cotten brings Valli flowers, I placed a cat on her bed whom Cotton tries to get to play with the string around the gift. But the cat just turns and jumps off. Then the cat jumps through the window. Whilst Cotten had been trying to get the cat to play, I had him say, "Bad-tempered cat." Then I worked in the line for Valli: "He only liked Harry." We next look out of the window, see a man come down the street, and watch him enter a doorway. So far as we know, it might be anyone. But by going over to him and playing with his lace, the cat establishes that it is Harry . . . We used so many cats: one in Vienna, running down the street; another in the studio on the bed; another to play with the lace . . . What was difficult was to get the cat to walk up to it.' Reed used an obvious lure: sardines.

The Vienna shooting concluded without incident. Or at least without incident from Welles. Trevor Howard, however, was arrested in his major's uniform for impersonating a British Army officer.

Welles took his location work very seriously, but inevitably some studio work was also necessary. Many locations demanded by the plot could not be found in Vienna; there was, for instance, no spiral staircase leading to a manhole in the street, and the fatal shooting of Lime had to be filmed in the studio. In the studio, however, Welles was simultaneously co-operative and disruptive. The set was prickling with anticipation on the day Welles arrived at Shepperton. The crew were looking forward to what they guessed would be a battle of wills between Reed and Welles, who was thought of in film circles as the greatest director alive. Even Alexander Korda turn up to watch the genius at work. Welles was conscious of the impact his presence was making and looked around at the faces staring at him. He started telling jokes and laughed loudly at his own humour. Then he got down to work.

Reed asked him to follow the instructions of the script. Welles looked puzzled. 'Now, I want you to play the entrance like this,' said Reed. Welles looked perplexed. 'I want to know the reason. Why do I have to do that?' Reed explained in his quiet way. If Welles wanted motivation, then Reed would give the reason. If he wanted a scrap, he would have that, too. But it didn't come to a battle of wills. Reed's ability to charm and flatter actors into doing exactly as he wished vanquished even Welles. Reed acted it all out before him, lifting his arms in the air, clenching his fists, walking and talking the lines.

Welles slowly became engrossed in Greene's sinisterly charming character and softened up, doing as he was told and speaking to Reed as if he were a schoolboy addressing a teacher. 'This is just a rough sketch, Mr Reed,' he told him. 'I'll fill in the details later.' Welles explained to Reed that much of his mischief-making was caused by a low boredom threshold. 'Unless I'm trying something new, I get bored with everything.' And he was full of praise for Reed, calling him 'a wonderful director. He's different from me though. Sometimes I break off and say: "This whole business is crazy. What are we doing it all for?" Carol never does that. He's serious the whole time and he loved that sewer in Vienna where we were filming. We had to kidnap him to fly home. As a director I soft-soap the actors. I caught Carol Reed doing that with me the other day and what was worse I found myself believing him. Carol and I have one thing in common: we are both awfully patient with me.' On the film's release *Time* magazine recognised the scale of Reed's achievement: 'The ultimate proof of Reed's powers as a director: he has managed to get a temperate, first-rate performance out of Orson Welles.'

When it came to shooting the Great Wheel sequence, however, Welles wrested control from Reed. Although some background shots had been taken in Vienna, it proved impossible to erect a camera position outside the ferris-wheel. It was decided, therefore, to mock up the carriage in the studio, using carefully matched back-projection of the view from the wheel. There was little movement necessary, for Joseph Cotten and Welles had merely to stand in the carriage and talk to each other. Welles took liberties with his lines from the very beginning. In a location scene among the carousels, he delivered an approximate version of what he was meant to say. At the door of the car, he started inventing his lines.

Instead of speaking of the lovers who had used the Great Wheel before the war to find some privacy, as in the script, he added extra cynicism to the part of Lime by referring to the lost pleasures of the children of Vienna. 'The kids used to ride this a lot in the old days. Of course, they haven't got the money now, poor devils.' The change was an improvement. He then added

an element to the scene which had a double irony. Lime chews
on some indigestion pills which, he tells Martins, cannot be
bought in Europe any more, and he is running out of them.
Again, Welles adds to the callousness of Lime's character: while
sending children to their doom with his vile trade in drugs, he
still troubles himself over his indigestion. Later he complains to
Martins, patting his chest and looking ill, 'I wish I could throw
this thing off.' Before saying farewell to Martins he again refers
to his dwindling reserve of stomach pills and tells Martins that
he regrets not having asked him to bring some from the United
States.

The plight of an American who cannot obtain the right pills in
Europe was based on Welles's personal experience. Living at the
Excelsior in Rome, waiting to make Korda's planned *Cyrano de
Bergerac*, Welles discovered that he had forgotten to pack his
Proloid diet pills and his Dexedrine, both of which not only kept
his weight down but kept him awake and hyperactive. He sent
to the States for some replacements, but they would take some
time, and he therefore made a long and desperate tour of Roman
chemists to track down pills which would work as effectively as
his American supply.

For the rest of the Great Wheel scene, Welles added and
rearranged his lines to suit himself, with Cotten staying as close
to the original script as Welles would allow him. In the final part
of the scene, where Lime bids farewell to Martins, Greene's
screenplay has Lime asking about old schoolfriends and
suggesting to Martins that he join him in the black market. What
Welles added instead has become one of the best-remembered
speeches in cinema: 'You know what the fellow said: In Italy for
thirty years under the Borgias they had warfare, terror, murder,
bloodshed; they produced Michaelangelo, Leonardo da Vinci
and the Renaissance. In Switzerland they had brotherly love,
five hundred years of democracy and peace, and what did they
produce? The cuckoo clock. So long, Holly.' There was not much
point in Reed attempting to curtail Welles's invention on the set.
Nor, when he heard the line, did he have any wish to.

Working first in Vienna, shooting twenty hours a day in three
shifts, then at Isleworth, then Shepperton, and despite a fire in
the cutting room which damaged some footage, Reed brought
the film in on time in March 1949.

Finding the right music for *The Third Man* had troubled Reed from the start. Vienna was, after all, the home of Schubert, Beethoven and the Strauss family, yet all of these obvious choices seemed to jar with the tone of the story and the wartorn condition of the city. In November 1948, while shooting on location in Vienna, Reed had made one important decision: there would be no Johann Strauss waltzes.

His ultimate solution was inspired. Because Reed gave a number of fanciful accounts of how he came to find the zither player Anton Karas, it is worth giving two of them in full, as between them they may contain the truth. The first he gave to the *New York Times* when the film was released in the United States. 'I and some of my friends went into a little café, a Heurigen where new wine is served, at Sievering, a suburb of Vienna. Toni [Karas] was playing the zither but nobody noticed him particularly. I don't just remember how I happened to think about the zither, except a thought came to me that its music mixes well with wine and conversation. Then I wondered if it would be possible to use Karas to make some background music. I asked Toni about it and he seemed to think it would be all right. Then he came to my hotel in Vienna, sat on the bed and played. We made a five-minute recording which I took back to England. I asked Toni if he would go to England too. He didn't seem amazed. He just nodded. I didn't speak German and he doesn't speak English. I wasn't quite sure he understood.'

Reed gave the second version to Charles Thomas Samuels in 1972: 'When we were on location I used to store props in a studio outside the city. Whilst the boys were unloading, I'd go to a store to get carafes of wine for them. Nearby there was a tiny beer and sausage restaurant, with a courtyard in which this fellow played a zither for coins. I'd never heard a zither before, thought it was attractive, and wondered whether we could use a single instrument throughout the film, especially since the zither is so typical of Vienna. I got Karas to come back to my hotel one night, where he played for about twenty minutes. I then brought a recording of that back to the studio to see if the music fought against the dialogue – and some did – but a good deal of it worked well. Karas then came to London to live.'

In London, Karas stayed with Reed in his house in the King's Road, with Pempie translating between them. Karas played dozens of different pieces over and over. One became the 'Harry Lime Theme', an unnamed tune he had composed himself and which he had not played for fifteen years. When Reed asked Karas why he hadn't played it for such a long time, he replied: 'When you play in a café, nobody stops to listen. This tune takes a lot out of your fingers. I prefer playing "Wien, Wien", the sort of thing one can play all night while eating sausages at the same time.'

The 'Harry Lime Theme' was recorded for commercial release, became a great hit, and began a craze for zithers which took the musical instrument shops completely by surprise. But Reed revealed something about the recording which has thwarted those who tried to copy Karas. 'What's driven other zither players mad (they can never figure out how it's done) is that he played the tune, then with an earphone re-recorded it, adding thirds. In the ordinary way, no zither player could do it.' There was one other trick. Reed found that the exact sound he wanted could be obtained by Karas playing his zither underneath the kitchen table. Attempts to replicate this sound in the studio failed until Reed arranged for his kitchen table to be brought to the studio, where Karas gamely sat underneath and played.

Selznick instantly recognised the power of the music to sell the film and attempted to delay the release of the record in the United States until he had enough copies of the film to be able to fully exploit the public's demand. The music critic Antony Hopkins wrote at the time: 'The much discussed zither music was, as music, both trite and commonplace in the extreme. Had it been orchestrated, however consummately, even the average cinemagoer would have felt it to be inadequate. But the true genius of Carol Reed showed itself when he realised that the zither, as sheer sound, was something fresh enough and new enough to excite the listener's interest and attention whatever the quality of the music played.' Part of the brilliance of the music is the way Reed used it to reinforce various scenes with incidental music, the most effective being the moment that Lime reappears from the shadows. As Reed later explained: 'In the cat scene, I asked Karas to play a few sort of walking notes while the cat crossed the street and then, as it looked at Harry's shoe, ascending chords, which break into *The Third Man* theme when it finally sees Harry and we hold on the cat's little face.'

The Third Man did not attract universal praise from critics on its release in Britain in August 1949 or in the United States the following February. Few saw that it would become a cinema classic, a favourite with critics and successive generations of audiences. C. A. Lejeune, the *Observer*'s critic, who had stead-fastly supported Reed throughout his career and had become a close professional friend, missed the point of the film, accusing Reed of using too many tricks. 'Mr Reed has never before elaborated his style so desperately, nor used so many tricks in the presentation of a film.' One trick was the zither, 'which thrums its way through the story and sends the audience away half-maddened and half-intoxicated. The most distracting is a habit of printing his scenes askew, with floors sloping at a diagonal and close-ups deliriously tilted.'

Dilys Powell, who had resisted much of Reed's charm hitherto, was more enthusiastic: 'With *The Third Man* Carol Reed establishes his claim to be considered one of the most accomplished living film directors. I say this not because his new work seems to me his best: in certain respects I like it less than *The Fallen Idol* and *Odd Man Out*. But the assurance with which he has handled his theme marks a decisive stage in his career.'

The film's release in the United States brought accusations of too much artifice from Bosley Crowther, critic of the *New York Times*. 'The simple fact is that *The Third Man*, for all the awesome hoopla it has received, is essentially a first-rate contrivance in the way of melodrama – and that's all. It isn't a penetrating study of any European problem of the day (except that it skirts around black markets and the sinister anomalies of . . . "zones"). It doesn't present any "message". It hasn't a point of view. It is just a bang-up melodrama, designed to excite and entertain. In the light of the buzz about it, this is something we feel you should know.'

No one took much notice of the critics. *The Third Man* became a success on both sides of the Atlantic through the topicality of its subject matter, the perfect performances, particularly from Welles, Greene's sense of adventure, the unusual photography and the contagious theme music, all of which have ensured the film's lasting appeal. The film heaped awards upon Reed. He won the first prize at Cannes, was nominated for a 'Best Director' Oscar and won the New York Film Critics' Award for best direction. Of all Reed's films, this was the one by which posterity would remember him. Without *The Third Man*, Reed's reputation would depend on *The Fallen Idol* and *Odd Man Out*, which have a more subtle appeal. *The Third Man* was the height of Reed's career. After such praise, he might have relaxed a little. But what troubled him was the question of how he could possibly follow a run of three such highly successful films.

9

An Island Castaway

'It's dull to stick to the same sort of subject and bad for one's work into the bargain. Repetition makes a director grow stale in his job, and lose his grip as an entertainer. I happen to love a dark street, with wet cobbles, and a small furtive figure under a lamp at the corner. Whenever I go on location, I instinctively look for something of that kind. Now that is bad; thoroughly bad for me, and tedious for the public. Variety is an essential exercise to a director. Every new film should be a new beginning, and nobody should ever be able to say with certainty, "Oh, that's a Carol Reed subject," or "That's not a Carol Reed subject." It's doing the particular job well – any and every sort of job – that primarily interests me. I don't think the type of subject matters much.'

To some extent Reed's philosophy was born of necessity, for early in his career, like any young British director, he had had to take what was offered, and the resultant need for versatility became a matter of pride to him. If the story was a good one, he believed that he could make a good film from it, as long as he was able to employ talented actors. As has been seen, he had little admiration for Hitchcock, despite his distinctive style, because he believed that a great director should attempt all sorts of subjects, and Hitchcock stuck to thrillers. Reed never thought of himself as a celebrity, and had little time for those who revelled in the fame brought by success in the film industry. C. A. Lejeune wrote: 'Mr Reed is difficult to interview. He is eager to help, to tell you anything you may want to know, but there are no firecrackers nor show phrases in his speech. He talks quickly and quietly behind half-closed teeth. He is invariably friendly and frank, but he simply cannot seem to realise that he's a man in the news. He has never quite outgrown, you feel, the days when he was just a novice.' Others who tried to explain Reed's curious diffidence about his success repeatedly refer to his eternal boyishness, his childlike enthusiasm, his reserve and lack of interest in adult matters.

Reed's reluctance to answer the questions of probing inter-viewers about his private life appears to have stemmed from his self-imposed silence about anything to do with his father. Reed came to shun publicity of any sort, saying: 'I don't think people care what sort of kitchen curtains I have. I don't think they care about the technical people. Stars are the draw. They earn their publicity. It brings the people in. But no one would go to see a film because it was directed by Carol Reed.' He was wrong; after *The Third Man*, a great number of cinemagoers looked forward to the next film by Carol Reed.

The immediate temptation was for him to continue his association with Graham Greene. Alexander Korda thought that Greene's novel *The Heart of the Matter* could do well as a film. Greene himself was very happy with the outcome of his two collaborations with Reed. In an explanatory preface to the reissuing of 'The Basement Room' as 'The Fallen Idol', he made his affection and respect for Reed clear. 'Of one thing about both these films I have complete certainty, that their success is due to Carol Reed, the only director I know with that particular warmth of human sympathy, the extraordinary feeling for the right face for the right part, the exactitude of cutting, and not least important the power of sympathising with an author's worries and an ability to guide him.' It would have been possible for the Reed/Greene partnership to continue for another film. They discussed a further collaboration and this leaked out to the press in March 1950. Reed commented on the rumour: 'There is no story yet – just an outline. It won't be a suspense thriller. I must have something different – a new groove – after *The Third Man*.'

Korda had announced, in the summer of 1948, his intention of making two films to which Reed's name was automatically linked. The first was Thomas Hardy's *Tess of the D'Urbervilles*, 'to be produced in Technicolor and directed by Carol Reed', and to which Korda had already appended the name of Jennifer Jones, Selznick's wife, as Tess. The Selznick connection alone would have been enough to ensure that Reed would have nothing to do with the project. Dutifully, however, he took the script home to read. The second Korda project was an adaptation of Joseph Conrad's *An Outcast of the Islands*, starring the American actor

Robert Mitchum. Reed was well aware that Alex Korda's announcements often amounted to little, and that it was by no means certain that Mitchum had agreed to play the part. Reed also had subject ideas of his own.

With no fear of unemployment at this stage of his career, he greatly enjoyed the period between one film's end and the beginning of the next. 'Picture-making is often sheer misery,' he said. 'Planning them is great fun. Making them is rather like riding on a switchback at a fair; you hardly dare imagine what is coming next.' What he was certain of, however, was that he did not wish to do anything which would invite comparison with *The Third Man*. By the end of 1949, when *The Third Man* was complete, Reed was making daily journeys to Korda's office at 146 Piccadilly to sift through ideas.

He wished to make a comedy and was seriously considering a story called 'Lunatic at Large' and Jerome K. Jerome's *Three Men in a Boat*, which had been filmed once by his apprentice-master Basil Dean in 1933. Reed also tried to buy the rights for Maurice Hewlett's historical novel *The Spanish Jade*, in which a British traveller in nineteenth-century Spain spends forty-eight hours travelling with a band of gypsies.

But first Reed turned his mind to a three-minute film for charity, which would star none other than the husband of Princess Elizabeth, the heir to the throne. It was intended as a filler for cinema programmes which would draw public attention to the Duke of Edinburgh's favourite charity, the National Playing Fields Association. The Duke had agreed to appear in the film, in which he would be seen talking to underprivileged cockney children before handing over to Kathleen Harrison, a Reed favourite, and Wilfred Pickles for the appeal for funds. One problem was that when Reed had time to make the picture, the duke was in Malta. Reed flew there and shot the footage of the duke, then spliced it into film of the children, who were filmed in Korda's offices. When the film was completed, Prince Philip sent a telegram to Reed: 'The Princess has told me that she considers your film to be very good indeed, and I want to thank you for all the great care and obvious interest you put into the job . . . I would like you to know what fun it was working with you at San Anton.'

There was more to come. On 1 January 1950 an aide at

Buckingham Palace conveyed this news: 'Michael Parker tells me that Princess Elizabeth has just telephoned to him concerning the Playing Fields picture. She said that it was slipped into the film programme at Sandringham last evening without warning. The audience were spellbound. They found it a very moving little picture. Ginger [one of the cockney boys] was a favourite with them all and they laughed a lot. They think it perfectly directed and could not be bettered in any respect. The King, the Queen and Princess Elizabeth wish their thanks to be conveyed to Sir Alexander Korda and Mr Carol Reed.'

Early in 1950 Reed agreed to Alex Korda's suggestion to film *An Outcast of the Islands*. Little could have been further from the corrupt post-war world of Greene's Vienna than this story of trading and treachery in the Far East. Reed had been a keen reader of Conrad as a teenager and was very familiar with the novel, which he had considered filming when contracted to Gainsborough Pictures.

An Outcast of the Islands was written as what the film industry now calls a 'prequel'. On the success in 1894 of his first novel, *Almayer's Folly*, Conrad had asked his friend Edward Garnett whether he should try his hand at a second. Garnett told him, 'You have the style, you have the temperament; why not write another?' Conrad went straight home and wrote the first page of an explanation of how the events in *Almayer's Folly* came about. The hero, Peter Willems, was loosely based on a man Conrad had met in the Dutch East Indies who was loathed by all Westerners living in the East because he had revealed a secret river and trading post to Arab merchants.

Conrad made Willems the friend of two characters from his first novel, Captain Tom Lingard, a merchant seaman, and Almayer, who keeps the location of his trading post secret so that he can do business with the native traders without fear of competition. Willems betrays the location of Almayer's concern to Arabs, having been duped by a one-eyed tribal statesman, Babalatchi, and having become infatuated with, then rejected by, a native girl, Aissa, who pursues him relentlessly. At the end of the novel Willems is left to a wretched existence, shunned by his former friends and forced to live primitively among the locals.

Making a film from a Conrad novel was notoriously difficult, and Reed was aware of the previous efforts, in particular Hitchcock's *Sabotage*, shamelessly lifted from *The Secret Agent*. H. L. Mencken had offered his advice to those stage directors and film-makers who aspired to translate *An Outcast of the Islands* into drama: 'The world fails to breed actors for such roles, or stage managers to penetrate such travails of the spirit, or audiences for the revelation thereof.' Reed was undeterred, and hoped to stay as close to Conrad's intentions as possible. He hired William Fairchild, who had just completed the screenplay of *Morning Departure*, to write the script.

Some important changes were decided upon from the beginning. Conrad had written to Garnett that the final chapter of the novel, which described the plight of Willems when his Western friends desert him, was 'simply abominable. Never did I see anything so clearly as the naked hideousness of that thing.' Reed agreed and decided to lose the final chapter, leaving Willems friendless in the remote Far East, without the postscript which describes the misery he later endured.

Other amendments were more intrusive. Rather than the native girl Aissa forcing her attentions upon Willems, it was decided that she was to be pure and innocent, with Willems the one who presses himself on her. This allowed Reed to cast an unknown actress in the role, without expecting her to do much except look seductive. Some changes were dictated by casting. Conrad had made the wives of both Almayer and Captain Lingard resentful half-castes, illustrating how closely their husbands were bound to the ways of the East. The difficulties of finding two suitable actresses or hinting at their mixed race proved too much for Reed, who simplified the roles by having both women quite white, a travesty of Conrad's intentions. (American distributors were also thought likely to object to such racial ambiguity on the screen.) And it was decided that Babalatchi would have two eyes rather than one, a detail which would have been only mildly awkward for Reed to keep authentic.

The part of Willems was plainly the key to the casting. Korda favoured Stewart Granger, who had just completed his first Hollywood film, a remake of *King Solomon's Mines*, and was the sort of new international star from Britain Korda wished to encourage. But Reed preferred Trevor Howard, one of his regulars, whose first film part had been in *The Way Ahead*, and who had appeared in *The Third Man*. Reed explained, with more affection than disapproval, 'I knew of no one among contemporary film actors better suited to play Willems, the moral degenerate, than Trevor Howard,' and he was quickly signed for the part.

Other key casting decisions also brought together actors with whom Reed had worked before. Ralph Richardson, the star of *The Fallen Idol*, agreed to play Captain Lingard, Robert Morley, Charles James Fox in *The Young Mr Pitt*, would play Almayer and his daughter Annabel would play Almayer's daughter. Also fresh from *The Third Man* was Wilfrid Hyde-White as Vinck. Wendy Hiller was to play Mrs Almayer. George Coulouris, the fine British character actor, was to black up for the part of Babalatchi.

Reed's West End stage army again dominated the minor parts, with Betty Ann Davies, who had appeared in *Kipps*, as Mrs Willems, A. V. Bramble as Badavi and Frederick Valk. One of the key roles was more difficult. Reed wanted a new female lead to play the irresistible Aissa, and he decided that on his trip to the Far East to reconnoitre locations he would look for a woman with no acting experience and coax a brilliant performance from her, as he had with Bobby Henrey in *The Fallen Idol*.

Reed set out for the East in June 1950, heading for Singapore, Malaya, Indonesia and Borneo. He took with him his wife Pempie, the screenwriter William Fairchild, his associate producer Hugh Perceval, who had done such a splendid job with locations in Vienna on *The Third Man*, his first assistant director Guy Hamilton, and his lighting cameraman John Wilcox.

In Singapore, Reed put up at Raffles and, wearing a khaki suit and dark glasses, threw out his net for Aissa, hoping that among the Malay community he might find the right girl. He was mindful of Conrad's specification, that Aissa should be 'startlingly beautiful – deeply, savagely beautiful with a suggestion of underlying passion – a beauty that comes from strength of character, great dignity and a proud and graceful carriage.' Soon after his arrival in Singapore, Reed was sitting in a café and saw a woman he thought was exactly what he was looking for. He approached her and she, perhaps misunderstanding his advance, told him that she was not interested in becoming a film star. As Freud might have said, sometimes a fountain pen is only a fountain pen; and sometimes a film director promising to make an attractive girl a film star is just that. Reed auditioned a long queue of models, hostesses, air stewardesses, dancers, typists, even actresses, but found no one who matched his imagined Aissa.

While in Singapore Reed decided to film some background footage. He recruited twelve members of the Singapore Repertory Club, hired five junks and a collection of extras and began shooting from the back of a truck. Filming went so well that soon he had thousands of feet of film, about three hours of material, which he sent back to Korda in London for processing. In Borneo he shot similar background material, including all of the scenes with the little boy who tags along in a canoe after Willems. Trevor Howard was never to meet the child who followed him around in the film; like Prince Philip and the cockney boys, they met only in the editing room. Reed also discovered that the Korean War, which was three thousand miles away, was to affect his shooting plans. Although the war would be nowhere near the locations he had planned in Indonesia, he found that insurance companies considered such a costly venture so close to the action to be a bad risk. He was, instead, forced to base his extended foreign location work in Ceylon, now Sri Lanka.

On his return to Britain Reed found that he had more problems. The background shooting which he had completed was deemed by the cinema technicians' union, the ACT, to infringe their agreements. They claimed that there should be a minimum number of crew, whereas Wilcox had merely stood up with a camera mounted on his shoulder, and that contracts should have been arranged in London before any shooting took place. Reed swallowed his anger. He had never been a member of the union and held the view that camera and studio crews were far too large to be effective and that the cost of them was slowly killing the British film industry. He said as much whenever asked, and his views had been widely reported in the technical press. Just as shooting was beginning on a large-budget film was not the time, however, to take a stand about the issue. Korda's advice was to keep quiet and allow him to fix a retrospective deal with the union.

Reed finally found his Aissa through a friend in Paris, who recommended the twenty-two-year-old daughter of an Algerian Arab businessman and his French wife. Her screen name was to be Kerima, although everyone who worked on *Outcast* called her Miriam. She had never acted before and intended becoming a medical student when the film was finished. The filming was an amusing diversion for her, a means of earning enough money to pay for her studies and create a small nest-egg. She spoke no English, which did not matter, for in the film she had no lines at all. She merely needed to disturb Trevor Howard with her sultry beauty and, at one stage, to give him an extended kiss. She turned out to be nobody's fool, and refused to condone the sexual gossip and innuendo which the studio publicity machine manufactured to give her screen presence some titillating mystery.

Filming began in Ceylon in November 1950 and lasted two months. Reed took with him for the first time the film editor Bert Bates, a no-nonsense cockney character with whom he forged a close and amiable working friendship which lasted the rest of his career. Bates could say things to Reed which others, including the assistant directors, could only think. Whereas Bates was all for quick decisions and getting on with it, Reed constantly asked the opinion of others. At this stage of his career he kept his costs low by ensuring that, according to Bates, each scene used in the final footage took an average of only two takes; an almost miraculous number compared to the industry average of more than ten. Reed was as generous with Bates as he was with actors, saying: 'I believe it is essential that the director and the editor should work closely together right through the picture – and I like working with the same editor. You get used to working together – otherwise you're only beginning to know each other at the end of the picture.'

Vincent Korda had gone ahead to Ceylon to build the sets, including the native village on stilts at the riverside village of Hanwella, employing two hundred workmen and two elephants, which were needed to drive the bamboo poles into the ground under the water. There was also shooting to be done in Colombo Harbour and at Kandy. All of the cast and crew, with the exception of Ralph Richardson, who arrived a little later, settled themselves in.

As on all foreign locations, there were mishaps, misunderstandings and small disasters. The local hired men would not work on the sets until a priest had blessed the project. One morning Reed woke to discover that one of the precarious stilt houses had been washed away by a flood from the mountains. At Anaradapurra, in the far north of the island, the cast and crew were kept awake night after night by the barking of dogs. Reed was a devoted animal-lover, but the noise of the dogs was too much. He summoned Leigh Aman, the production manager, to do something about the noise. Aman went out the next day, bought the dogs from their owners and had them shot, to Reed's anger when he heard of this chillingly permanent solution to his insomnia.

Trevor Howard had been brought up in Ceylon, where his father was an agent for Lloyd's insurance, and his father's old office found its way into the film's final footage. During a gap in filming he was invited to give the prizes at his old school at Haddon Hill, Nuwara Eliya. Christmas was spent on location and Christmas lunch in the sweltering heat was concluded by an impromptu speech from Ralph Richardson.

The unit returned to Shepperton for eight weeks of studio filming, and Reed adopted the fast shooting system he had perfected on *The Third Man*, working on two sets simultaneously; while he was shooting on one, the other was being lit and prepared. His method was to have two rehearsals of the shot, then two takes, then to cover the scene in a close-up.

Vincent Korda had flown planeloads of artefacts from Ceylon and Borneo to maintain authenticity and continuity. The most difficult scene was solved partly by Reed's inventiveness. Robert Morley as Almayer is hoisted up in a hammock and swung over a fire. Reed employed the Kirby Flying Ballet, the experts in stage flying identified with the annual *Peter Pan* pantomime on the London stage, to swing Morley and F. E. Moore, the cameraman, across the set. There was one moment of high drama when Moore became caught in the rigging with the fire below licking the hammock, though he escaped with a little singeing of his bottom. The fire scene alone took four days to shoot. By June 1951 all filming was complete and British release was scheduled for January 1952.

Although the shooting had gone smoothly and efficiently,

there was something odd about the film. Wendy Hiller had sensed it and regretted not mentioning it to anyone earlier. The filming did not appear to be holding Reed's full attention. 'Of course, Trevor was too fond of Carol to question him. We should all have questioned him,' she said. In his preface to the 1919 edition of *An Outcast of the Islands*, Joseph Conrad had written: 'The mere scenery got a great hold on me as I went on, perhaps because (I may as well confess that) the story itself was never very near my heart. It engaged my imagination much more than my affection.' From the finished film, it appeared that the story had never been very near to Reed's heart either.

Reed was to suffer too from the heightened expectations which *The Third Man* had aroused in the public and the critics, who gave *Outcast* a very lukewarm reception. His problem was expressed by Fred Majdalany in the *Daily Mail*: 'The difficulty of poor Carol Reed is that he has been the best English film-maker for so long. It is a harsh responsibility. He has himself created the dazzling standards by which he must be judged. A new Carol Reed film is automatically a special occasion. He cannot afford the luxury of being merely good. He is doomed to be outstanding. His past sorceries have taught us to take this for granted. In the circumstances, therefore, it is necessary to go almost out of one's way to record the view that Mr Reed's new picture, *Outcast of the Islands*, is a profound disappointment.'

The *Manchester Guardian* touched on a point which others, too, would articulate. 'Everything, in short, about this film is excellent except the heart of its matter. Its story is one which should arouse terror and pity; it fails to do so. The reason for that may be, in part, that Mr Reed, in spite of his brilliant gifts as a film-maker (or because of those gifts) is more technician than artist.' It was a cruel judgement, but one which many of Reed's film-making col-leagues shared, and which would plague Reed for the rest of his life. Asked what Reed was like as a film-maker, Michael Powell, speaking a dozen years after Reed was dead, said: 'A watch-maker. He was technically perfect, but displayed no passion at all.' When *Outcast* was released in the United States in May 1952, this lack of passion was commented upon. *Newsweek* thought that 'Carol Reed exhibits people charged with emotion but the camera views them with an effect of aloof detachment; it seldom enters into the scene dramatically in a way to get feelings out.'

More technician than artist and incapable of passion. Having made a trio of brilliant films, Reed had stumbled. At the top of his profession and with sound financial backing, he had attempted a subject beyond his grasp. From this point on, he would never recover the freshness of his films up to and including *The Third Man*. *An Outcast of the Islands* hinted that, good as Reed was as a technician, he had very little to say. Given a subject which Conrad had laden with profound questions about civilisation itself, Reed had no views to express. His inability to stretch himself and break out of the confines of his screenwriter's imagination meant that those who had invested so much in supporting him as 'Britain's leading film-maker' would quickly become disillusioned with him. After *The Third Man*, Reed seemed destined to make a succession of first-class films of great originality; after *Outcast*, it appeared that such ambition was beyond his reach.

For all the harsh reception which *Outcast* received from the critics, Reed could take some comfort in the fact that, in Britain, at least, the film brought queues of eager cinemagoers outside the Plaza Cinema in Regent Street. *An Outcast of the Islands* was a natural choice for the annual Royal Film Show, for it was a British film with a British director and a large British cast. The organisers of the event, however, always anxious not to offend the royal family, believed that the story was not suitable and that the notorious lingering kiss between Trevor Howard and Kerima was altogether too steamy. Princess Elizabeth thought differently, and in October 1951 asked that she be given a private screening. The private cinema in Alexander Korda's sumptuous offices in Piccadilly was often used by the royal family, because it was very close to Buckingham Palace and because the house was familiar; it was next door to the pre-war home of George VI and his family in the years before Edward VIII's abdication thrust the crown upon him.

In June 1952, the new queen awarded her first honours, on the recommendations of the prime minister, Winston Churchill. Among them was Sir Carol Reed, the son of an acting knight and the first British film director to be knighted for his craft. Writing in *Harper's Bazaar*, Kenneth Tynan described how Reed looked at the time of his knighthood: 'In appearance he is a tall, restless, butcher-looking man, with a large blunt nose; his face, amiably expressive after the manner of some Alsatian dogs, is crowned by leathery hair. He might be an Arnold Bennett character. He both looks and sounds notably unravaged by the toils of his craft: he will tell you that he has no ulcers, but simply indigestion. His aspect, a raw pink, glows with energy, a rapacious, upstart energy.'

The knighthood was popular among the British film community, even if some, like Michael Powell, thought it a typical establishment honour for one so close to Korda and his friend Churchill. The news brought Reed an avalanche of congratulatory telegrams. Laurence Olivier wrote cryptically: 'Go away my good man, oh I beg your pardon sir!' Margot Fonteyn was 'delighted to read of your honour which is so well deserved.' Brendan Bracken wrote: 'Dear Sir, Yours sincerely.' There were notes from Iris Tree, Celia Johnson, Basil Wright, Peggy Ashcroft, Diana Cooper, Robert Morley, J. Arthur Rank, Felix Aylmer, Graham Greene, Sybil Thorndike, Michael Balcon, Paul Rotha and Trevor Howard.

And there were touching messages from Reed's past. Jack Bligh, a friend from his days as an actor at the Lyceum during the twenties, reminded Reed of how he and his friend John Turnbull had scoffed at his suggestion that the cinema was the entertainment of the future: 'Well, time has proved that you were very right.' Congratulations also came from Alfred E. Johnson, who owned a sweetshop in Canterbury: 'No doubt you have passed it a hundred times and probably, too, have been in it when you were at the King's School.'

Diana Wynyard also wrote. After Carol and Pempie married she had joined the Shakespeare Memorial Theatre Company in Stratford for two seasons and travelled in Australia before returning to the West End. In 1951 she married Tibor Csato, relieving Carol of any financial obligations to her. But Diana and her husband were obliged to sell the house in the country she had bought with Carol, The Oyster House, to raise some capital. She wrote: 'Darling Carol, I am so glad about your honour because I know how pleased and happy it will make you underneath the giggles and laughing it off.' Mingled with her generosity was some sadness: 'I was rather upset that you should have asked after your share of the Oyster House when sold. You really must have forgotten me if you had any doubts that I would send it to you at once. There is no sign of a buyer yet and it is all rather a sweat and trouble, but I must sell it because it is too far off and is an endless responsibility, expense and harassment. I want to use some of the money when it's sold to have lovely holidays which otherwise we cannot afford in spite of both working idiotically hard. Blessings on you dear Carol, how pleased your mother must be. I thought of her at once. Love Diana.'

May Reed was indeed proud of her son and had followed his career with interest. Reed looked after his mother's welfare as she grew into old age and sent his secretary Dorli Percival each week to visit her house in Wimbledon crammed with memorabilia of Tree and her children. May was still a handsome woman, with well-groomed white hair and tall and statuesque despite her age. She treated Dorli with charm and courtesy, always asking about Carol and the other members of the family.

Reed saw very little of his brothers, Robin, Peter and Guy, and his sister Judy, who had married a businessman, Norman D'Arcy. And he saw nothing of Claude Beerbohm, although he made provision for his welfare. Claude's drinking problems grew worse and worse until he became a fantasist, too ill to run his own life. Carol paid for him to be lodged in a home in Brighton and sent him books in a vain attempt to rehabilitate him.

Carol Reed's knighthood was the high point of his life, and he was never happier than at this time. He had everything he wanted: success as a film-maker and an apparently endless demand for his talents, but above all a happy home life. With Pempie's help he had managed to recapture something of the warmth of his own childhood in Daisyfield.

Reed suffered from a vice which afflicts many fathers who leave it late to have children; he spoiled them. He had long been used to buying off Tracy, bundling her off with Nanny Rocher so he could be alone with Pempie at a time when he was, in principle at least, still married to Diana. And he was devoted to his son Max, showering him with gifts and affection. Max had been born without a right hand, and for Reed this was a tragedy, a spectre which stalked all the Beerbohms for it was lodged in the genes. His own brother Robin had a similar deformity. Max's hand became the subject of long and anguished discussions between Carol and Pempie which eventually concentrated upon the awkward decision of whether to send him away to school, where Carol believed he would be mercilessly ragged for his imperfection, and Pempie's belief that the practicalities of boarding-school life would ensure that Max came to ignore his affliction. Pempie won the argument, and Max was eventually sent to Stowe.

Carol was passionately fond of Max. The affection shines out of a tape recording made when he was five. Carol asked such philosophical questions as 'Who is God?' in order to explore his son's infant views, and his love for the boy is obvious. Carol showed his affections to everyone, men as well as women, in a bold, physical way which was a rare departure from the English reserve he usually displayed. But he felt a special closeness for Max, and cuddled and petted him to such an extent that once, on a walk from Chelsea across the Albert Bridge to Battersea Park, his paternal hugging attracted the attention of the police.

He liked children and would recruit the offspring of Judy Campbell, now married to John Birkin, Pempie's sister Angie Lacock, Vincent Korda and the Harrison family who lived next door. Battersea Park was Carol's favourite place to take children for a walk, for there was a permanent funfair, a remnant of the 1951 Festival of Britain, which was similar to the Prater in Vienna, where Harry Lime rode on the ferris-wheel.

Some visitors to the Reeds' home considered that he spoiled Tracy and Max. In the household Pempie had arranged Carol had very few daily responsibilities of any sort, and was not expected to look after the children, who were mostly taken care of by the nurse. Carol was temperamentally unsuited to the petty chores and strict routines that a well-ordered childhood demands, but film-making would have made such tasks impossible anyway. When he was working he barely saw the children at all, living elsewhere while on location and working around the clock when in the studio or editing. It was hardly surprising that when living at home in the periods between films Carol indulged his children.

Superficially, many aspects of the Reeds' family life were typical of others of their social standing. Pempie looked after the house and children, enjoying a little photography and charity work while Carol went out to earn the family's income. But

Carol was hardly a conventional father. He was forever disrupting Pempie's order and demanding outings or surprise foreign trips. He treated his children as equals, rarely attempting to impose a father's authority upon them. Tracy's only memory of a reprimand was of one evening when she was a teenager, and was out so late that Pempie, who usually went early to bed, had stayed up waiting for her into the early hours. Even then, although his words were cross, Carol merely appealed to Tracy not to upset her mother so.

There was little for Carol to do about the house, as Pempie had taken her housekeeper from Albert Mansions, Rose Barbieri, to Chelsea, and later a Mrs Hodder would also help with cleaning. There was a maid, a Hungarian woman called Veronica, who was one of the few who could keep Carol in order when he started disrupting the smooth running of the house. She usually turned him out to walk up the King's Road, where he would happily waste a few hours observing people. An odd-job man called Walker doubled as a chauffeur.

Carol was always passionate about cars, and would proudly have his photograph taken with the latest acquisition. Motoring for Carol was hardly a family pursuit, however, as he drove badly and erratically. When driving abroad in the early 1960s he would progress very slowly, refusing to stop for long and preferring to sleep in the car, a practice which Pempie disliked so much that she made alternative arrangements for herself and the children to go by plane. On a trip to Venice one year, Carol persuaded Dorli Percival to travel with him, which she did only on condition that they would stop for meals and stay in hotels en route.

When they owned a flat in Cannes, sited at Carol's insistence not amid the olive groves and pines of the countryside but in the middle of the town, looking out onto the busy harbour, Carol was obliged to drive to and from the south of France alone, although he could speak no French. On one journey, always on the look-out for company, he picked up a hitch-hiker heading for Toulon. The stranger fell asleep, waking now and then to ask, 'Toulon?' to which Carol would reply, 'No, not too long.' The misunderstanding took the passenger many miles out of his way. Carol's solution was typical; he drove to the nearest railway station and bought his passenger a ticket to Toulon.

Reed's working life after *An Outcast of the Islands* was some-what confused. The delay between choosing the subject of a film, its long and intricate casting and preparation, the shoot-ing and editing, then, finally, the film's release can disguise the true chronology of a film-maker's life. In October 1951 Reed accompanied Alexander Korda to New York to tie up the American distribution deal for *Outcast* and other Korda films. He had on his mind something which was referred to merely as 'The Tangiers Film'.

The following month, Reed and Pempie flew to Germany. He had become intrigued with the possibility of making a film about the desolation of Berlin, perhaps a cold-war thriller like *The Third Man*, but as always he was wary of repeating himself. The option of working again with Greene passed. In January 1952 it was announced that Greene was setting off for Holly-wood to write a screenplay of his new novel, *The End of the Affair*. The same month, *Outcast* was released, and its hostile critical reception was wounding for Reed.

Even at the height of the war, when there was little point in planning for the future, Reed had continued to note down a steady stream of plot ideas, just as Edgar Wallace had logged his ideas for thriller plots. When he had lived as a bachelor in his flat at 20 Grosvenor Gardens, Reed had kept a common-place book in which to jot down, in his bold but barely legible pencil script, notional films which would never be made. On 2 January 1941, he had written: 'News Chronicle Reporter with other Press men going to "Somewhere in England" misses train with others – no story – at press Club gets friend to get copy – writes it up its easy – headings and leader article – "Never again shall the same Mistakes be made as in 1914". Owner of Newspaper was at that time in Charge of Production.' On 14 February he wrote: 'Man returning on leave – booring [*sic*] wife knows it all – explaining the whole war away – not interested in him at all.' There were a series of detailed jottings, including descriptions of specific shots of men in bunks and what they each have in their wallets, for a film about the tour of duty of sailors depth-charging for German submarines which would end: 'Man looks at notice, turns to others – this evening at the movies there is Clark Gable in "Living Dangerously", should be exciting.'

In fact, apart from *No Parking* in 1938, Reed was never to have any of his own ideas filmed. The quick sketches in his notebook are seldom more than movie clichés, like this piece of dialogue: 'A: How do you do. B: How do you do. A: Darling, I love you. B: I love you too. A: John, I remember when we first met.' A detailed shooting script describes a similarly mundane camera rake across a busy main street on the day the circus arrives in town, with a series of visual cameos of children being sold patent medicine by a hawker, a strong man breaking chairs, a carousel turning – a composite of opening shots from many American films of the thirties.

In later years Reed made more serious attempts at writing screenplays himself. They included: 'The Gander Story', written in 1950; 'Honor [*sic*] Among Thieves'; 'Judy and Peter', which progressed no further than handwritten notes; and 'The Old Bags'.

Reed spent the spring of 1952 working on a treatment of his own, which he had come to call by a number of titles: 'The Tangiers Story', 'The Man Who Was' – the same title as a play his father had appeared in – and 'The Three Knives'. It was set in a world of intrigue similar to that of *The Third Man*, among a group of spies and amoral businessmen who discover that they share many of the same assumptions about life. In the weeks before the Allied North African landings, two British agents travel to Tangier to murder Skouras, a rich and powerful hotelier who is the city's counter-espionage chief. They poison him with cyanide, dump his body and presume him to be dead. One of the spies is killed. Many years later, one of the agents returns to the North African coast and joins the crew of a rich man's yacht, only to discover that the man is none other than the spymaster he thought he had murdered. They eventually confront each other and admit mutual admiration for each other's skills in their shared black trade. The former agent joins Skouras as a bodyguard, then things turn very nasty for all concerned.

Reed made a number of attempts at bringing the story to life, but he realised that he was incapable of writing convincing dialogue. Although the story is plainly derivative of many others set in the fictional world of honourable, bored spies and crooks with uneasy consciences, this did not trouble Reed. He knew he was incapable of giving a screenplay the gift of life and that he needed a writing partner. Greene was unavailable and in any case would not be interested in fleshing out Reed's story. A surrogate Greene was therefore called for. There was one brilliant British novelist who was capable of such work, and who was known to be prepared to take on any semi-respectable task as long as the money was right: Evelyn Waugh.

Waugh was a friend of Greene's and a great admirer of the Reed-Greene collaborations. He was on the panel of the *Daily Express* film awards in September 1948 and had attended the press showing of *The Fallen Idol*, which he described in his diary as 'clever and funny and original'. In May 1952, Waugh wrote to A. D. Peters, his literary agent: 'I have seen Carol Reed and he has sent me a treatment of a story named "The Man Who Was". I have told him on the telephone that it needs not only dialogue, but, in my opinion, many alterations of plot. He seemed agreeable to this, but is by no means certain of doing this film at all. I suggested that I should write a new treatment, of about the length of the present one, and that you should fix a price for this. He said he would consult Korda. In view of the vagueness of his plans and the probability that my treatment will not prove the prelude to more lucrative employment, I think we should ask a substantial sum.'

Waugh soon became sceptical about the whole enterprise, writing to Peters: 'C. Reed keeps coming here in a motor car. I think he is disposed to employ me. All he wants really is a listener. I will listen for £250 a week but I think it essential to have a contract signed. He is to consult Sir Alexander [Korda] on Tuesday and give an answer by noon Wednesday. Will you get in touch with Korda's paymaster on Wednesday morning and let me know by telegram when the contract is signed?' He continued: 'Two points about contract. 1) Full expenses to, from and in London. 2) No use of my name in publicity or "credits" without my authorisation. This is not a necessary condition but a desirable one. I have explained it to C. Reed and he agrees. Korda may not. The point is *not* that I shall be ashamed of the association, but that the film may well turn out in the end, not to be *my* film at all, and I would not like to give my name to a film, however good, that was not my own work. I am perfectly willing to subordinate my taste to my employers' work and work under their rules, but I shall prefer, if it can be arranged, that they accept sole responsibility.'

On 13 May A. D. Peters wrote to Waugh, having spoken to Reed and Bill O'Bryen of Korda's London Films, who confirmed that they were definitely going ahead with the film. Reed had said that it was Waugh's idea to write a complete new treatment, which would take about a week. The agent suggested that Reed would probably be satisfied with a full story outline, but without dialogue and much shorter than a full treatment. Reed wished to go to Tangier with Waugh in two or three weeks if it was decided to go ahead with the treatment. A fee of £250 a week had been agreed in principle, and at least seven weeks' work were expected of Waugh, although 'the period would turn out to be quite a bit more because Reed usually takes a very long time to prepare his scripts.' Peters strongly recommended that Waugh accept the work, as 'all expenses abroad would be paid and I think that the style of living would be luxurious. Reed is the white-headed boy at London Films and does pretty well what he likes.' The deal was signed with London Films the same day.

The following week Waugh wrote to his agent saying that he had delivered 'a fairly full treatment' and had been commissioned to write a full screenplay. However, Waugh was to be deprived of his trip to Tangier, as Reed decided that the script work should take place under his supervision at Brighton, as he had done with Greene. Waugh set to his task with some keenness, in fact he was far too enthusiastic for his agent's liking. 'Pleased work goes well,' he wrote, 'not too pleased it goes briskly. You are guaranteed min. of seven weeks; if longer, so much the better.'

In Waugh's hands, the screenplay instantly took life. The two British spies became bookend characters like the Naunton and Wayne duo from *The Lady Vanishes* and *Night Train to Munich*, and Skouras something like Sidney Greenstreet in *The Maltese Falcon*. The screenplay went through a number of revisions and began to take proper shape. By July, Waugh believed he had come to the end of his work for the time being. He betrayed his feelings about the screenplay to his agent. 'The film as it stands is very silly – the plot all Reed, quite unintelligible and implausible. I don't want my name associated with it. I don't want to hurt Reed's feelings by being snooty. I haven't told him explicitly how bad I think the film. Perhaps the best thing will be to say that they mustn't use my name until I have seen the finished production. They are bound to make radical changes, I think, and those will excuse me.'

Although Waugh was prepared to continue work, writing a full shooting script, the project ran into the sand at London Films. Perhaps Korda, too, thought the plot 'unintelligible and implausible'; perhaps, too, Korda vetoed having anything further to do with Waugh following an awkward incident at the Reeds' home at 213 King's Road.

It was a rare thing for the Reeds to entertain formally for dinner. Carol's idea of entertaining was to bump into people in the King's Road and bring them home for an impromptu meal of some sort, much to Pempie's annoyance. What was even more annoying to her was that when she arranged a lunch party, Carol would, as like as not, stay for the drinks before lunch, then claim he was due at an important meeting and leave the house. Pempie would be furious, knowing full well that he would only be going to the Six Bells public house around the corner. Reed was also incapable of thinking ahead. When they were invited for dinner, he would ask why they could not go right away. 'I would like to go now. How can they know they'll want to see us next week? And how can we be sure that we'll want to see them?'

He found it difficult to endure the small-talk and chat associated with entertaining and preferred the company of friends he knew well. Although he enjoyed being with film people while working with them, he had little interest in them between films. He did remain friends with Vincent Korda, who lived in Chelsea with his second wife Leila, and with Alex Korda's friend Moura Budberg. Moura was constantly looking for stories for Reed to make into films and would coax him out to events she thought he would enjoy. Otherwise his friends included Pempie's cousin John Birkin and Judy, who lived nearby, Angie and Bob Lacock and the Harrisons next door. He also befriended Pempie's cousin Bindy Lambton, and would go with her to nightclubs, simply to watch the people and take in the atmosphere. Pempie hated nightclubs and the drinking associated with them, and stayed at home. She also had an independent life. She had a much wider selection of friends than Carol and would often go out alone, leaving Carol to his own devices.

Although he could be charming, Reed was a most awkward conversationalist, uninterested in anything unless it was to do with films, even among some of his closest friends. Peter Ustinov, who lived next door to the Reeds in the King's Road for a number of years during the fifties, gave up trying to talk to him about anything except story ideas. 'Carol lives in a world of film,' he explained. 'To him, films are reality and all the rest is shadow show. He is the kind of man who breaks up a conversation by asking "Who is Mendes-France?" or "What is a cold war?"' While shooting a film Reed was open, approachable and full of enthusiasm; between films he became chronically shy and reclusive.

He did make an effort at social entertaining in an attempt to make his 'Tangiers Story' a success by properly introducing Waugh to Alex Korda and Pempie. Waugh had met Korda before, in 1936, when, much as Greene had been summoned to his studio, Waugh was sent for and asked whether he would like to write a screenplay of a story called 'Lovelies from America' about chorus girls. Waugh agreed and delivered a script, which Korda said was good, though the film was never made. The two had subsequently met over lunch at Korda's, when Waugh found him 'intelligent and reasonable'. Around the Reeds' table, however, Waugh was thoroughly objectionable to Korda, making pointedly offensive, largely anti-semitic remarks. Pempie Reed was angry and forbade his return to the house. Waugh claimed to Reed later that he was indignant that Korda should offend Pempie by bringing his mistress to the table. Korda had divorced his second wife, Merle Oberon, in 1945 and had taken Alexandra Boycun, a singer with whom he had recently fallen in love, to the Reeds'. They were married the following year. Waugh's behaviour was plainly inexcusable and may well have ensured that 'The Tangiers Story' was shelved for good.

Reed looked elsewhere for a good story. By November 1952 he announced that he would be making a film set among the ruins of Berlin and dealing with the trade in human lives between the two sides of the Iron Curtain. The film was plainly to be close to *The Third Man* in subject and tone, but Reed hoped that he would be able to overcome the inevitable comparisons by highlighting the story's topicality. There was little doubt that in 1953 Berlin was an ideal place to locate a mystery thriller. The city had become the focus for the battle between the competing post-war political ideologies ever since the Russians had tried to cut off the German capital from Western influence in 1948. And 1953 was an important year for the city, as it saw the death of Stalin and a workers' revolt in East Berlin which was put down by Russian troops and tanks.

Reed had read Lothar Schuler's novel *Susanne in Berlin*, set in the city and, in buying the rights, discovered that the author was in fact Walter Ebert, working under a *nom de plume*. Ebert was unavailable to write a screenplay from his novel, so Reed hired Harry Kurnitz, an American screenwriter with a broad range who had written some of the early 'Thin Man' comedy thrillers. Many of David O. Selznick's objections to *The Third Man* had been based on his belief that the screenplay made little sense to Americans and that it was too subtle and too slow. If the intention in hiring Kurnitz was to produce a slick comedy thriller with sharp American dialogue, it did not work. The script was the first of a number of catastrophes which would plague what was to become *The Man Between*. The experience of the film was to leave Reed exhausted, bewildered and, for the first time in his career, uncertain of his talents.

The close relationship between director and screenwriter which Reed had enjoyed with Greene did not exist with Kurnitz. The first draft of the screenplay was sloppy and insensitive and needed some urgent revisions. Reed had not been able to work closely with Kurnitz as he had with Greene, and the American had produced a wordy script, without a trace of humour, which was poor on characterisation and riddled with movie clichés. What was worse, Kurnitz was unavailable for the endless bouts of revision which Reed felt the screenplay needed. Reluctantly, and pressurised by Korda and the urgency of the film's timetable, Reed had to go ahead with the casting and the location shooting before the script was amended to his satisfaction. For the first time he began filming without an impeccably prepared shooting script.

'The Berlin Story' concerned the visit to Berlin of an English girl, Susanne, to see her brother Martin, a British officer in the occupying force whose job it was to administer the arrival in West Berlin of refugees from the East. Martin is married to a German woman, Bettina, whose anxious demeanour seems related to the arrival in the West of Ivo Kern, a spiv from East Berlin.

To play the key part of Ivo, Reed sought out James Mason, who since *Odd Man Out* had played more than a dozen Hollywood screen roles. His best-known performance, perhaps, was as Rommel in *The Desert Fox* (1951) and *The Desert Rats* (released in 1953), and Reed believed his association in the public mind with the Nazi general would act in the film's favour. He sent the script to Mason, apologising for its inadequacy but promising to make amendments. Mason agreed that it was 'somewhat dry and humourless', but said he would be delighted to work with Reed again. 'A director like Reed can make bad actors seem good and a good one even better,' he said later.

The casting of Susanne was equally important. In his regular journeys to the West End theatres, looking for ideas for film subjects and casting, Reed had seen Claire Bloom in *Ring Round the Moon* and had marked her out as a likely heroine for a future film. Bloom's appearance in Charles Chaplin's *Limelight*, still to be released, gave her added box-office appeal, which was particularly important to Korda.

As for the German parts, Korda had stressed to Reed through Bill O'Bryen that the film would only earn money in Europe if everything from casting to location work was authentic. Local German actors were therefore to be used wherever possible. To reduce costs, German parts needed for studio work at Shepperton should be given to German actors living in London. Assuming that Mason could be considered an honorary German for his performances as Rommel, which many British and Americans had considered too sympathetic, the only principal part which needed to be played by a German was that of Bettina. Reed chose Hildegarde Neff, who, after a stage career in Germany, had become an American citizen and made half a dozen English-language films. Hilde Sessak was cast as a prostitute; Albert Waescher as the sinister Communist police chief Haladar; and Dieter Krause was to play the boy on the bicycle who follows Ivo around the city, much as Trevor Howard was shadowed by a native boy during *An Outcast of the Islands*.

Both Mason and Bloom were in great demand and therefore very expensive, and their time in Berlin would be strictly limited. Reed needed Mason for five weeks in Berlin and a further nine weeks in the studio. Mason confused matters by declaring that he was not prepared to fly and therefore had to make the journey to Berlin overland. This was not only costly in time but was severely impractical, given the current high tension between East and West. Mason would have to travel by military train across Russian-occupied Germany, requiring British Foreign Office, American State Department and Soviet permission, which would take a great deal of time and patience to obtain. Korda cabled Mason's agent that 'even if he gets permission in Washington to travel by road, we refuse every responsibility for his safe arrival in Berlin as our contract starts only on the day he reports for work in Berlin.' After a great deal of trans-Atlantic haggling, Mason finally agreed to fly to Berlin, but the arrangements had already caused havoc to Reed's schedule.

Reed decided to begin shooting on what had by then been retitled 'Dangerous Holiday' early in 1953 without Mason, using a double for scenes in which Mason should appear. He was based at the Am Zoo hotel on the Kurfürstendamm, and discovered to his horror that his earlier trips to discover locations had been overtaken by events as the Western sector of the city was rapidly being rebuilt. Although the Eastern sector remained in ruins, the Soviet authorities there had taken exception to the implication in *The Third Man* that the Russians were prepared to harbour a criminal like Harry Lime and had therefore forbidden Reed from filming in their sector of the city. Reed had to settle for working on bombsites as close to the Russian zone as possible, where he could use the East Berlin ruins as a background. His decision to work close to the Russian zone in streets like Moritzplatz was not merely to ensure authenticity. 'First, I wanted the ruins, which are mainly in the Russian zone,' he explained. 'Secondly, I hoped to convey something that is not visual, the jittery feeling that pervades the area. I wanted our actors to feel it. They did.'

To reproduce the Eastern zone in the West he erected enormous portraits of Stalin and had actors dressed as East German policemen, which caused inevitable and often comic confusion among the West Berliners. In an attempt to capture as much of the fast-disappearing ruins as possible, Reed was obliged to work around the clock, using two crews back to back and directing both, one after the other, at twenty-hour stretches. By day, dressed in a flowing camelhair coat and scarf, he used a German crew led by the lighting cameraman Hans Schneeberger, who, with Gunther Rittau, had photographed Josef von Sternberg's *The Blue Angel* in 1930. At night, wearing a duffle coat, a Commando cap and huge Royal Air Force boots, he worked with a British crew led by the lighting cameraman Desmond Dickinson, who had given such power to the dark photography of Laurence Olivier's *Hamlet*. As in *The Third Man*, the West Berlin fire brigade hosed down the streets to make them gleam in the spotlit darkness. Reed filmed in as many Berlin landmarks as possible, including the Resi Restaurant, where customers could talk to each other on telephones linking the tables, and the Funk Tower Sports Arena, one of the city's eighty-five camps for refugees from the East.

On 18 February Mason arrived in Berlin, followed a week later by Claire Bloom. By this time Reed was haggard, harassed and tired. Mason recorded in his diary that Reed was 'glittering with enthusiasm and benzedrine', which he was taking in large quantities to stay awake. A side-effect of the drug was that he was not eating enough. It was hardly surprising that Reed confided to Mason that 'making a film is like going down a mine for eight weeks.'

Reed was under intense financial pressure. As the producer as well as the director, he had made a contract with London Films but was not an employee of them. They had an interest in the film, and were anxious that he should not go over budget because of difficulties with the German authorities. Korda wrote stressing that the responsibility to finish within budget was Reed's, and that he was not being suitably economical. He cabled Reed: 'To shoot night after night extreme long shots requiring a large organisation not right', and told him it would make very little difference to the final picture. He demanded that Reed start drastic economies immediately and finish in the shortest possible time. As usual, Reed was sending back the early shots to Korda in London for examination. Korda cabled Reed on 27 February that they were 'excellent impressive rushes', adding the warning: 'greatest worry that according all our calculations your money will finish about 7 March and we are completely unable get new allocation from German Government'.

Mason's late arrival had made life difficult for Reed, but what made it impossible were the demands from Korda's accountants to trim his budget. Reed tried to avoid direct contact with London and even stopped taking Korda's calls. Korda was angry and upset and sent a plaintive cable on 28 February: 'Trying phoning you whole week. As left messages cannot regard but personal discourtesy your not calling back. Studio complains now they have no precise info as to order in which you want your sets built.' He concluded that detailed instructions about the building of the sets were needed and that 'Failing give these immediately any delay in studios your sole responsibility.' By the beginning of March, with Reed already shooting with a full cast and crew on locations in Berlin, the London office began to put the pressure on, cabling him that 'Preliminary examination detailed budget based on [Hugh] Perceval's breakdown and company's past record indicate proposed shooting schedule v. seriously underestimated. Consider it essential full discussion with you earliest convenience. Can you return London w/end for meeting Monday morning? Regret production seems impossible.'

Reed returned for a major row with Korda's money people, shifting the blame back onto them for mistakes in the budget estimates and errors in getting the key members of the cast to Berlin on time. Claire Bloom was a week late and Mason was three days late, even though he had flown. Reed was blamed for overshooting the budget 'due to your method of working and the complicated shots'. The problem was Reed's insistence that he direct all of the shooting himself, instead of filming with a second unit under an assistant director. The labour costs had almost doubled as the crew claimed overtime payments. To offset the difficulties of obtaining more German currency, the British crew were paid in sterling.

In April, Reed arrived home two weeks ahead of schedule to begin work in the studio. His problems now were not merely financial. Others were caused by the poor quality of Kurnitz's script, which had become increasingly evident in Germany. Kurnitz had been on hand to help with script changes in Berlin, but when Reed returned to London he began travelling in Europe, from Germany to Italy to France to Britain, and his efforts at revising the script became hasty and slipshod. His attitude was unhelpful and he did not appear to understand the seriousness of the screenplay's shortcomings.

Reed decided to take advice on Kurnitz's work from Graham Greene, who agreed to look at the screenplay. He sent six pages of notes which began: 'A general criticism I have of the first 50 scenes is that I have no idea yet what the story is about. Perhaps this would not matter, if the events were startling and mysterious enough, but they are neither startling nor very mysterious.' Some paragraphs later he writes: 'Now I have reached Scene 68 and I have no idea of what the story is about.' By scene 96, he thought: 'The whole business of spying by means of one bicycle ridden by a boy seems to be too childish and fantastic. So far I get no sense of reality whatever out of the script.' He concluded: 'I am afraid this isn't the case simply for new dialogue. It seems to me that the whole story is meaningless and flat without a living character in it. A thriller about Europe today has surely got to have some significance about it and not simply end in long exciting chases . . . I am afraid that to me the whole film is meaningless.'

Reed, in despair, looked around for another writer and used Bill O'Bryen from Korda's office to hire Janet Green, a young British playwright, to start work on the screenplay immediately. Green had written mystery thrillers, including *Murder Mistaken*, for the London stage and had co-written with Eric Ambler a film, *The Clouded Yellow*, which was greatly influenced by Hitchcock. Her first reaction to the screenplay was one of hardly concealed horror, and she shared Reed's belief that it was unuseable in its present form. She read it overnight and wrote an assessment of the work which needed to be done.

She praised the main thrust of the story and the surprise element of the plot, which revealed that Ivo was married to Bettina, making her subsequent marriage to Martin invalid, but she found Kurnitz's dialogue 'repetitive, verbose and almost all without glamour', and believed that the dialogue must be tightened for the film to be effective. The script was too long and the same dramatic effect could be achieved without words, simply by action. She thought that there was a problem, too, with the characterisation. 'I know that C.R. could direct tension and conflict into the telephone directory, but would it not be so much easier if he could have it in the script already?' The characters appeared 'like cardboard figures' and were not credible because they did not appear to have any motivation. The vocabulary was poor and all the characters spoke in the same way. The relationship between Ivo, Bettina and Susanne should have been riddled with undercurrents of suspicion, but was lifeless and barely comprehensible. The character of the British officer Martin was incredible, and she believed that even strong casting would not make him flesh and blood. Reed had not helped by casting the wooden British stage actor Geoffrey Toone as Martin. Where Graham Greene had been accused of writing lines in previous films which could not be understood by American audiences, Kurnitz had made jarring errors about the behaviour of a young English girl. Green recommended that she completely rewrite the dialogue within the existing storyline.

There was, however, a problem of time. Reed attempted to get Kurnitz to amend his own work, but his efforts were mostly ineffective. In particular Reed was concerned about a scene where Ivo and Susanne, trapped in East Berlin, take refuge in a prostitute's room, where they acknowledge for the first time that they are sexually attracted to each other and make love. The scene as Kurnitz had written it was implausible. Reed wrote to Kurnitz in Rome, asking him to try yet again. Kurnitz replied that he had left his copy of the script in Cannes, had forgotten the order of the scenes and had become confused by the constant rewriting he had already done. Kurnitz's tone was sarcastic and unhelpful. He was happy to make suggestions as long as Reed didn't consider it 'presumptuous and an infringement of [his] Divine Right'.

In a series of letters Kurnitz accused Reed of being too demanding and inconsiderate. Reed, in turn, complained that what should be straightforward, quick amendments became enormous acts of rewriting. Kurnitz forcefully objected to the employment of a script-doctor to solve the problems, yet he was slow and unhelpful at making the changes himself. Even the timing of his work was out of pace with Reed: Kurnitz wrote at all hours of the day and night, while Reed demanded that ordinary office hours should be kept so that he could contact him. Reed asked for amendments, then more amendments, and Kurnitz became depressed and disillusioned. In one letter, when Reed had sent back a draft by return, asking for a different approach, Kurnitz wrote: 'Is that supposed to fill me full of confidence?' Kurnitz blamed the original novel for his inability to make the script come alive, and asked Reed to 'show me in the entire book one – just one – skilfully plotted passage, one great device, or one great surprise trick'. Shooting continued at Shepperton with a script which changed by the day.

A script-doctor was eventually hired, and one of great distinction. Although he had no experience of screenplay-writing, Eric Linklater was tempted by the fee of £250 per week to try to amend Kurnitz's inadequate dialogue. He did not find it easy going. He wrote to his wife: 'The work is interesting because Carol Reed is so clever at making something out of nothing; and that is what I have to do, too. Because the story of the film is utter nonsense . . . and although I have written quite a lot, I'm still not quite sure what the film is about.'

By the end of shooting, Reed was depressed and conscious of having wrestled with a task which had beaten him. But he kept his sense of humour, as is revealed in a cod job reference given to Linklater at the end of shooting.

> Linklater has been employed by me for five weeks, and leaves only at my request. His job was to create dialogue, for which my minimum requirements were that it should be at one and the same time
>   a) simple
>   b) dramatic
>   c) exciting
>   d) funny but not vulgar
>   e) fraught with tears
>   f) immortal
> His failure to reach this standard has been admirably consistent and shows real integrity. He is clean, diligent, and frequently sober; and I can recommend him for employment elsewhere.

Reed's love of practical jokes and spontaneous surprises was endured by all who liked him, including the long-suffering Pempie, who had no time for them. When not filming, he was very reluctant to get up in the morning but was happy to work on scripts or entertain friends well into the night, always playing the gramophone loudly. He did not share Pempie's interest in classical music, his choice always being popular and raucous. This preference for loud music was partly caused by his growing deafness, which had become evident since the war. Pempie used to wear earplugs to sleep, as Carol liked to remain in the drawing room listening to loud music. Sometimes, talking into the night with Judy Birkin, formerly Judy Campbell, he would turn the volume up to maximum to rouse Pempie to rejoin the party. Carol thought such behaviour playful; Pempie was not amused.

There was nothing Carol liked better than surprises. He was impulsive about everything from travelling abroad to going out to a restaurant, and always expected Pempie to be fully prepared for any eventuality. Judy Birkin was a regular visitor to 213 King's Road. Once, out shopping in Chelsea, Pempie said she had to go to the bank to exchange some money into French francs. Judy expressed surprise that they were going away without mentioning it to her, to which Pempie replied that she did not know whether they would be going abroad, but Carol usually decided such things at the very last moment and it would be best it she were to have some francs just in case.

It was typical for Reed to decide on a whim one morning to take Pempie and Max to Paris for lunch. On one impromptu visit to Dublin they arrived so late at the Gresham Hotel that they were drenched by rain while trying to rouse the porter. Despite this erratic, eccentric and egocentric behavour, Reed was constantly indulged by everyone close to him, who appeared to consider his childlike behaviour a small price for the mayhem and the magic which surrounded him.

His practical joking extended sometimes to his more sedate friends. Once in the George V Hotel in Paris with the dramatist Alan Melville, both of them quite sober, he came across a row of gilt chairs and was determined to see how many he could leap over. He ended up with a twisted ankle. When he and Pempie were invited by Alex Korda to stay on his yacht the *Elsewhere*, Reed chased Graham Greene around the deck with a soda siphon and introduced Peter Ustinov to a British admiral as Admiral Ustinov of the Red Navy.

In May 1953 Reed was awaiting the release of what had finally been retitled *The Man Between*, a further encouragement for the public and the critics to compare the new work to *The Third Man*.

And that is exactly what happened. At a press conference after the first screening, Reed was given a rough ride. He was a nervous man in public and was described at the time in an *Observer* profile as 'an unusually big, shy man, with small hands and feet, and a disarming and sensitive manner. In the film studio, amongst the crowd of actors and technicians, the bits of scenery, huge camera trolley, wires and cables, Sir Carol glides as smoothly as a waiter in a crowded restaurant or stands with his hands spread on his hips, head on one side, watching every detail. In his work he is infinitely patient, though outside he is fidgety and restless, hardly able to sit through someone else's film.' This time he was right to be nervous; he was about to experience failure.

In the past Reed had deliberately avoided repeating the same themes, but in *The Man Between* he forced a comparison with *The Third Man* which would inevitably damage his reputation. The months of worry about the story, the screenplay, the rewriting and, above all, the hectoring from Korda about the budget culminated in a reception from the press which put his efforts into clear perspective. Dilys Powell thought: '*The Man Between* is bound to be judged not simply on its merits but as a Carol Reed film. It will be expected to excel its predecessors, for while everybody agrees that a dead artist may have his ups and downs, nobody thinks that a living one ought to stop improving for a second. In particular it will be expected to excel *The Third Man*. And here I must say the comparison is justified: Carol Reed has asked for it.' She then went on, point by point, to mark Reed down against himself.

The Communist *Daily Worker*, which had a lot to say about the division of Germany, could not accept that Reed did not. 'The main failure is Sir Carol's. Without any solid point to illuminate, his sinister atmospherics are meaningless and absurd. He has taken his technique to one of the key points of the world and has shirked the challenge.' It was an astute judgement. Even when retracing his steps and perilously re-entering *Third Man* territory, Reed's purpose was not to reveal a different truth about the human misery of a divided city; he had simply attempted to repeat the box-office success of his earlier film.

American critics, more sensitive to commercial demands and more familiar with the Hollywood convention of the near-identical sequel, were more generous. In October 1953 Carol and Pempie flew to New York for the United States premiere, and were met with understanding notices in the American press. To a director anxious for commercial success, the *Variety* notice might have appeared ideal. It said the film's 'three star names, coupled with the marquee value of the director, give the pic strong showmanship possibilities, and although it is unlikely to repeat the b.o. triumph of its predecessor, it is destined for healthy grosses'. But Reed also craved praise for his artistic efforts, and on both sides of the Atlantic this was missing.

Reed acknowledged that it had been a mistake to return to familiar ground for *The Man Between*. Years later, his verdict on the film was: 'It wasn't a particularly good story, but I liked the atmosphere of Berlin after the war, and I wanted to work again with James Mason. It didn't come out quite right because we were forced back from Berlin before the location work was finished and we had to match a lot in the studio.' The picture earned its money back, but no more.

There was now a general demand among British critics for Reed to return to a domestic subject. *The Times*'s anonymous film columnist wrote: 'What one would like Sir Carol Reed to do now is to turn his camera on contemporary England and to remember at the same time that he possesses the gift of being modestly, illuminatingly, unexpectedly amusing.' His friend C. A. Lejeune told her *Observer* readers: 'It is the greatest mistake to believe that anything Carol Reed does is done without reason, without taste, or in any way haphazard; and I sometimes wonder if our chief complaint against our most distinguished director is not really that he will insist upon making such striking pictures about life in foreign countries, and nary a one nowadays about life at home.'

Reed took the point. Still working under the auspices of Alexander Korda, his next film would be set in Britain, as far as possible from the rubble of ideologically divided Europe. There were other lessons to be learnt from *The Man Between*. The tightness of control over budget and shooting schedule which had been Reed's professional trademark had led him to be trusted with filming overseas. Foreign location work was the most notorious means for film-makers to squander money, out of sight of their producers and far from the tightly-run studios.

Reed had mastered working abroad within budget during the filming of *The Third Man* by his rigorously pared script which allowed for no wastage. In *An Outcast of the Islands* he had been working in a low-cost country, again to a tight script. But *The Man Between* had shown what could happen when both script and filming schedules went awry. Reed was determined that his reputation for financial continence would not be damaged again and decided to work at home with a British author whose script he could keep tightly under control. His choice for this low-budget, domestic movie was *A Kid for Two Farthings*, to be adapted by Wolf Mankowitz from his own short story.

The film was set in the East End of London, had a young boy as its hero, deliberately employed popular actors, mixed realism with fantasy and was shot in colour. It was a strange gamble, a small film with a British cast, a sentimental story and, like *Bank Holiday*, a largely working-class setting. Mankowitz had established a reputation for his cockney morality tales, in which he imposed allegory upon tales of Jewish East London characters, and his first book, *Make Me an Offer*, had just been filmed by Cyril Frankel, with a distinguished cast including Peter Finch and Wilfrid Lawson. When Reed read the short story 'A Kid for Two Farthings', it appeared at once to have the makings of a film. It told of an East End boy who, reading a story about a magic unicorn, sets out to find one in his own neighbourhood and discovers a sickly kid goat with a single horn. He buys the 'unicorn' and finds that it makes wishes come true. A wrestler wins the match which will enable him to marry; a tailor obtains a much-needed steam press. But the kid dies before the boy's own wish, to travel to Africa to rejoin his father, comes true. Reed approached Mankowitz and asked him to write a screenplay from the story.

Casting was easy. For authenticity, many of the actors would be Jewish. Most important was the central part of the Jewish tailor Kandinsky, which was given to David Kossoff, a radio and film actor who had appeared in two of Peter Ustinov's plays, *The Love of Four Colonels* and *No Sign of the Dove*, and whom Reed had seen in a television play, *The Bespoke Overcoat*. The parts of Sam, a circus strong man, and Sonia, a glamorous young woman with whom he falls in love, were filled by 'Tiger' Joe Robinson, a former heavyweight wrestling champion, and Diana Dors, whom Reed and Pempie had seen on the stage in a variety show in Chiswick, West London. Dors was a sex starlet whose dyed-blonde hair and prominent bosom disguised the fact that she had been top of her class at the Royal Academy of Dramatic Arts, the London stage school founded by, among others, Herbert Tree. Primo Carnera, the pre-war world heavyweight boxing champion, was chosen to play Python Macklin, Sam's rival in the ring.

The other key part was that of the boy Joe. Mankowitz describes him in the book as looking 'no more than six, but is a year or so older. He is a solemn boy who takes life as a serious game in which he has an important part to play. A boy who already sees himself adult, and often behaves accordingly, nevertheless a boy, though not a jolly, raucous, bouncing one.' Reed knew of a boy who would fit the part and approached his actress mother, Rosalie Crutchley, who was a friend. Like Madeleine Henrey, she was at first reluctant to allow her son Jonathan Ashmore to become involved in films at such an early age. Apart from anything else, it was illegal for studios to use actors under thirteen years of age, but, as usual, the rules were bent to avoid prosecution. Jackie Green was employed as an acting coach and playmate for the boy.

Also among the predominantly Jewish cast were Celia Johnson, Brenda de Banzie, Sidney Tafler, Sidney James, Irene Handl, Alfie Bass, Joseph Tomelty, Derek Sydney and Anita Arley. As for the goat, a number of kids of varying sizes were bought from a pedigree goat farm near Windlesham, Surrey, and their mother was brought along to the filming to continue their suckling.

Shooting began in the East End of London in July 1954, around Petticoat Lane, renamed 'Fashion Street', and Aldgate, with the production offices in Whitechapel Baths. Picturesque background shots shrank the City of London, making St Paul's, a good mile away, appear to be at the end of the street. Filming was to take place among the barrows and crowds of the real street market at work. The busy shoppers became so involved that market traders complained of loss of trade. Reed found himself swamped by interested onlookers and set up a dummy film crew to distract attention from the genuine filming nearby. Then work moved to Korda's studios in Shepperton. In the final cutting a rich soundtrack of London sounds was added and, as in the films of Orson Welles, dialogue was allowed to overlap as it does in life.

The film began well, with a pigeon making the journey from Trafalgar Square to Petticoat Lane. In an extended introductory sequence the boy Joe walks the length of the market, the camera alternating between his point of view and those of the stall-holders. If the film became a little studio-bound after that, this was in keeping with Mankowitz's intention of making the story allegorical, almost magical. It was a trim little film which Reed cut to a bare ninety-six minutes and, although conscious that he had not created a masterpiece, he was pleased with it. He was relieved to have brought the film in on time and under the meagre budget of £200,000.

Reed took his film to Cannes, where it aroused controversy, liked by most of the British critics but heavily attacked by some of the Europeans and, according to *The Times Educational Supplement*, 'violent opposition from some intellectual quarters'. Some British critics thought that Reed's usual confidence had been upset by having to deal with two elements which were new to him, the use of colour and the fantasy aspects of the story. *The Times* reported from Cannes that the film 'seemed to show that Sir Carol Reed's search for a scenarist as suited to his dextrous talent as Mr Graham Greene is not at an end'. Everyone appeared to agree, however, that the subject had been delicately handled.

When the film was released in London in April 1955, after a royal charity premiere attended by Prince Philip in aid of the London Federation of Boys' Clubs, the critics were uninhibited by the need to support the local team, as they may have been in Cannes. The *Spectator* voiced the by-now common complaint: 'Life is full of disappointments and it is foolish to expect too much from anyone, even Carol Reed. Yet his *A Kid for Two Farthings* falls so far below the high standard he has so consistently maintained, it is impossible not to feel cheated.' Derek Hill, writing in *Films and Filming*, told the blunt truth: 'It is usual to say that a Carol Reed failure stands high above other British directors' biggest successes. Unfortunately, this observation has steadily become less and less true . . . Worse, this overblown trifle hints strongly that Reed's notorious willingness to tackle any kind of subject is fast reducing his work to insignificance.'

Reed took the criticism to heart. Missing some of the reviews when they came out, he compiled a typewritten summary of their observations for his cuttings book, and the worst comments were written in capital letters. The emphasis is revealing. The review in *The Times* had the following highlighted in capitals: 'The puzzling thing is this: in spite of the film's many merits, the 96 minutes it takes to run seem long.' The *Manchester Guardian*'s review went into upper case where it said: 'Nevertheless, he must forgive his admirers if they are conscious, at this fairly late point in his distinguished career, of a certain exasperation. Why will he not chance his arm just a little more – on some really worthwhile task? He is certainly one of the very few who, in terms of finance as well as artistry, might get away with it.' Also written in capitals was the line: 'The question will obtrude itself – is it quite enough for Sir Carol to be doing?'

Reed's final verdict on the film, in an interview some years later, was: 'I loved that book! The film was all right in part and not in others. It cost very little money, but did well.'

Reed now decided to make a deliberate shift away from the comfort of Alexander Korda's embrace in favour of working for the first time with American money pure and simple. It was to be the wrong cure for his malady. What he needed above all was a point of view, but beyond an enjoyment of observation he had none. He read books simply to find a storyline for a film. He went to the theatre merely to discover if there was a property worth buying to turn into a film. He had little intellectual interest in anything, even films. His favourite directors were never those who took a strong line on anything or had a striking visual style. He preferred the old Hollywood workhorses who could turn out a commercial, well-made film in six weeks.

Having worked hard since leaving school and never having enjoyed the benefits of a university education, Reed had learned his craft in the succession of jobs he had taken in the theatre and film industries. He knew how to make a good film from a good script, but he did not appear to have any need within him to make large points or to reveal important truths. He disguised this lack behind a cloak of modesty, a preoccupation with technical details and a warmth with actors. Yet Reed was expected to deliver something more than mere technical efficiency, and he now hoped to arrest the slump in his career by working in a new environment.

10

Our Man Adrift

Reed made plans to work without Korda. He wanted to continue to produce his own films, allowing him to keep control of his working methods, and if this meant making films in the United States, so be it. It was not something he looked forward to. He had enjoyed more independence than a Hollywood studio would offer, but he did not rule out working there for four or five months at a time. What was more important to him was to find a suitable story for a film.

He made his wishes clear to an American journalist in March 1955: 'It would have to be the sort of story with a background that was not too American. There is nothing worse than a film that is directed by someone who has little or no knowledge of the habits or ways of the country concerned in the picture. For instance, I would never make a film with an American college background, I would be bound to make too many mistakes.'

His words reveal the oddness of his position. Having directed some of the most extraordinary and imaginative films ever made in Britain, he was still content merely to be a freelance director of any project, so long as the storyline took his fancy. He not only avoided adopting a point of view in his films – which suited the purposes of a collaborator like Greene, who wished his story to be translated to the screen with the minimum of directorial interpretation – but he seemed to have no desire to make films which might stretch the mind. He had established himself as a highly talented technician, a human catalyst who could bring disparate and often difficult talents together and make them combine with dazzling results. His own contribution, however, remained merely that of a facilitator, a man between.

Reed, like his father, distrusted cleverness or intellectualism of any kind. His view was, 'I make films for the public, but in a manner that I like myself. I don't know what the public wants, and I doubt whether the public does either. People like a good picture, so you have to make a film on trust, knowing that if it is good people will like it.' In a 1950 interview he had said: 'The point you have to bear in mind is that the *audience* don't care how clever you are. All they notice is somebody up there on the screen. All that really matters is, do they feel for that person? Do they like him? Are they interested in him?' This explains, perhaps, why Reed, in the age of Laurence Olivier, never ventured into filming 'difficult' subjects like Shakespeare, one of his father's great inspirations for his idiosyncratic brand of popular theatre. Reed was content simply to entertain.

In 1955, Reed was in his late forties, and it was too late for him to make the break from Britain and join the American film industry in Hollywood, which also put entertainment before art. In retrospect he should, perhaps, have gone to Hollywood in the 1930s, before war was declared. Still, if going to America was the only way he could continue to make the films he wanted to make, he would go to America.

An immediate solution to his problem came by cablegram from the United States. Burt Lancaster and Harold Hecht had formed an independent production company, built on the box-office attraction of Lancaster's acting. Theirs was the biggest and the busiest of the moves to independent production which were now dismantling the power of the Hollywood studios. Hecht had met Lancaster when the actor was appearing on Broadway in *A Sound of Hunting* and had put him under contract, saying, 'Sign with me and we'll be producing our own pictures within five years.'

Within eighteen months they were producing *Vera Cruz*, a Mexican western, with Gary Cooper appearing for a 10 per cent stake of the gross. The success of that film led them the following year to produce *Marty*, directed by Delbert Mann with a screenplay by Paddy Chayevsky, which won four Oscars. With critical and financial success behind them, the team of Hecht-Hill-Lancaster – they had joined forces with the producer James Hill – was looking for a suitable subject for their third picture.

Lancaster had been a circus acrobat before turning to straight acting and, because this had made him the butt of many jokes about his past, he was determined to make a film which dignified the life of circus people. Max Catto's novel *The Killing Frost*, about the tension between two circus high-wire acrobats and their rivalry for the attentions of a woman, was full of drama, love interest and colour, and appeared just the story he was looking for. He proposed acting himself in the principal role of the part-crippled triple somersaulter who agrees, reluctantly, to pass on the secret of how to perform this rare trick to a young acrobat.

By coincidence, Reed too had read Catto's novel and realised its cinema potential, but had concluded that it would prove too expensive to buy the rights and to mount the production. In 1949 he had been seriously considering directing a picture about the circus and had had a long conversation with the impresario Charles B. Cochran about the idea, borrowing from him two illustrated books on the circus. Cochran suggested a film about Grimaldi; Reed thought that the life of Barnum, the great showman, would make 'a great film – but I am afraid it would be impossible to attempt it in this country. So far we have been unable to find a circus . . . I believe that the only way to go about this is to have an original written, and do it at a very much later date.' Cochran, by now eager to hatch something with Reed, sent him a copy of Granville-Barker's version of Sacha Guitry's *Deburau*, but Reed believed this would also be impossible to film.

Hecht and Lancaster's message to Reed in London, asking him to consider directing the film of Max Catto's novel, which was to be named *Trapeze*, was therefore doubly welcome. Here was a chance to make a film for Americans but without going to America, as all the filming would take place in Paris. Reed was also impressed by the scale of the budget which Hecht and Lancaster were proposing – $4 million, with an expected income of $20 million. Reed was offered a stake in the profits, a full say in casting and complete independence of direction. He accepted at the beginning of 1955 and immediately threw himself into research about the circus.

In 1971 he explained, 'I wanted to work with Burt Lancaster and Hecht-Hill-Lancaster owned this Catto novel, which, in fact, we used very little of in the end. Eventually, we decided the book was hopeless, but we got the idea of this crippled acrobat trying to help a novice learn the business. I'd committed myself before ever seeing the script. The story wasn't very good, but the photography was.'

When the contract was signed, only Lancaster had been cast. Reed was despatched to Rome to persuade Gina Lollobrigida to play the girl in the middle of the love triangle. 'La Lollo', as the Italian actress had been dubbed by her publicity department, was more intelligent than her hourglass 37-21-35 figure might have suggested. She spoke as little English as Reed spoke Italian, but, helped by the interpreting skills of her husband, Reed was able to describe the importance of the role and convince her that appearing in the film was in her best interests.

The choice of the young acrobat who was to be taught the triple somersault was more difficult, and several French and English actors were considered before the young Tony Curtis, who had been thought unavailable because of his contract with Columbia, agreed to take the part. Reed had only seen him in one picture, and had not grasped the importance of Curtis's quiff when he asked the young actor whether he would mind having the traditional close-cropped haircut which all aerialists had. Curtis agreed without a qualm, but the decision was to become a hot topic among his American fans, branding Reed 'the man who dared ask Tony Curtis to cut off his hair'. Reed chose Michel Thomas to be the ringmaster. Sidney James, who had appeared in *A Kid for Two Farthings*, took the part of a snake handler and backing the actors was a company of true circus performers: the Arriolas, a Spanish troupe of trampolinists; Folco Cipriano, one of the great equestriennes; Sampion Bouglione, the elephant master, and his elephants; a team of acrobats, the Gimma Boys; and clowns Zavatta, Mylos, Lulu and Tonio. Reed's corps of character actors was also there, including the massive Thomas Gomez, Minor Watson and, playing the circus midget, Johnny Puleo, a member of the Harmonica Rascals.

The domed, five-thousand-seat Cirque d'Hiver in Paris was hired for the summer of 1955 instead of a studio. Reed believed that no set could reproduce the unique atmosphere of the place, and the few outside locations needed could be filmed on the Paris streets. The Cirque would also solve Reed's problem of how to fill the wide CinemaScope screen which he was to be working with for the first time. Hecht and Lancaster were insistent that, in order to wrest the growing numbers of television viewers from their small monochrome screens at home, *Trapeze* should use the latest in cinema technology, Eastmancolor and CinemaScope.

Since 1952, when Twentieth Century Fox bought Henri Chrétien's wide-screen process for commercial exploitation, the enormous rectangular area which the CinemaScope lens embraced had proved a problem for film-makers. It was useful in epics like *The Robe* (1953), where crowd scenes and spectacles could be shown to great advantage. What was more difficult, however, was how then to move to intimate scenes between actors. Some of the results had been laughable, with characters shouting at each other across a great gulf. The French artist, writer and film director Jean Cocteau had ridiculed the whole process: 'Next time I write a poem, I shall use a wider piece of paper.'

The circus offered plenty of colour, but how best to use the wide screen was a genuine difficulty. Reed knew that the width of the screen would be ideal for the main action of the picture, which involved high-wire acts and vertiginous views from the top of the dome, but shooting the ring below would prove more awkward. His solution was simple, ingenious and effective. While he concentrated on the action in the foreground, he would fill the background with all of the spectacular and colourful activity of a circus in rehearsal. In the completed picture there are few moments when the screen is not crammed with elephants circling, ballet dancers leaping, jugglers juggling or clowns tumbling. A soundtrack which included circus noises and rehearsal music by the Cirque d'Hiver's twelve-piece band added to the busy atmosphere.

Another, less fundamental, problem was how to deal with the aerial action. Reed's three principals were not aerialists, although Lancaster had acrobatic experience and was determined to do as much as he could himself. Lollobrigida was surprisingly game to learn as much as possible about climbing ropes and falling into nets and was a nimble pupil. Curtis, however, was afraid of heights, and it took a great deal of time to accustom him to working at the top of the Cirque. Reed was keen to maintain his reputation for authenticity and therefore keep all trick camera-work to a minimum. In the final cut of the film, only three shots – one a ludicrous in-flight kiss between Lancaster and Lollobrigida – involve trick photography, and they look horribly conspicuous against the rest.

Reed's lighting cameraman was again Robert Krasker, who had just completed shooting Renato Castellani's colourful *Romeo and Juliet* on location in Verona. Their close working relationship allowed them to agree quickly on some of the methods to be used in photographing action on the high wire. Even on the wide screen, it was impossible to see whether the principal or a double was involved in the high-wire acts and so, although the launches and landings would be performed by the three main actors, the genuine aerial acrobatics could be performed by doubles. Eddie Ward stood in for Lancaster, Sally Marlowe for Lollobrigida and Fay Alexander for Curtis.

By comparison with the technical aspects of the film, the screenplay was deemed of minor importance, but Liam O'Brien and James R. Webb went to work on Catto's novel, completing a final draft which Reed approved by the beginning of the summer. Wolf Mankowitz, who wrote *A Kid for Two Farthings*, joined the crew in Paris to write additional dialogue. Reed collected his work permit and temporary resident's card on 12 July 1956 and work began in earnest eight days later. He spent six weeks in preparation at the Cirque, followed by eight weeks' shooting.

Each day Reed rose at six, drove to the Cirque d'Hiver and worked without a break until the evening. Hiring the circus performers was expensive, as the summer touring season is their most lucrative time, but considering the size of the cast and crew, drawn from fifteen countries, and the number of animals around the Cirque – tigers, apes, wolf-dogs, snakes, alligators, camels, horses and lions, among them one employed to feign mauling Lancaster's hand – the shooting was uneventful, although some public consternation was caused when the circus company was filmed marching along the Grand Boulevard and the Champs Élysées, attracting a crowd of 9000 Parisians.

Circus pictures do attract odd incidents, however. As a convinced animal lover, Reed was concerned about some of the cruelty which he saw being inflicted on the circus beasts, in particular the treatment of a camel, but there was little he could do except complain. His response was to go to an expensive restaurant where fish were held in a tank for the customers to choose. One day he bought the whole tankful and had the fish liberated into the Seine. When told that they would die there, too, he said, 'Isn't it better that at least they should end their days in their own environment.'

The actors were more trouble than the animals, particularly when jealousy broke out between Lollobrigida and Katy Jurado, a Mexican actress, who threatened to walk off the set. There were high-wire accidents, too, in which Lollobrigida's double fell; she was taken to hospital with a broken nose and severe lacerations. A prancing circus horse stepped on Katy Jurado's toe, breaking it. And the cast and crew endured a plague of circus fleas.

The Cirque became a place for film people to visit when passing through Paris, and Kirk Douglas, Robert Rossen, Robert Siodmak, Marilyn Monroe's husband Joe di Maggio, and Reed's next-door neighbour in Chelsea, Peter Ustinov, paid visits. When the shooting was finished, Reed returned to London to edit the picture and to apply the musical score, commissioned from Malcolm Arnold.

A personal and business tragedy overtook Reed in April 1956 when Alexander Korda died. Although Reed had already broken with London Films to make *Trapeze*, Korda had provided the money, the stability and above all the confidence for Reed to make the greatest films of his career. They were also personally very close, and a number of Reed's family and friends believed that a father-son relationship existed between them. On Alex's death his widow Alexa moved in with the Reeds in Chelsea until the complicated affairs of the dead movie mogul had been sorted out. If Reed did not consider Korda a father substitute, he certainly enjoyed Korda's avuncular friendship, which gave his advice added weight. No one since Edgar Wallace had provided Reed with so much backing and support.

The end of Korda's empire coincided with great changes throughout the film-making industry, both in Britain and in the United States. The old studios were crumbling. The cinema-going habits of the public were changing. Television was stealing audiences and keeping them at home despite great technical advances in film-making to try to ensure that a weekly visit to the cinema remained a habit. Actors, directors and producers had started to form companies of their own so that they could keep more of the huge profits which successful movies made.

Directors increasingly found that if they wished to make films of their own choice, they had to raise the capital themselves. There was, above all, a crisis of confidence in an industry which had enjoyed nearly thirty years of unrivalled success in entertaining the public. Exactly how film-making was to develop in the mid-1950s was a matter of intense debate. The studio chiefs argued that only the resources of a studio could rival those of the new industry of television; independent producers and directors believed that only a thrusting, imaginative approach would satisfy an increasingly fickle public.

In Britain the argument of studios versus independents was less pertinent because the studios were, in any case, fast fading. By the time Korda died, Reed had already broken his ties with him. It would take some time for him to discover exactly how much he would miss Korda, however, for *Trapeze* was a huge financial success.

Carol and Pempie Reed flew to America for a three-week publicity tour for *Trapeze* culminating in a grand premiere in Hollywood on 29 May 1956. The film was an instant success on both sides of the Atlantic, although it failed to excite the critics. After the first week of its general release in the United States, the film had broken the world record for gross box-office receipts, taking over $4 million. Cinemas, used to changing their programme at least once a week, were holding over *Trapeze* for a second and third week. In London the film broke records at the Odeon, Marble Arch, where it had opened after an old-fashioned celebrity-filled charity premiere for the Variety Club and Actors' Orphans, co-hosted by Reed and Laurence Olivier.

The technical achievement of cramming the big screen and filming the aerial shots provided an unprecedented Cinema-Scope sensation, for which the critics gave Reed little credit. *Sight and Sound* had hoped for 'a return by the director to an earlier, more personal style and even, perhaps, for a film that really conjured up the harsh and somehow sad atmosphere of the circus', but found that 'it might have been made by any competent director'. *The Times* agreed, saying 'it is indeed possible to watch *Trapeze* for long stretches at a time without connecting it with Sir Carol at all'.

For Reed, the arrangement with Hecht-Hill-Lancaster had proved a productive one, resulting in an international picture with a large budget, no interference from the producers and a chance to develop his skills in colour and the wide screen. *Trapeze* was also hugely profitable, which was encouraging to both parties. As Reed later explained: '*Trapeze* made more money than any of my films. It was the simplest subject in the world, with scenes that were almost like musical numbers. It paid for itself in a single country: Japan. It did well everywhere.'

It was little wonder, therefore, that he was tempted to continue the association. James Hill took the initiative, and in July 1956 invited Reed and Pempie to visit Hollywood and discuss possibilities. Hill understood Reed's impatience to get working again, saying in a letter, 'this inactivity must be killing you. I certainly thought by now we would have something in work together.' He was excited about a screenplay being worked on by John Van Druten called 'First Love', but Reed was working on something of his own, a treatment called 'The Amazon Story', which he described in great detail in a letter to Hill in August 1956. Like Reed's other attempts at writing stories, it was heavily derivative, in this case a reworking of *The Treasure of the Sierra Madre* and similar tales. His story concerned the crash somewhere in the Amazon basin of a plane laden with gold which three dubious types decide to hunt for, announcing their mission to the press as being to rescue the survivors. He made several drafts before writing a full-blown treatment.

Reed and Pempie reached Los Angeles for a three-week, all expenses paid business trip during the early summer of 1957, staying at the Beverly-Wilshire Hotel. He made a tentative agreement with Hecht-Hill-Lancaster to make three pictures for them, though 'The Amazon Story' was not among them. The first was an adaptation of Ray Bradbury's short story about the end of the world, 'The Rock Cried Out', for which it was agreed that the author would travel to London to work with Reed on a screenplay. Reed spoke with Bradbury each day for three weeks and they met in London at the end of June to discuss a full outline of the story. The second was to be Robert W. Krepps's novel *Tell it on the Drums*, to be retitled 'Kimberley', with a screenplay by Philip Yordan, with whom Reed had an extended conversation and who had already started writing. The cast was to include Burt Lancaster and Montgomery Clift. Reed described it as 'rather a Western-cum-crime story, but I always felt that if we could make it with a background of Kimberley it would give it a bigger canvas than they have agreed to'. The third picture was to be developed from Reed's own story, with action spread over five countries. As it transpired, all three projects came to nothing.

Reed was considering a number of other projects suggested by Hecht. One which particularly took his fancy was *My Fair Lady*, Alan Lerner and Frederick Loewe's musical adaptation of Bernard Shaw's *Pygmalion*. Herbert Tree had acted in the first British production of the play at His Majesty's Theatre, with himself as the elocutionist and Mrs Patrick Campbell as Eliza Doolittle, and Reed welcomed the chance of overlapping with his father. Hecht negotiated unsuccessfully to buy the rights of the stage show, which at the time were being offered to American television. Six years later George Cukor's film, with Rex Harrison and Audrey Hepburn in the cast, and with costumes by Cecil Beaton, won four Oscars. Hecht also suggested a property which his company had developed, 'The Racing Story', which would be set in England. Reed agreed to approach a number of British writers – among them Daphne du Maurier, Hammond Innes and Nancy Mitford – to write a screenplay.

With all the Hecht-Hill-Lancaster projects, it was agreed that Reed should be both producer and director, but that there should be as much consultation between all of them as had taken place on *Trapeze*.

While in Hollywood, Reed also met producers from other studios. He had just made one of the most profitable films in recent times, and others wanted to lure him away from Hecht-Hill-Lancaster. For once in his life, Reed found himself inundated with offers and ideas. But all were to prove illusory. At MGM he had lunch with Benny Thau, who immediately proposed 'Theatre', which Ingrid Bergman and Rex Harrison apparently wished to make, Harrison reportedly being so keen that he was prepared to take a sabbatical from *My Fair Lady*, which was running on the New York stage at the time. Reed became very enthusiastic about the project and said he would talk to Bergman about it as soon as he returned to London, but he soon discovered that the truth was not always told over a Hollywood lunch. Passing through New York on the way home, he stopped in to see Harrison at the theatre, who confessed to not yet having read the book. Reed then travelled to Paris to see Bergman and reported that she was 'in two minds about the project. She believed that I was keen to do it and that Rex Harrison was keen to do it. We discussed it for a couple of mornings and left the situation vague.'

Talking with producers at Twentieth Century, Reed suggested his own 'The Amazon Story', but although further screenwriters were discussed, it was left to Twentieth Century's London office to make any subsequent progress. Again the project came to nothing.

There were other subjects suggested, many of which Reed would have to finance himself. But after *Trapeze* he was confident that the money would be forthcoming if the story and the stars were right. Reed was prepared to pay £2000 of his own money for the rights to *The Black Virgin of the Golden Mountains*, which belonged to the American producer of *Edward My Son*, Edwin H. Knopf, and Reed also agreed to pay Knopf's expenses when he came to London to discuss the project further. Reed was convinced in June 1957 that shooting on this would begin within the year. Then there was *Rapture in Rags*, a Parisian stage play which Reed had seen and liked. Andrew Hakim, who had already commissioned a screenplay, wanted Reed to direct a film version later in the year. Reed balked and told him that he was already committed to a number of projects, none of which, it transpired, came to anything. There was also a project called 'The Reason Why', which Ray Stark was keen to make in England, although Reed told him that it would be very expensive. According to Reed, 'He said money was no object as long as we get the best cast.'

Reed, as enthusiastic as ever, took the Americans at their word and believed that he could work solidly from now on. He was so confident that he was prepared to start on a number of different projects at the same time, preparing one screenplay while shooting another. But, for all the ideas mentioned and the projects which might get off the ground, Reed knew that it would be some time before he was able to do the only thing which kept him happy; directing a picture. American films were more expansive, with bigger stars and bigger budgets and they took longer to make, but they also had longer periods of inactivity between them.

Reed found the constant promises of future work combined with his present inactivity immensely frustrating. He had never been short of money, and his films had made him very rich, even the less successful ones usually making money. The lack of anything to do each morning, however, made him unhappy and antisocial. When not working, Reed spent the whole time in search of stories or watching people. He could spend hours in a hotel lobby, observing people, and would also go to a gambling club called The Pair of Shoes, where again he would watch intently, pointing out what he had seen: 'Look at all those people losing money, pretending they do not care.' He took his son Max to the Cumberland Hotel in London and told him: 'This is where I come to learn to make films. You learn about people and how they move and what they do and you have to guess what they do.' When he bought a house in the south of France it was not a villa in the countryside surrounded by pines but a flat looking directly over the old harbour at Cannes, with a perfect view of everything that was going on in the bus station. There he mounted one of his directors' chairs, and he would sit for hours each day looking through binoculars at the life below. He did not need company, just people to watch.

When he was not working, his day began late. He would miss breakfast, finally emerging into Pempie's well-run household late in the morning. He would pour himself a gin and tonic, the first of many during the course of the day, and smoke the first of forty or more cigarettes. Often he would go out at lunchtime to a nearby public house, where he would drink until closing time at three in the afternoon. The rest of the afternoon he might spend reading a book or having a snooze.

He barely had any hobbies or interests which might keep him permanently amused. Pempie, Max and Tracy knew that life would only return to normal when a film was under way and Reed was leaving the house each morning to go to work.

His working days, by contrast, were filled with purpose. He would rise in the morning with enormous difficulty, prompted by Pempie, alarm calls and alarm clocks, one of which played the 'Harry Lime Theme'. He was invariably too late for breakfast or, often, a shave, but set out on time for the studio at 7.30 a.m.

He always preferred to drive himself in his modest British car, an Austin Princess, then eventually a Jaguar, and he rarely resorted to the luxury of a chauffeur, which most successful people in the film industry considered mandatory. To travel with him could be hair-raising because he drove very slowly and with apparently intense concentration on the road which turned out to be preoccupation about the work ahead. Guy Hamilton, assistant director on several of Reed's later films, remembers accompanying him one morning and witnessing a bicycle accident. Reed remained totally silent for fifteen minutes, which Hamilton imagined was because of shock. In fact Reed had not noticed the accident at all.

On one of the rare times he used a chauffeur, during filming of *The Third Man*, he only learned one German word, *'schnell'*, which he believed meant 'slower', and he was indignant that not only was the driver too fast, but he took no notice of his instructions.

At the studio Reed was a different person. He appeared entirely calm and collected, with infinite patience and charm, although this disguised his acute anxiety. He smoked in-cessantly, and told one interviewer: 'Films are made in fear and worry and work and panic. There is no happiness in this business.' His solution was to be entirely purposeful and fully prepared, with a detailed shooting script. He explained to the *New York Times*: 'The whole thing is in the preparation. I like to work three months or more on a script and come on to the floor with it finished to the last letter.'

He forwent lunch each day, eating sandwiches while watch-ing the rushes of the previous day's shooting. This allowed him to amend the film as he went along. 'After you've been shooting awhile and are looking at your footage as you go, you begin to see the picture taking shape, establishing a rhythm of its own. Things begin to fall into place of themselves. That's when you begin to feel the picture's natural pace and you develop it. You can then work with the actors to mould and shape it.'

Reed dearly hoped that Hecht-Hill-Lancaster would quickly put him back to work, and one project he discussed with them in Hollywood did eventually get off the ground. By August 1957, Reed was deeply engrossed in planning a film of Jan de Hartog's novel *Stella*, which would finally reach the screen as *The Key*. The story concerned the ill-starred link between three tugboat captains, sent to rescue merchant ships crippled by U-Boats.

Each captain passed on to the next the key of his apartment on shore, which contained a beautiful woman who became the wife of each in turn.

The picture, to be shot in monochrome CinemaScope, was really the inspiration of Carl Foreman, the American writer-producer-director, who had been chased across the Atlantic by the McCarthyite witch-hunts because of the radical nature of his writing. He had a short, distinguished film-making career culminating in *High Noon* (1952), which he had written and whose liberal tone was the cause of his coming to the attention of the House UnAmerican Activities Committee. He moved to Britain where he worked, uncredited, on the script of *The Bridge on the River Kwai* (1957), then wrote the screenplay based on *Stella* and raised the money to produce it.

With Foreman as executive producer and screenwriter, Reed could concentrate entirely on the direction. Foreman's view of the link between a good screenplay and a good director gave Reed confidence. He was on record as saying, 'A director should never be subjected to budgetary pressure once the film has started,' that 'the writer should be on the set throughout the production' and that 'just writing a script and handing it over completely to someone else is like having a baby and giving it out for adoption'. However, Reed did not get on well with Foreman. He once told him: 'Yes, I do like you. I can assure you I like you more than anyone else does.'

The cast boasted William Holden, straight from *Kwai*, who would be paid $250,000, and Sophia Loren, who was in Hollywood filming *Desire Under the Elms* and would be paid $225,000. Reed agreed a fee of $150,000. As much of the action was to take place at sea, Loren was not needed until halfway through the shooting. Reed cast Trevor Howard as the second of the three tugboat captains and filled up the smaller parts with character actors of his choice, among them favourites such as Bernard Lee, Renee Houston, Oscar Homolka, Carl Mohner and the young Bryan Forbes. He had hoped to cast Stanley Baker as the third captain, but Baker was under contract to Rank, who would not release him. Instead Reed reluctantly chose Kieron Moore.

Before the fifteen-week shooting schedule began in mid-July, a last-minute hitch emerged over Sophia Loren's working schedule. She had been engaged to arrive for studio work at

Boreham Wood in October, once shooting at sea was completed. She completed *Desire Under the Elms* in July and signed to make another Hollywood picture the following month, when filming had already started on *The Key*. Foreman's anxious enquiries about Loren's availability in October met with evasive answers and he concluded that she had overbooked herself and would be unable to make Reed's shooting schedule. Reed was therefore despatched to Paris to invite Ingrid Bergman to join the cast. Bergman agreed and a sum of £90,000 – the same fee that Loren was to have been given – was fixed. When this news reached Loren in Hollywood, an urgent cable was sent to Foreman declaring that she would arrive on time, as arranged, and that any attempt on Foreman's part to break the contract would be met with court action. Bergman's participation was therefore cancelled and Reed had to wait to see whether he would have a female lead by the time she was needed.

Faced with a story which took place half at sea and half on land, Reed was determined that the naval scenes should be as authentic as possible. He set up his headquarters at the Gloucester Hotel, Weymouth, and recruited the services of the Royal Navy at Her Majesty's Naval Dockyard at Portland and a tug called *Restive*, a genuine relic of the Atlantic convoy rescue fleet. In addition he had at his disposal three naval commanders as advisers, a camera ship, a communications launch, an explosion ship, a freighter, an oil tanker and a submarine, *Trespasser*, posing as a German U-Boat. The location shooting in the English Channel was to take six weeks with actors, followed by four weeks taking background shots, before returning to the Associated British Studio at Boreham Wood.

As *Restive* was to appear before and after enemy action, it often looked spick and span at the bows while weatherbeaten at the stern. The cast and crew totalled 104, with an additional 150 Royal Navy sailors available. At sea the crew of the *Restive* became so enmeshed in the filming that actors and sailors intermixed, which added to Reed's desired authenticity. And life was to imitate art. *Restive* was leased to Reed on the understanding that if it were needed at short notice by the Navy, it should be immediately released. One Saturday a yacht named *Tarifa* got into serious difficulties and *Restive* was called out, with Reed, Holden, Howard and the rest on board. The full cast was aboard a month later when the ship was called out a second time, to rescue a 2,610-ton Daring-class destroyer, *Decoy*. Persistent bad weather and stormy seas ensured that authenticity was maintained, even if the cast and crew became almost permanently seasick.

In his autobiography Bryan Forbes remembered how Reed's desire to make the film look real resulted in him and the rest of the crew perpetually hanging over the side of the boats. 'Carol was determined to make the film as authentic as possible and since the story demanded that the tug seek out and find crippled merchant ships, much of the action was spectacular and highly dangerous. He was the worst sailor of all and seemed to have a mental block about the mechanics of operating a ship at sea. He was consumed with his own private visions, and once he had decided how he was going to shoot a particular sequence he couldn't understand why some of his instructions were impossible to carry out. He thought that if he shouted "Stop" the real-life captain of the tug could apply disc brakes. Yellow of face, chain-smoking and denying himself any solid sustenance, he stared without comprehension as those around him argued the impossibility of his suggestions.'

For one scene Reed, hanging onto the ship's rail with one hand and looking through the camera-viewfinder with another, wanted the British submarine, posing as a German U-Boat, to rise to the surface and stop. 'This is the shot, Ossie,' he said to Oswald Morris, the cinematographer. 'The U-Boat comes up there, and we pan across to hold Bill and Bryan in a tight two-shot as they stop the tug and open fire with the Bofors gun.' Morris agreed that it would be a good shot. Reed took the megaphone and told the submarine commander of his plans. 'You'll surface there, where you are, if you'll mark that, Captain.' Then he addressed the captain of the tug from which he was shooting: 'And when that happens – we'll give you a cue, of course – you stop. Stop everything.' The tug captain had tried many times to explain to Reed that ships could not stop dead in the water, and this latest command made him exasperated. 'What do you think I am, the last tram-driver? I've told you before, sir, I can't stop this bloody thing to order.' The captain walked off the bridge in despair.

Now it was the submarine captain's chance to explain to Reed the difficulties in manoeuvring a large vessel to order. 'You quite clear, are you, Captain?' Reed enquired through the megaphone. The captain responded: 'Are you some sort of berk, or what?' Reed didn't hear the reply and asked the crew: 'What's he say?' Morris, aware of exactly what was going on, decided to intervene and spoke himself to the captain of the sub, who aimed his megaphone at Reed on the bridge of the tug: 'Look! I don't know what sort of jokers you've got on board there, but if you think I can bring this up from the bottom on a sixpence, you've got another think coming. It'll be a bloody miracle if I get within half a mile of it.' Reed again claimed not to have heard the response and, pleading seasickness as an excuse, left the bridge, asking Morris to sort out the matter. The submarine captain decided to waste no more time and set off for shore. Reed was shocked that his commands were not obeyed, although he must have known as well as the rest of the cast and crew that he was asking the impossible. He reasoned that if the impossible were not demanded, nothing extraordinary would be achieved.

The final cut of the film proves his point. Although the main plot is rather pedestrian, the film comes alive whenever the cameras are at sea, in particular an exceptional panning shot in the opening moments which runs the whole length of the ship.

When the studio work was complete, Reed completed the editing, again with Bert Bates, and the film was scheduled for a royal premiere on 29 May 1958, before Princess Margaret, and on 2 July, in time for Independence Day, in the United States. The film was greeted with some hesitation in Britain, where the hybrid films which demanded American money, a clutch of established international stars and merely British facilities were acquiring a bad reputation. These were not 'British films' in any genuine sense, nor were they American, which were considerably more popular, and in *The Key* it appeared as if Carol Reed had been leased out as part of the fixtures and fittings of a wider deal involving studio space and British distribution.

For the most part the film was Carl Foreman's, with Reed merely translating Foreman's script onto the screen, albeit with his usual competence. Reed admitted as much some months later, when he revealed that he was forced to shoot two endings, one for the Americans in which the final, surviving captain married the woman, another for the British in which they went their separate ways. He added: 'That was absolutely silly. I believe it was a mistake. I did not produce that film as I usually do. I took on a script that had been quite developed. When we were nearly done I was persuaded that too much rode on the success of this picture to be risked on a downbeat ending. The picture was much stronger with the two missing one another. I don't like to tie things up too neatly. Life isn't like that.'

Only in the early Atlantic scenes, with Oswald Morris's camera sweeping along the ship's side, was Reed's hand truly evident, and those scenes remain a most effective and dramatic use of black-and-white CinemaScope. Certainly the critics played down Reed's contribution, concentrating instead on Trevor Howard's performance, which upstaged both Holden and Loren. Reed was referred to as if he were merely a technician who had overcome with some ingenuity the slenderness of the story and the lack of coherence between the incongruous casting of three such disparate actors as Holden, Loren and Howard.

Dilys Powell described the film as 'a director's triumph – and a writer's – all round', but even she did not welcome *The Key* as a triumph for Carol Reed. *Sight and Sound*, usually so caustic, was generous, declaring: 'With this film Carol Reed is right back on form. It is the best thing he has done since that interesting but puzzling work *An Outcast of the Islands*,' which was hardly a recommendation. Derek Hill, writing in *Tribune*, put the praise in context: 'There's little point in being disappointed in anything Carol Reed turns out since *A Kid for Two Farthings* and *Trapeze* showed his talent hurtling to rock bottom.' The *Spectator* hoped that *The Key* 'might be that famous, long-expected Great Film from Sir Carol Reed at last', but came to the conclusion that it wasn't.

The Americans were more generous, although they did not share the great expectations which the British had once invested in Reed. John Carden in *Saturday Review* wrote that 'perhaps never before has there been such an impressive visual counter-point between the moods established by forces of nature, exemplified by the stormy North Atlantic, and the emotional tribulations of the very human characters'.

Reed's two American films, although made in Europe, proved a chastening experience for him. He had moved far away from his preferred working method of finding a good story and collaborating with the author on a screenplay. It was now ten years since his successful collaboration with Graham Greene on *The Third Man* had led to him being spoken of as the greatest director working in Britain. Since then he had endured a string of disappointments. His reputation was dropping with each film while his compatriot Alfred Hitchcock made one solid success after another. Hitchcock maintained a consistency of theme – American suspense thrillers tinged with romance – which Reed would not consider. But with his next project he was to beat Hitchcock at his own game, with help from his old friend Graham Greene.

Like Reed, Hitchcock was always looking for suitable subjects, and he too preferred a good literary basis for his script. Hitchcock was at the top of his form. *Vertigo* in 1958 was followed by *North by Northwest* in 1959 and *Psycho*, to be released in 1960. He now wanted to find something which would contrast with the terror of *Psycho*, and thought he had found it in the latest Graham Greene novel, *Our Man in Havana*, which the author described as an 'entertainment'.

Since *The Third Man* Greene had sold the rights of four novels which had been made into films, none of which had been as faithfully and sensitively translated to the screen as his two films with Reed. Each time the director had appeared to be trying to replicate *The Third Man*, and each time they had failed. *The Heart of the Matter* (1953), which Reed had shied away from as it came so soon after *The Third Man*, was made for Alexander Korda by George More O'Ferrall. The screenplay had taken liberties with the novel, and even with Trevor Howard in the lead and a strong cast, including Peter Finch and Denholm Elliott, the film had been an embarrassing failure. This was swiftly followed by the similarly awkward *The Stranger's Hand*, again starring Trevor Howard and the heroine of *The Third Man*, Alida Valli. *The End of the Affair* (1955) was given the full Hollywood treatment by Edward Dmytryk, although it was made in Britain with a cast which was almost entirely English. Again, the result had not pleased Greene. Joseph L. Mankiewicz's film of *The Quiet American* (1958) used the talents of *The Third Man*'s lighting cameraman Robert Krasker and had Michael Redgrave leading the cast. Yet again the plot, set in French Saigon, was altered in a damaging way, turning Greene's anti-Americanism into a cold war anti-Communist message.

It was with some trepidation, therefore, that Greene floated onto the market the film rights to *Our Man in Havana*. The Americans arrived first, offering large sums, with Hitchcock at the head of the pack.

Although written as a novel, *Our Man in Havana* had always been intended by Greene as a film. Shortly after the end of the war he had been invited by his friend Alberto Cavalcanti, the Brazilian film-maker working in Britain, to write a screenplay for him and had set to work on a treatment. He decided to plunder his own wartime experiences in the years 1943-44 as a reluctant spymaster in Kim Philby's section of the Secret Service. Greene's responsibility was Portugal, where those German Abwehr agents who had not already joined forces with the Allies, sending false reports back to Germany, had abandoned any serious efforts at spying and had filed fictional reports about Allied activity. They reasoned that inventing information was easier than discovering it and, as the tide of the war had turned, the Germans were no longer in a position to complain. Besides, their German income was too useful to abandon. Greene's experiences in East Africa had shown him how seriously agents' reports were taken at home base, however untrue or absurd. What is more, the headquarters staff always appeared grateful for even the most useless information, as long as that information kept coming. Greene wrote Cavalcanti a one-page synopsis of a story woven around this combination of sloth in the field and gullibility at headquarters.

The original plot for Cavalcanti was set in Tallinn, the capital of Estonia, in 1938 and concerned a man so besotted with his extravagant wife that in order to maintain his spying income he files false reports to prove his worth to his British paymasters. As the war approaches, his enemies and the local police begin to take him increasingly seriously. The story bears an uncanny resemblance to real British Secret Service activity in the Baltic states directly after the war when a ring of British agents and armed rebels was infiltrated wholesale by the Russians, who sent back fictional accounts of underground activity to London, which paid them handsomely for their information. Stalin joked that his espionage service was being funded by the British taxpayer, as indeed it was.

When Cavalcanti came to prepare Greene's idea for the screen, he decided to clear the plot in advance with the British Board of Film Censors, and was told that no certificate would ever be issued to a film which made fun of the Secret Service. Or so he said. Greene was suspicious that Cavalcanti may have disliked the idea and used the censors as an excuse. Either way, the film was abandoned.

Fifteen years later, however, Greene revived the germ of his original plot for his 'entertainment' – according to him, a story which was less depressing for him to write than a novel – to be called *Our Man in Havana*. He set the story in Cuba, to which he had made a number of visits in the fifties. According to Greene, he went there 'for the sake of the Floridita restaurant (famous for daiquiris and Morro crabs), for the brothel life, the roulette in every hotel, the fruit-machines spilling out jackpots of silver dollars, the Shanghai Theatre where for one dollar twenty-five cents one could see a nude cabaret of extreme obscenity with the bluest of blue films in the intervals.'

Greene realised that in his story of an Estonian agent who peddled false information to his bosses he 'had been planning the wrong situation and placing it at the wrong period. The shadows in 1938 of the war to come had been too dark for comedy; the reader could feel no sympathy for a man who was cheating his country in Hitler's day for the sake of an extravagant wife. But in fantastic Havana, among the absurdities of the Cold War (for who can accept the survival of Western capitalism as a great cause?) there was a situation allowably comic, all the more if I changed the wife into a daughter.'

Greene invented the character of Jim Wormold, an English vacuum-cleaner salesman in Cuba who is recruited by Hawthorne, the British Secret Service chief in the Caribbean, to assemble a ring of agents and to spy on the crooked Batista regime. At first reluctant to become involved in the spying trade, Wormold incompetently attempts to recruit spies but fails. However, he is determined to provide for his acquisitive daughter and so, rather than confess his failure and therefore lose his tax-free income, he begins to peddle make-believe information to the head of the Secret Service, code-named 'C', in London. All the characters except Wormold were based to some extent on people Greene had encountered during his own time in intelligence, with the exception of Dr Hasselbacher, who was inspired by a sad, overweight friend who lived near Greene in Capri. The novel was Greene at his most lighthearted and provided obvious material for a film.

Hitchcock began negotiations for the rights with Greene's agent, and after some months they had reached a figure of £25,000. Greene's agent demanded double the amount and Hitchcock sent his reply: 'Much too high.' Greene had seen his work emasculated by directors before and, although it would have been intriguing to see how Hitchcock would have coped with his plot, the thought of the master of visual gimmickry and suspense moulding *Our Man in Havana* for his own ends proved too much. The alternative, in any case, was a return to the old team of Reed and Greene, even if that would not enable Greene to earn anywhere near the £50,000 he had been demanding. Greene would be able to write his own screenplay, and although it had been ten years since he had worked with Reed, he knew that his friend still believed that above all a film director's purpose was to translate the intentions of the author onto the screen.

After *The Fallen Idol* and *The Third Man*, Greene had praised Reed's sensitivity as a film-maker, describing him in his preface to 'The Fallen Idol' as 'the only director I know with that particular warmth of human sympathy, the extraordinary feeling for the right face for the right part, the exactitude of cutting, and not least important the power of sympathising with an author's worries and an ability to guide him'.

In October 1958 Greene and Reed visited Columbia Pictures in New York, for whom Reed had, indirectly, made *The Key*, and a deal was struck. The pair then returned to London before setting out for Cuba to search for locations. Batista was running a regime of violence and suspicion, which Reed feared might interfere with the shooting. Greene's book was hardly reverential, and no dictator likes to be made fun of. But Greene told him not to be concerned. Reed explained: 'I was worried about how the old regime would react to the nasty suggestions about them in the book but [Graham] said, "Don't worry, they'll all be washed up by the time we're ready to come back here for production."' Columbia Pictures were not worried about filming amid the horrors perpetrated by America's ally Batista, so the plans for shooting went ahead, hotel rooms were booked and locations hired.

Reed persuaded Alec Guinness to play the central part of Wormold. Guinness admired much of Reed's work, but was taken aback by his interview-cum-audition in an office which Reed had decorated with photographs of actors. Reed explained, unflatteringly, that he put as much importance on finding the right face as on acting ability, which even amateurs could accomplish with a little careful tuition on the set. Guinness was also taken aback by Reed's explanation that the part of Wormold, although central, was to be a background figure around whom all the most interesting action would take place. He was a bewildered character, out of his depth, and Guinness would understand, suggested Reed, if for the most part he was left in the background of the picture. Close-ups would be very rare.

Greene and Reed established a screenwriting base in the Metropole Hotel, Brighton, in order to isolate themselves from the distractions of London, although, importantly to Reed, the capital was only a short train journey away. Reed installed himself in Room 221, with Greene next door. Greene explained their tried and proven system: 'I had a bedroom, there was a sitting room where a secretary worked and beyond that another bedroom where Carol slept. I would get up fairly early, do a quota of pages, hand them to the secretary who would type them before passing them on to Carol in bed. Carol and I would meet at lunchtime and discuss progress before going back to work again the same way in the afternoon. In the evenings we amused ourselves. We had that kind of closeness.' As before, there were disagreements and some anguish, but Reed always kept his temper. According to Greene, 'There was always a moment during the writing – usually about midway through the script – when one despaired and said "For God's sake, let's chuck this up!" followed by some hard words. Always coming from me, I'm afraid.' After three weeks' semi-isolation, they returned to London to continue their collaboration on the script. They then took a trip to Cadiz in Spain, to look for locations, where work carried on for several more weeks.

While the script was taking shape, important casting arrangements were made. There was pressure from Columbia to ensure some American presence for the all-important US market, but Reed kept it to a minimum. In casting the key parts, he settled some old debts. For the important role of Hawthorne, the British Caribbean spymaster, he chose Noël Coward, who had not made a film for some years. The deal was struck over lunch at the Aperitif Grill in Jermyn Street, St James's. Guinness called the decision 'a very amusing piece of casting. I am overjoyed.' Coward had been one of Selznick's choices for Harry Lime, but this part was altogether more suitable. Greene described Hawthorne as 'tall and elegant, in his stone-coloured tropical suit, and wearing an exclusive tie, he carried with him the breath of beaches and the leathery smell of a good club; you expected him to say, "The ambassador will see you in a minute."' Importantly, Coward was also popular in the United States.

For 'C', the Whitehall-bound head of the Secret Service, Reed chose his old friend Ralph Richardson, star of both *The Fallen Idol* and *An Outcast of the Islands*. A more difficult choice was the Batista police chief, which Reed gave to Ernie Kovacs, an American comedian with an inventive line in profanity and a penchant for ostentatiously smoking large cigars. Guinness, who had never met Kovacs before, considered him 'an outrageous extrovert, wild, rash, gipsy-like and, in a Goonish way, just about the funniest man I have ever met'. He grew a beard for the part. Burl Ives, fresh from his Oscar-winning performance in *The Big Country* (1958), agreed to play Dr Hasselbacher, and Maureen O'Hara took the part of the female agent sent to help with Wormold's huge workload. Finally Reed had to find a suitable young actress to play materialistic Milly, Wormold's seventeen-year-old daughter.

Reed had set his mind on Jean Seberg for the part, but she was signed to play an American student caught up with a young French murderer in Jean-Luc Godard's *À Bout de Souffle*, which was filming on the streets of Paris. It was Ernie Kovacs who suggested Jo Morrow, a nineteen-year-old blonde Texan actress who was already under contract to Columbia and had appeared in two teen-movies for them, though it was a third, *Gidget* (1959), a Sandra-Dee-type surfing picture, which was flown to London for Reed to judge her talents. She came with good references from the studio's drama coach, but it was plain that she had little acting talent. Reed, however, believed he could coax a good performance out of her. She was to play a child and teaching children how to act was something Reed prided himself on. In any case, she looked right for the part. Choosing her turned out to be a serious mistake.

Another important decision was whether or not to use colour and CinemaScope. Reed had now worked with both, with colour and Scope for *Trapeze*, and black-and-white Scope for *The Key*. He had enjoyed working in colour, but had considered it an experiment. It had worked for circus scenes, but he believed that the crude early Eastmancolor system was too artificial for either drama or comedy. Somehow, black-and-white, which audiences were used to, was less intrusive and therefore more realistic. And he believed that the key to any post-war film was above all that the audience should find it authentic. For *Our Man in Havana*, therefore, he decided to stick with monochrome CinemaScope. He explained: 'I've never seen a comedy in colour, not a good one. You cannot seem to get it. Colour is just not real enough yet. Perhaps it is for television, where your audience is sitting in a room with the lights on. But in a dark theatre, confronted by that huge screen, I feel that it is just not convincing.'

On 1 January 1959, Alec Guinness was made a knight in the New Year Honours List. The following day Fidel Castro overthrew Batista's regime in Cuba. Guinness was unperturbed. He said: 'Graham Greene is a good friend of Fidel Castro. He was in touch with him when he was out there getting the material for his novel and he was one of his supporters. So we're hoping it will be all right.' Ten years before, Reed had not dared take a cast and crew east of Singapore for fear of becoming embroiled in the distant Korean War; now he was about to film, with Columbia's blessing, in the immediate aftermath of a Communist revolution on America's doorstep. Whenever there was American nervousness, Reed stressed Greene's intimate link with Castro.

Before shooting began in March, Reed and Greene set off to pave the way for the cast and crew while Sir Alec Guinness and his wife Merula went to Jamaica at the invitation of Noël Coward, staying for ten days in a small guest house close to Coward's windowless hill-top villa. All three flew to Cuba together, where they were put up in the principal hotel in

Havana, the pink-and-white Capri Hotel. In Batista's day it was an up-market casino-cum-whorehouse, and little had changed in the two months since Castro's revolution. Coward was given a room based on a Mandarin's palace; the Guinnesses one in the style of Louis XVI. The hotel was gradually being vacated by American businessmen who were winding down their commercial interests on the island. All of Cuba's American tourists had been frightened away by the tales of life under Communism. Merula Guinness was unable to reach the hairdressers because of the queues of Castro's officers 'having their shoulder-length hair permed and their beards curled while they sat, with submachine guns across their knees, being flattered and cosseted by adoring Cuban hand-maidens'. Wagons laden with peasants in chickenwire cages were being drawn through the streets, taking their human cargo for questioning. On the first night Guinness walked into the hotel's gentlemen's lavatory to find a man loading a pistol. Kenneth Tynan, the theatre critic and journalist, was in Havana watching the spectacle of the young revolution wreaking its revenge on the former regime. It seemed a strange time to start filming a light comedy about spying. So thought the Cuban authorities, at least.

On the second day of shooting Reed, dressed in a *guayabera*, the traditional Cuban open-necked shirt, was approached by an official from the Ministry of the Interior demanding to see Greene's screenplay. They were concerned most of all that the part played by Kovacs, which was loosely based on Major Esteban Ventura, the deposed head of Batista's police repression squad, should not put the tyrant in a good light. While Dr Orlando Rodriguez, the new Minister for the Interior, was having the 30,000-word script translated for his perusal, he sent a government observer to keep an eye on the filming. Graham Greene, a Cuban lawyer friend and a man from Columbia Pictures began negotiations with the ministry, while work continued more or less as normal. Three weeks before, Reed and Greene had sent their script to the Ministry of Labour and work permits had been issued for the crew and cast. In the unsettled new government the Ministry of the Interior had intervened, claiming that it, too, had a right to oversee the project. Reed and Greene stressed to Castro's representatives that the film was concerned with events before the revolution. Since Castro's guerrilla army had taken over, a beard had come to represent a hero of the revolution, so Kovacs, playing a Batista police chief, had to take a razor to his. The local population, who took a keen interest in the filming, gave their instant verdict on the scenes being shot in front of them. Extras dressed in the blue uniforms of the Batista police were hissed, booed and spat at by the spectators.

Shooting retreated to the relative calm of the Havana Biltmore Yacht and Country Club. Coward and Guinness retained their English cool, Guinness by drinking iced tea, Coward by retiring to a hired air-conditioned car. Then an invitation came: Sir Carol Reed, Graham Greene, Sir Noël Coward and Sir Alec Guinness were cordially invited to meet Fidel Castro in his bungalow. The interruption would probably cost a whole day's shooting, but Reed told the cast and crew and the man from Columbia that it would be expedient to go. Guinness remembered the scene in his autobiography: 'When we arrived at the place we were shown up to the first-floor sitting room of an apartment from which Castro and his advisers could be seen through the slatted blinds of the bungalow below, all bearded, long-haired, forage-capped and gesticulating to each other in a cloud of cigar-smoke. Every ten minutes or so a henchman appeared and announced, "Fidel will be here in a minute." Ninety minutes passed and no Fidel came. We were all getting impatient when Carol firmly said, "This is a bloody waste of time. Let's go." Even Graham, an ardent admirer of Castro and a personal friend of his, thought it proper to leave; which we promptly did. The distressed henchman wrung his hands in despair but we pushed him aside. It was Noël, I think, who gave the fellow a reassuring smile and mouthed "mañana" at him.'

The shooting continued into May, with spasmodic co-operation from the new government, who happily closed streets and laid on crowds. The on-set censor had asked that a shoeshine boy, dressed in rags, be given a clean pair of trousers, and one alteration to the script was demanded. Where Greene had written, with English diffidence, that the murderous police chief was 'not such a bad fellow after all', the Cubans wished this to be changed to 'he's a man not without humour', a small price to pay for the shooting to continue without a hitch. The man from the ministry, explaining the change, confirmed that 'our revolution repudiates all censorship', but said that the change would be helpful to the film-makers because 'the book is a little weak'.

They were even allowed to restore the Tropicana, Greene's favourite blue nightclub, bringing back some of the pre-revolution strippers and filling the bar with the old sugar-daddies, for a scene where Wormold sprays soda over the police chief. A censor sat among the extras, leaping up every time he thought the girls were showing a little too much leg or breast. At one point he demanded of Reed that footage for the whole day's shooting should be handed over for cuts to be made. Reed, by now confident that Greene's friend Castro would protect them, stood firm and there was no comeback.

The film unit was visited by a number of distinguished visitors, including Ernest Hemingway, who lived in a beach house not far away and invited Greene, Coward and the Guinnesses to dinner one evening. And on the last day of filming Castro himself paid a visit to the location. Maureen O'Hara described his appearance on the set: 'He arrived in a large car with several of his lieutenants, quite unexpectedly. The word that he was there spread like wildfire and an enormous crowd gathered. He seemed to be very popular with the people. We stood talking in the square in the blazing sun.' He told Reed: 'Any film company can make any picture they want in Cuba,' and then continued: 'There is no censorship in my country. If you had trouble with my officials I apologise. It was all a mistake. It happened because I was away. You are to make your film exactly as you please. Those are my orders.'

On 15 May the shooting was completed and Reed returned to London. It had been an eventful seven weeks, but everything had gone very smoothly, with immense professionalism all round. Ernie Kovacs had at first appeared a disruptive presence, starting his first scene by wedging his head in the clapperboard. He also provided an obscene running commentary of events, to the amusement of Coward, Guinness and even Reed. Kovacs was pleasantly surprised by their benevolent attitude. He told Guinness: 'You know something? I was dreading working with all you toffee-nosed Brits: Sir Carol Reed, the Noël Coward, Sir Guinness. There'll never be a laugh, I thought, but you're the ones who laugh with me – not all those American broads and clapped-out bores.'

Alec Guinness, however, did not return to London happy. Reed was a great admirer of Guinness's technical brilliance and absolute professionalism, saying: 'Location is difficult. The sky is too high. You can't project personality in the street. But Alec is wonderful. He lets everybody run wild all around him, yet he disassociates completely. A great actor is completely selfish, self-centred and alone.' Yet Reed and Guinness had differed on how Wormold should be played. As Guinness wrote later: 'Carol wanted me to play the part . . . quite differently from the way I envisaged it. I had seen, partly suggested by the name, an untidy, shambling, middle-aged man with worn shoes, who might have bits of string in his pocket, and perhaps the *New Statesman* under his arm, exuding an air of innocence, defeat and general inefficiency. When I explained this Carol said, "We don't want any of your character acting. Play it straight. Don't act." That might be okay for some wooden dish perhaps but was disastrous for me. "Mustn't act, mustn't act," I kept repeating to myself; and I didn't. The director, particularly a world-famous one like Carol, is always right. Or often so.'

It was the acting, in the end, which undermined *Our Man in Havana*. Guinness was like a cypher, although his presence holds together the more colourful performances of Coward, Ives, Richardson and Kovacs, with Coward and Richardson quietly and ruthlessly upstaging each other whenever they appeared together. There were, however, some exceptional pieces of direction, beginning with the opening scene, with the camera gazing on a swimming girl then moving beyond the pool to reveal that it is perched on the roof of a building with a view of the whole of Havana. The script is tight and amusing, full of glorious jokes such as the pick-up of Wormold by Coward in the gent's lavatory of Sloppy Joe's Bar.

But some of Reed's plans went awry. After the success of the constantly teeming backgrounds in *Trapeze*, he had decided to construct a counterpoint to the main action by having a secondary plot involving a young woman and her lover take place among the extras on screen. It was a time-wasting gimmick which was largely removed from the final cut of the film. Guinness disliked 'the introduction of that totally phoney Latin-American couple, always munching apples and eyeing each other. It was a boring linking process.' But the most obvious flaw in the film was Jo Morrow, who demonstrated that she had little acting talent and humiliated Reed for his boast that he could glean a good performance from any non-actor. Greene blames Morrow for blowing a hole in an otherwise well-cast, well-acted, well-directed film. He explained: 'Poor Alec got the blame but his performance was ruined by Jo Morrow, the girl who plays his daughter. I remember we were all in the bar in Havana – Alec and Noël had arrived in from Jamaica – and Carol brought in the girl to introduce her to everyone. We went on to dinner without her and sat at a table outside a seafront restaurant. There was a long, long silence then Noël said: "Carol, what on earth induced you to hire that girl?" Carol replied that she had been shy "meeting all you famous people". "That little tart shy!" said Noël. And all Alec did was rub his hand up and down on the edge of the table, saying nothing with a look of despair on his face. Later on during the shooting I found myself talking to her and she told me that she was engaged to be married: "Of course," she said, "I don't know what he will feel about being known as Mr Jo Morrow."'

Reed returned for studio work at Shepperton and a single location session in Parliament Square for the film's final scene, then took a ten-day holiday in Salzburg with Pempie. On his return, he and Bert Bates set about editing the film into its final form. At one stage, worried that the film would be too long, Reed removed a scene where Guinness clowns around with a fruit bowl on his head to amuse his daughter; a little later he slipped the scene back in. In late November 1959, Reed delivered a print of the completed film to the managing director of Columbia in Britain. It was scheduled for release on 30 December at the Odeon, Leicester Square. Reed had come to dread the verdict of the critics, often being violently ill the day before an opening, and this time he was no less nervous. The film had all the ingredients of success, but it did not have the power and the certainty of his previous collaborations with Greene.

On the day of the film's release, Reed invited Guinness to his home in Chelsea for a drink. Both had a great deal riding on the film, and both knew that it did not represent their best work. What was particularly galling for Guinness was that he had worked so hard; seventeen weeks in a row with only one day off.

Reed was deeply upset by the tone of the press reviews. As they stood at the window, a crocodile of schoolchildren walked past. Reed turned to Guinness and said: 'At least they can't read.' Guinness remembered: 'We shrugged the whole thing off.' The critics concluded that, even with a brilliant Greene script and a fine cast, Reed had failed to recapture the magic of his films of the late forties.

11

Mutiny in Tahiti

Carol Reed's favourite director was not one of the great art directors like Sergei Eisenstein or Luis Buñuel, but the versatile Hollywood stalwart William Wyler, who made commercial films like *Mrs Miniver* and *The Best Years of Our Lives* and who became a close friend. Reed, like his father, believed in the values of the West End theatre, with popular stars acting in solid, entertaining stories made with high production standards. Wyler represented those West End values in Hollywood. Reed's other favourite directors included René Clair, John Ford, Vittorio de Sica and Joseph L. Mankiewicz, and his favourite actors were Greta Garbo, Cary Grant, Jean Gabin, Spencer Tracy, Vivien Leigh, Jean Arthur and Marlene Dietrich. The directors were all storytellers and the actors all entertainers.

Reed also believed in much of what the Hollywood studio system represented. He too understood commercial necessities and made well-crafted pictures for a large, middle-market audience. And as a professional film-maker he admired the technical facilities which Hollywood had to offer. His temperament, and lack of education beyond a basic level, made him suspicious of those directors who used their fictional films for a serious purpose. In a *New York Times* interview in 1950 he commented: 'I don't believe the cinema is a place for little lectures on how everybody should live. I don't think audiences want them either, unless they are very original and striking. Personally I dislike the infusion of amateur politics into films. Certainly that is not the director's job.' He did not much like politics in anything. By nature conservative and apolitical, he enjoyed all the establishment values and believed that Labour would take his money away. He had little notion of 'art' and considered his trade something done as a business. A great film-maker was above all one who pleased his audience.

He once summed up his attitude to film-making and to films:

'The most important purpose of the commercial film-maker is to produce entertainment which will draw the largest possible number of the paying public into the cinema, and (this is a most important condition) keep them there. You could gather a large number of people together to gaze at a two-headed dog, especially if you had a man with a loud enough voice announcing it; but the number of times people can be induced to pay money to see the dog is strictly limited; the wise showman provides also a bearded lady and a living skeleton – all, be it emphasised, strictly genuine. The public may be gullible, but there is a limit to its credulity. The swindling or unimaginative showman, like the man who deliberately makes bogus or otherwise unworthy films, may be successful for a while; but he has no future.'

By 1960, it appeared that the old Hollywood studio system had no future. The popular habit of a weekly or bi-weekly visit to the cinema was being undermined by the growth of television. In the late fifties, studios discovered that the new cinematic tricks like colour, wide screen and 3-D were not enough to lure the audience from their homes. What they believed was needed was a dramatic spectacle which an audience would be so eager to see that they would book tickets for it as they would for the theatre. The epic picture, a throwback to the days of silent movies, was revived.

In the twenties, epics were made to impress audiences with spectacles, usually historic – the American Civil War or chariot racing in ancient Rome – which only a cinema screen could embrace. During the second wave of epics in the fifties and sixties, studios turned again to the subjects they had used in the silent days, then to classic stories which had proved popular before. They assumed that public taste had changed very little and that contemporary reworkings of old box-office hits would therefore be successful.

Metro-Goldwyn-Mayer had built its reputation from its earliest days upon the mammoth scale of its productions, and in the late fifties it decided to remake a number of its early epics. MGM had made the ancient Roman epic *Ben Hur* in 1926, and in 1959 they made it again, with a chariot race the centrepiece as before. This time, however, the film was in colour, on a wide screen, and was so long that an interval was needed to restore the audience's flagging concentration. Television could not compete with such huge resources and with such spectacle.

Inspired by the profits of *Ben Hur*, MGM announced that other epics would be remade, among them *The Four Horsemen of the Apocalypse*, originally filmed in 1921. At the same time the studio announced their intention to remake *Mutiny on the Bounty*, which Irving Thalberg had produced in 1935, with Charles Laughton as the hateful Captain Bligh forever screaming for a Mr Christian played by Clark Gable. Eric Ambler, who with Peter Ustinov had scripted *The New Lot* and *The Way Ahead* for Reed during the war, was being wooed by MGM to write a screenplay for *The Four Horsemen of the Apocalypse*, which was eventually handed over to Robert Ardrey and John Gay, then to write a second version of *Mutiny on the Bounty*, a subject which appealed to him rather more.

He found himself employed by Sol C. Siegel, the head of the studio, who sat him in the comfort of his private screening room, armed him with a bottle of bourbon and projected the Thalberg film. When the lights went up, Siegel turned to Ambler and said: 'You know who wants to do *Mutiny on the Bounty* again?' Ambler waited in nervous anticipation. Siegel delivered the news: 'Marlon Brando.' Ambler was innocent enough to ask which part Brando wished to play and was told, 'Gable's.' He was pressed to write a script with Brando in mind and he agreed, on condition that extensive research was done to discover the historical truth of the mutiny. That would at least give him something new to work on, rather than having to slavishly follow the pattern laid down in 1935. Ambler hired a researcher in London to trawl the Admiralty for information about the mutiny which would give him a new pitch. The research revealed that the events portrayed in the Laughton/Gable film, directed by Frank Lloyd, were largely fictional. This had been brought about by the original screen-writers, who had followed the three-part historical novel about the mutiny by Charles Nordhoff and James Hall for which MGM had bought the rights. The film had also departed from the facts in order to accommodate Charles Laughton's interpretation of William Bligh as a sadistic bully.

Ambler's research in the Royal Navy archives uncovered elements of Bligh's life which had not been shown on the screen before. He had been navigator for Captain James Cook, the discoverer of Australia, and was a brilliant navigator and cartographer. When one of Cook's captains died, Bligh had not been preferred by the Navy and had harboured deep resentment about his treatment. Bligh had often captained merchantmen and had sailed with Fletcher Christian a number of times as ship's mate. It was also discovered that many of the mutineers suffered from venereal disease.

Ambler was pleased with these findings, and believed that he had discovered a new story worth telling. He wrote a script and delivered it to the picture's producer, Aaron Rosenberg, 'a big, All-American football player, a Jew from an orthodox family, who refused to play football on the sabbath. He was a very nice man, a very decent man.' The film was to suffer from the inability of a number of very nice, very decent men to harness the uncontrolled ego of Marlon Brando.

To Hollywood producers, Reed appeared the safest of safe pairs of hands, unlikely to take any financial risks. Sol Siegel thought Reed an ideal choice to direct Brando in a film which was to be so expensive that no detailed budget had been prepared and no upper limit fixed. Nor had a shooting schedule been prepared, for this was to be new territory. MGM said that they were prepared for the film to take as long as it took. Reed was slightly nervous of this way of working; during the filming of *The Man Between* he had endured budget restrictions imposed from head office, and he did not wish to repeat such a bruising experience. He was confident, however, that he would make a good picture and keep costs to a minimum.

Ambler was glad that Reed was to be the director, as he knew him to be a reasonable man with whom a screenwriter could argue and be given a fair judgement. The problem was going to be Reed's working relationship with Brando. By the end of the fifties, Marlon Brando was at the height of his powers as a box-office star. The early integrity of his acting in *The Wild One* (1953) and *On the Waterfront* (1954) had given way to unremitting commercialism. He appeared as Napoleon in a remake of *Desirée* (1954) and was to be found singing in the star-laden *Guys and Dolls* (1955). His most recent films, in which he had taken a closer interest, *The Teahouse of the August Moon* (1956) and *Sayonara* (1957), had awoken in him a passion for the Oriental and the exotic. So it was that Aaron Rosenberg, Eric Ambler and

Carol Reed found themselves kneeling, without shoes, in Brando's Japanese drawing room at 12900 Mulholland Drive in Coldwater Canyon, above the San Fernando valley, discussing the character of Fletcher Christian. Reed was enjoying his first experience of the indignities of working in Hollywood.

Mutiny on the Bounty was one of the first films to humour every whim of a star actor. Previously the studio chiefs and their producers had been in control, with directors merely overseeing the shooting of a film. Although actors appeared to be able to control their work, few were given the opportunity unless they became producers themselves, like Charles Chaplin and Douglas Fairbanks. Even the most popular actors were considered by producers to be of minor importance and something of a nuisance. Hitchcock's remark that actors were little more than cattle to be prodded and ushered around a set was the prevailing attitude.

By the fifties, with the studios in disarray and desperate for survival, actors who had the proven ability to attract audiences back to cinemas were in great demand. Brando had a string of bravura acting performances behind him, and had just finished directing himself in *One Eyed Jacks*, which had whetted his appetite for total control of his performance. Such was Brando's pulling power with audiences that he could not only ask a colossal fee but ensure that extravagant conditions were included in his contract.

Reed had never worked in such circumstances before. His two most recent films, both American, had been made in Europe. To be given Brando and a limitless budget was to place a great deal of faith in him, so it was with some surprise that he found himself kneeling, barefoot and in braces, somewhere in the Hollywood hills on a sweltering night, while Brando lectured him on the part of Fletcher Christian, the state of the screenplay and his interpretation of the events surrounding the mutiny.

Brando was gently spoken and said that he agreed with the structure of Ambler's original three-act script, in which Christian would dominate the third act when the mutineers reached Pitcairn Island. When Ambler pointed out that life on Pitcairn for Christian's sailors did not match Brando's preconceptions, the actor sagely told him: 'Eric, no man is an island unto himself.' Ambler remembered: 'It became quite extraordinary.

Carol sat there sweating in his braces while this self-regarding fathead told us it was to be *his* picture.'

Brando was thirty-seven, and had negotiated a fee of $500,000 from MGM. As far as Sol Siegel was concerned, this was Brando's film. Rosenberg was under no illusions that he was anything more than a studio nursemaid to ensure that the great man was kept happy.

Reed, though, was not only new to the ways of Hollywood, but imagined that he had been chosen by MGM because of his ability with money and with temperamental actors. He believed that the picture was his, despite Brando, and his experience with both Burt Lancaster and Carl Foreman had convinced him that it was possible to work as an equal partner even with Americans who were being paid substantially more than him. He considered himself a professional, like a doctor or perhaps a psychiatrist, whose opinion, when sought, would be followed because of his experience and his knowledge of film-making. Reed had lived a charmed life, almost permanently working in a business which offered no security of employment. He retained an honesty and gentle naivety of character which was about to be shattered by the antics of an egotistical method actor.

Reed inherited a film which had already been two years in the making. A replica of the *Bounty*, powered by diesel engines and a third larger than the original to accommodate the cameras, was being constructed in Nova Scotia. Its Canadian crew were to sail the ship through the Panama Canal to Tahiti, where the cast and film unit would join them after filming some early scenes in Hawaii. A film crew aboard would take background shots of the new *Bounty* at sea.

The studio had not told Reed that they were prepared to invest $5 million in the film, believing that they would soon be able to recoup their money, such would be the pulling power of Brando. And Sol Siegel did not tell Rosenberg, or Ambler, or Reed, that Brando had agreed to play Christian on condition that he had total veto powers over the script. In previous pictures he had become used to having his lines tailor-made for him, matching his understanding of how the part was developing, and because the daily rewrites were often done overnight, he had also become accustomed to having his lines written out on boards for him to read in front of the cameras.

The appointment of Reed, the actors' director, appeared to be a sop to Brando. Reed saw it differently. He wanted to make a big Hollywood picture and this was as big as they came. He believed that there was a Hollywood ethos which would protect him from the demands of a single actor, and thought that he would be able to do what William Wyler and others would have done in similar circumstances and be tough if necessary. He did not know that the studio had given Brando control of the picture. Reed took Max out of school and set off for Tahiti with Pempie, letting his house in Chelsea to Judy Garland, who was living briefly in London while performing at the Palladium.

According to Ambler, Reed was determined to succeed and thought that he could handle Brando. After all, he was an actor. 'Look here, Eric, we'll manage. These Americans!' he said as they set out for Honolulu and the first scenes of the vague shooting schedule. Reed's optimism was understandable. He had ensured that Brando was the only American in the cast, and as usual had packed the film with familiar players, among them Trevor Howard as Bligh, Hugh Griffith and the young Richard Harris. Extras would be taken on at Tahiti. Brando would be outnumbered. In fact an early worry was that Brando would be overwhelmed by his acting colleagues. Reed gave an assurance, which was to prove sadly ironic, that Brando would be allowed to maintain his own acting style and way of speech. 'His style is his own, just as his personality is his own. But this does not mean that his style will clash with that of English actors.' Always intrigued by actors and how they appeared on the screen, Reed became fascinated by Brando's evident appeal. He would take Trevor Howard off to a drug store, order two jumbo-sized chocolate malted milks and ask him, 'What has Brando got? What is it?' It was to remain a mystery.

Delays in the construction of the boat, followed by its long journey to Tahiti, meant that the film started late. Nonetheless, Ambler was still writing drafts of the screenplay when the company set off in November 1960 for the Royal Hawaiian Hotel at Diamond Head, Honolulu. All the principals were given suites and Ambler sat down to write yet another version of the script, hoping that this time it would meet Brando's ever-changing interpretation of Christian's character. The difficulty was how to portray Christian's attitude to the mutineers. Was he to be a co-conspirator, a father-figure or a saint? Brando wavered and Ambler kept writing.

Many weeks later, at one of the many drinks parties thrown to bring the unit together, Brando was charming to the rest of the cast, none of whom had worked with him before. He spoke very little in the mornings and ignored everyone until lunchtime, but in the evenings he warmed up. And gradually the extent of his sexual appetite became apparent. He had toured the islands looking for locations, and had made love to a number of local women. At a party to welcome Bengt Danielson, an anthropologist who was an expert on the Tahitian Islanders and their habits and had been hired to ensure the film's authenticity, Brando pounced on him.

'Tell me, Dr Danielson, what is the incidence of V.D. on the island? I did pick up a couple of nails in Paris . . . '

Danielson answered: 'Ninety-five per cent?'

Brando blinked. 'Oh. How do people get along?'

Danielson explained the system: 'You ask a girl; you send her to hospital; she brings you a certificate.'

Brando was aghast. 'For Christ's sake . . . '

A new member of the production team was promptly sent out from Los Angeles to administer to Brando's individual venereal needs.

The lack of an agreed screenplay meant that the production became almost frozen. Yet Brando continued to ask for the script to be rewritten. 'I'm not getting to you. You don't understand,' he told Ambler, who wrote and rewrote until he came to the end of his patience. Ambler was earning $3,000 a week for his pains, but it was not enough. He told Reed and Rosenberg that he was at the end of his tether. Then one evening, after Reed and Ambler had drunk a great deal of whisky, an argument broke out between them.

Ambler confessed: 'I don't want to go on with this. I don't think it is going to get anywhere.'

'Oh Eric . . . ' Reed replied, as if giving up at that moment would be to abandon a project just as it was about to succeed.

'I don't think he wants to finish the picture,' said Ambler.

'I agree with you on one thing,' said Reed. 'He should have been Bligh and we could have had Trevor as Christian.'

Ambler thought that Brando would never agree to that and declared his intentions.

'I'm going back to L.A. I have nothing more to write.'

'You're deserting me,' said Reed.

'Yes. I don't think there is anything left to salvage here.'

'Please stay. We'll do what *we* want.'

But Ambler was determined to go. 'We will never appease this bastard. I want to get out.'

The following day, Ambler held a farewell party in the grounds of the hotel and another row broke out between him and Reed, who appealed to his patriotism. 'You should stay and help. After all, you're British.' Ambler returned to the west coast and Howard Clewes, the first of an eventual nine replacement writers, arrived from Los Angeles.

Ambler took with him fourteen draft scripts for the final third of the screenplay. He felt sorry for Reed, and knew that it would be impossible for a good picture to come out of the situation Brando had created, that Reed would not be able to direct and that eventually Brando would demand that *he* be allowed to take over.

Without a trial script nothing but background shots could be filmed. The company arrived at Bora Bora and two hundred Polynesians were hired to take part in a spectacular stone-fishing scene, in which a bay full of fish was surrounded by colourfully clothed islanders who splashed their way to the shore, driving the fish before them. By the time the company, which included 110 Hollywood film technicians, reached Tahiti, the rainy season had started and filming progressed slowly. Pempie and Max arrived in Tahiti and she tried to quell what was fast becoming a mutinous team of British actors, frustrated by the lack of filming, the weather which kept them captive and the low morale caused by Brando's dominance over Reed.

Brando's promise that Tahiti would be like paradise now seemed hollow, as his self-indulgent behaviour was dragging out the filming. Trevor Howard muttered, 'I'm miserable and fed up and sick of everything.' Richard Harris was in a worse condition. 'Since the scriptwriters write the next day's lines in the evening, there's the added pleasure of sitting up all night memorising a script held in one hand while swatting insects with the other.' Reed was at the sharp end of Brando's demands, and maintained a dignified silence. He was determined not to give up. The arrival of Tarita Terriipai, the nineteen-year-old Polynesian girl who would play opposite Brando, only made matters worse, as Brando fell openly in love with her and became increasingly reluctant to appear in front of the cameras at all. Reed came to the conclusion that he had a disaster on his hands and that Brando was to blame. One day, when Reed asked Brando to try a certain way of playing a scene, the actor refused. When Reed asked him why, he said: 'Well, I don't see it that way.' Reed replied in his quiet voice: 'I think it is time for me to go.'

In February 1961, Reed, by now suffering acute stomach pains caused by gallstones, despatched Pempie and Max on a slow tour around the world while he took the company back to Hollywood. He hoped that the studio would realise that whoever directed Brando would find the task impossible, and that he should be discarded in favour of Trevor Howard. Sol Siegel, the head of the studio, did not agree. The picture would be a success because of Brando, however unlikely that might seem to Reed. It was Reed who would have to go. Reed told Howard how things stood and a delegation from the cast was quickly sent to Siegel, declaring that if Reed was sacked, all the British actors would rip up their contracts. Reed was embarrassed by this show of solidarity and convinced them that, far from being sacked, he was quitting. A combination of Siegel's threats and Reed's cool reason ensured that the cast remained intact. Reed accepted defeat and, in a noble but futile gesture, returned his fee to the studio. Brando and the cast returned to Tahiti, where the film continued under the direction of Lewis Milestone.

The studio was desperate to get the picture finished. Milestone demanded an enormous fee and it was quickly granted – anything as long as some of the studio's investment could be salvaged and Brando appeased. Milestone remembered: 'I thought, this is one way of getting rich quick – I get the salary and, at most, it couldn't take more than two or three months. After I'd signed the contract, I found out that in that year all they'd had on screen was about seven minutes of film. I spent a year on it.'

An indication of the insults Reed had been silently accepting from Brando comes from Milestone's memory of his experience: 'Everything went off fine for the first couple of weeks, and then suddenly we were doing a scene and Marlon spoke to the cameraman, right past me. He said: "Look, I'll tell you, when I go like this, it means roll it, and this gesture means you stop the camera. You don't stop the camera until I give you the signal." Well, I was amazed, but I didn't say anything about it.' Milestone walked away and read a magazine. When Rosenberg asked why he wasn't watching the filming, he replied, 'I hate to see movies in pieces, so you let him do this and when it's all finished and cut, for ten cents I can walk into the theatre and see the whole thing at once. Why should I bother to look at it now.'

Reed's name does not appear on the final credits and, apart from the stone-fishing and Captain Bligh's awkward dance scenes, little of his footage remains. He could take small comfort from the fact that *Mutiny on the Bounty* finally cost MGM over $27 million, recouped $10 million and brought the studio to its knees. The cost to Reed had been a personal crisis of confidence and an enormous blow to his prestige. To be sacked from any project is a humiliation, but to be so conclusively shown that Hollywood does not want your talent was a profound rejection. Reed appeared to have aged considerably.

He went back to work as quickly as possible, and it is a mark of the quality of his work for Columbia that in the summer of 1962 he was provided by them with another project, *The Running Man*. The story was a slender one, from a novel by Shelley Smith, adapted into a screenplay by John Mortimer. Two young British actors were to play the main protagonists: Laurence Harvey, as a commercial pilot who crashes his own plane then plots revenge on the insurance company which refuses to compensate him for the loss, and Alan Bates as the insurance investigator who follows him to Spain. The woman who links them in romance was to be played by Lee Remick.

Harvey and Bates were products of the new realistic British stage movement. Bates created the role of Cliff in John Osborne's *Look Back in Anger*, made his film debut in Osborne's *The Entertainer*, appeared in the film of Stan Barstow's *A Kind of Loving*, and had just completed a film of Harold Pinter's *The Caretaker*. Harvey had spent more time in poor British pictures. But by the early sixties he had worked in the United States in *The Alamo* and *Butterfield Eight* as well as British films like the screen version of John Braine's novel *Room at the Top* and Wolf Mankowitz's adaptation of Willis Hall's play *The Long and the Short and the Tall*, known in the United States as *Jungle Fighters*.

Reed had little time for the new movements in British theatre, nor for the New Wave directors in France. He said: 'If the public can watch good artists in dramatic situations with colourful backgrounds in a way of life they may never experience for themselves, why should we drag them into the cinema to look for an hour or two at a kitchen sink, a one-set film, the greasy dishes and the mental and moral miasma of certain elements in society?' In a radio interview he said that he was firmly an Old Wave director and had been weaned and brought up on conventional movie-making methods and felt it would be a mistake for him to change.

There was certainly no intention of taking any risks in *The Running Man*. As if to emphasise Reed's points about the new trends in both the theatre and the cinema, he hugged the security of an old working friendship by once again joining forces with his favourite cinematographer, Robert Krasker, and his old editor, Bert Bates. He was joined by Kits Browning, Daphne du Maurier's son, as his assistant.

Reed also fell back on his old trick, devised for *Trapeze*, of filling the background of the CinemaScope screen with action, leaving the story in the foreground to look after itself. Once again, however, an actor's demands dictated his working schedule. Laurence Harvey had earned so much in Hollywood that he was reluctant to return to Britain because he would be liable to pay income tax. He therefore placed in his contract a clause which said that all filming should take place outside Britain. At first Reed planned to begin shooting in Barcelona, working up towards the mountains of Andorra, but he switched to taking the company south, with the film's grand finale a spectacular crash into the Rock of Gibraltar, not only a recognisable location but, to fit in with the ironies of the plot, the symbol of the Prudential insurance company.

Reed took the cast and crew off for a ten-week location schedule in Malaga, Algeciras, San Roque and La Linea on the Costa del Sol. Harvey thought that the film was a non-starter, Lee Remick remained icy throughout and only Alan Bates emerges with credit. The plot twisted and turned, but Reed found few ways of heightening tension. There was a painful reminder of his lost ability to keep an audience on edge when an open-air showing of *Odd Man Out* was screened in his honour at the bullring at San Roque.

Reed was looking and feeling his age. He was now considerably overweight and felt unwell a great deal of the time. He was losing his hearing and his concentration. He never took any exercise, drank far too much alcohol and had been overeating for the whole of his life, although his height and his large frame disguised his fatness for many years. He ate irregularly, rarely sitting down at the table with Pempie at mealtimes. Instead he would drink one gin and tonic after another, then descend on the kitchen whenever he felt hungry. He could not cook anything except bacon and eggs, which he did by creating the maximum mess.

Once, staying in a New York hotel, he confined himself to his room in order to be able to plough through some scripts. After three days he was feeling very ill and summoned a doctor, who asked him what he had been eating. He said he had eaten nothing. The doctor, perplexed, could not understand why a man who had eaten nothing was showing all the symptoms of chronic indigestion until he left the hotel room. Outside, waiting to be cleared away, were half a dozen empty ice-cream bowls. The doctor returned to Reed and put it to him that he *had* been eating, he had eaten ice cream and nothing else. Reed confessed, but said that he did not consider eating ice cream to be eating.

For Bert Bates, who had been at his side through so many films, Reed's growing indecisiveness was immensely frustrating. Bates attempted to goad him into action and grew increasingly impatient with Reed's by now genuine inability to make decisions. In the past Reed had always welcomed comments from anyone on a set, however humble, but on *The Running Man* he started acting on the contradictory advice. It was as if all power of discrimination had left him.

In September a stunt pilot and a cameraman crashed into the sea and were seriously injured. There was some relief when the studio shooting began at the Ardmore Studios at Bray, near Dublin, soon afterwards. During the period of editing, Bates found Reed's dithering increasingly irritating and attempted to force him to be decisive. What had previously been a genuine interest in others' opinions had become a fundamental lack of confidence in his own decisions. Bates would say to him, 'Well, I haven't got all day. I've got some roses to prune,' and would leave the cutting room to tend his rose garden. Reed was still paying the terrible toll of Brando's humiliation of him during *Mutiny on the Bounty*.

The Running Man was dismissed by the critics when it was released in London in August 1963. *The Times* found the whole thing too old fashioned and obvious. The *Sunday Telegraph* believed that 'something awful has happened to the cool professionalism of Carol Reed. The old theme of love and betrayal (magnificently explored in *The Third Man*) goes for nothing here. The style of the film is casual. The tension doggedly refuses to build. Fishing for compliments to pay, one latches thankfully on the fact that the colour photography is splendid. But for a Carol Reed film, it isn't much to say.' The *Guardian* was sterner still. Richard Roud wrote: 'I defy anyone, however, on the basis of a viewing of *The Running Man*, to detect any trace of Reed's former talents.' It was universally thought that Reed was in terminal decline. In France the decline was stressed by the insensitivity of a switch in the film's title to *Le Deuxième Homme*.

What Reed needed was for some confidence to be shown in him, and it came from the Americans, who did not regard falling out with Brando or losing a job as anything more than the routine scarring of a rough, tough trade. The vote of confidence came from an unlikely source.

In the summer of 1963, Charlton Heston was considering a number of films, among them a screen adaptation of Irving Stone's historical novel *The Agony and the Ecstasy*, about the life of Michelangelo. Stone was a highly successful writer of popular historical biographies, researching extensively before writing a long fictional account of his subject's life. His biography of Vincent van Gogh, *Lust for Life*, was filmed by Vincente Minnelli for the wide screen in 1956, with Kirk Douglas as van Gogh, and his life of Michelangelo, published in 1961, had sold fifty-one million copies by 1963 and was an obvious subject for film treatment. Heston became interested in Michelangelo and in the screenplay written by Philip Dunne, which concentrated on the years in which Michelangelo painted the Sistine Chapel ceiling. By October 1963 Heston had found a studio, Fox, who believed the picture could be profitable.

Heston was in constant demand. His sculpted looks and dominant presence were ideal for the scale of monumental acting needed on a wide screen, and his muscularity meant that he wore the armour and togas of epics with conviction. His problem over *The Agony and the Ecstasy* was not that he was uncertain of the part of Michelangelo – he believed the script to be 'possibly the best-written that's ever been submitted to me' – but how to make time for it among his other offers, for *War Lord*, *Fate is the Hunter*, *Satan Bug* and *Khartoum*.

By October 1963 he had signed a deal with Fox. The rest of the cast and the choice of director remained undecided. At the time of signing, Darryl F. Zanuck, Fox's executive producer on the movie, was considering Fred Zinnemann, the maker of *From Here to Eternity* (1953) who had recently directed *The Sundowners*. The important part of Pope Julius II was hovering between Laurence Olivier and Spencer Tracy. It had been decided that, to reduce costs, all filming would take place in Italy. At the end of October Rex Harrison became interested in playing the Pope and by mid-November he signed a contract, but there was still no director, Zinnemann having declined the project. The studio suggested Guy Green, the British director who had recently worked with Heston on *Diamond Head*.

By mid-December Fox were negotiating with Reed. There could be no better indication of the decline in Reed's status after the disaster of *Mutiny on the Bounty* and the lacklustre direction of *The Running Man* than the way his name was ultimately picked for *The Agony and the Ecstasy*. The studio had become desperate. Reed offered years of experience with actors and of economical work on location, yet even when all a studio needed was an efficient technician, he was far from first choice. Heston, however, was pleased. He wrote in his diary on 31 December 1963, 'They want to make a firm offer to Carol Reed to direct. That's fine with me.' When Reed agreed to direct the film at the beginning of January 1964, Heston wrote: 'The word from Fox is that we have Carol Reed . . . This is good, I'm sure. We have a chance for a superior film with him; he confers class on the whole project.'

At the beginning of January Reed left London for New York and had a meeting with Zanuck and three days of conferences with his associates before flying to California on the 11th. On the 14th Reed and Heston met for the first time. Heston recorded: 'A full morning meeting with Carol Reed on *The Agony and the Ecstasy*. These first meetings are always spent largely convincing each other you're both men of high artistic purpose. Nonetheless, I think he can do this film. He's intent on getting rehearsal time before shooting begins on the scenes between me and Rex Harrison. I'm for this. We have to find a way to keep them from being simply a series of quarrels.' He concluded, 'So far, this one smells OK.' Heston returned to work on two other films, *The War Lord* and *Major Dundee*.

At the end of January, Reed and Zanuck met in Paris before Reed, on $1,000 a week expenses, and the screenwriter Philip Dunne set off for Rome, for location-hunting and two weeks of forging a shooting script between them.

By May, while Reed was scouting around Tuscany, Heston was undergoing make-up tests. He had been much criticised for looking exactly the same in each of his movies and he was determined to make himself look quite different as Michelangelo. His nose was already broken from a sporting injury, but with the help of the master make-up artist Ben Nye, greasepaint and a small rubber tap-washer, the break was emphasised. He also grew a beard for the part and cut his hair into a Florentine bang. At the end of the month he flew to join Reed and Harrison in Rome.

Reed had arranged many of the locations. A set representing St Peter's Square as it was in 1508 had been constructed in the medieval town of Todi. The ruins of Michelangelo's villa were rebuilt. But the main action would be shot in the Dino de Laurentiis Studios at Cinecittà, in the Via Pontina outside Rome, where a replica of the Sistine Chapel had been erected.

At first it was assumed that filming would take place in the chapel itself and Reed was surprised to discover that the Vatican were willing, but before contracts were signed it was decided that using the genuine ceiling as a background would cause too many problems. There would be immense insurance cover against damage, the actors might be intimidated by working in the holy surroundings of a church and, most importantly, the ceiling was very different from when it was first painted: the colours had faded and changed over time and there were large, inch-wide cracks in the plaster. A replica would be expensive, but more versatile for filming. Reed considered it very important, however, to have a ceiling as closely resembling the original as possible. Instead of having the studio ceiling painted by artists, he had the true ceiling photographed and reconstructed, with the original colours restored and cracks in the original painted out. Plaster would be spread over the studio ceiling and removed as Heston acted painting the Biblical scenes.

As soon as Heston arrived in Rome, Reed took him on a tour of the locations and, in the long car journey to the village of Todi, explained the changes he had made to the script. Heston wrote in his day-book: 'I'm drawn to Carol. He's a very available man, easier to reach than Willy [Wyler].' And the following day: 'I feel I'm learning a great deal from him . . . He's made changes that tighten and intensify the story as well as the character.'

Reed warned Heston that Rex Harrison would not necessarily be easy to work with. According to Heston: 'Perhaps he's insecure over who has the best part, which is understandable.' Harrison, however, saw the matter quite differently. He remembered that he 'had been persuaded, against my better judgement' to take the part, not least perhaps because of his fee of $250,000. He looked forward to working again with Carol Reed, 'my old friend from the Home Guard days', for the first time since *Night Train to Munich*, but was disturbed to find that the years had changed Reed. After his bruising at the hands of Brando, he had become very wary about Hollywood actors and the power they had to cause misery. In his autobiography Harrison remembered: 'I don't think Carol was himself. I think Charlton Heston was absolutely himself, and by the end I didn't know who I was. Pope I knew I was, though the real star was Michelangelo, and Heston very politely and very nicely made me feel that it was extremely kind of me to be supporting him. Carol did little to disabuse him of this notion, so I did everything I could to make myself believe that the picture was about Pope Julius rather than about Michelangelo. In this I was not too successful.' In June Diane Cilento joined the cast as the Contessina de' Medici.

Before filming began, Reed declared: 'I see this as a study of a genius, not a hero in the conventional sense. What interests me most is that Michelangelo was a man tormented by self-criticism, anxious about the work still left to do, who thought of his art as an act of self-confession.' Shooting started in the village of Carrara, north of Seravezza, at the site of the quarries where Michelangelo found the marble for his sculpture of Moses for the tomb of Pope Julius. An extended scene would show masons cutting the marble and Michelangelo hiding from the papal troops sent to bring him back to Rome to work on the ceiling of the Sistine Chapel.

Reed was worried about the wildness of Heston's beard, but there was no need for immediate action because the first day's work amounted to nothing. Although it was June, the mist rolled off the sea and shooting came to a halt. When it resumed the following day, Reed was in confident form. Heston, unlike Brando, liked to be made to work hard and enjoyed positive criticism, but was a little unnerved by Reed's apparent insouciance. 'Carol prints very quickly . . . maybe too quickly, though I don't see how such simple shots could have been done very differently . . . So far, Carol seems straightforward; he knows what he wants and is pleased with what I give him. Let him not be too easily pleased.' The relationship continued to prove fruitful. Heston wrote in his diary for 17 June: 'Carol gives a great deal in rehearsal; I agreed with all he said today. We cut a lot of literary crap out of the dialogue . . . writer's decoration that's just frosting on the scene . . . and Carol took a little actor's crap out of it, too.'

The shooting made slow progress, with Reed and the cast only allowed on the set for short periods, the rest of the time taken up by the demands of Leon Shamroy, the lighting cameraman. It was not Reed's way of doing things, but he was not working in a studio like Shepperton, where he could force the pace. When it came to epics, Shamroy knew his business, having photographed *Cleopatra* and *The Cardinal* the previous year. Heston, however, still thought Reed was too relaxed. He wrote: 'Carol's not happy over this [the slowness of the schedule] or with what the second unit did on the siege. I think he rides with too easy a hand for a director of his reputation.'

By July, after shooting at Moneterano, where Reed had found a deserted village and a ruined villa, location work came to an end. In the studio, the ceiling of the Sistine Chapel had been recreated, and a seventy-foot-high tower of scaffolding constructed to Michelangelo's original plans. It was unsafe and had to be bolstered except when the camera looked up its whole height to Heston lying on his back, painting chocolate pudding onto the ceiling so that if any fell in his mouth it would taste better than plaster. Heston continued to be unnerved by Reed's easy-going approach. 'Carol works in terms of praising his actors, which I can't object to, but it makes me a little uneasy. ("Why is he praising me? I must be screwing up.")' Relations remained good except for one day when, according to Heston's diary, 'Twice today I came as close to quarreling with Carol as I ever could. (He was wrong both times, in fact: about how to block in a figure before painting and how the pulley would react to my fall.)'

By the beginning of September, all the shooting was complete, and Reed retired to edit the footage. He had had some extraordinary shots taken from a helicopter hovering above St Peter's Basilica in Rome to lead in to a ten-minute introductory history lesson about Michelangelo's artistic achievements, giving a guided tour of his most famous sculptures. The film then broke into a spectacular fighting sequence, shot by the second unit director Robert D. Webb, which Reed had not at first been happy about. The contrast between the tranquillity of the opening and the brutality of the fighting during the siege, with Roman soldiers overrunning innocent bystanders, was a glorious introduction to Rex Harrison as the warrior Pope. Most of the location work and some of the ceiling scenes also contained considerable power. However, the script was often ludicrous, in the tradition of biographical movies, including Michelangelo's remark on being introduced to Raphael: 'I've seen your work – shows promise.'

The off-screen hostility between Harrison and Heston spilled over to some effect into the film, as had Trevor Howard's contempt for Brando in the final cut of *Mutiny on the Bounty*. And Reed used his Todd-AO lens and De Luxe colour to great effect, particularly in a long panning shot which sweeps through 180 degrees as it takes in the whole of the completed ceiling. The only serious lapse in taste was a scene on a mountaintop where Michelangelo receives a vision of how he should paint Genesis.

Reed could congratulate himself on much of the final version, cut down to 136 minutes, excluding the mandatory interval, which Reed intended to mark the transition from Michelangelo the tormented to Michelangelo the inspired. Heston believed that he had excelled himself: 'I don't think I've made a better one, or acted better, either.' In November, Reed met Heston again at a dinner party at the home of William Wyler, where they discussed Zanuck's positive response on seeing an early screening of the completed film. Reed remained in Hollywood, where he attended a party hosted by Irving Stone, the author of *The Agony and the Ecstasy*, and enjoyed a party thrown in his honour by Heston, at which *The Third Man* was screened.

Heston became friendly with Reed and respected his treatment of actors. When, the following March, he was looking for a director for *Khartoum*, in which he was to play General Gordon, Heston asked his agent to discover whether Reed, his first choice, was available to direct; Reed declined, and the film was eventually directed by Basil Dearden. In March Reed and Heston attended the sneak preview of *The Agony and the Ecstasy* in Minneapolis and the audience showed their approval by stamping their feet and cheering. At the end of the month Reed returned to London, hoping that the Minneapolis reception indicated that the film would be at least a moderate success.

The Agony and the Ecstasy was given a royal premiere in London on 27 October at the Astoria Theatre, Charing Cross Road, before the Duke of Edinburgh, in aid of the Duke's playing-fields charity. Gerald Kaufman, in the *Listener*, wrote: 'Some twelve years ago, when Sir Carol was regarded as Britain's foremost cinematic artist, a film like *The Agony and the Ecstasy* would have been greeted with moans of opprobrious despair. Now, however, when works such as *The Key* and *The Running Man* have conditioned us to expect from him no more than the efficiency of a brilliant technician, we can settle back to enjoy this screen biography of Michelangelo with uncritical self-indulgence.' This was hardly praise, but at least Kaufman found the film 'agreeable fiction'.

Most British critics regarded *The Agony and the Ecstasy* as a Charlton Heston picture, not the latest in the Reed canon, and the American critics took the same view. Heston, stung by the reviews, blamed himself and saw the poor reaction to the picture as caused by the critics' dismissal of him as an actor. John Fairbairn, the London head of publicity for Fox in Britain, wrote to Reed at the beginning of November 1965 enclosing the disappointing American reviews. He wrote: 'I am sorry that not all of the reviews in Britain were as good as I hoped they would be but I am sure that you will be pleased to know that the business, since we started, has been very good indeed.' Good 'business' was little consolation to Reed.

After *The Agony and the Ecstasy* Reed decided to take things easy. He was now fifty-nine and was rich enough to relax and make only those films which he wished to make. But inactivity did not suit him. He became increasingly depressed and began drinking heavily, convinced that no one would ever ask him to make a film again. The result was that he would accept projects which he did not believe in, simply to be working again. Yet he always expected every film to be a success, and they were not. He would fortify himself with drink before a film's release, desperately hoping that everything would be all right.

During the filming of *The Agony and the Ecstasy*, on 13 May 1964, Diana Wynyard died. Her second marriage, to Tibor Csato, had ended in divorce. Her acting career, however, continued on its steady course, and she appeared in a succession of important roles, among them Candida, Sara Muller in *Watch on the Rhine*, Lady Macbeth, Dilys Parry in *The Wind of Heaven*, Portia in *The Merchant of Venice* and Helen of Troy in *Troilus and Cressida* at Stratford-upon-Avon, and enjoyed a central position in John Gielgud's Phoenix company, as Beatrice in *Much Ado About Nothing* and Hermione in *The Winter's Tale*. She was an international star, appearing in the Soviet Union and on Broadway.

In the final years of her life she was cast as Gertrude in Laurence Olivier's 1963 production of *Hamlet* which opened the National Theatre. She remained with the National company until her death, and it was during rehearsals for *The Master Builder* that she was taken ill. She had lived a full and an interesting life, even if she never quite fulfilled the promise of her early career. In 1953 she was awarded the C.B.E., and she certainly never became the suburban housewife Reed had so feared.

12

Asking for More

In February 1952, Reed had given a rare interview to *The Picturegoer*. He had recently completed *An Outcast of the Islands* for Alexander Korda, and told the reporter: 'Some time in the future I'd like to make a musical, but I don't think I'm capable of it yet.' He did however have some experience of making musicals.

In the thirties, as part of his long apprenticeship with Basil Dean, he had directed *Who's Your Lady Friend?* followed by *Climbing High*, the non-singing, non-dancing Jessie Matthews vehicle which started as a musical. He had also made *A Girl Must Live*, which included some musical numbers, even if they were stagebound and incidental to the film's main plot. But Reed was certainly strange to the world of contemporary film musicals.

Before the war, an archetypal musical, made in black and white, might concern show people trying out a would-be hit in the extensive grounds of a country house in front of an invited audience which included a powerful theatrical producer. After the war musicals were made in colour and were more operatic, with dramatic events punctuated by musical numbers. Rodgers and Hart had given way to Rodgers and Hammerstein. *Babes in Arms* had been superseded by *State Fair*.

Few in Britain thought that they could compete with American musicals any more, and it is not surprising that in 1952 Reed did not think himself 'capable' of making a musical; they were beyond the reach of anyone working outside Hollywood. But by 1968 the high cost of American production meant that Britain was a cheap alternative location, as long as the expense could be kept to a minimum. Reed was no director of musicals, but he combined a number of abilities which few others could offer: a brilliance with child actors, a reputation (albeit dwindling) for visually interesting films, proven success in remaining faithful to the spirit of difficult literary properties and, perhaps above all, all-round competence and a skill in handling large budgets.

For once, Reed and the men from Columbia were thinking about exactly the same property. Lionel Bart had translated Charles Dickens's *Oliver Twist* into a highly successful musical, *Oliver!*, which was playing in the West End of London. Reed, who had no recent experience with the complex choreography of musicals or of working with singers, had special reasons for wanting to make *Oliver!* In the year before he was born, 1905, his father had appeared in a similarly popularised version of the Dickens novel adapted by J. Comyns Carr, his barrister-turned-dramatist friend. Carr's adaptation of *Oliver Twist* was able but inevitably simplified, and the action centred not on young Twist but on Tree's larger-than-life impersonation of Fagin, the Jewish pickpocket-tutor. Tree's rendition, accompanied by Constance Collier as Nancy and Lyn Harding as Bill Sikes, filled His Majesty's Theatre for three months in the autumn of 1905.

Eleven years later, in 1916, Tree revived Carr's *Oliver Twist*, for one night only, in Hollywood, where he was filming first *Macbeth* then *The Old Folks at Home*. He had promised his close friend the wartime prime minister Herbert Asquith that when he was in the United States he would raise money for the war effort and remind the American public that their contribution to the European war was important. Tree's single repeat performance as Fagin, in aid of the British Red Cross, turned out to be of considerable historic significance, although it may not have appeared so at the time, for playing the Artful Dodger was his new friend Charles Chaplin. They had not shared a hall since Henry Irving's funeral in 1905, when Tree was a pall-bearer and Chaplin a mourner.

So, fifty years later, Reed embarked upon his own version of *Oliver Twist* with a mixture of pleasure and apprehension. It was the only subject which both he and his father had attempted, and the inevitable comparison was intimidating. When Lionel Bart's dramatised musical adaptation opened on the London stage in July 1960, Reed went to see it and promptly made a bid for the film rights, but the price proved to be too high. It was plain from the beginning that the show would be a considerable success, and five years and more than two thousand London performances later, the decision by Bart's agents to hold out for a higher bid was vindicated.

As soon as *Oliver!* opened on Broadway in 1963, an American film version was not only inevitable but its success was almost guaranteed. The mid-sixties was a time for grandiose film musicals, from *The Sound of Music* to *Half a Sixpence* (based on H. G. Wells's *Kipps*, which Reed had filmed in 1941), although some, such as *Dr Dolittle*, had lost large sums. *Oliver!* seemed a natural choice, if the costs were kept reasonably low. What was less obvious when the film rights were bought by the British company Romulus Films, made up of the brothers John and James Woolf, was that the film should be made in Britain by Carol Reed. British costs were lower than in America and a budget of $8 million was set aside, but no British musical of any stature had been made, in Reed's opinion, since Victor Saville's films with Jessie Matthews, like *Evergreen*, in the thirties.

Reed's recent efforts had been neither critical nor financial successes, and the feeling among film producers was that he had lost his nerve on being removed from *Mutiny on the Bounty* and had never regained his confidence. However, it was Reed's known ability for coaxing superb performances from children which encouraged Columbia to agree to him directing *Oliver!* They were also aware that he was a meticulous craftsman whose precision in preparation and love of detail would ensure that the massive cast and crew of between two and three hundred people would be economically marshalled. Their judgement was to be profitably rewarded.

The production of a film musical is one of the most complex tasks which a director can perform, a team effort of extraordinary complexity. Reed would be responsible for the overall organisation, the casting, the direction and the final edit, but he would have to delegate a great deal of work. He was not particularly musical, and his knowledge of choreography was minimal. The sets would of course be created by a designer, but in this instance they were an essential key to the structure and movement of the action.

Above all Reed was obliged to remain true if not to Dickens then at least to Lionel Bart's view of *Oliver Twist*, a novel already submerged in popular myth and coloured by a succession of prior screen versions, beginning with silents by Pathe (1909),

Vitagraph (1910), an independent producer in 1912 and Herbert Brennan's 1922 version with Lon Chaney Sr as Fagin and Jackie Coogan as Oliver. Perhaps the most daunting was David Lean's superb 1948 adaptation, with a brilliant portrayal of Fagin by Alec Guinness, Robert Newton at his eye-rolling best as Bill Sikes and Anthony Newley as the Artful Dodger. Reed recruited Vernon Harris to adapt Bart's musical into a screenplay.

As always, Reed believed that casting was the key. The most important part was not Oliver himself, who was to be played by the eight-year-old Mark Lester, but Fagin. Reed felt that Ron Moody, who played Fagin on the London stage, was ideal for the part. He was captivated by both the actor himself and his singing voice. As he prepared for the film, he repeatedly played the soundtrack of the stage production, challenging anyone within earshot to deny that Moody was an exceptional performer. But Reed's judgement was doubted by Columbia, who were nervous of elevating an unknown actor, however brilliant, to the lead part in such an expensive venture. For a time Peter Sellers was suggested as a more obviously commercial piece of casting, much to Reed's annoyance.

Moody had some film experience, but the Columbia executives were unimpressed, wanting American audiences to have a star to turn out for. As with the casting of Orson Welles in *The Third Man*, Reed waited until he had brought the rest of the cast together before making his demand that Moody must play the part. There were difficulties too about the casting of Shani Wallis, a British cabaret singer, as the hapless Nancy. Reed had hoped to cast Shirley Bassey in the part, but Columbia vetoed the idea, believing that the murder of a black woman would cause unnecessary offence to American audiences, particularly to southern blacks.

Jack Wild, the fifteen-year-old non-actor who was chosen to play the Artful Dodger, was found playing football in a London suburb by an actors' agent. His parents had to be persuaded that his snub nose, photogenic looks and lively personality could give him a lasting career in film acting. When Reed saw him he thought he had the bumptious charm of a young Mickey Rooney.

For the key part of the evil Bill Sikes, Reed chose his nephew Oliver Reed, but the choice was far from nepotistic, except in the literal sense. Reed had gone out of his way to dissuade Oliver from becoming an actor. When Oliver visited his uncle at his home in the King's Road, wanting him 'to point me in the direction of that elusive bottom rung', Reed was unhelpful, even if he did not mean to be. He suggested: 'Best thing is to get yourself into a repertory company. Or, better still, try for RADA,' which had, after all, been founded by Oliver's grandfather, Sir Herbert Tree. The young man was in too much of a hurry for that, so Reed told him to 'get some acting experience and then go into films', which was easier said than done. His advice was to 'put yourself around a bit at the Ritz Grill', a suggestion which was not only thirty years out of date, but which the impoverished Oliver Reed could hardly afford. His uncle then advised him to join a few private clubs and become known about the place. Oliver began to realise that Reed was either deliberately throwing him off the track or was simply out of touch. He concluded: 'I had a feeling that dear Uncle Carol was drifting about in an Edwardian summer.'

Reed did, however, end up giving his nephew two useful pieces of advice. The first was: 'Seek out the people that can help you and pitch a tent outside their front doors and every morning when they come out, step out of your tent and say, "Excuse me, I'm Oliver Reed, I would like you to give me a job."' The second was to go to the cinema as much as possible. 'If you think a film is bad, watch it over and over again until you are convinced that you know why it is bad. The same with good films, only when you are convinced that you know the reason a film is good, try to emulate those finished performances.'

Oliver Reed followed his uncle's advice and had established a distinctive niche as a burly, earthy character actor in a number of films, some more worthwhile than others, by the time Carol Reed began casting for *Oliver!* Reed had no intention of giving his nephew a job and suggested someone else for the part of Sikes, but John Woolf proposed Oliver Reed. There was no argument that he would fit the bill, but it was telling that Carol Reed had not even considered him suitable until Woolf suggested it.

As for the rest of the cast, Reed, as ever, drew upon Britain's rich tradition of stage acting. He found casting for a musical slightly different to what he was used to, because his characters would have to be able to burst into song without undermining their often grim demeanour. He explained: 'This is Dickens. There are problems of a special kind. You say to yourself: "Fagin as a character would never dream of singing anything, nor, perhaps, would the Artful Dodger or Bill Sikes." They would probably get a laugh. The only way we could do justice to these characters was to cast them as well as we knew how, and you can only do that in England. We concentrated upon them and made them the centre of attraction. I never visualised *Oliver!* as a show dominated by a single big star. In fact there are seven very good parts.'

Some casting decisions suggested themselves. The former Goon Harry Secombe not only looked ideal as the rotund Mr Bumble, but was a fine singer. In the other parts Reed placed a number of his favourite stage actors, among them Leonard Rossiter, Hugh Griffith, Fred Emney, Peggy Mount and Hylda Baker. As in all Reed's films, his wish for perfect detail extended to even the smallest parts.

Woolf ensured that Reed's overall direction was underpinned by three tested experts – a musical director, set designer and choreographer – which left as little to chance as possible. Reed later explained: 'I discovered that in a big musical the man who directs it is far more dependent on other people than in a straight film. He has to learn from experts and consult with them all the time. He has none of the autonomy he's accustomed to exercise in a non-musical subject.'

The task of orchestrating Lionel Bart's score for the film fell to John Green, the former head of music at MGM who had already won two Oscars, for *Easter Parade* (1947) and *An American in Paris* (1951), and had been nominated for his work on the film of *West Side Story* (1961). The sets were to be created by John Box, who had distinguished himself with his brilliant work on epic films such as David Lean's *Lawrence of Arabia* (1962) and *Doctor Zhivago* (1965) and Fred Zinnemann's *A Man for All Seasons* (1966).

Onna White was appointed the film's choreographer on the strength of her work on the musicals *Irma la Douce* and *Half a Sixpence*, but it was on *The Music Man* that she had displayed the ability to orchestrate dancers and actors which was needed for *Oliver!* She set about regimenting the dance sequences, beginning with a workhouse scene in which the young Oliver has the audacity to ask for a second helping, which was drawn extensively from the mechanical movements in Fritz Lang's *Metropolis*. At one stage, for a scene involving dancing soldiers, she recruited the services of a sergeant major from the Scots Guards to give precise instructions.

Reed planned the exact logistics of the shooting schedule, perfecting the screenplay and approving the sets, music and dance sequences, for eight months before he moved the company into Shepperton Studios for an exceptionally long shooting schedule of seven months, which to minimise costs would run continually, weekends included. He then set aside six months for post-production work and editing.

He described how he unravelled the complicated overlaying of songs, dances and plot. First, he stayed true to Bart's original structure. 'If you're adapting Lionel Bart's *Oliver!* you are committed to playing the story with his characters and numbers and all the rest of it – Oliver running away from home, going back, walking the streets and so on. The pattern is complex, it opens into Clerkenwell and fills out a London square. We sometimes changed the order or spacing of the numbers. The story, too, had to be cut. We had to eliminate Dickens's subplot, and that amounts to a quarter or third of the film. The rest is story and the story is found in Lionel Bart's numbers – "Food, Glorious Food", "You've Got to Pick a Pocket or Two", "Who Will Buy?" The choreography, while belonging, is in a sense a separate film needing its own exteriors.'

Reed's impeccable organisation paid off, with the shooting schedule running so smoothly that he was able to exercise his uncanny ability to draw out fine performances from children. This film would test his skills to the full, for there were fifty children waiting to be coaxed into action.

His method in *Oliver!* depended, as in his previous films, particularly *The Fallen Idol*, on his understanding of a child's psychology. 'The worst thing one can say to a child when aiming a camera at him is "Act naturally." That will shrivel him on the spot. Children are natural actors but you must give them something to act. However many children you are going to film, give each one a separate identity. Tell the little boy to pretend the bicycle is one he has just won in a competition. Tell the little girl she is a princess in disguise. Give them something to work with and think about before the filming begins. Watch how one boy flicks his hair or rubs his nose, how a girl twists her braids and rubs one foot behind her leg. How they eat, how they smile, how they show shyness or jealousy by jumping up and down or pouting in a certain way. Then, when you're ready to film, re-enact their own mannerisms to them and ask them to imitate you. In fact, they will then be doing what comes naturally to them.'

An example of how Reed used tricks to generate the right reactions from his child stars is how he encouraged a look of wonder from Mark Lester when Fagin opens his box of treasures. After a number of attempts at imagining something wonderful inside the box, it became plain that the boy could not summon up a look of suitably astonished awe. The following day, Reed bought a white rabbit from a petshop and hid it in his coat. The cameras were set up and Lester was placed in front of Fagin's box. Reed said: 'Oh, Mark, I think I've got something that might rather amuse you,' and brought the rabbit out from his coat. Lester's face lit up and the shot was achieved.

Reed found himself on solid ground once again. He was doing what he knew how to do, working hard on a worthwhile project, and was very happy once more, although he was dogged by ill health. His hearing was becoming worse and he had started wearing an aid, and during the filming he was nagged by a permanent feeling of illness. Members of the cast noticed a vagueness and a crippling sense of indecision about him which he could no longer disguise behind his natural diffidence.

When the final cut of the film was completed, running to 148 minutes, Reed showed it to Woolf, who was ecstatic. There was no doubt that Reed was back on form and that the picture would be a huge success. A print was rushed across the Atlantic for the executives at Columbia to see, and they too were thrilled with it. At last their British outpost had produced something which was certain to make money, and any doubts which had been expressed about Reed were soon forgotten.

The publicity machine swung into action. A royal premiere was hastily arranged for September 1968 at the Odeon, Leicester Square, in front of the queen's sister, Princess Margaret. The top brass from Columbia all booked flights to London to share in the glory. For once it didn't matter what the critics would think of a film, everyone was confident that *Oliver!* could not fail. Only

Reed remained nervous, unused to such attention since the high days of *The Third Man*.

As it happened, the British press mostly liked the film. Typical was the reaction of Alexander Walker of the *Evening Standard*, who said it represented 'the restoration of Sir Carol Reed to the top flight of film directors'. Only Penelope Houston, in sharp mood, had her doubts: 'Mistrust a movie with too many close-ups of Bisto Kid children and doleful dogs: they suggest a director cleverly boxing his way out of some very tight corners.'

On the strength of London's royal premiere, Columbia planned a similar series of high-profile openings throughout Europe, all in aid of UNICEF, the United Nations International Children's Emergency Fund. In Paris the premiere was attended by Prince Rainier and Princess Grace of Monaco, the former Grace Kelly; in Rome by Senator Montini, Pope Paul VI's brother. In Sweden and Denmark there were royal premieres; leading political figures attended those in Austria, Belgium and Switzerland. Rarely had a film been so supported by the massed international establishment.

The New York premiere followed on 11 December, with a view to rush-releasing the film in fourteen cities by Christmas. The American press was even more generous than the British, many of them remarking upon the film's obvious commercial appeal. But for Pauline Kael, the doyenne of American film critics, Reed had produced a work of art. Writing in the *New Yorker*, she extolled its virtues at length, comparing Reed's old-fashioned ability to make a film well with other movies of the late sixties.

> Maybe the most revolutionary thing that can be done in movies at the moment is to make them decently again. *Oliver!* has been made by people who know how; it's a civilised motion picture, not only emotionally satisfying but so satisfyingly crafted that we can sit back and enjoy what is going on, secure in the knowledge that the camera isn't going to attack us and the editor isn't going to give us an electric shock . . . Carol Reed is in the tradition of the older movie artists who conceal their art, and don't try to dazzle us with breathtaking shots and razorsharp cuts. They are there, all right, but we hardly notice them, because there is always a

reason for the camera to be where it is . . . Reed uses tact and skill to tell a story that can be enjoyed by 'everyone', and it's a very great pleasure to see a movie that can be enjoyed by everyone that one really does enjoy . . . Reed sustains the tone that tells us it's all theatre, and he's a gentleman: he doesn't urge an audience to tears, he always leaves us our pride.

According to Kael, the film totally eclipsed the stage musical – 'No one who sees this movie is likely to say, "But you should have seen *Oliver!* on stage!" The movie of *Oliver!* is much more than a stage production could be; it's not only a musical entertainment but a fine, imaginative version of *Oliver Twist* that treats the novel as a lyrical macabre fable.' In her opinion the film also outclassed David Lean's *Oliver Twist*, which she found 'simply too painful, and the trumpery of the Dickensian plotting was too stylised and conventional to go with the pain of the child's suffering and the horrible murder of Nancy'. She had the highest praise for the sheer craft of the film. 'The musical numbers emerge from the story with a grace that has been rarely seen since the musicals of René Clair. It isn't really surprising that Carol Reed, a master of planned montage, should be so adroit.'

At the end of an extraordinary piece of concerted praise, she reached to the heart of Reed's achievement:

I admire the artist who can make something good for the art-house audience, but I also applaud the commercial heroism of a director who can steer a huge production and keep his sanity and perspective and decent human feelings as beautifully intact as they are in *Oliver!* I'm not being facetious when I suggest that the quiet, concealed art of good craftsmanship may be revolutionary now. It's more difficult than ever before for a director to trust his accumulated knowledge and experience, because on big commercial projects there's so much pressure on moviemakers to imitate the techniques of the latest hit, to be 'up to date', which means always to be out of date.

Reed could barely credit this sudden turnabout in his fortunes. Since the humiliating debacle of *Mutiny on the Bounty* he had been afraid that perhaps his talents had deserted him. It was comforting to discover that there was still some appreciation for directors who made films in an old-fashioned way.

Oliver! started to pick up prizes. It received the Golden Globe Award for best musical in 1968. In February 1969 the film was nominated for eight British Film Academy Awards, for best film, best director, Ron Moody for best actor, Jack Wild as the most promising newcomer, John Box for best art direction, Phyllis Dalton for best costume design, Ralph Kemplen for best film editing and John Cox and Bob Jones for the best soundtrack. The greatest triumph was to come in April when *Oliver!* swept the Academy Awards in Hollywood. It won Oscars for best picture, best art direction, best achievement in sound, best musical score, and best special choreography. Most important of all, Reed won the Oscar for best director.

Reed drove to the Oscar ceremony in a Rolls-Royce, as befitted a successful British director. In his acceptance speech he said: 'You can imagine that never having made a musical before I owe a lot of thanks to a lot of people. I don't know how to sing or dance, so it was all a matter of teamwork.' He was genuinely surprised to win the award, believing that the best director's prize traditionally went to the Directors' Guild award-winner. He had therefore expected Anthony Harvey to win for *The Lion in Winter*.

When the names of the Oscar-winners were released, Reed's name was omitted from the list. He was confident enough to believe that it was an innocent mistake. 'You know those rumours about the British fleet leaving the Mediterranean and heading westward?' he joked. 'I want to assure you that the fleet is purely on manoeuvres and there is no real danger to Americans, particularly those who live inland. I advise everyone to remain calm.'

The success of *Oliver!* meant that Reed could now make another film without delay. It would have been obvious for him to undertake another musical, but he could not wait for such a large project to be assembled, and wished to take advantage of his triumph by working immediately. Besides, one of his strengths had always been the variety of the work which he could handle, and he was anxious to maintain his reputation for versatility. His choice was very different from anything he had done before: it was based on a modern-day western novel called *Nobody Likes a Drunken Indian*, and was finally released in the United States as *Flap* and in Britain as *The Last Warrior*.

By the time of the Oscars, Reed's stock was running so high that Warner Brothers-Seven Arts had already given him a budget of $6 million for the film. He would direct for the first time on American soil, on location near Santa Fe, with Anthony Quinn in the cast. He described the film as not so much a western as a social commentary, 'a comedy with an undercurrent of seriousness, like Sean O'Casey's *The Plough and the Stars*'. It was hardly an obvious comparison.

The plot concerned a tribe of deadbeat Indians in contemporary America, a menace to the local community who wreak their revenge upon the descendants of those who had deprived their tribe of its land and its dignity. The subject-matter immediately caused concern amoung defenders of Indian rights, as far from portraying Indians as noble victims, it presented them as workshy drunks whose idea of nationhood was only fleetingly glimpsed in that brief moment between apathetic sobriety and incoherent alcoholic poisoning. Reed agreed that members of the Indian rights lobby should see the screenplay to ensure that the image of the American Indian would not be harmed by the film.

The novel on which the film was based was written by Clair Huffaker, and Reed promptly signed him to write the screenplay which until the end of shooting was called 'Nobody Loves Flapping Eagle'. Flapping Eagle was the film's hero, a huge, drunken, immensely proud Paiute Indian who had become the scapegoat among the local police for all their unsolved crimes.

From the moment Anthony Quinn agreed to take the part the film became type-bound, with Shelley Winters playing a busy whore who was also Flapping Eagle's girlfriend. The bad language in the screenplay meant that Reed's old sparring partners the Motion Picture Association, still trying to censor American films, demanded changes to the dialogue and to what they considered 'undue violence'. As they put it, more deferentially than when they had objected to *The Fallen Idol* and *The Third Man*, 'We would welcome the opportunity of discussing possible modifications and would be pleased to meet with you at your convenience.' Reed gave them short shrift, and began filming.

Reed had always held out against the spirit of the sixties, but stranded with Pempie in Santa Clara in the hostile New Mexico desert, among actors whose tradition he did not understand, he found himself immersed in a semi-fashionable piece of Indian-rights propaganda dressed up as a conventional Holly-wood film. It is hardly surprising that *The Last Warrior* demonstrates few of the Reed virtues and was given only limited release on both sides of the Atlantic. American critics tended to discuss the merits of the American Indians' case rather than the merits of the film, about which they were mostly very rude. In Britain the critics barely noticed it at all, except to point out that Reed should never have associated himself with it.

The failure of *The Last Warrior* ensured that Reed would have to spend months in search of his next project. He came to the conclusion at one stage that, having wasted the credit he had gained for *Oliver!*, he would never be given another chance to work, but at last an opportunity to make a further film came from the American producer Hal B. Wallis. Reed said: 'I had nothing on my plate when Hal Wallis offered this. That's the value of producers. As an independent, from finding the story to finding the money to casting, you've spent two years before you can start shooting. If you like making pictures, you've got to go from one to the other – within reason. It's like being a boxer – there's no good just sitting down.'

The subject, however, did not amount to much. It was based on *The Public Eye*, a half-hour long one-act play by Peter Shaffer which Reed had seen in London when it opened in 1964. The movie, to be known in the United States as *The Public Eye* and in Britain as *Follow Me*, would expand this slight piece of theatre into a full-length screenplay, adapted by Shaffer himself.

After his less than happy encounter with Warners, Reed went back to Wallis for money to make the film, for Universal. Like *The Last Warrior*, the story was a product of the sixties, the account of a hiccup in the marriage of a staid, unadventurous English accountant and his dreamy, hippy American wife. The jealous husband sets a conspicuous private detective onto his innocent wife, then comes to believe that he is being cuckolded by him. The play was written with a specific cast in mind, Julie

Andrews as the wife and Peter Ustinov as the detective, but Reed cast Mia Farrow and Topol, with Michael Jayston as the unbending husband.

Like *The Running Man*, although ingenious, the plot was hardly the stuff of a great movie. Shaffer was forced to over-extend his material, changing a single-joke short play into an overlong film with an over-indulged plot idea. Reed shot the film in his usual efficient way, taking just six weeks, but he was becoming slower and less decisive and was not on good form. The completed film, which was released in Britain in May 1972, contained no magic and no hint that it was Carol Reed behind the camera, and even Reed was under no illusions about it. 'It's a light comedy; very, very slight. I think it's amusing and Mia Farrow's very good in it. And Topol. It's just a simple story.'

Reed was to spend the rest of his life in search of suitable subjects to make into films, but never to find quite what he was looking for, or, more importantly, anyone willing to invest money in his talents. After the late burst of *Oliver!*, by the mid-seventies he had become almost unemployable. He had grown noticeably older, was very hard of hearing and, although tall, was overweight.

Eric Ambler and his wife met Reed and Pempie by chance in Harrod's at this time, and were shocked by how old the once-debonair Reed had become. He was also sad. According to Michael Korda, 'He missed his friends terribly. Alex was dead, Zoli [Zoltan Korda] was dead and Graham [Greene] had moved to the south of France. He was no longer a major force in motion pictures or even a minor one, and therefore all that life that had been built up around who he was and what he did no longer existed. He was drinking quite heavily and just sat in his house much of the time. My father came to see him, but perhaps that was no consolation since he was even older and more forgotten than Carol.'

Various attempts were made to find work for him. John Woolf, the producer of *Oliver!*, asked him to make a film of Barry England's courtroom play *Conduct Unbecoming*, but Reed eventually declined. And there was a late try to revive the most successful partnership of his career, with Graham Greene.

When Reed was at his flat in Cannes he often dined with

Greene, who lived in Antibes, and they discussed filming a story Greene had found, set at the time of the Napoleonic wars, and featuring a Wandering Jew. Reed could find no guaranteed money for the picture, although he tried his usual friends at Columbia. The best offer was to make the film in stages, with the script treatment completed first. Reed thought it would be insulting to Greene to have to work in such a way and the project was dropped.

Reed had never taken a day's exercise in his life and was carrying a great deal of extra weight. Once, when asked by an American how he stayed in such good physical condition, he had replied, 'I stand in queues,' and he also joked that he occasionally went to St Moritz to watch others ski. In early 1976 he suffered a mild heart attack. He recovered, and went to convalesce in his flat overlooking Cannes harbour.

On 25 April, back in his home in the King's Road, he was lying in bed reading the paper while Pempie was in the adjoining bathroom, filling a hot-water bottle. Pempie could hear him making a great chuckling sound, and thought he was making a joke. She told him to stop making the noise, because she found it frightening, but when she entered the bedroom, she found that the chuckles were nothing of the sort. Reed was gasping for breath. He was suffering a second, fatal heart attack.

Pempie left him lying where he was, and the undertakers, who wanted to take him to a chapel of rest in Shepherd's Bush, were instructed to leave him in bed until the funeral. Pempie decorated the counterpane with flowers and allowed close friends like Judy Campbell to come and see him. Daphne du Maurier was among the first to be telephoned with the news. Pempie continued to sleep in the bedroom, on a sofa at the foot of the bed, until the funeral, ten days after Reed died. She told her daughter Tracy, 'I always slept with him before and don't see any reason to change now.' She cut off a lock of his hair and enclosed it in a locket, which she always wore.

The funeral was held in Chelsea Old Church, which was crowded with family and friends from the film business. From the balcony came the sound of a zither. The congregation turned their heads to see Anton Karas playing a slow-march version of the 'Harry Lime Theme'. It was a *coup de théâtre* which Reed would have enjoyed. The memories it evoked, however, caused many in the church to weep.

Trevor Howard read the lesson, from *The Wisdom of Solomon*. 'In the sight of the unwise they seemed to die: and their departure is taken for misery, and their going from us to be utter destruction: but they are in peace.' They sang 'Love divine, all loves excelling' and 'Abide with me' and an anthem to the tune of the Londonderry Air. Reed was buried in the cemetery in Gunnersbury, in a plot which Pempie had chosen for them both, her mother, the family nanny and other members of the family. The gravestone was made from two stones decorated with daisies, a reminder of his mother's home, Daisyfield.

Pempie Reed died within six years of Carol, on 23 January 1982, of a brain tumour.

The Times obituary of Reed declared that he was 'one of the few English directors who could be reckoned the equal of the best that Hollywood could produce.' The view was shared on the other side of the Atlantic, the *Washington Post* saying that 'Sir Carol and Alfred Hitchcock have been the most famous and respected film-makers to emerge from the British motion picture industry'.

In the following years, his reputation slumped. Although key films like *The Third Man*, *The Fallen Idol* and *Odd Man Out* were popular and well remembered, mainly due to regular television screenings, among film people Reed was not considered a director of the first order. This was mainly because he had worked entirely as a commercial director, had shunned a personal style and had kept his own personality, in so far as that is possible, out of his pictures. Kenneth Tynan described Reed as 'the intuitive craftsman without a point of view'.

When the New Wave of French directors arrived in the fifties, Reed was dismissive of them, describing their visual tricks as old-hat and playing down their autobiographical approach to their work. He gave the impression that there was something undignified, unEnglish, even demeaning, about putting a little of his soul into his work. A critic told him, 'We like you, but we don't *know* you,' receiving the reply: 'In that sense you never will.' He argued that film was not art, it was simply a form of entertainment, and a film-maker's job was merely that of a translator of authors' stories.

Reed always preferred to discuss the technical side of his art, not the reasons for his decisions. Hence he always put great emphasis on the editing process and the need for judicious snipping to make a perfect film. 'Following the picture through to the last detail is critical, terribly important,' he explained. 'You know, not enough directors are willing to do this. They are too eager to run off and play in the south of France – they want their money fast and easy. As soon as shooting is over they're thinking of their next picture and are willing to turn the current one over to the studio to cut. They're apt to say, "I'm too close to the picture now." That's nonsense. To make a good film you've got to sit down at the moviola day after day – all day – running the footage over and over, trying combinations.'

But inevitably elements of Reed's character do surface in his films, for he was not able to purge his own point of view entirely from his work, even though he had become used to disguising who he was for most of his life. The glimpses of Reed in his films are to be found among the many children who wander helpless and innocent through an adult's world, and in the amoral heroes who suit themselves whatever distress they may cause to others.

While he genuinely had no pretensions about the job that he did and denied that he had a distinctive style, it was the very precision of his films which reveal Reed's character. Kenneth Tynan caught the mood of Reed's approach to film-making when he wrote: '"Never have so many talents," it was once said of Alexander Pope, "been allied to so much drudgery."; and you could say the same of Reed. No genius can ever have had more of the journalist in his soul. The older critics used to write about art in terms of what they called "the long wrestle" between reason and imagination. In Reed there is no such struggle: in him, common sense and insight have marched always side by side: he was commercial – contentedly, productively so – from the beginning.'

Reed's description of his trade as essentially mundane and inexact, a craft like so many others, meant that he could hardly credit himself with great achievements. Having argued for so long that there was little of himself in his films, he found it easier to deny their success. Asked which film he was most pleased with, he said: 'They're all disappointments in the end. You only see the things you wish you had done. In the theatre you can take a play and then change it on tour or cut it down, but once you have finished a film and shown it, that's it . . . No, I have no favourites.'

The Career of Carol Reed

STAGE

Actor

1924
Heraclius
St Joan
Henry VIII
1925
The Eternal Spring
Swank
The Fool
1926
The Merchant of Venice
A Midsummer Night's Dream
1927
The Corvan Conspiracy
The Winter's Tale
The Terror
1928
The Flying Squad
1929
The Calendar
1931
Charles the Third

Director
1929
Persons Unknown
The Calendar
1930
On the Spot
Smoky Cell
1931
The Last Mile
Charles the Third

1933
Twelfth Night
As You Like It
A Midsummer Night's Dream

Producer
1930
On the Spot
1933
Poet's Secret

FILMS

Actor
1929
The Flying Squad

Assistant
1929
The Valley of Ghosts
Alias
Chick
The Flying Squad
Red Aces

Dialogue Director
1932
Nine Till Six

Assistant Director
1934
Autumn Crocus
The Constant Nymph
Java Head
Sing As We Go
The Sign of Four
Three Men in a Boat
Loyalties

Love, Life and Laughter
Looking on the Bright Side
1935
Lorna Doone

Director
1935
It Happened in Paris
(Co-directed with Robert Wyler)
Sc: John Huston, H. F. Maltby (from Yves Mirande's *L'Arpète*).
Cast: John Loder (Paul), Nancy Burne (Jacqueline), Edward
H. Robins (Knight), Dorothy Boyd (Patricia), Esme Percy (Pom-
mier), Minnie Rayner (Concierge), Laurence Grossmith (Bern-
ard), Jean Gillie (Musette), Bernard Ansell (Simon), Paul Sheri-
dan (Baptiste), Billy Shine (Albert), Warren Jenkins (Raymond),
Val Norton (Roger), Kyrle Bellew (Elvira), Nancy Pawley
(Ernestine), Eve Chipman (Mrs Carstairs), Margaret Yarde
(Marthe), Roy Emerton (Gendarme), Bela Mila (Mme Renault).
Prod: Bray Wyndham. Rel: A.B.F.D. 68 mins. GB release: 9
December 1935.
Midshipman Easy (US title *Men of the Sea*)
Sc: Anthony Kimmins from *Mr Midshipman Easy* by Frederick
Marryat. Ph: John W. Boyle. Art dir: Edward Carrick. Ed:
Sidney Cole. Music: Frederick Austin. Music dir: Ernest Irving.
Sound: Eric Williams. Ass dir: Cecil Dickson. Dial dir: Tyrone
Guthrie. Prod and Ed Supervision: Thorold Dickinson. Cast:
Hughie Green (Easy), Margaret Lockwood (Donna Agnes),
Robert Adams (Mesty), Harry Tate (Mr Biggs), Lewis Casson
(Mr Easy), Roger Livesey (Captain Wilson), Tom Gill (Gas-
coigne), Dennis Wyndham (Don Silvio), Norman Walker (Fitch),
Arthur Hambling (Lt Sawbridge), Arnold Lucy (John Rebiera),
Esme Church (Donna Rebiera), Frederick Burtwell (Mr East-
hupp), Donald Tester (Gosset), Jacky Green (Allsop), Anthony
Rogers (Vigors), Roy Sharpe (Phillips). Prod: Basil Dean for
Associated Talking Pictures. Rel: A.B.F.D. 76 mins. GB release:
20 April 1936.

1936
Laburnum Grove
Sc: Anthony Kimmins from J. B. Priestley's play. Ph: John

W. Boyle. Art dir: Edward Carrick, Dennis Wreford. Sup ed: Jack Kitchin. Mus dir: Ernest Irving. Sc ed: Gordon Wellesley. Sup sound eng: Paul Wiser. Cast: Edmund Gwenn (Radfern), Cedric Hardwicke (Baxley), Katie Johnson (Mrs Radfern), Francis James (Harold Russ), James Harcourt (Joe Fletten), Norman Walker (Man with glasses), David Hawthorne (Inspector Stack), Frederick Burtwell (Simpson), Terence Conlin (Police sergeant). Prod: Basil Dean for Associated Talking Pictures. Rel: A.B.F.D. 73 mins. GB release: 16 November 1936. US release: 1 December 1941.

1937
Talk of the Devil

Sc: Anthony Kimmins and Carol Reed. Ex dir: R. Norton. Ph: Francis Carver. Cast: Ricardo Cortez (Ray Allen), Sally Eilers (Ann), Randle Ayrton (John Findlay), Fred Culley (Alderson), Charles Carson (Lord Dymchurch), Gordon McLeod (Inspector), Dennis Cowls (Phillip), Quentin McPherson (Angus), Langley Howard (Clerk), Margaret Rutherford (Stephen's housekeeper), Moore Marriott (Dart thrower), Pam Downing (Deidre), Stafford Hilliard (Head clerk), Aubrey Mallalieu (Director), Mac Callachan (Barman). Prod: Jack Raymond for British & Dominions. Rel: United Artists. 60 mins. GB release: 26 April 1937. US release: 1 June 1937.

Who's Your Lady Friend?

Sc: Anthony Kimmins. Story by Julius Hoest from Oesterreicher and Jenbach's *Der Herr ohne Wohnung*. Ph: Jan Stallach. Art dir: Erwin Scharf. Ed: Ernest Aldridge. Music: Robert Stolz, Ernest Irving, Vivian Ellis. Cast: Frances Day (Lulu), Vic Oliver (Dr Mangold), Betty Stockfield (Mrs Mangold), Romney Brent (Fred), Margaret Lockwood (Mimi), Frederick Ranalow (Cabbie), Sarah Churchill (Maid), Marcelle Rogez (Yvonne Fatigay), Muriel George (Mrs Summers). Prod: Martine Sabinet for Dorian. Rel: A.B.F.R.D. 73 mins. GB release: 27 December 1937.

Bank Holiday (US title *Three on a Weekend*)

Sc: Rodney Ackland, Roger Burford, Hans Wilhelm. Story by Ackland and Wilhelm. Ph: Arthur Crabtree. Ed: R. E. Dearing. Cast: John Lodge (Howard), Margaret Lockwood (Catherine), Hugh Williams (Geoffrey), Rene Ray (Doreen), Merle Tottenham (Milly), Linden Travers (Ann Howard), Wally Patch (Arthur), Kathleen Harrison (May), Garry Marsh ('Follies' manager), Jeanne Stuart (Miss Mayfair), Wilfrid Lawson (Police sergeant), Felix Aylmer (Surgeon), Arthur West Payne (Ken), David Anthony (Hector), Angela Glynne (Marina), Michael Rennie (Guardsman). Prod: Edward Black for Gainsborough. Rel: G.F.D. 86 mins. GB release: 6 June 1938. US release: 1 July 1938.

1938
Writer
No Parking
Dir: Jack Raymond. Sc: Gerald Elliott from Reed story, 'The Little Fellow'. Cast: Gordon Harker (The tramp), Frank Stanmore (Friend), Irene Ware (The moll), Geraldo and His Orchestra.
Director
Penny Paradise
Sc: Thomas Thompson, W. L. Meade, Thomas Browne, from a story by Basil Dean. Ph: Gordon Dines, Ronald Neame. Art dir: Wilfred Shingleton. Music/lyrics: Harry Parr-Davies, Harry O'Donovan. Ed: Ernest Aldridge. Sound: Eric Williams. Prod sup: Jack Kitchin. Ass dir: Basil Dearden. Cast: Edmund Gwenn (Joe), Jimmy O'Dea (Pat), Betty Driver (Betty), Ethel Coleridge (Aunt Agnes), Syd Crossley (Uncle Lancelot), James Harcourt (Amos Cook), Jack Livesey (Bert), Maire O'Neill (Widow Clegg). Prod: Basil Dean for Associated Talking Pictures. Rel: A.B.F.D. 71 mins. GB release: 20 February 1939. US release: 24 September 1938.
Climbing High
Sc: Sonnie Hale, Lesser Samuel, Stephen Clarkson and Marian Dix. Ph: Mutz Greenbaum. Art dir: H. Murton, Alfred Junge. Ed: Michael Gordon, A. Barnes. Music dir: Louis Levy. Sound rec: Alex Fisher. Cast: Jessie Matthews (Diana), Michael Redgrave (Nicky), Noel Madison (Gibson), Alastair Sim (Max), Margaret Vyner (Lady Constance), Mary Clare (Lady Emily), Francis L. Sullivan (Madman), Enid Stamp-Taylor (Winnie), Torin Thatcher (Jim), Tucker McGuire (Patsy), Basil Radford (Reggie), Athole Stewart (Uncle). Prod: Gaumont-British. Rel: MGM (GB), Twentieth Century Fox (US). 79 mins. GB release: 8 May 1939. US release: 28 April 1939.

1939

A Girl Must Live

Sc: Frank Launder, Austin Melford, Michael Pertwee from Emery Bonet's novel *Gold Diggers of Bloomsbury*. Ph: Jack Cox. Art dir: Vetchinsky. Ed: R. E. Dearing. Music dir: Louis Levy. Musical staging: Eddie Pola, Manning Sherwin. Cast: Margaret Lockwood (Leslie James), Renee Houston (Gloria Lind), Lilli Palmer (Clytie Devine), George Robey (Horace Blount), Hugh Sinclair (Earl of Pangborough), David Burns (Joe Gold), Mary Clare (Mrs Wallis), Kathleen Harrison (Penelope), Moore Marriott (Mr Bretherton-Hyde/Lord Grandonald), Drusilla Wills (Miss Pokinghorn), Wilson Coleman (Hoder), Kathleen Boutall (Mrs Blount), Muriel Aked, Martita Hunt (Mesdames Dupont), Michael Hordern. Prod: Edward Black for Gainsborough. Rel: Twentieth Century Fox (GB), Universal (US). 92 mins. GB release: 25 September 1939. US release: 25 April 1941.

The Stars Look Down

Sc: J. B. Williams from A. J. Cronin's novel. Ph: Mutz Greenbaum, Henry Harris. Art dir: James Carter. Ed: Reginald Beck. Sound: Norman Davies. Ass dir: Vincent Permaine, Hal Mason. Prod sup: Fred Zelnik. Cast: Michael Redgrave (David Fenwick), Margaret Lockwood (Jenny Sunley), Emlyn Williams (Joe Gowlan), Nancy Price (Martha Fenwick), Edward Rigby (Robert Fenwick), Allan Jeayes (Richard Barras), Cecil Parker (Stanley Millington), Milton Rosmer (Harry Nugent MP), George Carnet (Slogger Gowlan), Ivor Barnard (Wept), Olga Lindao (Mrs Sunley), Desmond Tester (Hughie Fenwick), David Markham (Arthur Barrass), Aubrey Mallalieu (Hudspeth), P. Kynaston Reeves (Strother), Clive Baxter (Pat Reedy), James Harcourt (Will Kinch), Frederick Burtwell (Heddon), Dorothy Hamilton (Mrs Reedy), David Horne (Wilkins), Edmund Willard (Ramage), Bernard Miles, Frank Atkinson, Ben Williams, Scott Harold. Prod: Isadore Goldsmith for Grafton. Rel: Grand National (GB), MGM (US). 104 mins. GB release: 26 February 1940. US release: 20 July 1940.

Night Train to Munich (US title *Night Train*)

Sc: Frank Launder, Sidney Gilliat (story by Gordon Wellesley). Ph: Otto Kanturek. Art dir: Vetchinsky. Ed: R. E. Dearing. Music dir: Louis Levy. Cast: Margaret Lockwood (Anna Bomasch), Rex Harrison (Gus Bennett), Paul Henreid (Karl Marsen),

Basil Radford (Charters), Naunton Wayne (Caldicott), James Harcourt (Axel Bomasch), Felix Aylmer (Dr Fredericks), Roland Culver (Roberts), Eliot Makeham (Schwab), Raymond Huntley (Kampenfeldt), Austin Trevor (Captain Prada), Keneth Kent (Controller), C. V. France (Admiral Hassinger), Fritz Valk (Gestapo officer), Morland Graham (Teleferic attendant), Irene Handl (Station mistress), Billy Russell (Hitler), Pardoe Woodman, Albert Lieven, Edward Baxter, J. H. Roberts, David Horne, G. H. Mulcaster, Ian Fleming, Wilfred Walter, Jane Cobb, Charles Oliver, Torin Thatcher, Pat Williams, Winifred Oughton. Prod: Edward Black for Twentieth Century Fox. Rel: MGM (GB), Twentieth Century Fox (US). 95 mins (90 mins in US). GB release: 24 June 1940. US release: 18 October 1940.

1940
The Girl in the News
Sc: Sidney Gilliat from Roy Vickers's novel. Ph: Otto Kanturek. Art dir: Vetchinsky. Ed: R. E. Dearing. Cutting: Michael Gordon. Music dir: Louis Levy. Sound sup: B. C. Sewell. Cast: Margaret Lockwood (Anne Graham), Barry K. Barnes (Stephen Farringdon), Emlyn Williams (Tracy), Roger Livesey (Bill Mather), Margaretta Scott (Judith Bentley), Wyndham Goldie (Edward Bentley), Basil Radford (Dr Treadgrove), Irene Handl (Miss Blaker), Mervyn Johns (James Fetherwood), Betty Jardine (Elsie), Felix Aylmer (Prosecuting counsel), Kathleen Harrison (Cook), Roland Culver (Chief Constable), Edward Rigby (Hospital secretary), Jerry Verno (Charlie), Allan Jeayes (Chief Inspector), Richard Bird, Michael Hordern, V. R. Bateson, Ben Williams, Pauline Winter, Bryan Herbert, Roddy Hughes, Aubrey Mallalieu. Prod: Edward Black for Twentieth Century Fox. Rel: MGM (GB), Twentieth Century Fox (US). 78 mins. GB release: 10 February 1941. US release: 31 January 1941.

A Letter From Home
Sc: Rodney Ackland. Cast: Celia Johnson, Joyce Grenfell, Georgina Goddard. Prod: Edward Black for the Ministry of Information. Rel: Twentieth Century Fox. 17 mins. No GB release. Released in US.

Kipps (US title *The Remarkable Mr Kipps*)
Sc: Sidney Gilliat (from H. G. Wells's novel). Ph: Arthur Crabtree. Art dir: Vetchinsky. Dress and sets: Cecil Beaton. Ed: Alfred

Roome. Music dir: Louis Levy. Sound: B. C. Sewell. Prod sup: Maurice Ostrer. Cast: Michael Redgrave (Kipps), Diana Wynyard (Helen Walsingham), Arthur Risco (Chitterlow), Phyllis Calvert (Ann Pornick), Max Adrian (Chester Coote), Helen Haye (Mrs Walsingham), Michael Wilding (Ronnie Walsingham), Lloyd Pearson (Shalford), Edward Rigby (Buggins), Mackenzie Ward (Pearce), Hermione Baddeley (Miss Mergle), Betty Ann Davies (Flo Bates), Arthur Denton (Carshot), Frank Pettingell (Old Kipps), Betty Jardine (Doris), Phillip Frost (Kipps as a boy), Beatrice Varley (Mrs Kipps), Diana Calderwood (Ann Pornick as a girl), George Carney (Old Pornick), Irene Browne (Mrs Bindon-Botting), Peter Graves (Sidney Revel), Viscount Castlerosse (Man in bath chair). Prod: Edward Black for Twentieth Century Fox. Rel: Twentieth Century Fox. 111 mins. GB release: 30 June 1941. US release: 27 March 1942.

1941
The Young Mr Pitt

Sc: Frank Launder, Sidney Gilliat (from story by Viscount Castlerosse). Add dialogue: Viscount Castlerosse. Ph: Frederick Young. Art dir: Vetchinsky. Ed: R. E. Dearing. Music: Charles Williams. Music dir: Louis Levy. Sound sup: B. C. Sewell. Cutting: Alfred Roome. Dress and sets: Cecil Beaton. Period adviser: C. H. Hartman. Costumes: Elizabeth Haffenden. Prod sup: Maurice Ostrer. Cast: Robert Donat (William Pitt, Earl of Chatham), Robert Morley (Charles James Fox), Phyllis Calvert (Eleanor Eden), John Mills (William Wilberforce), Raymond Lovell (George III), Max Adrian (Sheridan), Felix Aylmer (Lord North), Albert Lieven (Talleyrand), Jean Cadell (Mrs Sparry), Stephen Haggard (Lord Nelson), Geoffrey Atkins (Pitt as a boy), Agnes Lauchlan (Queen Charlotte), Ian McLean (Dundas), A. Bromley Davenport (Sir Evan Nepean), John Salew (Smith), Stuart Lindsell (Lord Spencer), Henry Hewitt (Addington), Frederick Culley (Sir William Farquhar), Frank Pettingell (Coachman), Leslie Bradley (Gentleman Jackson), Roy Emerton (Dan Mendoza), Hugh McDermott (Mr Melvill), Alfred Sangster (Lord Grenville), Herbert Lom (Napoleon), Leslie Dwyer (Servant), Hugh Ardele (Naval officer), Gertrude Massmore-Morris (Lady in waiting), Max Kirby (Third secretary), Frederick Leister (Lord Auckland), Ronald Shiner (Man in stocks), Esme Cannon,

Merle Tottenham and Aubrey Mallalieu (Servants at Lord Auckland's house), Margaret Vyner (Duchess of Devonshire), Austin Trevor (Registrar), Leo Genn (Danton), James Harcourt (Bellmay), Muriel George (Mrs Carr), Dalla Black (Napoleon's mother/Girlfriend of the young Charles James Fox/Daughter of the Duchess of Gordon), Louise Disarte (Napoleon's father), Townsend Whitling, Kynaston Reeves, Joan Rees, Johnnie Schofield, Ann Stephens, Bruce Winston, John Bradley, Joe Clark, Owen Reynolds, Billy Holland, Gerald Cooper, Jack Watling, Cecil Rayne, Ralph Roberts, Edgar Vosper, Edmund Willard, Alf Goddard, Frederick Valk, Lucien Camilliere, J. H. Roberts, Esme Percy, George Bishop, Ardele Sherry, Ellen Lewis, C. Jervis Walters, Bertram Wallis, Gibb McLaughlin, D. J. Williams, Morland Graham, Lloyd Pearson, W. E. Holloway, Charles Paton, Gordon James, Neal Arden, Gordon Edwards, Kathleen Byron, Stanley Escane, Ernest Verne, Leslie Harcourt, Sydney Pointer, John Patience, Charles Doe, Leonard Glasspoole, Maurice Maudie, Allan Burdell, Farmer Millard. Prod: Edward Black for Twentieth Century Fox. Rel: Twentieth Century Fox. 118 mins. GB release: 21 September 1942. US release: 26 February 1943.

1943
The New Lot
Prod: Thorold Dickinson for the Army Kinema Corporation. Cast: Robert Donat, Stanley Holloway, Raymond Huntley, James Hanley, William Hartnell. 40 mins. Not released.
The Way Ahead
Sc: Eric Ambler, Peter Ustinov from Ambler's story. Ph: Guy Green. Art dir: David Rawnsley. Ed: Fergus McDonnell. Music: William Alwyn. Cast: David Niven (Jim Perry), Raymond Huntley (Davenport), William Hartnell (Sergeant Fletcher), Stanley Holloway (Brewer), James Donald (Lloyd), John Laurie (Luke), Leslie Dwyer (Beck), Hugh Burden (Parsons), Jimmy Hanley (Stainer), Reginald Tate (C.O.), Leo Genn (Company commander), John Ruddock, Bromley Davenport (Chelsea Pensioners), Alf Goddard (PT Instructor), Johnnie Schofield (Territorial instructor), Renee Asherson (Marjorie Gillingham), Mary Jerrold (Mrs Gillingham), Tessie O'Shea (ENSA entertainer), Raymond Lovell (Garage owner), A. E. Matthews (Col-

onel Walmsley), Jack Watling (Marjorie's boyfriend), Peter Ustinov (Rispoli), Lloyd Pearson (Mr Thyrtle), John Salew (Lloyd's friend), Penelope Dudley Ward (Mrs Perry), Tracy Reed (The Perrys' daughter), Esme Cannon (Mrs Brewer), Eileen Erskine (Mrs Parsons), Grace Arnold (Mrs Fletcher), Trevor Howard. Prod: Norman Walker, John Sutro for Two Cities. Rel: Eagle-Lion (GB), Twentieth Century Fox (US). 115 mins. GB release: 10 July 1944. US release: 4 January 1945.

1944
The True Glory

Sc: Staff Sgt Guy Trosper, Pte Harry Brown, Sgt Saul Levitt, Maj. Eric Maschwitz, Pte Peter Ustinov, Capt. Frank Harvey, Flight Lt Arthur Macrae, Flight Off. Jenny Nicholson, Gerald Kersch, Paddy Chayevsky. Research: Capt. Peter Cusick. Ph: Army Film Unit and American Army Pictorial Service, with cameramen from Great Britain, USA, Canada, France, Poland, Belgium, Netherlands, Czechoslovakia, Norway, Germany. Ed: Lt Robert Verrell (supervision), Sgt Liberwirz, Sgt Bob Farrell, Sgt Jerry Cowen, Sgt Bob Carrick, Sgt Bob Clarke. Music: Marc Blitztein, William Alwyn. Prod: Ministry of Information (GB), Office of War Information (USA). Rel: Warner Brothers (GB), Columbia (US). 87 mins. GB release: 27 August 1945. US release: 4 October 1945.

1946
Odd Man Out

Sc: F. L. Green, R. C. Sherriff (from Green's novel). Ph: Robert Krasker. Art dir: Ralph Brinton. Ed: Fergus McDonnell. Music: William Alwyn. Cast: James Mason (Johnny), Robert Newton (Lukey), Robert Beatty (Dennis), F. J. McCormick (Shell), Fay Compton (Rosie), Beryl Measor (Maudi), Cyril Cusack (Pat), Dan O'Herlihy (Nolan), Roy Irving (Murphy), Maureen Delany (Theresa), Kitty Kirwan (Granny), Min Milligan (Housekeeper), Joseph Tomelty (Cabbie), W. G. Fay (Father Tom), Arthur Hambling (Alfie), Kathleen Ryan (Kathleen), Dennis O'Dea (Head constable), William Hartnell (Fencie), Elwyn Brook Jones (Tober), Ann Clery, Maura Milligan, Eddie Byrne, Maureen Cusack. Prod: Carol Reed for Two Cities. Assoc prod: Phil

C. Samuel. Rel: G.F.D. (GB), Universal (US). 115 mins. GB
release: 17 March 1947. US release: 21 June 1947.

1947
The Fallen Idol (US title *The Lost Illusion*)
Sc: Graham Greene (from his short story, 'The Basement
Room'). Add dial: Lesley Storm, William Templeton. Ph:
Georges Périnal. Design: Vincent Korda, James Sawyer.
Ed: Oswald Hafenrichter. Music: William Alwyn. Ass dir:
Guy Hamilton. Camera op: Denys Coop. Spec effects:
W. Percy Clifford. Sound: John Cox. Prod man: Hugh Perceval.
Cast: Ralph Richardson (Baines), Michele Morgan (Julie), Sonia
Dresdel (Mrs Baines), Bobby Henrey (Felipe), Dennis O'Dea
(Insp. Crowe), Jack Hawkins (Det. Ames), Dora Bryan (Rose),
Walter Fitzgerald (Dr Fenton), Bernard Lee (Det. Hart), Karel
Stepanek (Secretary), Joan Young (Mrs Barrow), Geoffrey Keen
(Det. Davis), James Hayter (Perry), Hay Petrie (Clock winder),
John Ruddock (Dr Wilson), Torin Thatcher (Policeman A),
George Woodbridge (Police sgt), Dandy Nichols (Mrs Patter-
son), Gerard Heinz (Ambassador), Nora Gordon (Waitress),
Ethel Coleridge (Housekeeper), Ralph Norman, James Swan
(Policemen). A David O. Selznick/Alexander Korda presenta-
tion. Prod: David O. Selznick, Carol Reed. Assoc prod: Phil
Brandon for London Film Organisation (US). 95 mins. GB
release: 30 September 1948. US release: 15 September 1949.

1948
The Third Man
Sc: Graham Greene. Ph: Robert Krasker. Add ph: John Wilcox,
Stan Pavey. Design: Vincent Korda, Joseph Bato, John Hawks-
worth. Assoc des: Ferdinand Bellan, James Sawyer. Ed: Oswald
Hafenrichter. Music: Anton Karas. Ass dir: Guy Hamilton.
Camera op: Denys Coop, Ted Scaife. Sound: John Cox. Sound
rec: Bert Ross, Red Law. Cast: Joseph Cotten (Holly Martins),
Orson Welles (Harry Lime), Alida Valli (Anna Schmidt), Trevor
Howard (Maj. Calloway), Paul Hoerbiger (Porter), Ernst
Deutsch (Baron Kurt), Erich Ponto (Dr Winkel), Siegfried Breuer
(Popescu), Bernard Lee (Sgt Paine), Geoffrey Keen (British
policeman), Hedwig Bleibtreu (Anna's old woman), Annie
Rosar (Porter's wife), Harbut Helbek (Hansl), Alexis Chesnakov

(Brodsky), Wilfrid Hyde-White (Crabbin), Paul Hardtmuth (Hall porter), Eric Pohlmann. A David O. Selznick/Alexander Korda presentation. Prod: Carol Reed for London Film Productions. Assoc prod: Hugh Perceval. Rel: British Lion (GB), Selznick Releasing Organisation (US). 104 mins. GB release: August 1949. US release: 4 February 1950. American Academy Award for Best Photography.

1949
Short appeal film for the National Playing Fields' Association. Cast: Prince Philip, Duke of Edinburgh, Kathleen Harrison, Wilfred Pickles. 3 mins.

1950
An Outcast of the Islands
Sc: William Fairchild (from Joseph Conrad's novel). Ph: Ted Scaife, John Wilcox. Design: Vincent Korda. Ed: Bert Bates. Music: Brian Easdale. Ass dir: Guy Hamilton. Camera op: Freddie Francis, Ted Moore. Spec eff: W. Percy Day. Sound: John Cox. Dancing: T. Ranjana, K. Gurunanse. Cast: Ralph Richardson (Capt. Lingard), Trevor Howard (Peter Willems), Robert Morley (Almayer), Wendy Hiller (Mrs Almayer), Kerima (Aissa), George Coulouris (Babalatchi), Wilfrid Hyde-White (Vinck), Frederick Valk (Hudig), Betty Ann Davies (Mrs Willems), Peter Illing (Alagpjan), James Kenney (Ramsey), A. V. Bramble (Badavi), Dharma Emmanuel (Ali), Annabel Morley (Nina Almayer), Marne Maitland (Mate). Prod: Carol Reed for London Film Productions. Assoc prod: Hugh Perceval. Rel: British Lion (GB), United Artists (US). 102 mins (93 mins in US). GB release: 25 February 1952. US release: 11 July 1953.

1952
The Man Between
Sc: Harry Kurnitz, Eric Linklater (from Walter Ebert's novel, *Susanne in Berlin*). Ph: Desmond Dickinson. Des: Andre Andrejew. Ed: Bert Bates. Music: John Addison. Music dir: Muir Mathieson. Sound: John Cox. Cost: Bridget Sellers. Ass dir: Adrian Pryce-Jones. Camera op: Denys Coop, Robert Day. Cast: James Mason (Ivo Kern), Claire Bloom (Susanne Mallinson), Albert Waescher (Haladar), Ernst Schroeder (Kastner), Karl

John (Insp. Kleiber), Hildegarde Neff (Bettina), Dieter Krause (Horst), Hilde Sessak (Lizzi). Prod: Carol Reed for London Film Productions. Assoc prod: Hugh Perceval. Rel: British Lion (GB), United Artists (US). 101 mins. GB release: 2 November 1953. US release: 18 February 1954.

1954
A Kid for Two Farthings
Sc: Wolf Mankowitz (from his story). Ph: Ted Scaife. Col: Eastmancolor. Des: Wilfrid Shingleton. Ed: A. S. Bates. Music: Benjamin Frankel. Ass dir: John Bremer. Camera op: Robert Day. Cast: Celia Johnson (Joanne), Diana Dors (Sonia), David Kossoff (Kandinsky), Joe Robinson (Sam), Jonathan Ashmore (Joe), Brenda de Banzie (Ruby), Vera Day (Mimi), Primo Carnera (Python Macklin), Sidney Tafler (Madame Rita), Sidney James (Ince Berg), Daphne Anderson (Dora), Lou Jacobi (Blackie Isaacs), Harold Berens (Oliver), Danny Green (Bason), Irene Handl (Mrs Abramowitz), Alfie Bass (Alf), Eddie Byrne (Sylvester), Joseph Tomelty (Vagrant), Rosalind Boxall (Mrs Alf), Harry Purvis (Champ), Harry Baird (Jamaica), Lily Kann (Mrs Kramm), Arthur Lovegrove (Postman), Madge Brindley (Mrs Quinn), Harold Goodwin (Chick man), George Hurst, Eddie Malin, Peter Taylor Gordon, Max Denne (Customers), James Lomas (Sandwichboard man), Bart Alison (Auctioneer), Arthur Skinner, Norman Mitchell (Stallholders), Marigold Russell (Third customer), Judith Nelmes (Alf's customer), Meier Leibovitch (Mendel), Locarno (Pigeon man), Mollie Palmer, Barbara Denney, Barbara Archer, Ann Chaplin, Anita Arley (Workroom girls), Raymond Rollett (China stallholder), Bruce Bebbey (Policeman), Lew Marco (Referee), Frank Blake (M.C.), Ray Hunter, Charlie Green (Wrestlers). Prod: Carol Reed for London Film Productions. Rel: Independent/British Lion (GB), Lopert Films (US). 96 mins (91 mins in US). GB release: 15 August 1955. US release: 14 April 1956

1955
Trapeze
Sc: James R. Webb. Add sc: Wolf Mankowitz. Adapted by Liam O'Brien (from Max Catto's novel, *The Killing Frost*). Ph: Robert Krasker. Camera technician: Gregory Wheaton. CinemaScope.

Col: DeLuxe. Art dir: Rino Mondellini. Ed: Bert Bates. Music: Malcolm Arnold. Make-up: Louis Bonnemaison. Cast: Burt Lancaster (Mike Ribble), Tony Curtis (Tino Orsini), Gina Lollobrigida (Lola), Katy Jurado (Rosa), Thomas Gomez (Bouglione), Johnny Puleo (Max), Minor Watson (John Ringling North), Gerald Landry (Chikki), J. P. Kerrien (Otto), Sidney James (Snake man), Gabrielle Fontan (Old woman), Pierre Tabard (Paul), Gamil Ratab (Stefan), Michel Thomas (Mr Loyal), Edward Hagopian (Third Pole). Aerialists (doubles): Eddie Ward, Sally Marlowe, Fay Alexander, Willy Krause, Betty Codreano. Circus acts: The Arriolas, Mme Falco Cipriano, The Codreanos, Sampion Bouglione, The Gimma Boys. The clowns: Zavatta, Mylos, Lulu, Tonio. Prod manager: Ruby Rosenberg. Prod: James Hill for Hecht-Lancaster/Susan. Rel: United Artists. 106 mins. GB release: 20 August 1956. US release: July 1956.

1957
The Key
Sc: Carl Foreman (from Jan de Hartog's novel, *Stella*). Ph: Oswald Morris. CinemaScope. Art dir: Geoffrey Drake. Ed: Bert Bates. Music: Malcolm Arnold. Sound: Peter Handford, W. Milner. Cast: William Holden (David Ross), Sophia Loren (Stella), Trevor Howard (Chris Ford), Oscar Homolka (Van Dam), Kieron Moore (Kane), Bernard Lee (Wadlow), Beatrix Lehmann (Housekeeper), Noel Purcell (Hotel porter), Bryan Forbes (Weaver), Sidney Vivian (Grogan), Rupert Davies (Baker), Russell Waters (Sparks), James Hayter (Locksmith), Irene Handl (Clerk), John Crawford (American captain), Jameson Clark (English captain), Michael Caine. Exec prod: Carl Foreman. Prod: Aubrey Baring for Open Road. Rel: Columbia. 124 mins. GB release: 28 June 1958. US release: July 1958.

1958
Our Man in Havana
Sc: Graham Greene (from his novel). Ph: Oswald Morris. CinemaScope. Art dir: John Box. Ed: Bert Bates. Music played by: Hermanos Deniz Cuban Rhythm Band. Sound: John Mitchell. Ass dir: Gerry O'Hara. Cast: Alec Guinness (Jim Wormold), Burl Ives (Dr Hasselbacher), Maureen O'Hara (Beatrice), Ernie Kovacs (Segura), Noël Coward (Hawthorne), Ralph Richardson

('C'), Jo Morrow (Milly Wormold), Paul Rogers (Carter), Gregoire Aslan (Cifuentes), Jose Prieto (Lopez), Timothy Bateson (Rudy), Duncan Macrae (MacDougal), Maurice Denham (Navy officer), Raymond Huntley (Army officer), Buckingham (Stripper), Ferdy Mayne (Prof. Sanchez), Karel Stepanek (Dr Braun), Gerik Schjelderup (Svenson), Elisabeth Welch (Beautiful woman). Prod: Carol Reed for Kingsmead. Assoc prod: Raymond Anzarut. Rel: Columbia. 107 mins. GB release: 21 March 1960. US release: 1960

1960
Mutiny on the Bounty
Sc: Eric Ambler, Charles Lederer and others. Ph: Robert Surtees. Music: Bronislau Kaper. Cast: Marlon Brando (Fletcher Christian), Trevor Howard (Capt. Bligh), Richard Harris, Hugh Griffith, Tarita, Richard Haydn, Percy Herbert, Duncan Lamont, Gordon Jackson, Chips Rafferty, Noel Purcell. Completed by Lewis Milestone.

1962
The Running Man
Sc: John Mortimer (from Shelley Smith's novel, *The Ballad of the Running Man*). Ph: Robert Krasker. Panavision. Col: Technicolor. Art dir: John Stoll. Ed: Bert Bates. Music: William Alwyn. Spanish prod man: Roberto Roberts. 2nd Unit dir: Harold Hayson. Ass dir: Peter Bolton, Pedro Vidal. Music dir: Muir Mathieson. Sound: Peter Thornton. Sound rec: Claude Hitchcock, Bob Jones. Cast: Laurence Harvey (Rex Black), Lee Remick (Stella), Alan Bates (Stephen), Felix Aylmer (Parsons), Eleanor Summerfield (Hilda Tanner), Allan Cuthbertson (Jenkins), Harold Goldblatt (Tom Webster), Noel Purcell (Miles Bleeker), Ramsay Ames (Madge Penderby), Fernando Rey (Police official), Juan Jose Menendez (Roberto), Eddie Byrne (Sam Crowdson), Colin Gordon (Solicitor), John Meillon (Jim Jerome), Roger Delgado (Spanish doctor), Fortunio Bonanova (Spanish bank official). Prod: Carol Reed for Peet. Rel: Columbia. 103 mins. GB release: 6 October 1963. US release: October 1963.

1964
The Agony and the Ecstasy

Sc: Philip Dunn (from Irving Stone's novel). Ph: Leon Shamroy. Todd-AO. Col: DeLuxe. Prod des: John de Cuir. Ed: Samuel E. Beetley. Music: Alex North. Art dir: Jack Martin Smith. Set dec: Dario Simoni. Costumes: Vittorio Nino Novarese. Make-up: Amato Garbini. Choral music: Franco Potenza. Sound: Carlton W. Faulkner, Douglas O. Williams. 2nd Unit dir: Robert D. Webb. Spec eff: L. B. Abbott, Emil Kosa Jr. Ass dir: Gus Agosti. Cast: Charlton Heston (Michelangelo), Rex Harrison (Pope Julius II), Diane Cilento (Contessina de' Medici), Harry Andrews (Bramante), Alberto Lupo (Duke of Urbino), Adolfo Celi (Giovanni de' Medici), Venantino Venantini (Paris De Grassis), John Stacy (Sangallo), Fausto Tozzi (Foreman), Maxine Audley (Woman), Tomas Milian (Raphael), Alec McCowen (Cardinal). Prod: Carol Reed for International Classics Inc. Rel: Twentieth Century Fox. 139 mins. GB release: 28 October 1965. US release: October 1965.

1968
Oliver!
Sc: Vernon Harris (based on the musical play by Lionel Bart, adapted from Charles Dickens's novel, *Oliver Twist*). Ph: Oswald Morris. Panavision 70. Col: Technicolor. Prod des: John Box. Art dir: Terence Marsh. Ed: Ralph Kemplen. Music: Lionel Bart. Music sup/arrangements: John Green. Assoc music sup: Eric Rogers. Songs: 'Food, Glorious Food', 'Oliver!', 'Boy for Sale', 'Where is Love?', 'Consider Yourself', 'You've Got to Pick a Pocket or Two', 'It's a Fine Life!', 'I'd Do Anything', 'Be Back Soon', 'Oom-Pah-Pah', 'Who Will Buy?', 'As Long as he Needs Me', 'Reviewing the Situation', by Lionel Bart. Cost: Phyllis Dalton. Choreo/musical sequences staging: Onna White. Assoc choreo: Tom Panko. Sound sup: John Cox. Sound: James Groom. Sound rec: Buster Ambler, Bob Jones. Prod sup: Denis Johnson. Prod manager: Denis Johnson Jr. 2nd Unit dir: Ray Corbett. 2nd Unit ph: Brian West. Ass dir: Colin Brewer, Max Reed. Cast: Ron Moody (Fagin), Shani Wallis (Nancy), Oliver Reed (Bill Sikes), Harry Secombe (Mr Bumble), Hugh Griffith (The magistrate), Jack Wild (Artful Dodger), Clive Moss (Charlie Bates), Mark Lester (Oliver Twist), Peggy Mount (Widow Corney), Leonard Rossiter (Mr Sowerberry), Sheila White (Bet), Kenneth Cranham (Noah Claypole), Megs Jenkins (Mrs Bed-

win), Wensley Pithey (Dr Grimwig), James Hayter (Jessop), Fred Emney (Chairman), John Baskcombe, Norman Pitt, Arnold Locke, Frank Crawshaw (Workhouse governors), Elizabeth Knight (Charlotte), Norman Mitchell (Arresting policeman), Clive Moss, Peter Lock. Prod: John Woolf for Warwick/Romulus Films. Rel: Columbia. 146 mins. Overture, Intermission and Recessional music 7 mins. GB release: 28 September 1968. US release: 11 December 1968. American Academy Awards for Best Picture, Best Director, Best Art Direction, Best Achievement in Sound, Best Musical Score, Best Special Choreography.

1969
The Last Warrior (US title *Flap*)
Sc: Clair Huffaker (from his novel, *Nobody Loves a Drunken Indian*). Ph: Fred J. Koenekamp. Panavision. Col: Technicolor. Prod des: Art Loel. Art dir: Mort Rabinowitz. Ed: Frank Bracht. Music: Marvin Hamlisch. Song: 'If Nobody Loves' by Marvin Hamlisch, Estelle Levitt, sung by Kenny Rogers and the First Edition. Set dec: Ralph S. Hurst. Sound: Alfred E. Overton Sr. Prod sup: Milton Feldman. Prod man: Carter DeHaven Jr. Ass dir: Reggie Callow. Cast: Anthony Quinn (Flapping Eagle), Claude Akins (Lobo Jackson), Tony Bill (Eleven Snowflake), Victor Jory (Wounded Bear Mr Smith), Don Collier (Mike Lyons), Shelley Winters (Dorothy Bluebell), Susana Miranda (Ann Looking Deer), Victor French (Rafferty), Rodolfo Acosta (Storekeeper), Anthony Caruso (Silver Dollar), William Mims (Steve Gray), Rudy Diaz (Larry Standing Elk), Pedro Regas (She'll-Be-Back-Pretty-Soon), J. Edward McKinley (Harris), Robert Cleaves (Gus Kirk), John War Eagle (Luke Wolf). Prod: Jerry Adler. Rel: Warner Brothers. 106 mins. GB release: 20 November 1971. US release: November 1970.

1971
Follow Me (US title *The Public Eye*)
Sc: Peter Shaffer (from his play, *The Public Eye*). Ph: Christopher Challis. Panavision. Col: Technicolor. Prod des: Terry Marsh. Art dir: Robert Cartwright. Ed: Anne Coates. Music: John Barry. Choreo: Sally Gilpin. Sound ed: Don Sharpe. Sound rec: John Aldred. Set dec: Peter Howitt. Prod sup: Denis Johnson. Ass dir: Allan James. Cast: Mia Farrow (Belinda), Topol (Julian Cristo-

forou), Michael Jayston (Charles Sidley), Margaret Rawlings (Mrs Sidley), Annette Crosbie (Miss Framer), Dudley Foster (Mr Mayhew), Michael Aldridge (Sir Philip Crouch), Gabrielle Brune (Lady Crouch), Michael Barrington (Scrampton), Neil McCarthy (Parkinson), Jack Watling (Client), David Battley (Writer), Lucy Griffiths (Bertha), David Hutcheson, Joan Henley (Dinner guests). Prod: Hal B.Wallis for Universal. Assoc prod: Paul Nathan. Rel: Rank. 93 mins. G B release: 9 May 1972. U S release: August 1972.

Bibliography

Eric Ambler, *Here Lies: An Autobiography*, Weidenfeld and Nicolson 1985

Cecil Beaton, *Persona Grata*, Wingate 1953

Herbert Beerbohm Tree: Some Memories of Him and of His Art, collected by Max Beerbohm, Hutchinson 1921

Madeleine Bingham, *The Great Lover: The Life and Art of Herbert Beerbohm Tree*, Hamish Hamilton 1978

Dirk Bogarde, *Snakes and Ladders*, Chatto and Windus 1978

The Noël Coward Diaries, Ed. Graham Payn and Sheridan Morley, Weidenfeld and Nicolson 1982

A. J. Cronin, *The Stars Look Down*, Victor Gollancz 1935

Basil Dean, *Seven Ages: An Autobiography 1888-1927*, Hutchinson 1970

Basil Dean, *Mind's Eye: An Autobiography 1927-1972*, Hutchinson 1973

The Dictionary of National Biography 1931-1940, Oxford University Press 1949

Frances Donaldson, *Edward VIII*, Weidenfeld and Nicolson 1974

Daphne du Maurier, *The Rebecca Notebook and Other Memories*, Victor Gollancz 1981

Daphne du Maurier, *Growing Pains: The Shaping of a Writer*, Victor Gollancz 1977

Daphne du Maurier, *I'll Never Be Young Again*, Heinemann 1931

Quentin Falk, *Travels in Greeneland: The Cinema of Graham Greene*, Quartet 1984

Bryan Forbes, *Notes for a Life*, Collins 1974

F. L. Green, *Odd Man Out*, Michael Joseph 1945

Graham Greene, *The Pleasure-Dome: The Collected Film Criticism 1935-40*, Secker and Warburg 1972

Graham Greene, *The Third Man/The Fallen Idol*, Heinemann 1950

Graham Greene, *The Third Man* (screenplay), Lorrimer Publishing 1973

Graham Greene, *Ways of Escape*, Bodley Head 1980

Graham Greene, *Our Man in Havana*, Heinemann 1958

Alec Guinness, *Blessings in Disguise*, Hamish Hamilton 1985

Leslie Halliwell, *Halliwell's Film Guide*, 4th Edition, Paladin Books 1985

Leslie Halliwell, *Halliwell's Filmgoer's and Video Viewer's Companion*, 9th Edition, Grafton Books 1988

Rex Harrison, *Rex: An Autobiography*, Macmillan 1974

Jack Hawkins, *Anything for a Quiet Life*, Elm Tree 1973

Robert Henrey, *A Film Star in Belgrave Square*, Peter Davies 1948

Charlton Heston, *The Actor's Life: Journals 1956-76*, Allen Lane 1979

Des Hickey and Gus Smith, *Laurence Harvey*, Leslie Frewin 1975

Charles Higham, *Brando*, Sidgwick and Jackson 1987

Harold Hobson, *Theatre in Britain: A Personal View*, Phaidon 1984

Anthony Holden, *Olivier*, Weidenfeld and Nicolson 1988

Michael Holroyd, *Bernard Shaw: The Search for Love 1856-1898*, Chatto and Windus 1988

John Kobal, *People will Talk*, Alfred A. Knopf 1985

Michael Korda, *Charmed Lives*, Allen Lane 1980

Karol Kulik, *Alexander Korda: The Man who Could Work Miracles*, W. H. Allen 1975

Margaret Lane, *Edgar Wallace*, Hamish Hamilton 1964

Barbara Leaming, *Orson Welles*, Weidenfeld and Nicolson 1985

James Mason, *Before I Forget: An Autobiography*, Hamish Hamilton 1981

Jessie Matthews, *Over my Shoulder*, W. H. Allen 1976

Leslie Mitchell, *Leslie Mitchell Reporting . . . An Autobiography*, Hutchinson 1981

Sheridan Morley, *The Other Side of the Moon*, Coronet Books 1986

Roy Moseley, *Rex Harrison: The First Biography*, New English Library 1987

Vivenne Knight Muller, *Trevor Howard: A Gentleman and Player*, Blond & White 1986

David Niven, *The Moon's a Balloon*, Hamish Hamilton 1971

The Oxford Companion to Film, Ed. Liz-Anne Bawden, Oxford University Press 1976

Michael Parnell, *Eric Linklater*, John Murray 1984

Hesketh Pearson, *Beerbohm Tree: His Life and Laughter*, Methuen 1956. 1988 paperback includes introduction by Sir John Gielgud.

Michael Powell, *A Life in Movies*, Heinemann 1986

Michael Redgrave, *In my Mind's Eye*, Weidenfeld and Nicolson 1983

Michael Redgrave, *Mask or Face*, Heinemann 1958

Oliver Reed, *Reed All About Me*, W. H. Allen 1979

Paul Tabori, *Alexander Korda*, Oldbourne 1959

Hilton Tims, *Once a Wicked Lady*, Virgin 1990

J. C. Trewin, *Robert Donat: A Biography*, Heinemann 1968

Olivia Truman, *Beerbohm Tree's Olivia*, Andre Deutsch 1984

Kathleen Tynan, *The Life of Kenneth Tynan*, Weidenfeld and Nicolson 1987

Peter Ustinov, *Dear Me*, Heinemann 1977

Hugo Vickers, *Cecil Beaton*, Weidenfeld and Nicolson 1985

The Diaries of Evelyn Waugh, Ed. Michael Davie, Weidenfeld and Nicolson 1976

H. G. Wells in Love, Ed. P. G. Wells, Faber and Faber 1984

Emlyn Williams, *Emlyn: An Early Autobiography 1927–35*, Bodley Head 1973

Basil Wright, *The Long View*, Secker and Warburg 1974

Index